Rob Gray is Mathew Professor of Accounting and Information Systems in the Department of Accountancy and Business Finance at the University of Dundee. He qualified as a chartered accountant with KPMG Peat Marwick, is Editor of the *British Accounting Review*, Director of the Centre for Social and Environmental Accounting Research, a Fellow of the Royal Society of Arts and author of over ninety books, monographs and articles. These include *Corporate Social Reporting: accounting and accountability* (Hemel Hempstead: Prentice Hall International, 1987) and *The Greening of Accountancy* (London: Chartered Association of Certified Accountants, 1990). He is actively involved with many organizations concerned with the issues of business, accounting and the environment and has been a member of the Green Party for fifteen years.

Jan Bebbington is a lecturer in accounting in the Department of Accountancy and Business Finance at the University of Dundee. She qualified as a chartered accountant with KPMG Peat Marwick in Christchurch, New Zealand, and lectured at the University of Canterbury before coming to work in Scotland. She has been involved in the Outward Bound movement and Youth Sail Training for some years.

Diane Walters is a lecturer in accounting in the Business School at Heriot-Watt University. After graduating in sociology she undertook two years of postgraduate research before transferring to accountancy. She qualified as a chartered accountant with Thomson McLintock (now KPMG Peat Marwick) and, having spent two years as a financial controller in industry, moved into lecturing in 1989. She has been an active member of the Green Party for a number of years.

ACCOUNTING FOR THE ENVIRONMENT

Rob Gray
with Jan Bebbington & Diane Walters

Editorial Adviser: Martin Houldin, KPMG National
Environment Unit

This book is based upon a research project
funded and supported by the Chartered
Association of Certified Accountants. The
views expressed are those of the authors and
do not necessarily represent the views of
either the ACCA or KPMG.

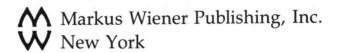 Markus Wiener Publishing, Inc.
New York

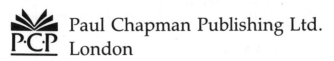 Paul Chapman Publishing Ltd.
London

Copyright © 1993 R H Gray and The Certified Accountants Educational Projects Ltd.

Paul Chapman Publishing Ltd
144 Liverpool Road
London
N1 1LA

For the USA and Canada write to:
Markus Wiener Publishing, Inc.
225 West 34th Street, Suite 1105,
New York, NY 10001

British Library Cataloguing in Publication Data

Gray, Rob
  Accounting for the Environment
  I. Title
  658.408

  ISBN 1-85396-230-9

Library of Congress Cataloging-in-Publication Data

Gray, Rob.
    Accounting and the environment; green accounting/Rob Gray with
Jan Bebbington and Diane Walters.
    Includes bibliographical references.
    ISBN 1-65876-075-X
    1. Corporations – Accounting – Case studies.   2. Industry – Environmental
aspects – Accounting – Case studies.   3. Environmental protection – Economic
aspects – Accounting – Case studies.   4. Environmental policy – Case studies.
    I. Bebbington, Jan.   II. Walters, Diane.   III. Title.
    HF5686.C70568   1993
    657 – dc20   93-6808 CIP

Typeset by Best-set Typesetter Ltd., Hong Kong
Printed and bound by The Cromwell Press Ltd., Broughton Gifford, Melksham,
Wiltshire SN1L 8PH, UK

A B C D E F G H 9 8 7 6 5 4 3

Contents

PART B: MANAGEMENT INFORMATION AND ACCOUNTING

Overview of Part B

We are pleased to acknowledge the considerable assistance received during the course of the research from the following:

Alcan International
BSO/Origin
British American Tobacco
British Gas plc
British Polythene Industries plc
Business in the Environment
Canada–United Kingdom
  Colloquia
Carron Phoenix plc
Centre for Environmental
  Management and Planning
Centre for Environment and
  Business in Scotland
Centre for Human Ecology
Centre for Resource
  Management (NZ)
Chartered Association of
  Certified Accountants
Chartered Institute of
  Management Accountants
Confederation of British
  Industry Environment Unit
Department of the Environment
Department of Trade and
  Industry
Dundee City Council
Electricity Corporation of New
  Zealand Ltd
Environment Council
Eurotherm
Fletcher Challenge Ltd
GB Papers Ltd
Hewlett Packard (UK)
IBM (UK) Ltd (Edinburgh and
  Portsmouth)
Imperial Chemicals Industries
  plc
Institute of Environmental
  Assessment
Institute of Environmental
  Auditors
Institute for Policy Analysis and
  Development

Integrated Environmental
  Management
International Institute for
  Economic Development
International Institute for
  Sustainable Development
  (Canada)
Jupiter Tarbutt Marlin
KPMG Peat Marwick: London
  and Scotland
Lancashire County Council
Management Institute for
  Environment and Business
Milburn New Zealand Ltd
Ministry for the Environment
  (NZ)
New Consumer Ltd
Nexus Television Ltd
Norsk Hydro (UK) Ltd
Ortech International
Parliamentary Commissioner for
  the Environment (NZ)
Petro-Canada
Pilkington plc
Pittencrief Ltd
Procter & Gamble Ltd
Rhône Poulenc Ltd
Rumenco Ltd
J. Sainsbury plc
Scottish Natural Heritage
Scottish Enterprise
Seaford Lodge Ltd
South London Industrial Mission
Stockbridge Engineering Ltd
SustainAbility
Todd & Duncan Ltd
Touche Ross
United Nations Centre for
  Transnational Corporations

And the 200-plus companies that
  most kindly responded to our
  postal questionnaire.

Preface and Personal Acknowledgements

Within less than five years, accounting for the environment has moved from being considered the most marginal and irrelevant of topics to its present position of occupying an increasingly central role in the deliberations of the worldwide accounting profession. Further, environmental accounting is now seen as an essential element in any organization's environmental response. EC proposals in 1992 in *Towards Sustainability* recognized that accounting must change its most basic concepts and practices if full environmental information is to be a central element in management organizational decision-making. Also in 1992, the State of Washington (USA) Department of Ecology issued guidelines on how to develop accounting systems 'for pollution prevention'. Such radical proposals from authoritative non-accountancy bodies would have been unthinkable only a few years ago.

This book follows on from *The Greening of Accountancy* published by the ACCA in 1990. It seeks to answer the question 'What can/ should accountants do in response to the developing environmental agenda?' The book lays out the best accounting practice with regard to the environment around the world and provides ideas for experimentation and future development. Whilst environmental accounting has come a considerable way in a very short time, it has now reached the stage where much wider – and more open – experimentation is essential. And this requires the very closest collaboration between practising and academic accountants. This book is the result of such collaboration and should provide a basis for the practitioner in industry and in partnership to start the environmental accounting ball rolling. Beyond that, the book should provide a basis for experimentation. In addition, the formation of the CSEAR (see below) is designed to facilitate the sort of more extensive academic/practitioner collaboration that is essential if our profession is to play its full part in the mitigation of the worst excesses of environmental degradation.

We have received considerable help and support throughout the research work for this book and in the preparation of the manuscript. In particular, we would like to express our especial gratitude to Roger Adams and the ACCA, who not only funded the project but also supported it in many ways, and to Martin Houldin of KPMG who acted as editorial advisor for the book and wrote the overviews for Parts A, B and C. We are also pleased to acknowledge the help we received from Rick Clarke of KPMG, Mark Campanale of Jupiter Tarbutt Merlin, Tony Clayton of IPAD, John Elkington of Sustain-Ability, Frank Jenkins of DTI, Nola Buhr, Sue Gray, Helle Bank Jorgensen, Linda Lewis, Meg Liston, Dave Owen, Ian Thomson, Jonathon Walesby and colleagues at the University of Dundee who have all given of their time, experience and ideas in different ways.

Rob Gray
Jan Bebbington
Diane Walters
August 1992

How to Use this Book

The book has been written with several different audiences in mind. First, it should provide a good basic introduction to the business and environment agenda for those who are not familiar with the issues – whether accountants, management, students, academics or the general reader and whether seeking a practical guide or a wider introduction to the issues at stake. Second, the book is not restricted to just the accounting issues. In recognizing that any developments in environmental accounting must occur in a context of increased environmental sensitivity within the organization, many of the basic management developments that must take place to mitigate an organization's environmental impact are introduced. Thus the book will provide a good introduction for the management of organizations of all sizes which can be used as a complement to the increasing number of excellent management texts and manuals in the field. The book thus should be of equal interest and relevance to practising managers and, for example, MBA students. Third, and most importantly, the book lays out the state of the art in environmental accounting and provides guidelines, ideas and proposals for ways in which accounting may become more responsive to environmental needs. As a result, the book should be of interest to all accountants and students of accounting.

We thus anticipate that the book may be used in a number of ways. It may be read as a whole. It may be used to support teaching at either undergraduate, professional or post-experience level. It can be used as a reference text for particular topics at particular times. It may be used as a preliminary 'how to go green' manual. Or it can be dipped into for practical examples or for general guidance.

Organizational response to the environment in general and accounting for the environment in particular are fairly recent developments. This is the first book – anywhere in the world as far as we are aware – that has tried to address the environmental/accounting relationship in a way suitable for all branches of the accounting and management professions. We have tried to put the text together in a way that will be amenable to as wide a range of approaches as possible and we hope that this text will help develop the accountants' role within the rapidly evolving environmental agenda.

About CSEAR, ACCA and KPMG

The Centre for Social and Environmental Accounting Research was established by the University of Dundee in 1991. Its principal purpose is to act as a networking centre between academics and practitioners in the field of social and environmental accounting on a worldwide basis. It achieves this by keeping open a flow of information about experiments and experiences between academics and between academics and practitioners in different countries. CSEAR has been base-funded by ACCA and KPMG, has contacts throughout the world and produces a newsletter. For more detail please contact the Centre at the address in Appendix B.

The Chartered Association of Certified Accountants is one of the world's major professional accountancy bodies and funds a wide range of original and practical research. The ACCA funded the research which underpinned *The Greening of Accountancy*, published in 1990, and has provided the funding and support on which the present text is based. In addition, the ACCA launched the Environmental Reporting Awards Scheme, which is a major initiative in developing environmental disclosure by organizations.

KPMG Peat Marwick are one of the world's largest accountancy firms. The UK firm has one of the longest-established accountancy-based environmental consultancies – the KPMG National Environment Unit. In addition to a wide client base in the public and private sectors, KPMG work closely with organizations like Business-in-the-Environment and the Environment Council and have been responsible for a number of environmental initiatives. They specialize in advising government bodies on matters of policy, supporting financial auditors and corporate finance teams with environmental expertise and in all aspects of environmental management.

Acronyms and Abbreviations Used in the Text

ABC	Activity Based Costing
ACBE	Advisory Committee on Business and the Environment
ACCA	Chartered Association of Certified Accountants
AEC	Association of Environmental Consultancies
AICPA	American Institute of Certified Public Accountants
ASB	Accounting Standards Board
ASC	Accounting Standards Committee
BATNEEC	Best Available Techniques Not Entailing Excessive Cost
BCSD	(i) Business Charter for Sustainable Development
	(ii) Business Council for Sustainable Development
BiE	Business in the Environment
BIM	British Institute of Management
BPEO	Best practicable environmental option
BS (e.g. 7750)	British Standard (e.g. 7750)
BSI	British Standards Institution
C&LD	Coopers and Lybrand Deloitte
CBI	Confederation of British Industry
CEAS	Corporate Environmental Accounting System
CEBIS	Centre for Environment and Business in Scotland
CEFIC	Conseil Européen des Fédérations de l'Industrie Chimique
CEP	Council for Economic Priorities
CERCLA	Comprehensive Environmental Response Compensation and Liability Act
CERES	Coalition for Environmentally Responsible Economies
CFCs	Chlorofluorocarbons
CHP	Combined Heat and Power
CIA	Chemical Industries Association
CIA RCP	Chemical Industries Association Responsible Care Programme
CICA	Canadian Institute of Chartered Accountants
CIMA	Chartered Institute of Management Accountants

CIMAH	Control of Industrial Major Accident Hazard
CIPFA	Chartered Institute of Public Finance and Accountancy
CIS	Counter Information Services
CMA	Society of Management Accountants of Canada
COD	Chemical Oxygen Demand
COSHH	Control of substances hazardous to health
CSEAR	Centre for Social and Environmental Accounting Research
CWS	Compliance-with-Standards
DCF	Discounted Cash Flow
DoE	Department of Environment
DTI	Department of Trade and Industry
EC	European Community
EC DG XI	Directorate General 11 (Environment, Nuclear Safety and Civil Protection)
EEO	Energy Efficiency Office
EIA	Environmental Impact Assessment
EIL	Environmental Impairment Liability
EIRIS	Ethical Investment Research Service
EIS	Environmental Impact Statement
EMS	Environmental Management System
ENDS	Environmental Data Services
EPA	(i) Environmental Protection Act
	(ii) Environmental Protection Agency
EPS	Environment Priority Strategies
EQM	Environmental Quality Management
ERA	Environmental Reporting Awards
FASB	Financial Accounting Standards Board
FRC	Financial Reporting Council
G7	The Group of Seven (major industrialized countries)
G77	The Group of 77 (lesser developed countries)
GATT	General Agreement on Tariffs and Trade
GEM	Gas Energy Management
HMIP	Her Majesty's Inspectorate of Pollution
HMSO	Her Majesty's Stationery Office
HSE	Health and Safety Executive
IAS	International Accounting Standard
IASC	International Accounting Standards Committee
ICAEW	Institute of Chartered Accountants in England and Wales
ICAS	Institute of Chartered Accountants of Scotland
ICC	International Chamber of Commerce
ICCBCSD	International Chamber of Commerce Business Charter for Sustainable Development
IEA	Institute of Environmental Assessment
IIEA	International Institute of Environmental Auditors
IISD	International Institute for Sustainable Development
INCPEN	Industry Council for Packaging and the Environment

IoD	Institute of Directors
IPAD	Institute of Policy and Development
JIT	Just In Time
LCA	Life Cycle Analysis/Assessment
LDC	Lesser Developed Country
MNE	Multinational Enterprise
NACCB	National Accreditation Council of Certification Bodies
NADS	National Association of Diaper Services
NPV	Net Present Value
OECD	Organization For Economic Co-operation and Development
Ofwat	Office of the Director General of Water Services
PCB	Polychlorinated biphenyls
PIRC	(i) Public Interest Research Centre
	(ii) Pensions Investment Resource Centre.
PPP	Pollution Prevention Pays
SARA	Superfund Amendments and Reauthorization Act
SEC	(i) Securities and Exchange Commission
	(ii) State Electricity Commission (of Victoria, Australia)
SETAC	Society of Environmental Toxicology and Chemistry
SEPTIC	Single Event Pollution Triggered Incident Clause
SFAS	Statement of Financial Accounting Standards (see FASB)
SNA	United Nations' System of National Accounts
SORP	Statement of Recommended Practice
SSAP	Statement of Standard Accounting Practice
SWOT	Strengths, Weaknesses, Opportunities, Threats
TQM	Total Quality Management
TRI	Toxic Release Inventory
TUC	Trades Unions Congress
UNCED	United Nations Commission on Environment and Development
UN CTC	United Nations Centre for TransNational Corporations
UN CTC ISAR	United Nations Centre for TransNational Corporations Intergovernmental Working Group of Experts on International Standards of Accounting and Reporting
UNEP	United Nations Environmental Programme
VAS	Value Added Statement
WARM	Waste as a Raw Material
WCA	Waste Collection Authority
WDA	Waste Disposal Authority
WEN	Women's Environmental Network

WICEM II	Second World Industry Conference on Environmental Management
WRA	Waste Regulation Authority
WRAP	Waste Reduction Always Pays
WWF	World Wildlife Fund for Nature

PART A

INTRODUCTION TO THE ISSUES

Part A: An Introduction to the Issues – an Overview

by Martin Houldin, KPMG National Environment Unit

Introduction

At a pragmatic level, the two most obvious reasons for accountants to be involved in environmental issues are that:

(1) Environmental issues are business issues. Above all this book seeks to show clearly that environmental issues, in terms of legislation and market changes, have implications for business in those areas which directly concern accountants of all shapes and sizes. From straightforward cost and P&L issues, to competitive advantage and cost efficiency, to the more complex issues in asset values, contingent liabilities and environmental risk, most accountants will have a role to play.

(2) Environmental issues have considerable implications for 'audit' in all its guises. In addition to the environmental implications for the statutory audit there are the growing demands of 'environmental audit' – over which there is much confusion. Environmental audits are put firmly in their place within a context of environmental management. Again, many accountants will find scope for involvement, although less directly in environmental audits (a tool for the review of environmental issues), whilst the more 'genuine' audits will call for much of the skills and experience of accountants.

The first two chapters do more than introduce environmental issues as they affect accountants. A strong case is made in support of the view that accountants have a major role to play, both through their traditional roles of recording and reporting financial details and through their roles as business managers. The authors go even further to suggest that there are five ways in which accountants can contribute to environmental management:

(1) Modify existing accounting systems (as in energy costing).
(2) Eliminate conflicting elements of the accounting systems (as in investment appraisal).
(3) Plan for financial implications of the environmental agenda (as in capital expenditure projections).
(4) Introduce environmental performance to external reporting (as in annual reports).
(5) Develop new accounting and information systems (as in eco-balance-sheets).

Research findings indicate that accountants are not yet as involved as they could be, especially when some aspects of the environmental agenda and the attitudes of different groups are taken into account. This is surprising when one considers the financial implications of incurring liabilities for cleaning up contaminated land, of being in breach of (environmental) regulations, and of being able to gain market share over competitors who have been slower in grasping the need to change (in response, for example, to the implications of the packaging standards in the German market). It is also remark-able when taking into account the shift of public opinion, and the thinking and actions of leaders in the business community. In spite of widespread efforts of, for example, the ICC and CBI, survey results seem to show a distinct lack of interest in meeting higher environmental performance standards unless there is pressure of legislation – although given the rapid change in the environmental agenda it remains to be seen how reliable these results still are.

A Practitioner's View

From wide experience in working with different companies on the full spectrum of the components of environmental management, it could be said that we can be assured of much greater interest from accountants in the near future. Indeed there are indications that this is already happening in perhaps the one area which you might expect to be in the vanguard, namely the arrangement of corporate deals/transactions.

Before delving into the body of the book, it is useful to consider the following issues.

Business and Environmental Issues

What are the business implications of environmental issues and how is business responding? The spectrum of environmental pressures (see Figure A.1) really has two broad categories: legislative (local, national, regional) and market-based. Each has implications for business and accountants.

UK legislation Mainly the EPA 1990, the Water Act 1990 and the register of contaminated land. Companies will need to:

Figure A.I.

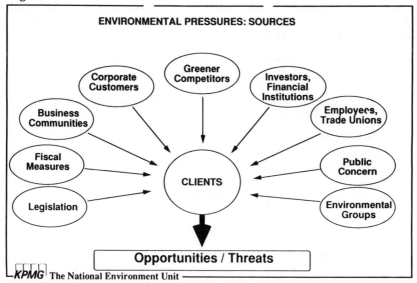

- invest in pollution protection;
- invest in cleaner technologies;
- change processes and products;
- review asset values;
- spend on waste treatment/disposal.

EC legislation   A much wider range of environmental legislation is due for enactment by the mid-1990s. By the early 1990s there were already some business implications:

- the nature of packaging is changing;
- packaging recovery/recycling schemes are needed;
- cost of waste treatment/disposal is rising;
- companies need to make more information available to the public;
- heavier industrial processes need to adopt environmental management practices.

Fiscal measures   Market or economic instruments to encourage environmental response – carbon taxes raising the cost of energy by 50 per cent likely in the EC.

Business community   Peer pressure and leadership through, for example, ICC, CBI, BiE, BAUM acting ahead of legislation.

Corporate customers   Cradle-to-grave and total life-cycle leading to 'responsible care' for use and disposal of products and 'environmental audits' of suppliers' standards.

Greener competitors   Competition is developing through cost-effective response to legislation and to customer needs, high environmental profile in markets and the development of products with better environmental performance.

Investors/financial institutions   Environmental issues mean new risks for financial institutions requiring more information from companies on: capital expenditure plans; the environmental effect on profits; potential liabilities; and ability to cope with existing and future environmental problems.

Public concern/environmental groups   Companies need to build closer working relationships with groups who are increasingly vocal and well informed by the greater amount of information available in the public domain. Despite the (temporary?) decline in the impact of the green consumer, the impact of these groups is rising.

Environmental Accounting

What do we mean by environmental accounting? This is open to interpretation. However, for the purposes of this book it can be taken as covering all areas of accounting that may be affected by the business response to environmental issues, including new areas of eco-accounting.

Environmental accounting will cover:

- accounting for contingent liabilities/risks;
- accounting for asset revaluations and capital projections;
- costs analysis in key areas such as energy, waste and environmental protection;
- investment appraisal to include environmental factors;
- development of new accounting and information systems;
- assessing the costs and benefits of environmental improvement programmes;
- developing accounting techniques which express assets and liabilities and costs in ecological (non-financial) terms.

But the development of the accountants' role will be set within an environmental management context. As with any new field of management, there will be differing ways of defining environmental management. One broad definition is 'the range of responses by companies to environmental issues in reviewing their environmental position, developing and implementing policies and strategies to improve that position and in changing management systems to ensure ongoing improvement and effective management'. And environmental management will consist of a range of functions which, in turn, will influence the role of the accountant.

Environmental Management Functions

- environmental review;
- policy/objectives development;
- life-cycle assessment;
- standards – BS7750, eco-audit, ISO;
- regulatory compliance;
- environmental assessment (including contaminated land);
- eco-label applications;
- waste minimization;
- research, development and investment in cleaner technologies.

Environmental Management and Accountants

How does all this affect different accountant roles when translated to the job level? It is evident from the above introduction to the business implications of environmental issues and the definitions given for environmental management and environmental accounting, that a variety of accounting jobs will be affected.

By mapping environmental issues to different accounting jobs we can begin to see more clearly how accountants will be involved, (see below).

How the Accountants' Jobs Will Change

Financial accountant
- Balance sheet issues:
    - valuation
    - liabilities
    - contingencies
    - provisions
- Profit & loss issues:
    - major cost items such as waste treatment/disposal and site clean-up
- Annual reports:
    - environmental performance figures
- Relationships with banks, fund managers, insurance companies.

Management accountant
- Business plans including new costs, capital items and revenue projections.
- Investment appraisal to evaluate environmental costs/benefits.
- Cost/benefit analysis of environmental improvement.
- Cost analysis/efficiency improvement programmes.

Systems accountant
- Changes to management information systems.
- Changes to financial reporting systems.

Project accountant
- Investment appraisal.
- Environmental auditing of proposed corporate deals (mergers and acquisitions).
- Environmental assessment for planning purposes.

Accountants as internal auditors
- Incorporate environmental auditing into internal audit programmes.

As these affect accountants in commerce and industry, then we also see corresponding roles for accountants within the professions, acting as auditors or specialist advisers.

From an accountant's point of view all this could be seen as unwelcome change; however, it can equally be regarded as a great opportunity for building on the proactive, business management roles that many accountants already enjoy. Environmental issues are of real interest to accountants because of the breadth and scale of potential business issues that arise, both profitable and cost-incurring. Many of us believe that, as accountants, we have no option but to tackle environmental issues at all points in the company. We do have the option, however, to get involved early and plan ahead, or to be forced to react to the negative effects of pressures.

1. Business and the Environment:

The Challenge for Accounting and Finance

In responding to the challenges posed by the environment, which is our natural wealth, all aspects of accountancy including financial reporting, auditing, management accounting and taxation will have to change. In doing so, there will be an impact on all members of the Institute whether in public practice or in commerce and industry and whether working at home or abroad.

(Mike Lickiss, ex-President of the Institute of Chartered Accountants in England and Wales, *Accountancy*, January 1991)

The Department of Ecology is most concerned that facilities make a good faith effort to make the economic analysis of pollution prevention alternatives as complete as possible, and to include environmental compliance and oversight costs. Many case studies show that such expanded cost accounting helps facilities implement pollution prevention projects that they would otherwise have felt required to reject because of costs.

Washington State Department of Ecology *Guidance Paper: Economic Analysis for Pollution Prevention*, Washington State, July 1992 (p3)

1.1 Introduction

The need for a substantial response to the worldwide environmental crisis from organizations in general and business in particular has never been clearer or more urgent. The need is one which demands imaginative and complete responses from all sectors of the business, commerce and professional communities because no one group, no single functional area of business, can on its own make the sort of profound change which is necessary. Despite the relatively considerable strides made by many businesses throughout the world by the early 1990s,[1] the response from the accounting and finance community as a whole had been fairly lukewarm and superficial. The role played by accounting in the early steps taken by corporations towards a 'greening of business' was small. Yet it was becoming brutally apparent that a more substantial move towards a sustainable economic framework could not be achieved without a more substantial response from accounting and finance.[2]

There are two principal reasons for this. First, it is quite apparent that, in the current political climate, if there is to be any major progress in reducing the rate of ecological destruction, business will have to play a major part – and, indeed, appear to be keen to do so.[3] Second, wide experience shows that: (a) business people need some guidance, some 'performance indicators', on their achievements in environmental activity – such an information system would need to run parallel with or be incorporated with the present accounting information system; (b) current accounting practice and the present accounting and financial frameworks both hinder environmental initiatives and positively encourage environmentally malign activity (see Figure 1.1 and Appendix 1.1). Thus, business cannot fully embrace the necessary environmental changes until accounting and finance have done so. For these pragmatic reasons if for no other, accountants must learn to incorporate environmental factors into their more traditional roles.

1.2   Accountants, Accounting and the Environment

Whilst there is no doubt that accounting is not the most obvious place to start if one is seeking to address either environmental issues in general or the business/environment relationship in particular, it is equally true that without a 'greener accounting' many environmental initiatives will simply not get off the ground. Throughout this book we have treated the accountant as a member of the organization's management team and therefore seen his or her role

---

[1] The advances made by the environmentally aware businesses can be seen to be considerable compared with their starting points. There is, however, a very strong case that compared to the extensiveness of the ecological crisis, the steps taken by business by the early 1990s were really very superficial and did not come close to addressing the real systemic issues at stake.

[2] Sustainability and its implications are explored in Chapter 14.

[3] The most obvious examples of this are the international initiatives of the Business Council for Sustainable Development (BCSD) and the International Chamber of Commerce (ICC), see, for example, ICC (1989) and Schmidheiny (1992). A word of caution, however, is appropriate. In part such initiatives could be seen as attempts actually to control, rather than respond to, the environmental agenda. It is noticeable that business-based publications on the subject generally avoid engaging the environmentalists' arguments in the debate. The most obvious example of this relates to 'growth' and whether it is the cause of or the cure for ecological desecration. No business-based publication of which we are aware has made any attempt to address carefully the 'anti-growth' arguments and evidence.

Figure 1.1

Some areas where traditional accounting and finance frameworks are in conflict with environmental initiatives

- Investment appraisal criteria
- Performance appraisal criteria
- Budgeting constraints
- Share price performance
- Reported earnings per share
- Priorities in the annual report
- Design costs
- Creation of new information systems
- Forecasting
- Assessing environmental costs
- Costs of sustainability

---

as greater than just that of maintaining the financial information systems. This will be apparent throughout the text but, in particular, it would appear to be the case that accountants in general need introducing to the wider business/environment agenda. That is, it is fairly self-evident that the accounting systems of any organization are effective only when related to the context of the organization itself. We have therefore used Chapters 2, 3, 4 and 5 to introduce many of the basic (but essential) environmental management initiatives in a way which should be relevant to the accounting and finance professional. With this background, we can then move on to those activities which are more specifically within the functional ambit of the accountant.

The accountant's role in helping organizations to become more environmentally sensitive will fall, approximately, into five phases.[4] The chapters and structure of the book reflect this.[5]

(1) The existing accounting system can be modified slightly to identify the environmentally related areas of expenditure (and, perhaps, revenue) separately. The most obvious areas for this to occur are in energy, waste, packaging, legal costs and suchlike

---

[4] We have generally chosen to ignore any tendency for accountants to treat environmental matters as 'nothing to do with me'. Such an attitude is usually predicated upon the grounds that their job is to record and account for financial transactions. When the environmental issues are reflected in changed monetary values the accountants will account for them. The changing environmental agenda has no direct affect on accounting. This would appear to be the predominant practice among accountants at the moment.

[5] This and other comments throughout the book are taken from the research we did via visits, interviews etc., working with organizations and via a questionnaire survey. More detail on this is provided in Appendix C. More detailed analysis of the interviews and questionnaires is given in a series of papers by the authors. Please contact us for further details.

(see, for example, Chapters 6 and 7) and in land remediation and liability – especially in North America (see Chapter 11).

(2) The environmentally negative elements of the existing accounting system need to be identified and, where possible, ameliorated. The most obvious examples of this relate to investment appraisal and performance appraisal (see, for example, Chapter 8).

(3) The accounting system needs to become more forward looking and, in the present context, to be more aware of potential issues arising from the rapidly changing environmental agenda. This will affect such matters as changing payback periods as energy costs change, looking forward to potential contingent liabilities, the potential costs of 'greener' financing, assessing the potential costs of *not* undertaking environmental initiatives, and so on (see, for example, Chapters 2 and 5 to 10).

(4) The external reporting function is changing. One extreme (but not unrealistic) description of current corporate reporting practice is that the accountants look after the statutory accounts and the public relations department looks after the rest. Environmental issues will not permit this hard delineation when the financial statements begin to reflect various aspects of the environmental costs, and the non-financial elements of the report need to be a great deal more substantive than self-congratulatory publicity material (see, for example, Chapters 11 and 12).

(5) New accounting and information systems will need to be developed. Whether these are physical quantity information systems or some sort of financial information system, they will need to be of a status equal to the present financial accounting systems. Experimentation and innovation will be crucial here whether one is talking about more subtle performance appraisal, the development of something akin to life-cycle assessment or really attempting to build a sustainability accounting system (see, for example, Chapters 4, 5, 8, 9 and 14).

Throughout any process of 'greening' accountancy and finance it is possible to allow accountants simply to be reactive within their conventionally conceived roles. However, whilst there is a lot of evidence to suggest that accountants *are* reactive, we have predicated much of the book on the belief that accountants are also professionals and can (and should) exercise professional attributes. For this, accountants need to recognize the responsibility which accounting bears for the environmental crisis[6] and, recognizing the skills and attributes which accountants bring to bear in their job, look for creative ways to mitigate the responsibility and to help organizations develop greater environmental sensitivity. Many accountants are *not* hostile to this view (see below) but they do not have the intention or wherewithal to put it into practice. This book is intended to help

---

[6] See Appendix 1.1, Appendix 1.2 and Gray (1990e).

Figure 1.2

What is environmental accounting?

- Recognizing and seeking to mitigate the negative environmental effects of conventional accounting practice;
- Separately identifying environmentally related costs and revenues within the conventional accounting systems;
- Taking active steps to set up initiatives in order to ameliorate existing environmental effects of conventional accounting practice;
- Devising new forms of financial and non-financial accounting systems, information systems and control systems to encourage more environmentally benign management decisions;
- Developing new forms of performance measurement, reporting and appraisal for both internal and external purposes;
- Identifying, examining and seeking to rectify areas in which conventional (financial) criteria and environmental criteria are in conflict;
- Experimenting with ways in which sustainability may be assessed and incorporated into organizational orthodoxy.

---

them do so. From a human, ethical and professional point of view, the accountant is committed to the 'public interest' and amelioration of the ecological crisis, and survival of the human species must fall within that interest. Professional accountancy bodies around the world have taken initiatives in response to the developing environmental agenda in recognition of the need for a reaction – perhaps even a lead – from the accountancy profession. Little of this (beyond material on contingent liabilities and disclosure in the USA and Canada) has yet found its way into practice. Further advance will have to come from the combination of academics and practitioners working together to meet these new challenges.[7]

1.3 Accountants and Environmental Attitudes

Our dealings with organizations have suggested that accountants are not widely involved in the changing environmental agenda. More worryingly, there is a widespread view that the accountant's conventional approach is acting like a dead hand on environmental innovation. Conventional short-term profit measurement, performance reporting, budgetary constraints and investment appraisal are highly likely to be in conflict with more environmentally benign initiatives – in the immediate term at least. For one of our correspondents this conflict is profound and the priorities clear:

I was disheartened to receive your letter of 5 Jan and to learn that a pragmatic and esteemed organisation such as yours had lowered its

---

[7] See, for example, Bebbington and Gray (1992); CSEAR was founded to facilitate this.

*standards to worry about c--p at a time when most of the nation is facing
economic hardship and your subject matter will add zero to the well-being
of this country.*

*We have therefore filed the Questionnaire in a place we believe
appropriate.*

Finance Director, Large International Trading plc (censorship by authors).

Our own survey (see Appendix C) suggests, more encouragingly,
that this is a minority view and, in fact, accountants are very keen to
innovate. However, accountants still have a strong attachment to
the conventional accounting activities – in particular financial
measurement – and, under a more favourable interpretation, are
largely unsure about whether they should become involved and, if
so, how to contribute to the development of environmental sensitivity in the organization. There seems to be little doubt that
accountants are fully aware of the changing environmental agenda
and of their own organization's responses to it. However, they
appear to be looking for a lead from the company or the professional
bodies – whilst retaining a deep-rooted suspicion of any attempt to
dilute the 'reliability', 'objectivity' and 'unbiasedness' of their conventional activity.[8] As we have argued elsewhere[9] this is an unten-
able position for the accounting profession to maintain.

These observations have a considerable importance in this book,
however. Following publication of *The Greening of Accountancy*[10] and
the continuing environmental accounting initiatives from the ACCA,
we sought to identify and describe 'best environmental accounting
practice' and, where possible, to work with organizations in the
development of their experimental environmental accounting
systems. (More details of the research process are given in Appendix
C.) It is apparent that very little that can be specifically identified as
'environmental accounting' is currently taking place. Where it *is*
taking place, many organizations are preferring to tend the seedling
growth away from the glare of publicity. Where we have identified
interesting environmental accounting practice it is reported in this
book. Elsewhere, unfortunately, we are left with inference and
(informed) speculation. Readers of this book looking for a complete
manual on 'Learn Environmental Accounting in a Weekend' will be
disappointed – as were we. Until there is a greater level of environmental accounting practice and experimentation, accounting for the
environment will remain speculative. The book has therefore been
written in a way that should provide maximum available assistance

[8] It does not (or should not) require us to rehearse why these characteristics are
rarely, if ever, present in accounting data. The continuing attachment to these
motherhood myths, if our inferences from the data are correct, is a perplexing and
worrying one.

[9] See Gray (1990c); (1990e) and Bebbington and Gray (1992).

[10] See the bibliography for Gray (1990e).

to accountants wishing to begin the process of developing greener accounting and finance systems.

1.4   Conclusions and Developing the Accountant's Role

Our research suggests that accountants are not seen as a major source of innovation – in the organization generally and in organizational response to the environment in particular. Indeed, whilst accountants *do* see themselves as potentially innovative, it is an innovation constrained within the existing financial information system. That there has been little seriously innovative environmental accounting to date is consistent with this. This will, however, have to change but in the short to medium term it seems most likely that the environmental initiative will tend to come from elsewhere in the organization. However, as the Overview to this Part notes, the rapidly changing demands upon the organization will bring an urgent demand for changes in accountants' activities. Few are yet ready to respond to this.

We have tried to provide support and encouragement for the accountant seeking to explore environmental initiatives and, as a result, have provided chapters on both potential and actual areas of direct relevance to the accountant as well as the broader environmental management areas. We have not attempted to be comprehensive on these latter topics, and refer readers to the works listed in the further reading sections. Our hope is, however, that we will encourage accountants to adopt the role that they *can* play in developing the environmental sensitivity of the organization and to see the ease with which their traditional – and perhaps limited – role can be put aside. The book cannot answer all problems and for this we have provided, in the Appendices, contacts at the Centre for Social and Environmental Accounting Research and KPMG Peat Marwick and contact points for many of the other appropriate and frequently excellent organizations.

Further Reading

General Introduction to Environmental Issues

For an excellent and beautifully presented introduction to a very broad range of the issues:
Ekins, P. (1992) *Wealth Beyond Measure: An Atlas of New Economics*, Gaia, London.

. . . or if you prefer highly glossy coffee table tomes:
Porritt, J. (1991) *Save the Earth*, Dorling Kindersley, London.

. . . an excellent but 'heavier' work is:
Jacobs, M. (1991) *The Green Economy*, Pluto Press, London.

. . . and see also the very popular:
Cairncross, F. (1991) *Costing the Earth*, Business Books/the Economist, London.

General Introductions to Business and the Environment

Chechile, R. A. and Chechile, S. (1991) *Environmental Decision Making: A Multidisciplinary Approach*, Van Nostrand Reinhold, New York.

Davis, J. (1991) *Greening Business: Managing for Sustainable Development*, Blackwell, Oxford.

Elkington, J. (1987) (with T. Burke) *The Green Capitalists*, Gollancz, London.

Elkington, J., Knight, P. and Hailes, J. (1991) *The Green Business Guide*, Gollancz, London.

Hutchinson, C. (1991) *Business and the Environmental Challenge*, Conservation Trust, Reading.

Stead, W. E. and Stead, J. G. (1992) *Management for a small planet*, Sage Publications, Newbury Park, California.

General Introductions to Accounting and the Environment

Arthur Andersen/Sidley & Austin (1990) *Environmental Liabilities: Is your company at risk?* Arthur Andersen/Sidley & Austin, Chicago.

Gray, R. H. (1990) *The Greening of Accountancy*, ACCA, London.

Molinaro, L. (ed.) (1991) *Accounting and the Environment: Reading and Discussion*, Management Institute for Environment and Business, Arlington, Virginia.

Macve, R. and Carey, A. (1992) *Business, Accountancy and the Environment: A policy and research agenda*, ICAEW, London.

Owen, D. (ed.) (1992) *Green Reporting: Accountancy and the Challenge of the Nineties*, Chapman Hall, London.

Price Waterhouse Environmental Services (1991) *Environmental Accounting: The Issues, The Developing Solutions – A Survey of Corporate America's Accounting for Environmental Costs*, Price Waterhouse, Pittsburgh.

General Introduction to (UK) Law and the Environment

Ball, S. and Bell, S. (1991) *Environmental Law*, Blackstone, London.

APPENDIX 1.1
The Accountant and the Environment:
A Systems View[1]

Whilst accountants use systems terminology (in, particularly, management information systems and auditing) there have been only a few attempts to take a wider systems perspective of the conventional accounting activity itself. One such view is given in Figure Appendix 1.1a.[2]

The figure is no more than a reinterpretation of what the accountant traditionally does. His or her world centres around the organization (the accounting entity – which is itself a system made up of various sub-systems; see Laughlin and Gray (1988) for more detail), which can be seen to be located in a 'substantive environment'. (The word 'environment' does not necessarily have ecological connotations in this context.) This 'substantive environment' is bounded with reference to only those events which the accountant traditionally recognizes – those economic events which can be described in financial terms. For simplicity, the flows that the accountant records can be categorized into three sets of inflows (debits) and three sets of outflows (credits) represented by information (e.g. debtors, creditors, ownership claims), funds (all receipts and payments) and physical resources/goods and services (e.g. labour, plant, vehicles, buildings, materials, sales).

This perspective can be used to capture all the accountant's book-keeping and financial reporting activities, but one of the major benefits of this view is that it makes explicit the very limited view we take of the world. In Figure Appendix 1.1b, a simple representation of the social world is introduced. Now we can see the accountant's perspective rather more clearly. The organization is a complex web of interactions drawing from and contributing to the social world in many ways (both positive and negative). Because many of these interactions are either implicit, and/or embedded into the very fabric of the society (e.g. the question of personal and group rights) and/or are matters of interpretation and perception they are not made explicit in a way that the price system – and therefore tradi-

---

[1] The material that follows is a straight adaptation of the material in Gray (1990e).

[2] Figure Appendix 1.1a and subsequent figures are based upon the excellent work of Lowe (1972) and Lowe and McInnes (1971). These ideas are summarized and employed in a financial accounting context by Laughlin and Gray (1988). A very good critique of systems theory is provided by Hopper and Powell (1985).

Figure Appendix 1.1a A Systems View of Accounting, Organizations and the Environment

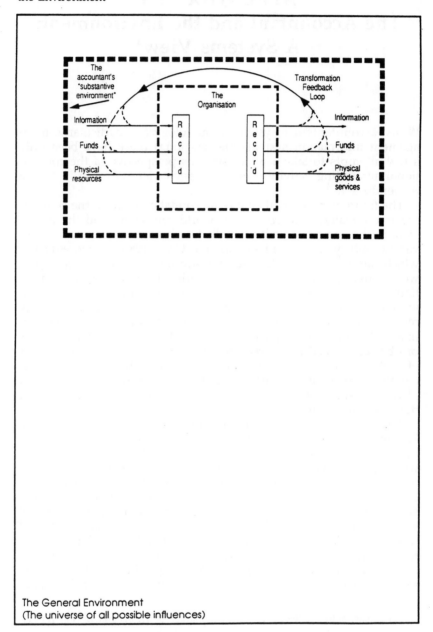

Adapted from Lowe (1972) and Laughlin & Gray (1988)

Figure Appendix 1.1b   A Systems View of Accounting, Organizations and
the Environment

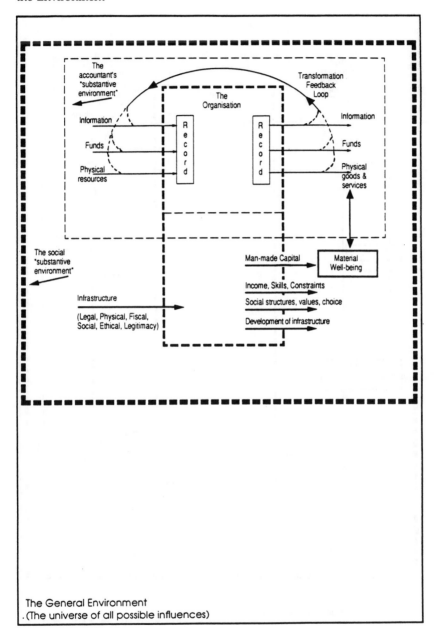

Adapted from Lowe (1972) and Laughlin & Gray (1988)

Figure Appendix 1.1c   A Systems View of Accounting, Organizations and the Environment

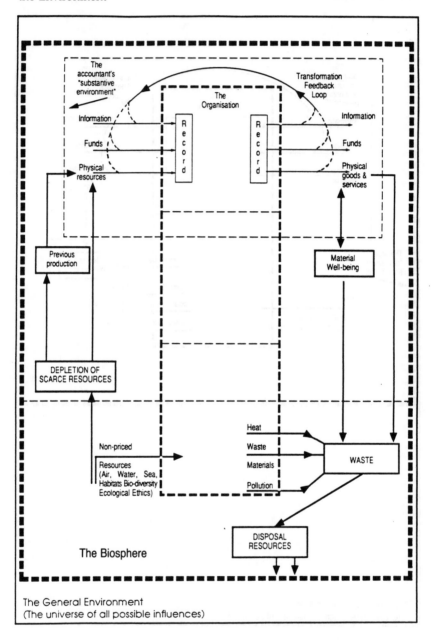

Adapted from Lowe (1972) and Laughlin & Gray (1988)

tional accounting practice – can recognize. Traditional accounting therefore largely ignores them, as does the traditional neo-classical model of economics (see, for example, Gray, 1990f). It is almost certainly the case that accounting ignores these interactions *because* of these omissions by the underlying economic model.

Our present concern is with environmental issues, and these are introduced into the model in Figure Appendix 1.1c. The activities of the organization in creating material well-being draw off from the biosphere some things for which prices exist (raw materials) and some things for which no prices exist (landscape, sea water). The biosphere in most cases is diminished by this. The processes of producing the man-made capital and the (presumed) subsequent material well-being as well as the subsequent consumption benefits lead to waste (immediately or eventually). This waste is injected back into the biosphere – there is nowhere else for it to go! The accountant's model cannot recognize these interactions and so they are ignored. The problems this raises are graphically put by Yankelovich (1972), in his 'Macnamara fallacy':

> The first step is to measure whatever can be easily measured. This is OK as far as it goes. The second step is to disregard that which can't be easily measured or give it an arbitrary quantitative value. This is artificial and misleading. The third step is to presume that what can't be measured easily really isn't important. This is blindness. The fourth step is to say that what can't be easily measured really doesn't exist. This is suicide.
>
> (Source: D. Yankelovich (1972) *Corporate Priorities: A continuing study of the new demands on business*, Daniel Yankelovich Inc, Stamford, Conn.)

The pictures painted by accounting must be incomplete – it can recognize only those things which can be measured, which can be measured in prices, and which are exchanged for prices. In so far as accounting is an important source of information about organizations, this incompleteness may be very dangerous. The information from the accounting system is used in a whole range of management decisions and is a major source of information to the external participants of the organization. It not only forms part of the basis of important decisions but, far more importantly and subtly, accounting helps define and measure the 'success' of actions and, ultimately helps construct our concepts of organization and of the world itself. Accounting is thus implicated in the construction of a 'social reality' (this point is especially well developed by Hines, 1988, 1989). With regard to (for example) the environment it is obvious that the accounting picture is one from which essential elements are missing and, if used as a basis for action and decision, it must mislead. The present environmental crisis is certainly a function of decisions taken for reasons of economic success or efficiency. To a large degree, accounting forms a major basis for the assessment of that success or efficiency – accounting is the scorekeeper. The 'score' takes no account of environmental matters and so, as a result, neither does 'economic' decision-making. Given the importance of accounting information and the way in which we account it seems inevitable therefore that 'economic' decisions must be environmentally malign. The environmental crisis is an inevitable result of the way we accountants do what we do. Accounting bears a serious responsibility for the growing level of environmental devastation.

APPENDIX 1.2
The impact of the environment on the conventional financial statements

PROFIT & LOSS ACCOUNT

REVENUE

Market growth

market decline

product taxes

COSTS

Clean-up
Effluent/emission control
or reduction
Waste Treatment/
disposal
Insurance
Fines
H & S Claims
Plant Depreciation
Compliance
Waste Minimisation
Licences/Authorisations
Research & Development

KPMG The National Environment Unit

BALANCE SHEET

ASSETS

Land Revaluations

Plant Write-offs

New Plant

Stock - net realizable

value

LIABILITIES

Breach of Consents

- fines/actions, damages

Remediation
(pollution damage)

Capital Commitments

Contingent Liabilities

KPMG The National Environment Unit

2. Business and the Environment:

Agenda, Attitudes and Actions

2.1 Introduction

The first question for any organization considering its response to the environmental agenda is to decide the importance of environmental issues. Until an organization comes to a view on this question, it is not possible to respond in an appropriate way. This chapter will briefly introduce the elements of the environmental debate and then attempt to outline the positions that individuals and organizations are taking on the environmental agenda. This should illustrate the range of views and help accountants and management to reach responsible conclusions.[1] However, the environmental issues *are* different in nature from other 'normal' business strategic issues in that the wrong decision may have the profoundest effects for a great deal more than one's business, one's employees, management and shareholders. Attitude to the environmental issues is therefore a crucial first step in the greening of enterprise (see Figure 2.1).

2.2 The Evolving Agenda

Environmental issues are evolving so fast and developments in thinking, law, practice and attitudes are so very rapid that no one individual could keep up with them. Figure 2.2 illustrates just some

[1] We should perhaps state that the authors share a 'deep green' view of the environmental issues in that we consider the planet to be in crisis and that the crisis must transcend other, shorter-term concerns. We know that this is a minority view. We also know it is not a view held widely in business and accounting circles. We fully respect the views of our 'lighter green' colleagues but would claim that all the evidence supports our case. We will try to be even-handed in giving 'both sides' throughout the text.

Figure 2.1

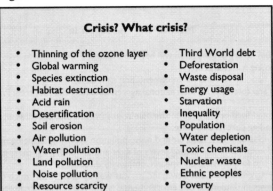

Crisis? What crisis?

- Thinning of the ozone layer
- Global warming
- Species extinction
- Habitat destruction
- Acid rain
- Desertification
- Soil erosion
- Air pollution
- Water pollution
- Land pollution
- Noise pollution
- Resource scarcity
- Third World debt
- Deforestation
- Waste disposal
- Energy usage
- Starvation
- Inequality
- Population
- Water depletion
- Toxic chemicals
- Nuclear waste
- Ethnic peoples
- Poverty

Figure 2.2

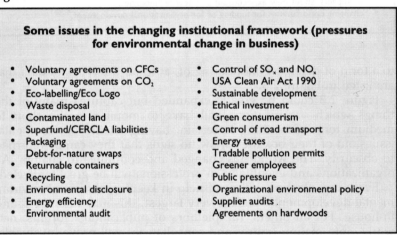

Some issues in the changing institutional framework (pressures for environmental change in business)

- Voluntary agreements on CFCs
- Voluntary agreements on CO_2
- Eco-labelling/Eco Logo
- Waste disposal
- Contaminated land
- Superfund/CERCLA liabilities
- Packaging
- Debt-for-nature swaps
- Returnable containers
- Recycling
- Environmental disclosure
- Energy efficiency
- Environmental audit
- Control of SO_x and NO_x
- USA Clean Air Act 1990
- Sustainable development
- Ethical investment
- Green consumerism
- Control of road transport
- Energy taxes
- Tradable pollution permits
- Greener employees
- Public pressure
- Organizational environmental policy
- Supplier audits
- Agreements on hardwoods

of the areas that are changing and from which further change will come. What must be grasped, is that each of these changes will produce a pressure for change – indirectly (for example, through changes in service or material availability) or directly (for example, through legislation). These pressures must be incorporated into the organization. That, in turn, will raise demands for innovation in the accounting and related information systems. All functional areas of accounting and management will be affected. Adjustment earlier in the process will avoid ill-advised change later. Thus, monitoring the agenda and all its developments (see Chapter 3) is a crucial element in coming to – and educating – one's view on the ecological crisis as it influences (and will influence) business and accounting. This leads

Figure 2.3

Monitoring the Agenda

At a minimum, every organization will have to monitor:
* forthcoming national law;
* existing national law and its implementation timetable;
* existing and forthcoming international agreements (e.g. the Montreal Protocol on CFCs);
* existing and forthcoming law in the countries in which one operates and in which one's trading partners operate;
* the activities of water, land, air and noise pollution agencies, changing methods and levels of enforcement, changing levels of fines and increasing tightness of consents;
* existing and forthcoming European Community directives;
* industry agreements – one's own industry as well as those with which one deals;
* the changes in thinking about environmental issues (e.g. on sustainability); public opinion and the attitudes and actions of the pressure groups;
* the ethical position of oneself, one's employees and colleagues and one's organization vis-à-vis the environmental issues;
* changing knowledge – about the impact of actions on the biosphere, about the scale of impacts; about new expectations and new technologies;
* changing opportunities for funding or for organizational development.

to a form of defensive monitoring of, at least, the types of data that are listed in Figure 2.3.

Figure 2.3 could be greatly expanded but captures many of the things which organizations will have to monitor in the short to medium term. One thing is certain: having let the environmental issues out of their box they show no signs that they can be returned to obscurity. The world has changed and continues to change. All organizations and eventually all professions will be greatly affected.

Every organization will need help in keeping abreast of environmental developments. For the very largest, this may often be found in-house. For all others, the plethora of publications, forums, networks, information centres and consultancies will prove invaluable. Figure 2.4 lists some of those from which we have drawn and with which we are involved. The list is not complete, nor are we prepared to state that it is the best. Other organizations, information sources, bodies, companies, etc. are listed in Appendices A and B at the end of the book, and each chapter recommends further reading and suggests (where appropriate) specifically helpful organizations. Each chapter also contains footnotes which refer to readings and information contained in the bibliography in Appendix D.

The developing business and environmental agenda has so far relied heavily upon voluntary initiatives.[2] In addition to the inter-

---

[2] Much in keeping with the move to the political right and the more open and enthusiastic embracing of liberal economic thinking. It would be difficult to see such a move as an unqualified success.

Figure 2.4

> ## Some sources of information and help
>
> * Business-in-the-Environment
> * Business and the Environment (USA)
> * *CBI Environment Newsletter*
> * Centre for Environment and Business in Scotland (CEBIS)
> * Environment Council
> * Institute of Environmental Assessment
> * *Integrated Environmental Management*
> * International Institute of Sustainable Development (Canada)
> * International Environment Reporter (USA)
> * *KPMG Environment Briefing Notes*
> * SustainAbility
> * United Nations Centre for Transnational Corporations

national agencies (such as BCSD and ICC) each country has its own voluntary bodies. Britain especially has an abundance of them.[3] These organizations are effectively rolling the environmental agenda along while taking a proportion of the business communities with them.

However, only time will tell whether this has been effective enough. There is no evidence to suggest that voluntary action alone will be sufficient to deal with the environmental crisis and there has been a steady trickle of information which suggests that voluntary initiatives are having only partial success.[4] Equally though, legislative solutions are not without their own major problems.[5] But the probability is that voluntary initiatives cannot make the necessary impact

---

[3] These include, in addition to those mentioned in Figure 2.4, the CBI's Environment Business Forum and the UK government's Advisory Committee on Business and the Environment, as well as a whole host of more specialized outfits. See Appendix B for more detail on some of these and see, for example, Forrester (1990) on the ways in which companies and environmental groups are co-operating – and can develop that co-operation – in the UK in the 1990s. For further information see also Deziron and Bailey (1991).

[4] For example, a Friends of the Earth Report in 1991 (reported in the *Guardian*, 12 July 1991) states that the voluntary action on CFC reductions is much slower than required by the target dates; the Conservative UK government, previously wedded entirely to the purity of 'market forces', is finding that they do not work as required (reported in the *Observer*, 5 January 1992); whilst there is a steady flow of examples in which corporate and environmental interests are in conflict – and where the corporate interests appear to usually be the winners (reports in, for example, *Financial Times*, 25 November 1991, on the conflict between Ofwat and the water companies, and in the *Observer*, 11 November 1990, on the conflict between a major environmental initiative in the USA opposed by many companies including three of the UK's leading 'green' organizations).

[5] The most widely reported example is that 'twenty years of US emission control have done little to improve air quality', especially with respect to automobiles (Bell, 1992).

Figure 2.5

The four principles of ecology

- Every separate entity is connected to all the rest;
- Everything has to go somewhere;
- You cannot get something for nothing from it;
- Nature knows best.

Source: B. Commoner (1972) 'The social use and misuse of technology' in Benthall J. (ed.) *Ecology: the shaping enquiry* London: Longman pp. 335-362

---

when there are clear clashes between short-term business interests and protection of the environment.

A critical major factor appears to be attitude and the extent of one's education in environmentalism and ecology. More especially, our experience suggests that *what* an individual knows about the environment and *how* that individual thinks about what he or she knows profoundly affects attitudes. In particular, the extent to which one does or does not believe in the possibility of 'environmental crisis' depends largely on whether or not one can consider the elements in Figure 2.1 as isolated, individually soluble problems or whether one sees them as connected, interrelated and systemic.[6] It is only when the elements are seen in this systemic way that a crisis – rather than a 'problem' – is perceived.

2.3   The Public, Media and Politicians

Whilst each individual will come to some personal, educated view on the facts of the environmental crisis (and their ethical response to those facts), it is likely that every organization will be more immediately concerned with how the environmental issues are constructed, perceived and construed by the public, the media and by politicians. As the CBI[7] (1992b, emphasis added) put it:

> *The public debate of environmental issues is growing. The heightened awareness it brings is welcome but* can lead to issues getting greater attention environmentally than they deserve. *The CBI believes it is*

---

[6] This is known as 'systems thinking', related to general systems theory and is apparent in most environmental books. For an introduction see Gray (1990e) from which Appendix 1.1 is taken.

[7] This quotation, and a great deal from the CBI, highlights an essential series of questions. In particular is there a conflict between business needs and environmental needs? The CBI would generally hope that there was not. The answer depends on how 'deep green' one is. A second major problem is whether or not business has the right, the moral position or the ability to set the environmental agenda *correctly* (see below). Too much of the environmental debate is conducted in a business-knows-best climate when business cannot *always* know best.

Figure 2.6

Public opinion and the environment

In the UK, 30% of people questioned in 1990 saw the environment as the (or one of the) most important issues facing the country and over 90% professed themselves sufficiently concerned about the greenhouse effect to consider doing something about it. By early 1991, less than 5% were giving the environment the same priority. In Canada, for example, 21% saw the environment as the biggest single issue in June 1989 but by January 1991 this was down to 10%.

In the UK, in early 1992 over 60% of respondents to a survey professed themselves 'worried' or 'very worried' about water pollution, oil spills, global warming, loss of wildlife, radioactive waste, insecticides and fertilizers, acid rain, air pollution, litter and rubbish, drinking water quality and loss of green belt. Over 50% were either active or expressed a willingness to be active on avoiding CFCs, picking up litter, avoiding pesticides, using bottle banks, reducing electricity consumption, recycling newspapers, using alternative – non-car – transport, using recycled paper, using lead-free petrol and using phosphate-free washing powder. In Canada, where environmental awareness at least appears to be better developed than in the UK, the continuing environmental concern expresses itself in fears over the threats to life, in changing consumption patterns, in beliefs about the growing responsibility of individuals, governments and business and in a recognition that environmental issues are likely to have a substantial impact on life-styles.

---

right for businesses collectively to help set the agenda *by stating their priorities, by enhancing their own awareness of the environment and by working more closely with Government and all those agencies, national and international, active in the field.*

Public, media and political opinion influences business practice, consumer attitudes and employee concerns and ultimately leads to regulation and the institutional framework within which organizations operate. Such opinion will have an immediate impact on organizations, whereas the environmental facts, no matter how pessimistic one might be, are unlikely to have much noticeable direct effect on organizations – in the developed world at least – for some time.

Public opinion on the environment is volatile and varies from country to country, but that volatility disguises the extent to which environment concern is an enduring issue – that continues to develop but with a lower, less excitable, profile. (See Figure 2.6[8]). From a business strategy point of view, the volatility of public opinion does not offer any real lead for business – except perhaps to encourage organizations to persuade the public that there is not much to worry about. In this, business in the UK and elsewhere

[8] Taken from (i) a MORI poll in the *Independent* in July 1990 and reported by Greg Neale to the Canada–UK Colloquium, 1991; (ii) an *Observer*/Harris poll reported in the *Observer*, 15 April 1990; (iii) a report from Barry Watson of Environics in a paper to the Canada–UK Colloquium, 1991; (iv) a report in the *Independent on Sunday*, 12 January 1992.

appears to be achieving 'success'. However, it is clear that although the public media have perhaps reduced their excitability over the issues, the quantity and – more importantly – the quality of environmentally related journalism, investigations and general programmes is continuing to increase. Organizations are almost certain to find themselves with increasingly environmentally better-educated public, customers and employees.

The media-vaunted rise of the 'green consumer' may have cooled off but consumption habits have changed and continue to do so. As we shall see in later chapters, no organization can ignore the green purchaser for much longer and there is every sign – not least with the arrival of eco-labelling – that environmentally motivated consumption will have an increasing effect on organizational life.[9]

The impact of the environmentally minded employee is not yet clear. A 1990 report in the UK suggested that environmental issues played a part in most graduates' thinking when seeking employment.[10] In times of recession and unemployment this may seem a little optimistic but reports from the USA have suggested that environmental concern is of increasing significance in highly competitive markets for the rare and best-potential employees.[11] Certainly, the retention and motivation of employees are closely linked to how they feel about the environmental impact of what they do. Many companies have spoken to us of the importance that they place on their employees' attitudes to the environmental posture of the company.[12]

Public perceptions of the environmental agenda are, by and large, constructed by the popular media: an increase in reportage leads to a corresponding rise in concern among an organization's public, local community, customers and employees – and perhaps even among its shareholders, bankers and insurers (see Chapter 10). And active environmental groups are increasingly successful in using the media to make known their points of view. For these reasons, if for no others, every organization must monitor media attention to environmental matters and must, as far as possible, stay in tune with the developing concerns of the environmentalists (see Chapter 3).

But public concern has its greatest impact when reflected in political concern. This is generally less of an issue in the UK than

---

[9] For more detail see, for example, Bruce (1989), Elkington and Hailes (1988, 1989), Ferguson (1989), Foster (1989), Krietzman (1988), Papworth (1990a,b), Redmond (1988) and especially Adams, Carruthers and Hamil (1991).

[10] KPH Marketing Report 'Student attitudes to corporate responsibility and environmental issues', 1990.

[11] For more detail see Baxter and Rarick (1989), Bennett (1988), Benson (1989), Cartwright (1990), Houldin (1989).

[12] A view shared – and much expanded upon – in Elkington, Knight and Hailes (1991), chapter 12.

in many other countries,[13] but it cannot be ignored altogether. A survey of UK politicians in early 1991[14] showed a relatively relaxed attitude to environmental issues and suggested that business has been fairly successful in persuading politicians that environmental issues must be good for business, and voluntary initiatives by business are infinitely preferable to the dead weight of legislation.[15] Despite this, the regulatory framework on environmental matters in the UK is increasing – prompted, in part, by the increasingly penetrating responses of the European Community. Monitoring this will soon be a prerequisite for continuing in business and illustrates that, to maintain position, each organization must watch developments throughout Europe and, indeed, in all its markets, areas of supply and locations of activity.

Much of this must appear self-evident and yet Elkington reports that, in 1990 (at the height of the first wave of public green concern) 30 per cent of companies considered that environmental issues had no relevance for their business and 50 per cent had taken no steps to adjust to the developing environmental agenda.[16]

2.4 Business Attitude and Business Response

Even by the early 1990s a large proportion of British management was still choosing to ignore environmental matters and the majority of companies were still struggling to get started – as the following headlines (from the BIM's (British Institute of Management) *Management News*) attest: February 1991 – 'More environmental awareness is vital'; September 1991 – 'Lip-service paid to the "green" cause'; February 1992 – ' "Greener" approach urged on managers: Survey highlights lack of policy'. It is this range of (lack of) concern – plus the problem we identified above of environmental issues relying heavily on personal opinion – that led us to develop the matrix shown in Figure 2.7.

The management addressed by the BIM are clearly of the view that they can stay in square A1. Whilst the vast majority of UK business would have been there until about 1989, matters have moved on and environmental issues *are* now accepted as significant – although not yet seen as life-threatening.[17] The more sensible

---

[13] See, for example, Friends of the Earth (1990).

[14] Reported in *Management Today*, March 1991, p. 100.

[15] This is not a view to which we subscribe – as will become apparent later in the book. The 1992 general election in Britain was startling in its almost total avoidance of environmental matters and this supports our assertion that environmental matters still do not have the profile that they need for either (a) the protection of the planet, and/or (b) the maintenance of British industry's ability to compete internationally.

[16] Elkington, Knight and Hailes (1991), p. 21. A survey by the Institute of Directors (1992) – a year and a half later – suggested that 30 per cent of board members *still* foresaw that environmental issues would take 0 per cent of board time. One is reminded of horses and water.

Figure 2.7 Business posture and the environment

Business Response	Belief about the state of the physical environment		
	A **Greening as a 'passing fad'**	**B** **Environmental issues are significant but *not* critical**	**C** **Natural environment *is* in crisis**
I. Do nothing	OK	Perhaps lose business? Catch up costs? Legal problems?	CRISIS (No natural environment)
2. Follow law and public opinion	Costs and advantages	OK	CRISIS (Perhaps delayed? No natural environment)
3. Aim for sustainable business	CRISIS (Probably out of business)	Costs and advantages	OK?

Adapted from Gray and Collison (1991b), p. 22.

organizations are moving into B2 in order to follow, stay ahead of and/or exploit a changing organizational climate.[18] For the laggard organizations – those that the BIM is addressing – B1 and the attendant costs must be beginning to loom large. Looking to the future, the targets of sustainability and 'sustainable business' raise many challenges that organizations – on a worldwide basis – are as yet ill-equipped to handle. Only time will finally tell whether or not organizations should be seeking to move into C3: the costs of moving to cell C3 when one does not have to are significant indeed for the business; the costs of *not* moving to C3, if the environmentalists are right, are appalling (see Chapter 14).

For most organizations, however, the environmental issues still remain a matter of judging the costs and benefits of action and inaction. Figure 2.8 has been developed to start the process of examining that trade-off. There are problems with the diagram[19] but, given that the theme from British business has been that

[17] The IOD survey in 1992 actually opens with the phrase 'Environment can no longer be seen as a passing fad'. The message is taking a long time to get through.

[18] While the most risk-averse strategy would quite probably be to seek out – or at least approach – B3.

[19] The problems include (a) the worrying idea that we assess the preferable environmental actions only on the basis of conventional profit; (b) the options for organizations in the list are over-simple; (c) the impact of costs will vary across industries and over time. All industries will feel the costs eventually but it is on the organizations in the front line – typically chemicals and extractive industries – that the incidence will first fall.

Figure 2.8 Going green: a cost or a benefit?

	No change in business environment	Probable that law and PR *do* change	Environment *is* in serious crisis
Light greening			
Unleaded petrol	+£	++£	Will make very little
Catalytic converters	−£	+£	difference
Initial use of recycled products	−£	++£	
Initial recycling	£	+£	
Waste management	+£	+++£	+++£
Energy management	+£	+++£	+++£
Significant greening			
Use of public transport	+£	+£	+++£
Substantial use of alternative resources	−−£	£	+++£
Substantial recycling	−£	+£	+++£
Change investment procedures	−−£	++£	+++£
Towards sustainability			
Reduce throughput	−−−£	−£	+++£
Change products	−−−£	£	+++£
Longer-life & repairability	−−−£	£	+++£

Key: £ = Break even; +£ = Profit likely; −£ = Loss likely.

'greening equals profit', it seems necessary at least to look at that suggestion. It *is* possible to equate certain environmentally benign activities with cost savings and profitable opportunities (we look at some of these in later chapters).[20] Indeed, many organizations have reaped some such benefits from so doing. However, there is the potential for rather more tension between environment and profit than there is congruence and, after several years of bullish 'talking up' the environment, many business leaders around the world are just beginning to recognize this.[21] At its simplest, the reaping of benefits from energy and waste management, for example (see Chapters 6 and 7), will often involve some considerable investment. For an organization with a cash-flow problem the option may be difficult to undertake (see Chapter 8). The costs of meeting legislation, clean-up costs (see Chapter 11), insurance costs (see Chapter 10), etc., are rising and will continue to do so. Companies which are 'environmentally impeccable' – by current standards anyway – are not proving as profitable as the bulk of companies (see Chapter 10). The probability is therefore that the financial benefits from going

[20] See also Elkington (1987) and Elkington, Knight and Hailes (1991) for many good examples of this.

[21] See, for example, the publications from IISD and BCSD which illustrate this point clearly.

Figure 2.9   A summary of business/environment surveys

Survey No.	I	2	3	4	5	6	7	8	9
When conducted	4/89	1/90	1/90	1/90	3/90	1/91	2/91	?/92	1/92
How many in sample	32	500	81	250	108	15	1420	320	180
Who addressed	CEO	Dir.	CEO	CEO	FD	?	CEO	Dir.	FD
Research method	Int.	PQ	PQ	PQ	Tele	?	PQ	Int.	PQ
Attitudes									
Environment is significant				85	87				
Will rise in importance	90	95						75	
Will raise costs	31			32	22				
Board/manager level responsibility	47	21	50	95	54	53	88	50	
Employees are trained	34		14						
Response in public									
Environmental policy?	31	79	37	88	41	46	39	22	56
Treated in Annual Report?	53		15		29				38
Will be in Annual Report?					44				53
Environmental Audit?			16		16	60	45	16	57
No legislation/information problems?	50	79		70				44	
Main motivation?									
Social responsibility				62	40		20	25	
Legislation				65	18		50	28	
Consumers	47	21		35	18			18	
Employees	47	25			2	20		18	
Suppliers		6							
Public opinion		49		32			10	10	
Family/conscience		48		20					
Shareholders/financial community	9								
Measures taken									
Energy conservation	94	71	70						50
Reduce/recycle waste	72		51						30
Lead-free petrol	75	62	83						
Catalytic converters			20						
Recycle paper	47								
Use recycled paper	34		24						
Investment procedures					59	20			45

Key:[22]

1 Adapted from Gray and Collison (1991).

2 Survey compilers: 1 Touche Ross (1990); 2 Nash (1990); 3 Burke and Hill (1990); 4 CBI/PA Consulting (1990); 5 Pimm (1990); 6 Bain (1991); 7 Hillary (1992); 8 IOD (1992); 9 the authors' preliminary data.

3 The dates refer to the quarter of the year and the year: hence 2/91 suggests that the survey was conducted between April and June 1991.

4 Results are expressed as a percentage of respondents.

5 NB: The questions in the surveys were rarely exactly comparable and insufficient information is given to assess the reliability of the surveys.

[22] It is noticeable that most of the surveys which we report here were not undertaken by academics and therefore the reports do not provide sufficient information to enable any reader to evaluate their reliability. However, surveys are notoriously tricky things to interpret sensibly under the most ideal of circumstances.

Figure 2.10

Conclusions from UK Business/Environment surveys

(1) A significant minority of companies still fail to recognize the environment as a major business factor;

(2) Not all companies recognize that the environment will increase in importance;

(3) Between 20 per cent and 50 per cent of companies do not have environmental responsibility at Board level;

(4) About half of British companies still have no environmental policy;

(5) There is widespread doubt about and resistance to environmental disclosure;

(6) The majority of companies have not undertaken any environmental audit;

(7) The principal motivation for taking environmental issues seriously is equally divided between legislation and personal, social, familial or public opinion;

(8) The primary areas of response are: energy management; waste management; lead-free petrol and the use of recycled paper;

(9) Investment appraisal is still conducted without environmental criteria.

---

green will – in general – be the benefit of severe loss forgone. Unless, that is, there is some very significant change in the financial, institutional and regulatory framework within which organizations operate.

Equally unclear are the strategic questions as to how 'deep' the greening will have to go, and over what time scale this will happen. It is quite clear that an organization which severely misjudges these questions may well put itself in dire trouble. It is equally clear that many organizations, small and large, are concerned about exactly where the goalposts are likely to settle. For all but the largest and most secure organizations this uncertainty tends to encourage a reactive stance on environmental issues. Whilst this is perfectly understandable it does not bode well for the future and clearly counsels for a stronger lead from governments.

Surveys of organizational response to the environmental agenda have produced oddly conflicting pictures about just what organizations are doing and why. Figure 2.9 reviews nine such surveys in the UK. A number of conclusions can be drawn and these are shown in Figure 2.10.

The conflicting messages from business and government ('voluntary is best', 'industry is taking the environment seriously', 'more must be done') disguise a considerable gap between aspiration and actuality. By the early 1990s, the evidence from Britain is that organizations – in general – are not yet taking the environment seriously enough. The messages from around the world are far more mixed but whilst some countries – notably parts of Europe and North America – are more advanced in integrating environmental matters into the business culture, few organizations anywhere in the world have come close even to beginning to address the substantive matters of sustainable development (see Chapter 14).

2.5 Conclusions

Whilst there is little doubt that environmental matters are on the organizational agenda to stay, the progress towards a more fulsome and enthusiastic embracing of the environmental agenda has been very much slower than predicted in 1990. Combinations of confusion, cost constraint, ignorance and too little a lead from government may all play a part. Much more substantial – and widespread – response is crucial: for both the environment and the life of organizations. Whilst one might be unsurprised at business choosing to ignore the environmental message from Friends of the Earth, Greenpeace and Earth First!, it is more surprising when that message is coming from the IOD, ICC, CBI, DoE, DTI, IISD, BCSD, UNCTC, BiE, etc. And the accounting profession? Most of the major accountancy bodies in Britain, North America and Australasia have nailed their colours to the mast of the development of environmental accounting systems and disclosure. This book will, hopefully, help the accountant in the field to answer that challenge but, in the end, it will be experimentation resulting from academic and practitioner co-operation that will make the real difference. Until accountants in practice and industry adopt a more positive attitude to the environment in general and environmental accounting in particular, the profession must remain in the realms of guesswork and speculation. This is not a very professional response to the challenge of the environment.

Further Reading

Most of the readings suggested for Chapter 1 are equally applicable to this chapter. In addition, each of the surveys covered in Figure 2.9 should make interesting reading. But see also:

Confederation of British Industry (1986) *Clean up – It's Good Business*, CBI, London.
Confederation of British Industry (1990) *Waking up to a Better Environment*, CBI/PA Consulting, London.
Elkington, J. and Dimmock, A. (1991) *The Corporate Environmentalists: Selling Sustainable Development: But Can They Deliver?*, SustainAbility, London.
International Institute for Sustainable Development (1992) *Business Strategy for Sustainable Development*, IISD/Deloitte & Touche/BCSD, Winnipeg.

PART B

MANAGEMENT INFORMATION AND ACCOUNTING

PART B

MANAGEMENT
INFORMATION AND
ACCOUNTING

Part B: Management Information and Accounting – an Overview

by Martin Houldin, KPMG, National Environment Unit

Given the range of environmental issues covered in Part A and the potential implications for business, especially where we can see the full range of business functions becoming involved, getting started can be a daunting task.

A multitude of different sources of guidance is available to companies, from books to consultancies of varying degrees of technical and business/management skills. Much of the published material, and even some of the consultancies, tend to give advice on *what* needs to be looked at rather than *how*. The solutions offered may at first seem somewhat confusing: 'Develop an environmental policy, set objectives, carry out an environmental audit, publish a report, appoint somebody senior', and so on. Key questions such as 'Do we need to cover everything?', 'Should we start bottom-up or top-down?', 'Who in the company should be involved?' etc., can be answered only by considering each company's individual situation.

Environmental Management

While there cannot be a panacea, all of these approaches can be fitted into a framework or context of environmental management. This is worth introducing at this point.

Managing the environmental impact of business activities is for many businesses a relatively new idea, and one which calls for a change both in business culture and in day-to-day management systems. Current thinking on environmental management is based on the recognition that it cannot stand alone as a discipline, and that environmental thinking must be integrated with normal business practices. So environmental management is essentially about changing management practices and systems in response to the business implications of environmental issues. It is the first stages of this which constitute the bulk of the 'new' work, and which provide the direction for change.

The starting point is to carry out a review of environmental issues (whatever it ends up being called – environmental review or audit). The aim is to understand enough about the current and planned activities of the business in relation to potential environmental impacts (on air, water, land and nature). This means looking not only at the possible environmental effects of materials and resources used, wastes and emissions, and of products, but also at business issues arising. These are likely to result from legislation and regulatory standards, market activity (such as by customers and/or greener competitors). At this stage, environmental impacts can be looked at on a cradle-to-grave basis by using life-cycle analysis techniques.

The results of the environmental review will provide a basis for identifying those areas where the company needs to improve its performance. This will mean forming some ideas of objectives. We will then have identified those key areas which need to be reflected in policy and in a strategy for action. This process, although sounding simple enough, is more often than not an interactive process of doing enough work at the review stage to identify priority areas, then focusing on these for more in-depth review to shape and refine policy and objectives.

Environmental policies and objectives will typically cover a range of key performance areas, and not just those which are prescribed by legislation and regulation. These include process emissions, wastes, supplier performance, product design, management systems and nature conservation.

While the policy can be used effectively to demonstrate the company's intent, the real measure of commitment lies in setting responsibilities and objectives at business unit and individual levels. As a consequence there will be increasing demands for information on environmental performance.

Recent Developments

A wide range of organizations which represent, support or regulate businesses have recognized the importance of environmental management. As a result an equally wide range of 'guidelines' have been developed for different purposes by, for example, the ICC, the CBI and industry associations (such as the Chemical Industries Association's Responsible Care Programme). There have been similar developments outside the UK through organizations such as BAUM (Germany), GEMI (USA), and UNEP (United Nations). There is no doubt that these initiatives are influencing business awareness and thinking.

There are developments, however, which are having a more direct effect in shaping environmental management practice. At the European level these include a British Standard (BS7750) for Environmental Management Systems, which is expected to provide the basis for an International Standard in the near future, and the European Commission's draft proposals for an Eco-Audit scheme to be introduced at national levels. Both of these developments reflect much of current thinking on how environmental management needs to be developed. They will, however, provide only a generic framework within which companies will operate. The organizations involved in their development recognize the need for a significant amount of work to be done at sector and individual company levels to determine how environmental management is to be implemented.

There are examples of practice in some sectors, notably the oil and chemical industries, and the business community is learning fast in areas such as environmental review, auditing, policy development and technology change. Areas such as performance measurement, which go far deeper into the workings of the business, remain a challenge for the near future.

Management Information and Accounting

Success in implementing effective environmental management will depend on the quality of information available to managers. While companies rely on the more traditional types of management information produced on a regular basis, there is a need for new information (such as emissions, product disposal impacts) and some refocusing of existing systems in areas such as energy and wastes.

There may be practical difficulties, resulting mainly from the lack of raw data, as many companies are thus far developing *ad hoc* information streams from environmental reviews. As a starting point this is not a bad approach, but one that needs to lead fairly quickly into an analysis of environmental information requirements within the business context. This would address data sources and gaps, and identify options for developing information on different application areas. There is no doubt, however, that accounting and financial systems need to be brought more into play, both in producing better information and aiding decision-making. The question is how.

In the short term, accountants can focus on those key performance areas identified in the policy and consider their contribution while working within existing accounting and financial systems. This is likely to be in two areas. First, by *costing* those areas relevant to environmental objectives, such as waste treatment and disposal, energy, site maintenance, in such a way that makes them separately identifiable and more controllable. Second, by working to resolve inevitable conflicts between environmental management and traditional financial management systems. This occurs particularly in *investment appraisal*, where new guidelines need to be developed.

Accountants need to find ways of taking into account quantifiable and tangible environmental factors. Otherwise some proposals that are economically and environmentally sound, in the longer term, may be rejected. This is where life-cycle analysis may have a role to play, and accountants need to assess whether it could be a useful tool in cost/benefit analysis.

In the medium term, accountants need to reorientate planning and forecasting systems to incorporate environmental improvement targets, and their financial implications. Part of this will involve assessing the need for new and/or modified information and financial systems.

In the longer term, there will be developments in eco-accounting or natural resource accounting, aimed at producing environmental accounts to reflect the full costs of production, even where monetary values cannot be assigned.

Accountants in Environmental Management

Remember the old maxim: if you can't measure it, then you cannot manage it!

In many companies, environmental policies and objectives are defined well enough for accountants to be able to begin to determine a role in measurement, analysis and control, and thereby contribute to environmental improvement. The chapters in Part B aim to put the accountant's role in the context of environmental management, and to give some guidance in those areas likely to be of immediate interest.

3. Greening the Organization:

Getting Started

3.1 Introduction

There is no unique way to start an organization on the path towards increased environmental sensitivity. Environmental response is the sort of issue that *must not* be quickly delegated to some remote, peripheral part of the organization and forgotten about. It must be central to the organization's whole programme. The environmental crisis itself arises out of the basic failure of organizational structures, business ethics, economic frameworks and accounting systems to recognize 'nature'. All life, obviously, derives from and is part of the 'natural environment', but until 'environment' is inescapably enmeshed with the organization, Western industrial systems will continue to treat it as though it were something which is irrelevant at best and distinct from life at worst – and thereby destroy it. Just as health, safety and respect for one's employees have become accepted – even essential – prerequisites for responsible organizations, so too must environmental concern be considered an essential element of responsible management.

Where to start? Everywhere at once is the most accurate, if the most bewildering, answer. Elkington's (1987) Ten Steps to Environmental Excellence continually prove to be a robust statement of the necessary – if not sufficient – conditions for incorporating environmental matters. The span of issues that must be considered is just some guide to the ubiquity of green thinking.

Throughout this chapter, we will attempt to provide an overview of the areas in which an organization can make some impact on its environmental sensitivity. However, our treatment must be superficial and the reader is recommended to consult that small number of excellent texts which develop these matters more fully. The further reading listed at the end of the chapter includes some

Figure 3.1

The ten steps to environmental excellence

1 Develop and publish an environmental policy.
2 Prepare an action programme.
3 Arrange organization and staffing including board representation.
4 Allocate adequate resources.
5 Invest in environmental science and technology.
6 Educate and train.
7 Monitor, audit and report.
8 Monitor the evolution of the green agenda.
9 Contribute to environmental programmes.
10 Help build bridges between the various interests.

Source: J. Elkington (1989) *The Green Capitalists*, with Tom Burke, London: Victor Gollancz

---

Figure 3.2

One company's approach to 'Going Green'

1. Develop corporate culture components on environmental matters;
2. Accept that the company's activities do disturb the environment and aim to minimize these and perhaps look for enhancement also;
3. Undertake environmental impact assessment on all major company proposals;
4. Provide environmental training for all levels of staff;
5. Build up networks with environmental groups.

Source: Reported in *Environment Update* (1990) New Zealand Ministry for the Environment, No. 17 p. 2

---

which we and the organizations we have worked with have found most helpful.

3.2   The Forces of Change

How the many potential forces for change actually succeed in creating change and the form that such change eventually takes is not well understood.[1] The 'environment' is not yet a *direct* force for change in itself (on organizations in the developed world at least). The pressure for environmental change comes *indirectly* as a result of changes in consumer taste, employee and management attitudes, law, etc. This is one of the reasons management seeking to manage the 'environmental agenda' have such a problem. It is necessary to monitor the development both of environmental facts *and* of the environmental issues and knowledge in the public domain,

---

[1] See e.g. Laughlin (1991).

Figure 3.3

```
The new 3 R's of an environmental culture

•   Reduce;
•   Re-use;
•   Recycle;

Popular also are:

•   Refuse;
•   Refill;
•   Repeat;
•   Repair;
•   Remediate;
•   Reclaim;
•   Return.
... and so on.
```

while attempting to assess the different ways in which these might eventually have a direct influence upon the organization.

However, there are some prerequisites for change, the most crucial being the attitudes and actions of the board. The 'tone from the top' is as important in environmental matters as it is in ethical ones.[2] This becomes even more apparent when it is realized that what is needed is a *cultural* change. An organization which was previously maximizing throughput, growth, profitability, etc. will have to start minimizing a few things – a new dimension will have to enter it.

In the broadest of terms, the forces of change can come from outside the organization, the employees and the senior management. We briefly examine these in turn before looking at the accountant's role.

3.3   External Influences for Environmental Change

It is that range of pressures external to the organization which provide the greatest influence on its environmental response. (See the Overview to Part A.) As such, however, they are forces over which the individual organization has little immediate or direct control. Good management control requires, therefore, that such influences be successfully anticipated.

The most obvious of these pressures arises from changes in legislation and the related institutional framework.[3] The surveys discussed in Chapter 2 showed that this was a principal reason cited by

---

[2] See e.g. Baumhart (1961), Bennett (1988), Benson (1989), Ermann (1986).

[3] For example in supervision, financing, taxation, penalties, incentives, etc.

Figure 3.4

Monitoring the developing environmental agenda

The organization must be monitoring:
  (1) the emergence of environmental facts, findings and research;
  (2) the emergence of environmental issues;
  (3) the media's portrayal of issues;
  (4) public opinion;
  (5) employee views and attitudes;
  (6) the activities of environmental groups;
  (7) the activities, profile and attitudes of suppliers and customers;
  (8) draft law and EC directives;
  (9) complaints procedure and complaints received;
 (10) what is considered 'best practice' in one's industry.

management for undertaking environmental change within the organization. Our own research has gone beyond this, however, and suggested that the most powerful forces for change have come as 'shocks', or otherwise largely unexpected. These may be in the form of unanticipated legislation but, equally, may arise from other sources. The characteristic is that it catches the organization unprepared. It was noticeable that where environmental issues remained significant within an organization (i.e. had not been given a superficial treatment) *and* had not been fully integrated (e.g. into a TQM culture; see below) it was usually because there had been some external shock to the system. Examples of such shocks included the attentions of organizations like Friends of the Earth, Greenpeace or Earth First!; an environmental disaster with attendant fines and publicity; or some other substantive change forced upon the organization from outside.[4]

It should follow, therefore, that careful monitoring of the agenda (see Figures 3.4 and 2.3) will have the effect of encouraging change. At least change will be encouraged once an organization recognizes that what has happened to Exxon, Shell, ICI, Rhône-Poulenc, Fisons, Union Carbide, BP, Nestlé, McDonald's, etc., can happen to it. Such a shock – or potential shock – can then be treated as a matter for aggression, of fear, of disdain or a matter for recognition that opinions other than those of the organization have intrinsic merit and it should seek to learn from them. Which response is chosen will depend on the organizational culture and, in particular, the attitude of the chief executive.

After the law and other external shocks, the pressures for change are equally powerful and intrusive – but much less dramatic. Such pressures include changing customer behaviour and the eco-labelling developments, changing public opinion, initiatives from the busi-

---

[4] We also observed two examples of changes of board membership, one takeover and two privatizations which had acted as the spurs for change.

ness community, eco-audit and BS7750, the developing 'supplier audits' and ethical investment. We will consider these and other pressures as appropriate in subsequent chapters. For the present, it suffices to say that monitoring, anticipating and responding to the external, environmentally related influences are therefore essential steps for the organization starting on the road to environmental sensitivity.

3.4   Internal Influences for Environmental Change: The Employees

Setting the organization on a greener path from the 'bottom up' has worked well for some companies (up to a point at least). Employees' actions have succeeded in educating senior management and can continue to do so. Equally, senior management can begin a 'light greening' process through encouraging employees in a variety of ways. This may be the most successful means of initiating the preliminary changes to the organization and its culture which will be necessary if environmental matters are to be taken seriously.

The first environmental experience for many organizations has arisen from some employee initiative that deals with the softer aspects of environmentalism. Examples have included the collection of paper for recycling in offices, canteen collections of cans and glass for recycling, transport-sharing schemes or, rather more innovatively, requests to undertake tree-planting schemes on land owned by the organization. The impact of such initiatives on the larger environmental programme is initially slight but in each case these small beginnings have had the effect of raising awareness among employees and of effectively introducing environmental questions into the workplace. Such an initiative may come from individuals, groups, or trade unions[5] either independently or as a result of contact through environmental groups, schools, local authorities, etc. Figure 3.5 summarizes the 'bottom-up' approach.

For such initiatives to be successful, they must be seen to be encouraged – not just patronized or tolerated. Depending upon the management/employee climate in the organization, care must be taken not to appropriate a genuine employee initiative and thereby impede the motivation that originated it. For one, medium-sized manufacturing company, it was the initiative of two (very junior) employees that eventually led to a series of recycling schemes throughout the organization, a presentation to the senior management organized by the employees and, subsequently, a complete rethink of the company's stance on environmental issues.[6] For

[5] See, for example, Trades Union Congress *Greening the workplace*, London: TUC, 1991.

[6] It is worth pointing out at this stage that many of the recycling initiatives are of dubious environmental value if not thought through. These matters are touched upon in Chapters 6, 7 and 9.

Figure 3.5

Greening from the bottom up

- What do the employees of the organization think about environmental issues?
- How do you know? Why don't you know?
- Encourage and support employees to establish schemes for recycling – start with paper, cans and glass – don't stop at that!
- Are any employees active environmentalists? Will they help the organization? If not why not? That deserves thinking about.
- Tree-planting scheme or nature reserve scheme on organizational land? Involvement with local authority?
- Give employees free time for environmental involvement.
- Suggestions from employees? Are they encouraged and acted upon?

Stockbridge Engineering the planting and landscaping of the site became a major factor in the organization's culture and self-image and has brought enormous benefits in terms of public relations, employee morale, contacts with schools, local authorities and local voluntary groups. IBM's 'community investment programme' is a totally embedded part of its culture, which helps define the organization and appears to be an essential element in employee self-esteem and motivation. For many schools and universities, the pressure for change has come from small initiatives from students to which, eventually, the organization has sought to respond.

The initial steps may be small, but in raising the profile of the issues, many substantive advantages accrue and environmental awareness, as a precursor to real environmental development within an organization, can successfully infiltrate all aspects of the organization.

The response of the management is, of course, crucial. Some of the simplest but most effective (in terms of environmental sensitivity) changes have come from employee suggestions. As is the case with all aspects of organizational management, there must be a culture in which suggestions are encouraged, seen to be encouraged and seriously considered. The worldwide fame of the 3M culture and, in particular, its PPP (Pollution Prevention Pays) programme and of Dow Chemicals' encouragement to employees to form environmental groups within the company demonstrates just how far such a process can go.[7]

Taking matters further will involve providing facilities for training employees – both general and job-specific. This, in the right climate, should have a roller-coaster effect. Of course, in the wrong climate any training can be a waste of time, money and effort and counter-

[7] See Elkington (1987) for further information. See also Dauncey (1988), Robertson (1985, 1990), Plant and Plant (1991) and Davis (1991) for further ideas on this participative innovation approach.

productive in terms of the frustration and demotivation it creates. Therefore, some degree of freedom within individuals' working lives becomes essential. There must be a degree of autonomy for issues – and even experiments – to be pursued. One company (reluctantly) gave an employee some freedom to explore the cost, use and disposal of the containers and wooden pallets it used. The analysis, although somewhat naive, raised a considerable number of issues which the organization had to address. The resultant savings more than paid for the employee's time and the employee had enjoyed himself – thus lifting morale. Another company (again reluctantly) had permitted an employee doing an Open University degree to use the laboratory facilities – including technician time – to explore land contamination on the site. The results came as a shock to management and stood up to further testing. This put the organization in a position to start to address the issue well before the matter became a legal one. A third organization has encouraged a school to undertake an inventory over time of the flora and fauna on the company site. Employees are responsible for the project starting in the first place (through contact with the school) and are also involved in supervising and supporting the activity. The investigation has generated enormous interest throughout the company and has led – inevitably really – to suggestions for increasing the habitat possibilities of the site.

The openness of the organizational culture has usually been the determining factor of successful developments along these lines. With the increasing complexity of and rapidity of change in the green agenda, the organization which encourages and responds to its employees is bound to be in better shape. Ultimately, the depth and adequacy of the organization's response to environmental matters will be a function of its management and, in particular, its directorate and performance appraisal schemes.

3.5   Senior Management: The 'Tone from the Top'

If environmental issues are to be addressed seriously by any organization, they must be 'championed' within the organization by a member of senior management – ideally a member of the board. Without board representation – and/or direct and real access to it by the environmental manager – the organization is only playing at going green. The representation and 'championing' must also be backed up in a number of specific ways (see again Elkington's ten steps, set out earlier). Whilst each organization will approach the matters with a somewhat different emphasis, it must ensure that, at a minimum, the 'environment' is sufficiently resourced in an active and effectual department. This may be a separate environmental department but much more usual is to tie environmental concerns to health and safety (SHE – safety, health, environment – departments), to current procedures for COSHH (control of substances hazardous to health)

Figure 3.6

Watching the environmental issues

- Environmental policy
- Performance targets
- Management structure
- Staff awareness and training
- Public relations
- Community involvement
- Investment
- Financial implications
- Legal compliance
- Purchasing policy
- Market pressures
- Emergency/contingency plans
- Insurance
- Site and building management
- Paper use
- Equipment and furniture
- Energy sources and use
- Waste management and disposal
- Water use and discharge
- Product design
- Raw materials
- Packaging
- Process design/operation
- Emissions
- Transport and distribution.

Adapted from Business-in-the-Environment (1991) *Your Business and the Environment (DIY Review for Companies)* London: BiE/Coopers & Lybrand Deloitte.

---

or to the mechanism in place or being developed for total quality management.[8] Environmental matters *must not*, however, be located and left in PR departments. Although PR is clearly a function which will wish to cover environmental matters, the environment is not a PR issue – it is substantive and must be treated as such. Figure 3.6 provides just some indication of how substantive and Figure 3.7 (from Business-in-the-Environment (1991a)) provides a guide to how to make an initial prioritization of issues.

Once the breadth and depth of the response the organization will have to make to environmental matters have been recognized, it becomes clear the 'environment' will be a strategic management issue for the board. Environmental response must permeate every aspect of the organization's activities and must, therefore, be bedded into its long- and medium-term plans for the positioning of the organization, its processes, structure and products. This must

---

[8] Leading to 'environmental quality management' as Elkington, Knight and Hailes, (1991) call it. See BS7750 in Chapter 5.

Figure 3.7

Identifying Environmental Priorities for your Company

L – Low
M – Medium
H – High

	Atmospheric Emissions	Water Use/ Discharge	Solid Waste	Energy	The Natural Environment	Corporate/ Market Pressures	Human Health	Accidents/ Emergencies	Legislation
Agriculture, forestry and fishing	L	H	M	L	H	M	H	M	M
Energy and water supply	H	H	H	H	H	M	M	H	H
Minerals, metals, chemicals, plastics	H	H	H	H	M	H	H	H	H
Metal goods, engineering, vehicles	H	H	M	M	L	M	M	M	H
Food, drink and tobacco	L	H	L	M	L	H	H	L	M
Pulp and paper	M	H	H	M	H	H	M	M	M
Other manufacturing	M	M	M	M	L	L	L	L	M
Construction	L	L	M	M	H	M	L	H	M
Distribution and transport	H	L	L	H	M	L	L	M	M
Communications, printing, publishing	M	M	M	L	L	M	L	L	L
Banking, finance and insurance	L	L	L	M	L	M	L	L	L
Retail	L	L	M	M	L	H	M	L	M
Marketing, advertising	L	L	L	L	L	H	L	L	L

Source: BiE (1991) *Your Business and the Environment: a DIY Review for Companies* (Legal Studies and Services on behalf of BiE/C&LD)

Figure 3.8

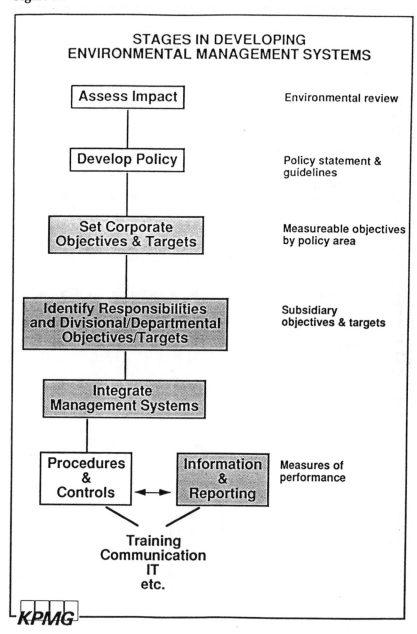

STAGES IN DEVELOPING
ENVIRONMENTAL MANAGEMENT SYSTEMS

Assess Impact — Environmental review

Develop Policy — Policy statement & guidelines

Set Corporate Objectives & Targets — Measureable objectives by policy area

Identify Responsibilities and Divisional/Departmental Objectives/Targets — Subsidiary objectives & targets

Integrate Management Systems

Procedures & Controls ↔ Information & Reporting — Measures of performance

Training
Communication
IT
etc.

KPMG

start from the development and implementation of an environ-mental policy (see Chapter 4). This must then be used to ensure that – from both an ethical and a (not entirely incompatible) business survival and strategy viewpoint – 'environment' receives as much priority as a business policy issue as do marketing, technology, product development, and so on.[9] A potential 'map' for the organiza-tion is provided in Figure 3.8 and environmental management systems are examined in more detail in a number of subsequent chapters but particularly Chapter 5.

From this, environment must flow into all procedures, policies and – most crucially – into the financial system and the system of performance appraisal, incentives and rewards. If a manager undertakes a project which is marginally less profitable than the apparently 'best' option but does it on environmental grounds, will the organization ignore, punish or reward him or her? Until that question is resolved, the organization is not serious about environ-mental matters. Although we cannot give detailed attention to them here, we do need to look at these and related matters, and this seems an appropriate moment to bring accountants back into the frame.

3.6   The Accountants' Role in the Initiation of Change

Whether one is considering a large multinational company, a small manufacturing enterprise or a not-for-profit organization such as a local authority, it is clear that the crunch comes when environmental matters are in conflict with financial criteria. Organizations have dealt with issues of this type before – most obviously in the area of employee protection, health and safety. A company may consider that employee protection is a good long-term financial investment or (more typically in a TQM culture) that accidents and injuries to employees are simply unacceptable to any reasonable, responsible and ethical organization. Either way, some basis upon which 'social', 'human' and/or 'ethical' matters can transcend immediate financial criteria has been established. So it is with environmental issues.

It is clear from all the organizations with which we had dealings that until environmental matters are embedded into the performance appraisal system, appropriately prioritized and the incentive, reward and budgeting systems similarly redirected, environmental matters will nearly always lose out to financial criteria. (There are, of course, as we have seen, exceptions where financial and environmental criteria are in harmony, and these are likely to increase – see particularly Chapters 6 and 7. This is not true

[9] For more guidance on this, see, for example, Davis (1991), Elkington, Knight and Hailes (1991), and Winter (1988) as well as the other further reading at the end of this chapter.

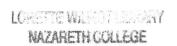

for all activities however (see Chapter 8), and this must be explicitly recognized and addressed.)

Perhaps the best illustrations of this can be given by a specific example. What was probably the most 'environmentally advanced' organization we dealt with had established environmental criteria as part of managerial job specifications. Every six months, managerial appraisals were held on the basis of the targets set at the previous appraisal. Each appraisal concentrated on three areas, one of which is environmental.[10] The company sees itself as operating in a TQM culture and expects all target areas to be met within a framework of zero complaints (internal or external), zero notifications from the regulatory authorities, zero transgressions of consents or internal standards (whether notified or not) and a rapid recognition of suggestions from external or internal sources. Financial rewards and promotion are dependent upon these appraisals and failure to meet environmental standards will be appropriately penalized. It was apparent that this had permeated the organization; employees were aware that their management were appraised upon environmental matters and that eventually environmental criteria would be built into their own job specifications. (This was warmly welcomed by the employees with whom we spoke – not least because the organization's close relationship with a number of local communities meant that employees, including management, were under pressure from friends and neighbours about the environmental impact of their employer's activities.[11] This had forced the BPEO[12] criteria into investment decisions (see Chapter 8), had raised the emphasis on, and detail contained in, environmental impact assessments (see Chapter 5) and discussions were taking place about establishing particular allocations within the budgetary system. It also required, obviously, establishment of the appropriate information and reporting systems. These were developing as the organization experimented.

Most of this sounded like accounting, so where were the accountants?

The accountants? We had never thought of getting them involved. They just concern themselves with the numbers. We just tell them what to do and if they start interfering and telling us it costs too much, we simply

[10] For example, one manager's targets ranged from the relatively trivial requirement to eradicate litter from his sites to the much more demanding requirement that he present to the board practicable proposals for eradicating – or at a minimum reducing – the pollution of water discharges from sites. This latter was regardless of consent levels.

[11] This is related to the crucial matter of transparency – the process of enabling (particularly) communities to 'see into' the organization in order to develop an informal environmental accountability. This matter is returned to in Parts C and D.

[12] Best practicable environmental option – see, for example, HMSO (1988) and Chapter 8.

override them. I'm not sure we'd want them involved really. They are
good at their job but they'd be more likely to prevent environmental
initiatives than to encourage them. I suppose I should talk to them about
it.

The Divisional General Manager, Medium sized extractive
and processing company.

We did speak with the accountants. They had not previously
thought about their role in environmental issues. Once the
possibility had been raised they *were* interested in helping but
seemed at a loss to make the connection between accounting and
the environment. This response from the organization and the
accountants is widespread (see also Appendix C) but must be
changed if organizations are to respond fully to the green agenda.

The accountant as neutral at best, obstructive at worst, is
illustrated by two other organizations – a local authority and an
international company – both of which experienced the same
problem. Both had a financial budget-driven culture, in which
environmental investment initiatives naturally fell against financial
return rates (see Chapter 8). Statements from the board that
apparently encouraged environmental initiatives to be undertaken
were not backed up by a change to the performance appraisal
system and thus all environmental projects had also to meet current
financial criteria; and no extra facilities, time or money were made
available, so that any environmental activities that were not directly
financially beneficial and/or avoided legislative complications
became – in effect – voluntary acts of the employees. Naturally
enough, very little (apart from falling morale) was happening.

Our own survey of accountants in the UK (see Appendix C)
suggested that accountants do see themselves as responsible for
innovation as well as keen and willing to undertake initiatives in the
development of financial information systems. In the environmental
domain, however, this has yet to translate into practice.

Interestingly, it is only when things like environmental matters
are considered that the ubiquity of financial information systems
within organizations becomes apparent. Figure 3.6 listed some of
the areas to which the environmentally aware organization will give
attention. Many will have financial implications in one form or
another, in which case the accountants (and the auditors, internal
and external, see Chapter 11) must be brought alongside. A number
of organizations have, for example, adopted a more environmentally
aware purchasing policy. Whilst imaginative approaches (and care
over wastage – see Chapter 7) can ensure that less environmentally
malign purchasing does not necessarily cost more, it may often
do so. The accountant, the accounting system and/or the internal
auditor may quickly put a stop to that if not properly integrated
into the system. An increasing number of organizations have also
recognized the importance of transport policy and, in particular,

Figure 3.9

Getting started

(1) adopt Elkington's 'ten steps';
(2) adopt the 3 (or more) Rs;
(3) monitor the developing environmental agenda;
(4) encourage employee initiatives and environmental schemes within the organization;
(5) set the 'tone from the top';
(6) ensure that environmental concerns permeate the organization;
(7) ensure that the company takes a multidisciplinary approach, bringing different functional managers together;
(8) raise company-wide awareness and ensure that the environment is 'owned' across the board;
(9) adapt the performance appraisal system;
(10) ensure that the accounting and financial systems are in harmony with the environmental initiatives.

---

personal transport.[13] Private car usage is clearly heavily subsidized (financially and environmentally) in general and company cars especially so. A particularly imaginative approach is to allow all personal travel on the organization's business to receive the standard car mileage rate – users of public transport, foot or bicycle are thus highly rewarded for their effort, the organization is no worse off and its environmental impact is reduced. In two organizations we know, this system floundered very quickly because the accounting system and the internal audit personnel had not received instructions and this practice was strictly counter to existing regulations and therefore (in the case of a local authority) actually illegal. The matter was quickly resolved but where the accountants had been involved from the beginning – with an environmentally educated and aware point of view – the system ran very sweetly from the start.

Organizations cannot reduce their environmental impact and become more environmentally benign if they have a strong financial culture *and* their accountants are not in at the design stage of environmental initiative and environmental information systems. Their exclusion will prevent initiatives, their inclusion brings their undoubted abilities into the frame.

3.7 Conclusions

There can be no single, ideal way in which any organization can begin the process of developing its organizational sensitivity. Each

---

[13] Despite the at-times reverential awe in which the sacrosanct private car is held, some companies do manage to get away from it. Body Shop is perhaps an unsurprising initiator but Ciba-Geigy is reported by Hutchinson (1991) as discouraging cars, issuing bicycles and encouraging public transport.

may choose a different route – some starting with an environmental policy (see Chapter 4), some with an environmental audit (see Chapter 5), others with environmental reporting (see Chapters 11 and 12). Others may wish to experiment with some of the suggestions in this chapter. However one approaches it, there is no need to do it alone. Contact with the support organizations listed in Appendix B and guidance from the further reading below and in Appendix A are essential – and economic – ways of getting started on the very difficult path of making the organization more environmentally sensitive.

Further Reading

Business-in-the-Environment (1991a) *Your Business and the Environment: A DIY Review for Companies*, BiE/Coopers & Lybrand Deloitte, London.

Business-in-the-Environment (1991b) *Your Business and the Environment: An Executive Guide*, BiE, London.

Business-in-the-Environment (1992) *A Measure of Commitment: Guidelines for Environmental Performance Measurement*, BiE/KPMG, London.

Davis, J. (1991) *Greening Business: Managing for Sustainable Development*, Blackwell, Oxford.

Earth Works Group (1989) *50 Simple Things You Can Do to Save the Earth*, Hodder & Stoughton, London.

Elkington, J., Knight, P. and Hailes, J. (1991) *The Green Business Guide*, Gollancz, London.

Forrester, S. (1990) *Business and Environmental Groups: A Natural Partnership?*, Directory of Social Change, London.

Kleiner, A. (1991) What does it mean to be green? *Harvard Business Review*, July–August, pp. 38–47.

Trades Union Congress (1991) *Greening the Workplace*, TUC, London.

Winter, G. (1988) *Business and the Environment*, McGraw Hill, Hamburg.

And for a legal approach to 'getting started' . . .

Handler, T. (ed.) (1992) *Regulating the European Environment*, Baker McKenzie, London.

4. Environmental Policy:

Adoption, Establishment and Implementation

4.1 Introduction

All aspects of a company's operations, from accounting and purchasing, to product design, manufacturing, sales and marketing and distribution, will have an impact on the environment. Your company environmental policy should reflect your recognition of this.

(Business-in-the-Environment (1991a), Annex 1)

The primary prerequisite for an organization intending to take environmental matters seriously is the development of an environmental policy. This will form the basis from which all the organization's environmental interactions and policies will be developed and it will be the principal signal to the internal and external stakeholders of the seriousness (or otherwise) of the organization's intentions with respect to the environment. It is therefore not a matter to be taken lightly.

It may be the case that an organization adopts one environmental policy for internal use but discloses to a wider public only extracts from or even a watered down version of it. Whilst it is difficult not to have sympathy for an organization nervous about offering hostages to fortune, the publication of bland policy statements (see below) or, more specifically, the refusal to open up to the environmental debate is not a constructive approach to one's commitment and contribution to the amelioration of the environmental crisis.

The present situation is *not* ideal. The proportion of companies adopting (and disclosing) environmental policy statements is significantly below 100 per cent. This is not a cause for complacency. Figure 4.1 illustrates this point.

These proportions are low – especially when it is remembered that they are taken from the largest companies, which are more likely to have adopted a policy. But there is also a gap between

Figure 4.1 Disclosure of environmental policies[1]

Country	World wide	France	Germany	N'lands	Sweden	Switz'd	Total Europe	UK
Survey	UNCTC			Roberts (1991)				Coy Report
Sample	222	25	40	15	15	15	110	670
% age Disclose	39	28	35	33	27	20	30	5

Figure 4.2

Some pros and cons for developing an in-house environmental policy

Advantages to the organization
- It can be tailored to one's own needs
- It can recognize what can be 'realistically' achieved in the foreseeable future
- It can be protected and tended in the dark, away from the glare of publicity
- Its feasibility can be assessed in privacy
- It can be much more general and less demanding
- It can be refined and developed in the light of experience
- It can be easier to defend against environmental groups
- Implementation may be cheaper
- It can be more adventuresome if it can be kept private

Disadvantages:
- It may be bland
- Implementation and monitoring may not be prioritized
- Derivation of the policy is more expensive
- It is not comparable – nationally and internationally
- It looks like a softer option – bad PR?
- It does not necessarily encourage transparency
- It may avoid the really difficult and important issues relating to the business

adoption and disclosure. Figure 2.9 suggested that about 40 per cent of UK companies had adopted an environmental policy; these figures show that disclosure rate is very much lower.[2]

The establishment of an environmental policy can take two main routes: development of an organization-specific policy; or the adop-

[1] These figures are taken from Roberts (1991), *Company Reporting 1991* and UNCTC papers E/C.10/AC.3/1992/3.

[2] In addition to the more obvious reasons of shyness and/or secretiveness, the predominant reasons given for non-disclosure in general (see Chapters 11 and 12) are the lack of demand for the information and the absence of a legal requirement to disclose. However, there is a further, more compelling reason. Companies may be (realistically) reluctant to disclose their environmental policy until they have conducted environmental reviews and undertaken attempts to perform to the level required by the policy. Only time will tell whether this reason has substance.

tion of one of the publicly established 'charters'. We will deal briefly with the tailor-made experience first before spending most of the chapter on the 'off-the-peg' possibilities. But a policy on its own means little, so the later sections of the chapter will cover some of the steps towards implementing the policy – embedding it into organizational practice.

4.2   The Company's Own Environmental Policy

The primary purpose in adopting an environmental policy is as a guide to future action. It therefore needs to be informed by reliable data on the organization's environmental interactions, consist of commitments which are as specific as possible and be supported by as many mechanisms for turning the policy into specific targets as can be established. The specific targets, which should be transitory and developing, should be referred to in the policy but *not specified* – that should be done in supporting documents.[3] Figure 4.2 lists some pros and cons.

It makes considerable sense for any initial environmental policy statement to be a draft only. Once the organization has carried out environmental reviews, assessed its own environmental position and assessed the feasibility of its environmental goals, *then* it can turn the draft into the 'real thing' in the knowledge that the policy is feasible and can be a long-lived document. Then, but only then, the organization can consider publishing the statement.[4] (A more detailed guide to this process is contained in Appendix 4.1.[5]) Figure 4.3 provides two examples of published statements that have emerged from this process, other examples are contained in Chapters 11 and 12.

The process of developing the environmental policy is not without its problems. One company, for example, was concerned that:

> *this emphasis on environmental policy is in danger of overshadowing other areas of policy. Isn't environmental policy just one more part of the organization's general policy? Shouldn't we be making the same fuss about health and safety for example?*

Indeed, it seems most appropriate that the organization should have a general mission and policy statement, but backed up by detailed policies in the appropriate areas – including environment

---

[3] It should also be recognized that the formulation of the environmental policy may come after the initial environmental review (see Chapter 5). Policy, to a degree at least, does need to be informed by a sound knowledge of the actual and potential environmental impacts of the business.

[4] A statement of intent or even a very general policy can usefully be disclosed earlier in the process, of course.

[5] See also BiE (1991a), which contains a draft outline policy statement for organizations to mould to their own needs. Much more detailed guidance on this process is provided in Elkington, Knight and Hailes (1991) and see also 3M/Environment Council (1991).

Figure 4.3A   Example of a published environmental policy

THE FUTURE

The detailed implications of the Environmental Protection Bill and any subsequent legislation are not yet clear, but there will certainly be further pollution control requirements and a need for more openness by industry with regard to activities which impinge on the environment. Additionally, because steel production is a major user of fossil fuel-derived energy, any legislation aimed at curbing either acid rain or the greenhouse effect will have an impact on the industry.

The Company recognises its responsibilities in this area and the Board has approved in outline an investment programme of almost £150m, mainly concerned with reducing atmospheric emissions at existing production plants. Such a programme requires careful planning to avoid undue disruption to customer service and will be phased over a five-year period.

A programme of progressive removal of all PCB-containing equipment has begun recently. It has required a rigorous investigation of the UK companies offering PCB removal and incineration services, before drawing up contracts for the work which will be completed over a five-year period at a cost of £8m.

Finally, the prudent use of energy is rightly seen as a major environmental issue and our energy conservation programme will be continued with renewed vigour. It will conserve natural resources, reduce emissions of greenhouse gases and drive down further the Company's production costs.

Management's progress against these targets will be audited regularly by the Board committee on environmental matters.

Published by Information Services. Designed and produced by Mike Horton & Partners 1990

British Steel plc
9 Albert Embankment
London SE1 7SN

This paper includes straw pulp to help the environment.

16

Figure 4.3B Example of a published environmental policy

PILKINGTON

Glass for Buildings and Transport

PGL ENVIRONMENTAL POLICY

Our aim is profitable continuity. The core businesses provide flat and safety products for architectural and automotive markets. These products make an important contribution to improving living standards, to people's safety, to the conservation of energy, and are ecologically friendly.

We strive for the highest standards in all our operations, motivated by an acute awareness of the best international practices. We integrate environmental considerations in our business decision-making. We have an overriding commitment to the market, and sensitivity to the needs and interests of our customers.

To sustain and protect the environment, we will:

— conduct environmental audits of all our operations to ensure that waste and pollution is minimised.

— regulate and improve our manufacturing processes to cause the least practicable impact on the environment, encouraging our employees to help and investing ahead of legislative requirements.

— develop and market products that have excellent environmental characteristics and which meet the highest demands for efficiency.

— liaise with suppliers and customers to facilitate the best possible environmental practices in the manufacturing and installation chain, and promote the recycling of glass and related materials.

— co-operate with the appropriate authorities and technical organisations in the formation of standards and the means of compliance.

— promote and undertake educational programmes and discussion on Green issues for employees, suppliers, customers, schools and the community at large, protecting health and safety.

— discuss environmental issues regularly at the highest levels of the Company, and take a lead in Group initiatives.

**Re-Confirmed by the
Pilkington Glass Limited Board
18th July, 1990**

Rodney Stansfield, Chief Executive

and health and safety.[6] In fact, such an approach seems essential in that environmental matters will permeate the whole organization and must therefore influence, and be integrated with, other areas of policy.

If the environmental policy-making process is working success-fully within the organization it will raise difficult questions. For example, should the policy state that the organization will comply with all laws or, even, go beyond them? Our experience suggests that the wider (and less cynical) elements of the public will assume that organizations comply with law. The publication of such a state-ment may not be seen as especially impressive. The irony is, of course, that most organizations either do not comply with all law or, far more commonly, have little or no idea whether or not they comply with environmental law. For this reason, if no other, reference to the law seems particularly appropriate.

Another major issue for multinational corporations is whether or not to adopt worldwide standards. Companies such as IBM, ICI and Norsk Hydro *have* committed themselves to such a policy even though this means that the operations in the country with the lowest environmental standards will be conducted by reference to the standards operating in the most environmentally stringent country. This is an expensive and brave policy. A number of other multinationals have consciously decided *not* to adopt this policy because it has a severe impact on their international competitive-ness, it costs far too much, they see no need for such high standards or, as one company said, they really have no idea what sorts of environmental standards are being applied in many of their sub-sidiaries. Such problems – and attitudes – suggest to us that a 'worldwide standards' clause must ultimately be the target of all environmental policies.[7]

The importance attaching to environmental policies, the need for all organizations to adopt them, the need for guidance on them and, especially, the perceived need for comparability against the highest (currently feasible) standards has led to the development of the 'charters' – independently derived and publicly adopted environ-mental policies.

4.3 The Environmental Charters

An environmental charter is a public document with a number of primary purposes. It consists of a number of guiding principles covering areas of corporate planning, activity and control where

[6] Whilst we might consider environmental matters should dominate all others, this is not an especially widely held view nor is it likely to achieve the sort of balanced organization that most environmental initiatives are intended to achieve.

[7] It is notable, however, that the charters we will be discussing below do not insist on this requirement. Some of the implications of this are touched upon in Chapter 15.

Figure 4.4

The primary purposes of the public environmental charters

(1) to provide information to external parties by signalling environmental intentions and commitments of the entity;

(2) to act as an internal guide for the organization of the broad areas of environmental concern – a blueprint for the development of more detailed environmental policies and practices;

(3) to act as a means by which external parties may place pressure on organizations to become more environmentally sensitive via (e.g.) providing investors with an investment evaluation tool and providing a standard which organizations can be asked to match.

Figure 4.5

Major advantages/disadvantages of signing up to the public environmental charters

(1) If sponsored by a body independent of the organization it is likely to be free of the more obvious forms of bias. As a result it is likely to contain clearer and more specific environmental objectives than the environment mission statements found in annual reports or other public relations statements.

(2) By providing a common mission statement, charters simplify the process of comparing organizations' policies.

(3) An organization can be assessed on its performance by comparison with the charter – either by the charter's initiators or some other body (e.g. Friends of the Earth, Greenpeace, EIRIS etc.). This potential for a monitoring function permits a potential enforcement mechanism.

(4) It provides an external standard for reference by which organizations – whether or not subscribers to the charter – may be judged.

(5) It allows the existence and identity of non-subscribers to be more readily available. This leads to the inevitable questions as to why an organization *did not* sign up to a particular charter.

---

environmental aspects should be incorporated. We shall briefly review the most widely known charters: the Valdez Principles and the ICC's Business Charter for Sustainable Development; look briefly at the Chemical Industries Association Responsible Care Programme; and touch upon the UK Environmental Investor Code, the Friends of the Earth's Environmental Charter for Local Government and the CBI's Agenda for Voluntary Action.[8]

An environmental charter has a number of advantages (or disadvantages, depending upon one's point of view) which can be summarized in Figure 4.5.

[8] Each of these charters we review can serve the purposes in Figure 4.4. However, it is quite obvious why the vast majority of companies are less then enthusiastic about adopting such policies and thus providing outside parties with a stick with which to beat them.

Figure 4.6

The Valdez Principles

We adopt, support and will implement the principles of:

1. *Protection of the Biosphere* We will minimize and strive to eliminate the release of any pollutant that may cause environmental damage to the air, water, or earth or its inhabitants. We will safeguard habitats in rivers, lakes, wetlands, coastal zones and oceans and will minimize contributing to the greenhouse effect, depletion of the ozone layer, acid rain or smog.

2. *Sustainable Use of Natural Resources* We will make sustainable use of renewable natural resources such as water, soils and forests. We will conserve non-renewable natural resources through efficient use and careful planning. We will protect wildlife habitat, open spaces and wilderness while preserving biodiversity.

3. *Reduction and Disposal of Waste* We will minimize the creation of waste, especially hazardous waste, and wherever possible recycle materials. We will dispose of all wastes through safe and responsible methods.

4. *Wise Use of Energy* We will make every effort to use environmentally safe and sustainable energy sources to meet our needs. We will invest in improved energy efficiency and conservation in our operations. We will maximize the energy efficiency of products we produce or sell.

5. *Risk Reduction* We will minimize the environmental, health and safety risks to our employees and the communities in which we operate by employing safe technologies and operating procedures and by being constantly prepared for emergencies.

6. *Marketing of Safe Products and Services* We will sell products or services that minimize adverse environmental impacts and that are safe as consumers commonly use them. We will inform consumers of the environmental impacts of our products and services.

7. *Damage Compensation* We will take responsibility for any harm we cause to the environment by making every effort to fully restore the environment and to compensate those persons who are adversely affected.

8. *Disclosure* We will disclose to our employees and to the public incidents relating to our operations that cause environmental harm or pose health or safety hazards. We will disclose potential environmental, health or safety hazards posed by our operations, and we will not take any action against employees who report any condition that creates a danger to the environment or poses a health and safety hazard.

9. *Environmental Directors and Managers* At least one member of the Board of Directors will be a person qualified to represent environmental interests. We will commit management resources to implement these Principles, including the funding of an office of vice president for environmental affairs or equivalent executive position, reporting directly to the CEO, to monitor and report upon our implementation efforts.

10. *Assessment and Annual Audit* We will conduct and make public an annual self-evaluation of our progress in implementing these Principles and in complying with all applicable laws and regulations throughout our worldwide operations. We will work toward the timely creation of independent environmental audit procedures which we will complete annually and make available to the public.

Whatever potential they may have, they must be essentially imperfect. The difficulties of interpreting and implementing the charters plus the absence (to date at least) of adequate monitoring and follow-up procedures[9] do place the charters at risk of becoming merely public relations statements rather than substantive commitments of policy. The charters are, however, widely promulgated and discussed and, generally, represent standards to which every organization must aspire – even if they currently represent standards which make most organizations perspire.

4.4   The Valdez Principles

The Valdez Principles (see Figure 4.6) were developed in the wake of the *Exxon Valdez* tragedy[10] by the Coalition for Environmentally Responsible Economies (CERES) project of the Social Investment Forum in the United States – a body which claims to have the backing of over US$150 billion assets.[11] In the UK, the Principles were launched in November 1989 by the Green Alliance and Jupiter Tarbutt Merlin. Although the Green Alliance has not maintained its involvement, Merlin, along with the UK Social Investment Forum (the UK equivalent of CERES, formed in July 1991), has done so and continues its active involvement in the promulgation of the Principles and their adoption.[12]

Corporations are invited to sign publicly the Valdez Principles and, in doing so, provide a highly public signal of corporate commitment to environmental excellence and to compliance with (what one analyst referred to as) 'a legal document which has direct financial consequences'. The Principles are the strictest of the public charters and the lack of general support for them by industry[13] reflects an understandable (if not admirable) preference for less stringent codes. The extent of the commitment required by the Principles prompted one public expression of why a company might refuse to sign them:

[9] Although the CBI's Business and Environment Forum (see below) does have monitoring procedures built into it.

[10] Exxon's oil tanker, the *Valdez*, spilt 11 million gallons of oil into Prince William Sound, Alaska after running aground in March 1989. The devastation to the fragile ecology of the region was such that there remain profound doubts as to whether it may ever 'recover'. The resulting devastation to Exxon, although considerable and measured in US$ billions, was *not* fatal.

[11] See e.g. Lander (1989).

[12] See e.g. Dobie (1990), Miller (1992) and Chapter 10.

[13] By August 1991, only 28 organizations (principally unlisted companies and ethical/green investment funds) in the USA had signed the Principles. Subscriptions to the Principles command about US$350 billion assets, but this low level does not prevent their use as a potent tool in the application of external pressure on organizations via such things as shareholder resolutions to companies. For more detail see, for example, KPMG *Environment Briefing Note*, Autumn 1991, no. 8, pp. 2–5.

Several of these Principles, while worthy in their aims, contain unqualified commitments to 'minimize' or to 'strive to eliminate' emissions or other environmental damage. We considered that such commitments with no regard to practicability, to cost, or to acceptable or sustainable levels of emissions are simply unrealistic if taken literally.

(Charles Donovan, Senior Managing Director of British Gas,
British Gas Views: Business and the Environment
(London: British Gas) 1991, p. 6.)

Non-subscription to the Principles revolves around either a fear of the 'blank cheque' or concern about the commitment to disclosure. There is a degree of irony in this. Article 7 of the Principles requires little more than that required in the USA under Superfund and likely to be required in the EC (see Chapter 11); Articles 8 and 10 require no more than Eco-Audit will require or information which, in the relatively near future, can be expected to be in the public domain. Articles 3, 4, 5, 6 and 9 are little more than the basic principles of environmental quality management and environmental management systems (see Chapter 5). Articles 1 and 2, which are undeniably strict and demanding, are concerned with sustainable development, which nobody (publicly at least) will admit to being 'against'. Thus, at a simple interpretation, the Principles are tailor-made for any organization committed to sustainable development, environmental management systems and being ahead of legislative development.

In this sense, there should be no organization which cannot sign them.[14] And, if there is, the public could be expected to ask why. In this sense the Principles have been successful. However, the demand from industry for a milder, more forgiving environmental code with which to work led to publication of the ICC's charter.

4.5   ICC Business Charter for Sustainable Development

The International Chamber of Commerce formally launched its Business Charter for Sustainable Development (ICC BCSD[15]) in April 1991 at the Second World Industry Conference on Environmental Management (WICEM II)[16]. By the end of 1991, it (see Figure

---

[14] There is some concern that not all elements of all the charters are equally applicable to every business. Certainly one would expect – from a business, as opposed to an environmentalist point of view – that an organization should assess whether the charter is relevant to the business and then set about the difficult process of prioritizing the elements of the charter. An environmentalist would argue that each charter *is* applicable to every organization. Business and environmentalists would agree on the need to prioritize but perhaps disagree on what that priority should be.

[15] Not to be confused with the Business Council for Sustainable Development.

[16] For further information see e.g. Burke, Robins and Trisoglio (1991).

Figure 4.7

ICC Business Charter for Sustainable Development

1. *Corporate priority*   To recognize environmental management as among the highest corporate priorities and as a key determinant to sustainable development; to establish policies, programmes and practices for conducting operations in an environmentally sound manner.

2. *Integrated management*   To integrate these policies, programmes and practices fully into each business as an essential element of management in all its functions.

3. *Process of improvement*   To continue to improve corporate policies, programmes and environmental performance, taking into account technical developments, scientific understanding, consumer needs and community expectations, with legal regulations as a starting point; and to apply the same environmental criteria internationally.

4. *Employee education*   To educate, train and motivate employees to conduct their activities in an environmentally responsible manner.

5. *Prior assessment*   To assess environmental impacts before starting a new activity or project and before decommissioning a facility or leaving a site.

6. *Products and services*   To develop and provide products or services that have no undue environmental impact and are safe in their intended use, that are efficient in their consumption of energy and natural resources, and that can be recycled, re-used, or disposed of safely.

7. *Customer advice*   To advise, and where relevant educate, customers, distributors and the public in the safe use, transportation, storage and disposal of products provided; and to apply similar considerations to the provision of services.

8. *Facilities and operations*   To develop, design and operate facilities and conduct activities taking into consideration the efficient use of energy and materials, the sustainable use of renewable resource, the minimization of adverse environmental impact and waste generation, and the safe and responsible disposal of residual wastes.

9. *Research*   To conduct or support research on the environmental impacts of raw materials, products, processes, emissions and wastes associated with the enterprise and on the means of minimizing such adverse impacts.

10. *Precautionary approach*   To modify the manufacture, marketing or use of products or services or the conduct of activities, consistent with scientific and technical understanding, to prevent serious or irreversible environmental degradation.

11. *Contractors and suppliers*   To promote the adoption of these principles by contractors acting on behalf of the enterprise, encourage and, where appropriate, requiring improvements in their practices to make them consistent with those of the enterprise; and to encourage the wider adoption of these principles by suppliers.

12. *Emergency preparedness*   To develop and maintain, where significant hazards exist, emergency preparedness plans in conjunction with emergency services, relevant authorities and local community, recognizing potential transboundary impacts.

13. *Transfer of technology*   To contribute to the transfer of environmentally sound technology and management methods throughout the industrial and public sectors.

14. *Contributing to the common effort*   To contribute to the development of public policy and to business, governmental and intergovernmental programmes and educational initiative that will enhance environmental awareness and protection.

15. *Openness to concerns*   To foster openness and dialogue with employees and the public, anticipating and responding to their concerns about the potential hazards and impacts of operations, products, wastes or services, including those of transboundary or global significance.

16. *Compliance and reporting*   To measure environmental performance; to conduct regular environmental audits and assessments of compliance with company requirements, legal requirements and these principles; and periodically to provide appropriate information to the Board of Directors, shareholders, employees, the authorities and the public.

Figure 4.8

The ICC's principal functions are stated as being to represent business at international levels such as the United Nations; promote world trade and investment based on free and fair competition; harmonize trade practices and formulate terminology and guidelines for exporters and importers; and provide practical services to business.

4.7) was the most widely supported charter, with over 400 organizations having endorsed it.

ICC is a non-governmental organization 'serving world business with membership in over 100 countries'. Figure 4.8 lists its principal functions. ICC has a history of supporting business in the environmental arena. Its environmental guidelines for world industry were first published in 1974, with the latest and fourth update being published in 1990. The ICC BCSD, in contrast with the 'absolutes' contained in the Valdez Principles, involves somewhat softer standards and vaguer undertakings. It is thus potentially less stringent – especially as it requires its signatories merely to endorse its aims rather than to have reached the standards set out. For instance, ICC BCSD refers to 'no undue environmental impact' (Clause 6) and speaks of 'foster[ing] openness and dialogue' (Clause 15). The ICC exhorts business to an environmental response rather than demands one.

The ICC is publicly opposed to disclosure in general (see Chapter 5) and so the 'tentative' nature of the requirements for systematic auditing and reporting comes as no surprise. While Clause 16 requires regular audits and periodic provision of 'appropriate' information, it neither insists on disclosure nor makes absolute the audit requirement. This allows organizations considerable flexibility in reporting and provides the public and shareholders with no guarantees on the quality of environmental performance or the regularity of environmental information (see Chapters 10 to 12).

Similarly, ICC does not monitor compliance with the Charter. Rather, it believes that the public interest will be an adequate monitoring mechanism.[17] That is, knowing that the organization subscribes

[17] Torvild Aakvaag, Chairman of ICC Environment Commission, in Burke, Robins and Trisoglio (1991), p. 88.

to BCSD will enable the public to evaluate its compliance with the Charter. However, given the absence of widespread public announcement of which organizations have signed the Charter and the lack of systematic audit and publication of results, how individuals will in fact be able to assess for themselves the level of compliance is unknown. Indeed the suggestion from the ICC that UNEP might act as an assessing body[18] seems equally without substance. Signing up to the ICC BCSD is thus a relatively relaxed affair. In the words of the Environment Director of a large plc:

The ICC policy is a very good set of the principles that must form the basis for discussion for any company deriving its own policy. It is the discussion which is useful – not the policy itself. It is this company's nature to be in the forefront and thinking about these issues will put you in the forefront – and this will give commercial advantage.

Ironically, one of the most interesting reasons expressed for *not* subscribing to the charter came from one of the world's largest and most environmentally advanced companies. It believed that it was improper to sign anything which committed it to sustainable development as currently understood. Not because the company was opposed to the concept (after all, who is?), but because 'buying into sustainable development' implies also 'buying into' the major social policies that would appear to go along with it – most notably population control[19]. The directors of the company did not believe that their authority extended to such a commitment. The irony is that the ICC BCSD, despite using the term 'sustainable development', makes no attempt to demonstrate that satisfaction of the Charter is in fact compatible with sustainability (see Chapter 14).

4.6 The Chemical Industries Association Responsible Care Programme

The Chemical Industries Association Responsible Care Programme (CIA RCP – see Figure 4.9), whilst less demanding than either the ICC or Valdez Charters, is a good example of an industry-based initiative which has the value of being 'realistic' enough to be acceptable to most of that industry. It was launched in May 1989 in order to 'improve the chemical industry's performance and to enable companies to demonstrate improvement to the public' (CIA Preface to the Guiding Principles).

In addition to its industry-based origin – a response to the chemical industry's increasingly environmentally malign public image – the CIA charter has three noteworthy characteristics[20]:

[18] Ibid.

[19] See Chapters 14 and 15.

[20] Of note is that the CIA RCP was also issued relatively early on in the modern development of the environmental agenda. It seems likely that this was motivated –

Figure 4.9

CIA Responsible Care Programme

GUIDING PRINCIPLES:

Members of the Chemical Industries Association are committed to managing their activities so that they present an acceptable high level of protection for the health and safety of employees, customers, the public and the environment.

The following Guiding Principles form the basis of this commitment:

- Companies should ensure that their health, safety and environment policy reflects the commitment and is clearly seen to be an integral part of their overall business policy.
- Companies should ensure that management, employees at all levels and those in contractual relationships with the Company are aware of their commitment and are involved in the achievement of their policy objectives.
- All Company activities and operations must be conducted in accordance with relevant statutory obligations. In addition, Companies should operate to the best practices of the industry and in accordance with Government and Association guidance.

In particular, Companies should:

- Assess the actual and potential impact of their activities and products on the health and safety of employees, customers, the public and environment.
- Where appropriate, work closely with public and statutory bodies in the development and implementation of measures designed to achieve an acceptably high level of health, safety and environmental protection.
- Make available to employees, customers, the public and statutory bodies, relevant information about activities that affect health, safety and the environment.

Members of the Association recognize that these Principles and activities should continue to be kept under regular review.

(1) It explicitly states the need to comply with legislation. (As we have seen, that is far from being as trivial as it might appear.)
(2) Although it falls short of actually committing itself to regular and widespread public disclosure, it does require that companies make information available upon demand to employees, customers, etc. – by implication – to the extent that these groups are affected by the organization's activities. In an atmosphere reluctant to disclose, this is a welcome development (see Chapters 11 and 12).
(3) Significantly, the CIA explicitly recognizes the developing nature of the environmental agenda and the need, therefore, closely to monitor and review the Charter.

Whilst the Responsible Care Programme may not be as demanding as the Valdez Principles – or as advanced as a growing environ-

in part at least – by 'good business sense' in order to provide a defensible position against either charters of the Valdez requirements or against the possibility of more demanding legislative requirements in the wake of a series of chemical and chemical-related environmental disasters.

mental crisis might require – it represents a major step forward. In particular, if all organizations could sign up to – *and comply with* – such a charter, the environment/business debate would be a great deal more advanced than it is.

4.7   Other Charters and Related Initiatives

It is tempting to infer that the number of different initiatives directed towards the development of public (or semi-public) environmental charters is a recognition of the importance attached to this first of Elkington's 'Ten Steps'. On a less grand scale than the charters reviewed above, more locally focused initiatives are developing all the time. The UK has seen, for example, a UK Environmental Investor Code, developed by Pensions Investment Research Consultants Ltd, which is intended to gain the full support of the pension funds so that pressure may be brought upon companies to develop their environmental excellence and, most significantly, undertake regular and systematic environmental disclosure. Local authorities have the Environmental Charter for Local Government launched by Friends of the Earth in 1989. This includes guidance both to the authorities and to members of the local community and encourages the adoption of a 'declaration of commitment' and a fifteen-point policy commitment. The Charter has been widely adopted – often in adapted form – by many local authorities.

In 1992 the CBI launched *its* Environment Business Forum with an 'Agenda for Voluntary Action on the Environment' (see Figure 4.10). This asked companies to sign up to the Forum and, having done this, the signatory organizations received a letter asking them for a statement of their plans and progress on the 'Agenda'. Failure to respond removed them from the Forum. Figure 4.10 outlines the elements of the CBI's initiative. Initiatives in the 'voluntary action on the environment' area need follow-up and monitoring processes if they are to be more than PR 'puff'. Other initiatives in the UK – such as the Business-in-the-Environment initiative – are also coming to recognize that some follow-up and monitoring of actual progress towards the environmental objectives for which organizations have signed up is now an essential element of any environmental policy.

4.8   Implementing and Monitoring the Policy

The publicly launched charters are learning something that organizations which have developed their own in-house environmental policy learnt some time ago: a policy on its own means virtually nothing; it must be translated into action.

On the face of it this follows the textbook approach of Figure 4.11 in which one simply follows a cookbook menu. In principle this is so: Alcan said in 1991 that the environmental (and related) policy drives all investment and R&D (see Chapter 8); IBM UK published

Figure 4.10

The CBI Agenda for Voluntary Action

* Designate a board level director with responsibility for the environment and the management systems needed to address the key issues.
* Publish a corporate environmental policy statement.
* Set clear targets and objectives for achieving the policy.
* Publicly report progress towards meeting those objectives.
* Ensure communication with employees, and training where appropriate, on company environmental programmes.
* Establish appropriate 'partnerships' to extend and promote the objectives of the Forum, particularly with smaller companies.

---

in 1992 its policy, targets *and* target completion dates (see also Chapters 11 and 12). Each of these steps is important. That is:

(1) Unless the policy can be turned into specifics it cannot be controlled – for example, all organizations may choose to think of themselves as sustainable without ever having defined sustainability or investigated the claim.

(2) Unless the conflicts in the policy(ies) are examined the policy may be ineffectual – an organization may reduce emissions 'as far as is practicable', or use technology which is the most environmentally advanced 'within budget constraints'. Both statements mean nothing at all until the financial implications of 'practicable' and 'budget constraints' are adapted.

(3) Monitoring is more important than often realized. Not only does it assess performance and provide a feedback and control mechanism, it should also fulfil two further functions. First, the existence of *no* monitoring is a strong signal to employees that the organization is not serious about environmental issues. It signals that despite warm words and exhortation, performance will still be measured by the old ways, promotion will still be on the same old criteria and no resources will be made available for environmental matters. No monitoring virtually equals 'don't care'. Second, the monitoring should be part of a wider monitoring system that can also provide early warnings to the organization. This is worth emphasizing. We have already discussed (see Chapter 3) the need to monitor the developing environmental agenda. This cannot be a precise, technical (or algorithmic) activity. Much will depend on instinct. This instinct needs to be informed by regular reviews. For example, an organization may be apparently meeting its consents but certain areas of the organization may be having more accidents than others. This is an area that a responsible management will wish to investigate – not least because it may prove to be an area of embarrassment at some time in the future. Similarly, if an organization is not

Figure 4.11

> ### Implementing the policy
>
> - Prioritize the goals of the policy.
> - Prioritize the goals of the organization in terms of the policy.
> - Identify interactions throughout the organization and decide how to harmonize them.
> - Turn the goals into specific targets.
> - Give the targets completion dates.
> - Assign responsibility.
> - Monitor performance.
> - Feedback and reward.

Figure 4.12

> Monitoring systems (including audit and review)
>
> - Performance against legal standards
> - Performance against consent levels
> - Performance against forthcoming law
> - Performance against organizational ethical policy
> - Performance against environmental policy
> - Performance in all areas of environmental policy
> - Analysis of complaints
> - Highest standards audits/reviews
> - Analysis of employee suggestion boxes
> - Review of regular organizational data on wastes, emissions, leaks, accidents etc.
> - Review of who gets the information and when. What is done with it?

making regular reviews of its activities, it needs to recognize that outside bodies may be doing so. The organization will wish to avoid the unpleasant surprise of discovering that part of its operations are breaching its mission and ethical statement or are in an area of increasing sensitivity.[21]

A monitoring system is outlined in Figure 4.12.

But all this involves time and energy. The intelligent design of information systems and the regular scrutiny of the data from the information systems are far from trivial matters. An organization can feel realistic confidence in its performance across environmental and related areas only if it has applied real manpower resources to it. Ignorance and assuming the best will no longer be enough.

[21] The experience of BP in 1989 is a good example when its activities in the South American rain forests, much to the amazement of its UK management, were suddenly front-page headlines. The company was caught unawares.

4.9 Conclusions

Setting and/or adopting an environmental policy is a major step. It is the first step that an organization must take in reassessing its environmental sensitivity but it is a step requiring serious commitment, careful thought and, most importantly, systematic follow-up. The policy will set the tone for the organization and, if it is to be believed by internal and external participants, it must be backed by real commitment. Organizations are increasingly under public scrutiny and, at a minimum, senior management must place their organization in a position which is publicly defensible. This has two major elements: are you complying with your own professed standards? and are these standards as high as (say) the Valdez Principles? If not why not? The environment is a public matter and reluctant though organizations may be to accept that, accept it they must. The environmental policy is both the first step and potentially the most contentious. Any organization serious about its environmental impact will recognize that anything less than the best is simply not good enough.

Further Reading

3M/The Environment Council (1991) *A Guide to Policy Making and Implementation*, 3M/The Environment Council, London.

Business-in-the-Environment (1991a) *Your Business and the Environment: A DIY Review for Companies*, BiE/Coopers & Lybrand Deloitte, London.

Business-in-the-Environment (1992) *A Measure of Commitment: Guidelines for Environmental Performance Measurement*, BiE/KPMG, London.

Confederation of British Industry (1992c) *Corporate Environmental Policy Statements*, CBI, London.

Elkington, J., Knight, P. and Hailes, J. (1991) *The Green Business Guide*, Gollancz, London.

Focus Report: Business and Sustainable Development – the role of environmental charters, *Business and the Environment* June 1992 Vol. 3. no. 7. pp. 2–4.

Hutchinson, C. (1991) *Business and the Environmental Challenge*, the Conservation Trust, Reading.

APPENDIX 4.1
Shandwick Environment:
'Creating a Corporate Environmental Policy Statement'

SHANDWICK ENVIRONMENT

CREATING A CORPORATE ENVIRONMENTAL POLICY STATEMENT

If your company wishes properly and fully to meet its environmental obligations, it must first articulate the commitment of management with a formal policy statement. This is not a large, long and complex document, but does need to be carefully thought out.

The policy, if not to be seen as empty posturing, must:

- address the agenda set by external audiences
- be seen accurately to reflect past action and future aspirations
- lead naturally to an action plan
- indicate yardsticks for measuring progress

A key audience for the policy statement is your own employees. If it is not credible and acceptable to them, it will be impossible for management to take it forward.

THE POLICY-MAKING PROCESS

Writing a policy is a multi-stage process. Not until these are complete is the organisation able to start taking position benefits from its environmental actions.

The stages are enumerated below. Although carefully ordered for clarity, many are actually carried out simultaneously.

1) Scoping

The general content of a formal policy has been reasonably well defined by environmental and industry organisations.

However, an effective environment policy is highly specific to the individual company. It must be practical and appropriate in technical scope, and cover the full range of corporate activities.

Action: Review policy guidelines by e.g. CBI, ICC, and environmentalists' proposals.

2) Establish Company-Specific Issues

Review all environmental issues relevant to your company, both now and predictions for the future. You should take account of both 'real' technical environmental impacts and public perceptions.

Action: Interview internal experts and external commentators for their views. Consultants may help, as they often have broader experience.

3) Positioning Content

For maximum usefulness, your policy must not be a pale imitation of competitor positions, nor fall

SHANDWICK ENVIRONMENT

CREATING A CORPORATE ENVIRONMENTAL POLICY STATEMENT

short of the expectations of activists, customers or staff. It must fit within any framework established by the parent company.

The policy needs to be phrased consistently with corporate values, habits and language.

Action: Obtain and review parent, competitor and customer policies. Interview sample of staff (all levels, but especially middle management) on their expectations. Review existing documentation, interview communications specialists.

4) Address Content

Whatever external and internal views may suggest, the policy *must* be consistent with the real level of management commitment. It must address as many areas as possible, but must not promise beyond what is intended.

Action: Interview senior management to determine extent of commitment.

5) Draft Policy

The policy is best written to last, and will therefore be quite generally phrased. It should make the firmest commitment possible.

The policy should make reference to company targets and actions, but these are better set out in full elsewhere.

Action: Prepare drafts and discuss in detail with senior management. Try to be as bold as possible with the first draft, it is more likely to get softened than strengthened as the consequences of the commitment become clear.

6) Amass Examples

To make it easier to understand the policy, it helps to describe actual examples of good environmental decisions already made. It is very rare for a good range not to be available. Often the reason for the action was not directly environmental (e.g. cost-based) but the effects are just as helpful. These examples can usefully be published in a policy booklet.

Action: Interview middle management against checklist of draft policy points.

7) Assess Present Position

Unless the extent of the company's present impact is known, progress will be difficult to identify. Measuring environmental impact is a technical matter. It can be carried out internally or with external support.

Action: Identify technical resource and priority areas to be examined. The issue analysis will be useful for this.

8) Set Targets

The policy statement defines commitment, targets define progress. Reaching targets is a clear demonstration of progress, and it is, therefore, better that they be set achievably. Targets are more credible with dates attached. They should be numerical, and can be either actual (e.g. average fleet mpg down to x) or relative (emissions to air cut by 10%).

The positioning benefit of targets varies according to the values set by receiving audiences, so targets must address perceived issues.

SHANDWICK ENVIRONMENT

CREATING A CORPORATE ENVIRONMENTAL POLICY STATEMENT

Action: Review issues in relation to operations, draft targets and discuss with management.

9) Define Action Plan
In order to meet targets and demonstrate management commitment to good environmental practice, actual action is required. Priorities must be agreed, and may be influenced by feasibility, external issues or competitive positioning advantage.

Action: Prioritise areas for action by reviewing possible options against external perceptions, ask operational managers to write action plans for approval.

10) Allocate Responsibilities
The action plans will languish unless someone is made responsible for carrying them out. Environmental improvement is no exception. Responsibility for each point of the agreed action plan should be clearly defined and progress reviewed regularly.

Action: Review existing managerial procedures and recommend structure for effecting environmental action plan.

For further information, please contact: Shandwick Environment,
Shandwick Public Affairs,
Dauntsey House, Frederick's Place, Old Jewry, LONDON EC2R 8AB
Tel: 071 726 4291   Fax: 071 726 2999

5. Environmental Audit:

Assessment, Review, Management and Attestation

5.1 Introduction

Environmental audit is a term which has become synonymous with organizational response to the green agenda and is an area growing in both complexity and importance. In Europe, with the development of the 'eco-audit', 'duty of care', 'eco-labelling', potential land remediation liability, supplier audits, BS7750 (on environmental management systems) etc., it is not a matter that can be treated as either trivial or simple.[1]

The CBI (1990, based on ICC, 1989) defines 'environmental audit' as:

> the systematic examination of the interactions between any business operation and its surroundings. This includes all emissions to air, land and water; legal constraints; the effects on the neighbouring community, landscape and ecology; and the public's perception of the operating company in the local area . . . Environmental audit does not stop at compliance with legislation. Nor is it a 'green-washing' public relations exercise . . . Rather it is a total strategic approach to the organization's activities.[2]

The term covers a multitude of different (although related) activities. The first step in environmental auditing which any organization must take is the precise determination of the sort of

---

[1] One medium-sized manufacturing company, for example, had no environmental audit, had no intention of conducting one and was entirely unaware that EC developments might require one. There is a real danger that the UK may be in danger of falling too far behind other European and North American countries.

[2] The Confederation of British Industry *Narrowing the Gap: Environmental Auditing Guidelines for Business* (London: CBI) 1990 which is based upon The International Chamber of Commerce *Environmental Auditing* (Paris: ICC) 1989.

Figure 5.1

Types of environmental audit

(1) environmental impact assessment;
(2) environmental survey;
(3) environmental review, monitoring and surveillance;
(4) environmental investigation;
(5) the 'eco-audit' and BS7750;
(6) independent attestation of environmental information – for internal or external participants.

'audit' it wants and the range of activities the audit must cover ('scoping'). This, itself, will be determined by a wide range of factors related to, *inter alia*, the nature of the organization, its industry and markets and how far it has advanced towards embracing the green agenda. Ultimately, 'environmental audit' should become a major and established element of an organization's environmental management systems (see below) but in the early stages it may be no more than the first tottering step towards the goal of environmental sensitivity.[3]

It therefore makes sense to recognize explicitly the range of things that are, at times, included within the term 'environmental audit' (see Figure 5.1).

They are all importantly different, require different skills and have a different orientation. Being clear about each one may also have legal implications. So the first word of warning is to proceed carefully and to ensure (as we emphasized in Chapters 1 and 2) that one is clear about where one stands with respect to the law. All we can do in this chapter is provide some general guidance. We will introduce and define these different elements of the environmental audit, provide some suggestions and illustrations on how to get started with the audit, share the experiences of others and suggest where to go for further help and information.

5.2   The Environmental Impact Assessment (EIA)

EIAs were probably first developed in the USA under the National Environment Policy Act of 1969. This lead was initially followed by Canada, Australia, Holland, New Zealand and Japan but it was a fairly isolated activity in the UK until July 1988 when, as a

---

[3] There is a very considerable literature and experience on environmental auditing in its widest sense. This chapter and its further reading can only scrape the surface. Other useful sources include Bins-Hoefnagels et al (1986), Bins-Hoefnagels & Molencamp (1989), Cardwell (1991), Dewhurst (1989), Roger Gray (1989), Greenpeace (1985), Moretz (1989), on Allied Signals' approach, and Humble (1973) and Hunt (1974) for a historical perspective to remind us that little in this area is actually new.

result of the EC Directive on Environmental Assessment (85/337), impact assessments were required in Britain. EIA can be defined as: 'essentially a process that seeks to identify and predict the impacts of a new development on the environment, to mitigate them where possible and to monitor the actual impacts'.[4]

As a general statement, all major projects that are subject to some form of planning permission and which are likely to have 'a significant impact on the environment' should be subject to EIA. (The EC Directive lays down in Annexes I and II some indication of what this might mean.[5]) Their initial purpose was to guide planners in coming to decisions on new initiatives although Fuller argues that the motivation for their introduction in the EC owed as much to attempts to 'level the playing field' as to protection of the environment. However, the situation in the UK has remained far from clear in that it is not obvious that EIAs are always conducted when required and neither is the quality of the resulting environmental impact statements (EISs) as high as it should be.[6] This situation appears to have arisen from a number of factors, including the apparent reluctance of the UK government to take an appropriate lead, the lack of accreditation of bodies equipped to produce EISs, the diversity of planning authorities to which the EIS goes and, as a result, the lack of expertise in evaluating the EIA.

There have been two major responses to this situation in the UK. First, the number of statutory EISs is now being matched by the number of voluntary EISs. This arises as organizations recognize the value of the EIA – both as a means to assist the planning process and as useful management techniques as part of their wider environmental management and audit (see below). Second, there has been a recognition of the need to establish guidelines and standards of good practice for EIA.[7] With the growing importance of EC direc-

[4] Taken from Fuller (1991) p. 12 from which more detail can be obtained.

[5] Department of the Environment (1989d). For information on the legal issues see, for example, Ball and Bell (1991).

[6] By way of comparison, in the Netherlands a single Impact Commission is involved in all EIAs, in Canada there has been a significant emphasis on the development of public awareness and involvement in EIAs and in New Zealand detailed guidelines are supplemented by Environmental Impact Report Audits carried out by the Commissioner for the Environment. For more detail on the UK see, for example, Ball (1991a).

[7] This led to the formation of the Institute of Environmental Assessment (IEA) in July 1990 and to the formation of the Association of Environmental Consultancies (AEC) – both bodies concerned with raising professionalism and standards in both assessment and in more general environmental audit. In broad terms the IEA, working with the National Accreditation Council of Certification Bodies (NACCB), seeks to develop the status of an independent, standard-setting professional body (the National Environmental Auditing Review Board) whilst the AEC acts more as a trade association. For more detail see ENDS Report 195/April 1991 (pp. 15–17), Gray and Symon (1992a) and Environmental Assessment Report No. 2 Winter 1991 (p. 3). The addresses and contact names of the bodies can be found in Appendix B.

Figure 5.2

Information in an environmental impact assessment

(1)   a description of the proposed project and, where applicable, of the reasonable alternatives for its siting and design;

(2)   a description of the environment that is likely to be affected;

(3)   an assessment of the likely effects of the proposed project on the environment;

(4)   a description of the measures proposed to eliminate, reduce or compensate for adverse environmental effects;

(5)   a description of the relationship between the proposal and the existing environmental and land-use plans for, and standards of, the affected area; and

(6)   an explanation of the reasons for the choice of the preferred site and project design rather than of the 'reasonable' alternatives.

All this information would, in addition, need to be published in a form which the public can understand, to ensure effective public participation.

Source: Elkington (1982) p. 26.

---

tives on environmental issues and, in particular, the developing eco-audit requirements (see below) there is need for greater clarity, professionalism and independence in this area.[8]

EIAs are not seen as especially onerous by most companies with a developed experience of them. In fact, the experience of, for example, British Gas, IBM and ICI is that they speed up, simplify and remove some of the risk from the planning process. Indeed, one company expects all planning formalities through in under sixteen weeks. This is as a result of the reputation of the company and the quality of the EIS. This feeds upon itself and increases the environmental reputation of the company.

However, a major decision for any organization is whether to undertake the EIA itself or to call in a consultant. Many of the big companies throughout the world have the experience and the very wide expertise necessary to undertake the EIA in-house. For other organizations this option is unlikely to exist, and taking some reliable expert advice at some stage in the proceedings seems necessary. Nevertheless, it can be helpful for any organization to have some idea of what an EIA might look like. Figure 5.2 provides an outline of the process.

The experience of companies such as ICI and IBM can also be useful. Both have developed over time and have produced useful guidelines. These can be integrated to produce the checklist shown

---

[8] The issue of independence is a most difficult one, as any commentator on the auditing profession would note (see e.g. Sikka, Willmott and Lowe, 1989, 1991). The problem arises in the potential conflict of interest between consultants and the professional body on the one hand and the development of a need for independent attestation on the other (see later in this chapter). The International Institute of Environmental Auditors has been established to try to address this problem but as a new and relatively small body has still fully to establish itself.

in Figure 5.3.[9] (It will be noted that the checklists, very sensibly, broadly follow the Directive's suggestions.)

The EIA is clearly an area in which experience and technical, legal and scientific knowledge are required. However, it must not be seen as a wholly unique activity. It differs from most other environmental information-collation activities in that it is specifically prepared for public consumption in a particular context. Whilst other environmental information is increasingly finding its way into the public domain (see Part C) much of it is prepared, in the first place at least, for management's consumption. Any organization with a well-developed environmental response, environmental management system, will integrate the EIA process with the other elements of 'environmental audit' to avoid duplication, to provide independent sources of data and to develop the overall organizational strategy with respect to environmental sensitivity.

5.3   The Environmental Survey

We have used the term 'environmental survey' to refer to the simplest type of environmental audit – the first step that any organization can take towards improving its environmental sensitivity.[10] Simple though it might be, it serves a number of important functions including orientating the organization to environmental issues, beginning the process of recognizing and identifying actual and potential areas of environmental impact, and laying out an initial agenda for undertaking further environmental audits and starting the move towards a more complete environmental management. Whatever the outcome, the experience at this and later stages should feed back into the issues we have discussed in earlier chapters – for example, organizational policy statements, initial green activities and changing the corporate culture. The importance of this step can be seen in the fact that surveys have suggested that perhaps over 80 per cent of companies have undertaken no environmental audit,[11] and that some companies in our survey referred to themselves as either 'having no environmental impact' or as being 'environmentally neutral'. As we discussed in Part A, no organization can justifiably make such claims.[12]

[9] The information for Figure 5.3 was obtained through interviews with the companies and from other public sources (see Further Reading at the end of the chapter, and Appendix A). Principally the same information can be found in Elkington, Knight and Hailes (1991).

[10] Sometimes also called the 'scoping' audit. Costs of audit vary considerably. Scottish Enterprise reckon that £1,000 should be sufficient for a scoping audit. Burkitt (1990) reports that environmental audits in the widest sense can cost between £5,000 and £400,000.

[11] See Chapter 2 and also e.g. Cardwell (1991), Walesby (1991).

[12] It is too simple to associate environmental audit and environmental impact only with extraction and manufacturing in its most intrusive forms. Recent reports have

Figure 5.3

Environmental Audit Checklist based on the approaches of IBM and ICI

Stage 1. Screening: Assessing whether the project qualifies for an EIA and, if not, whether the organisation should still undertake one.

Stage 2. The IBM Approach: in three stages:

(a) Site environmental assessment: a quick first appraisal to identify early on in the process any major issues – which may, in fact, screen out the project at an early stage.

(b) Environmental baseline study: the basis against which to assess any changes to the environment over the course of the study and the project – for both planning, EIA and 'defensive' purposes. Will include (*inter alia*) air, water, land, flora, fauna, habitat, noise, aesthetics and the community.

(c) Prepare for the EIA.

Stage 3. The ICI Checklist:

(a) Describe the project: including benefits, costs, potential issues, possible objections, legal issues etc.

(b) Describe possible alternatives to the proposed plan.

(c) Propose methods to reduce environmental impact.

(d) List possible effects on the environment.

(e) Measure the impact of the project on people, animals and their environment.

(f) Summarize and evaluate: involving economic versus environmental 'costs and benefits'.

Stage 4. After Project Begins Monitor Environmental Impact

In this section we suggest how any organization can undertake this first step. (The approach has been derived from the organizational visits we have made, informed by the more useful publications that are now widely available.) Subsequent sections will explore the development from this; meanwhile the appendices to this chapter and the further reading provide examples of flowcharts and checklists for the putative environmental auditor.

The first stage in the process may seem elementary but is often the most difficult – that is, actually sitting down and starting the process.[13] The second stage involves no more than paper, pencil and a knowledge of the organization. Applying the 'systems perspective' we discussed in Appendix 1.1, the flows into and out of the organization are broadly identified in the first place by the proprietor or manager. An extract from the first step in one initial such 'survey' (of a small hotel) is shown in Figure 5.4.

---

highlighted the effect of environmental audits undertaken by accountants (KPMG reported in the *Financial Times*, 12 June 1991); by banks (National Westminster reported in the *Financial Times*, 26 February 1992); and by newspapers (*Guardian*, 10 August 1991).

[13] For small organizations this can be especially difficult and so we recommend that some third party is invited in – even if this is just an intelligent colleague or friend with a basic appreciation of environmental matters.

Figure 5.4 A 'first step' environmental audit for a small hotel

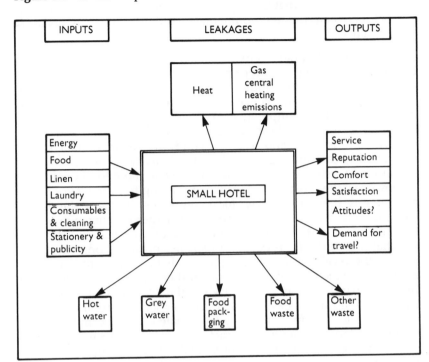

This was not, obviously, seeking any especially profound insights into the environmental impact but encouraging the manager (or whoever) to think the process through. Each of the categories was then itemized separately (which leads to recognition of other items originally missed, e.g. use of the car, use of a coal fire). Then each item and area of activity was discussed in terms of possible impact and how that could be minimized through 'refuse, reduce, re-use, recycle and substitute'. Current practices with respect to minimizing environmental impact were itemized and a plan of action, with maintenance of additional information systems as appropriate, was detailed. The most important part of the plan was the decision to appraise performance against the plan at subsequent meetings of the directors.

Such a simple approach had a profound effect on the thinking and subsequent actions of the proprietor/manager of several organizations we visited. It also explicitly raised two additional crucial matters:

(1) What were the costs and benefits – in hard financial numbers – of the plan agreed? In a tightly run organization, operating on small margins with no spare capital, most of the significant actions were impossible.

(2) What are the crucial business success factors, beyond which the business is unable to go – i.e the actual points of real conflict between the environmental standards and the business standards?[14]

This basic beginners' environmental survey must be refined before either relying upon it or moving on to the more sophisticated forms of environmental audit. Two of the basic ways of doing this are, first, to refine the conception of the organization into more useful sectors, for example upstream effects, people, housekeeping/office, processes, products/services, emissions, wastes and other downstream effects; and then, second, to separate analysis to individual sites and/or lines of business/activity in order either to repeat the exercise or to refine by reference to more local criteria.

However, the most important factor missing from the layperson's audit is any reference to law, local conditions, industry standards, consents, etc.[15] Experience suggests that larger organizations often find the law and its threat a major motivator in greening activities, but that a disturbing proportion of smaller organizations have little idea of the legal matters which govern them in this area or, more appositely, which are likely to concern them in the near future. On the other hand, the surveys and visits did seem to emphasize that smaller organizations have a much stronger sense of community and duty to the locality in which they are situated. They seem less likely to outrage local residents or attract the wrath of Greenpeace. (The steps for the beginner's environmental audit are summarized in Figure 5.5).

As a starting point, the beginner's survey is helpful. It most certainly is not sufficient. It can provide no more than a starting point to frame and identify areas for later development. Without specialist knowledge it cannot identify legal problems, it cannot identify potential chemical hazards and so on. For this, more advanced forms of audit – leading to environmental management – are necessary.

5.4   Developing the Environmental Audit

There is no simple cookbook approach to developing the environmental audit. Each organization is different, has different concerns and, perhaps most important, differs in the talents, time and cash available to it. Perhaps the first decisions any organization must make at this stage are: do we go it alone or call in outside help? and

---

[14] In the case of the small hotel, one such issue was the whiteness (not cleanliness) of sheets, which was considered essential to the success of the business.

[15] A number of consultants are developing computer software for use by small organizations as a guide to self-environmental audit. The market for this sort of support is growing rapidly and new products can be expected on a regular basis.

Figure 5.5

The beginner's environmental survey

Step 1. **Get started:** asking for assistance if necessary.

Step 2. **Draw a systems flow of the organization:** identifying the major categories of inputs, outputs and leakages.

Step 3. **Provide a detailed itemization of the elements in Step 2:** identifying the products and materials and the activities to which they relate. Pick up additional items involved along the way.

Step 4. **Review each item with a view to minimization:** refuse, reduce, reuse, recycle, substitute.

Step 5. **Assess financial costs and benefits (if any):** what can the organization realistically afford?

Step 6. **Identify crucial business factors:** what are the issues on which you feel you cannot compromise – where the environment loses out to the business?

Step 7. **Draw up a detailed plan of action**

Step 8. **Review progress at board meeting or equivalent**

Step 9. **Refine the organization:** identify (as appropriate) people, housekeeping/office; processes, products/services; emissions and wastes; and repeat on site and/or business basis.

And do not forget ...

Step 10. **Identify existing and potential law, industry standards, consents as appropriate:** the smaller organization relies here upon its trade association and related journals and trade magazines (but see Further Reading). This will become the first step as the organization begins to adjust.

---

do we undertake more investigation, or are we in a position to move directly to setting up our environmental management systems?

Many organizations of every size have found that further investigation is necessary as a precursor to the development of environmental management systems. The most widely reported approach is that of calling in an environmental auditing consultancy to provide an organization-wide review. These gain the greater public attention when the result, or summary, is published – as with companies like British Airways, Caird and Body Shop for example.[16] Other companies have chosen to do the matter entirely in-house – to keep the matter private whilst they start the process of getting their house into some sort of order. More common is a balance between these two – developing in-house environmental auditing team(s) and calling upon external bodies at different stages for advice and evaluation of what has been done. Perhaps the best known of these (in the UK at least) are the IBM(UK) liaison with John Elkington's

---

[16] See Chapters 11 and 12 for more detail.

Figure 5.6

Major elements in an environmental audit or review

- identify the most important of the organization's environmental interactions;
- assess the degree of environmental impact;
- learn about how to deal with and reduce or improve the organization's impact;
- identify a priority list of interactions to be dealt with (this will develop, in part, from the first two and in part in response to actual and potential changes in law and in society's attitudes;
- establish standards and policies;
- identify responsibilities;
- train staff;
- change practices and put policies into action;
- develop environmental information systems;
- monitor performance and performance appraisal;
- assess performance against standards;
- reappraise this list, starting from the top, on a systematic and continuing basis.

SustainAbility[17] and the widely publicized Norsk Hydro audit.[18]

The suggestions in the Further Reading section of this chapter will provide more detail on the stages and processes of this more developed environmental audit but we can lay down an outline of the basic steps as an illustration of what will be necessary in the move towards environmental management systems. These are shown in Figure 5.6.

By the time an organization reaches the stage of devising an 'environmental audit strategy' it is beginning to beg larger questions about its overall environmental strategy, aims, objectives and how environmental issues are to be fitted into the overall organizational context. (This we touched upon in Chapters 3 and 4 and will return to from time to time.) One approach to attempting this integration is the use of SWOT analysis.

Companies of the stature and experience of Pilkington Glass have found undertaking a SWOT (Strengths, Weaknesses, Opportunities, Threats) analysis, if done brutally and honestly, can provide useful guidance on where to place attention in the development of the organization's environmental response. Figure 5.7 illustrates generally the sorts of matters that may usefully come through such a process – to be really useful it would need to be a great deal more specific than this.

Such analysis has the distinct advantage of encouraging an

---

[17] See, for example, *IBM UK Environmental Programmes* published at the end of 1991.

[18] See Part C for more detail on Norsk Hydro.

Figure 5.7   An illustration of environmental SWOT analysis

XYZ plc: 1/1/92

Environmental SWOT analysis

Strengths	Weaknesses
1. Public image	1. Public impression of greenness, visible pollution
2. Staff morale	2. Trade-offs: cost versus emissions; different types of emissions
3. Product type	3. Worldwide standards
4. Technological advantages	4. Level of recycling
5. Recycling opportunities	5. Current technological limits on greening products and processes
6. Current position in meeting consent levels	6. Transport
7. Environmental awareness in the industry	7. Toxicity of wastes
Opportunities	**Threats**
1. Products' environmental strengths	1. Legislation UK/EC/overseas
2. Involvement with business and environmental groups	2. Energy costs
3. Involvement with community	3. Duty of care and landfill costs
4. Recycling opportunities	4. Worldwide standards and inter-company trade
5. Use and develop employees' goodwill and ideas	5. Cost of current and future monitoring
6. Position in the industry	6. Existing good public image makes us vulnerable to accidents and other discoveries
7. Exploit R&D advantages	

organization to take a hard look at itself and begin the process of identifying where its environmental efforts should lie. However, a successful SWOT analysis presupposes a significant knowledge of the organization's activities and this cannot be assumed. It became very apparent during our visits that many companies – major as well as minor – had no real idea of what was happening throughout their operations. This was especially noticeable in the multinationals where, for example, several household name companies had a sound knowledge of their USA and Canadian activities and a growing knowledge of their European ones but little or no knowledge of operations elsewhere. Here, there was a need to do more investigation before any more sophisticated development could take place. (As we discussed in Chapter 4, companies are recognizing that there is both a moral and a defensive case for attempting to operate worldwide standards.) Figure 5.8 provides an indication of the possible range of environmental audits.[19]

[19] Elkington, Knight and Hailes (1991) and Elkington and Jennings (1991) provide detail on the extent to which and the way in which BP makes use of several of these audits within its overall environmental management system. See also *Environment Business Supplement*, November 1991, Gray (1990e) and BiE (1991a) for more detail.

Figure 5.8

Forms of environmental audit

Within any particular management strategy, the following audits may be seen as the same in essence, differing only in terms of their objectives, scope, the risks they seek to assess and the management decisions which they support and inform.

- Compliance Audits I: Assessing compliance with current and future legal standards.
- Compliance Audits II: Assessing compliance with consents, industry and guideline standards.
- Compliance Audits III: Assessing compliance with corporate policy and standards ('Corporate', 'Policy' and 'Ethical' audits).
- Energy Audits (see Chapter 6).
- Waste Audits (see Chapter 7).
- Site Audits: Reviewing every aspect of a site or spot checks on sites having actual or potential problems.
- Activity Audits: Reviewing a particular activity or process, especially one which spans sites, business units and countries.
- Issues Audits: Review of corporate performance in a particular area – e.g., in the case of BP, BAT and B&Q, tropical hardwood forests and impact on habitats.
- Takeover/Merger Review: Assessment of potential subsidiary, associate or partner against corporate standards and any actual and potential legal issues.
- Process Audits: Related to the above and designed to ensure that policies, processes, documentation, responsibilities, monitoring and appraisal are in place.
- Emerging Issues Audit: Future scenario assessment, anticipatory and intended to assess the extent of the organization's ability to respond to new challenges.

And, as the environmental management system develops, these audits will be closely related to:

- Process Safety Audits: Hazards and risks arising from processes, safety and accident provisions.
- Occupational Health Audits: Exposure and conditions for the workforce.
- Quality Audits: Not only the product in use but the environment in relation to TQM.

5.5 Developing an Environmental Management System

As KPMG Peat Marwick explain in *Environment Briefing Note* No. 5, understanding of the role of environmental audit – and thereby making full use of the process(es) – can be achieved only within the broader context of learning to manage environmental performance. This is not simply because this may make good business sense or because limiting oneself to *ad hoc* reaction is inefficient but because 'environment' is embedded in every strand of organizational life and its impact will continue to grow. The environment is not a one-off issue admitting of one-off solutions. Thus 'environmental audit' must become a regular, critical and analytical part of organizational management. (As we shall see in the next section, the EC and BSI are ensuring that this must be the case.)

A constant message through the book has been the difficulty – if

Figure 5.9 Going green.

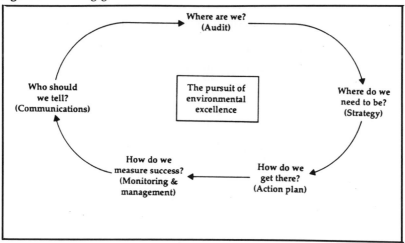

Source: Elkington and Jennings (1991)

not impossibility – of breaking down environmental response into discrete parts. Developing an organization's environmental policy and signing up to the charters (Chapter 4) required an understanding of the organization's environmental impacts. This is acquired through an initial environmental audit. To guide the environmental audit(s) efficiently and effectively they must be driven by policy. The whole process is circular rather than linear. This is nicely illustrated by Figure 5.9.[20]

In this way we can see the more developed function of environmental audit (more accurately called 'review', 'monitoring' and 'surveillance' now) as a means of assessing progress against targets and goals and as a means of monitoring new and emerging problems and searching for new and innovative ways of improving overall environmental quality – exactly the role designed for environmental audit at, among others, Hewlett Packard. Figure 5.10 provides a basic way of conceiving of this more developed approach.[21]

What any organization must be seeking by this stage is an integrated environmental management strategy similar in principle to a culture in pursuit of total quality management (TQM) – and, increasingly, good environmental management is being seen as an essential component of TQM: namely, EQM.[22] As with TQM, there is no simple method of buying in quality. The organization has to

[20] This is reprinted from *Integrated Environmental Management* from Elkington and Jennings (1991).

[21] These diagrams are reprinted from KPMG *Environment Briefing Note* No. 5 (1990).

[22] See Houldin (1992) for an especially helpful discussion of these matters.

Figure 5.10

Developing an environment management system

AN APPROACH TO MANAGING ENVIRONMENTAL PERFORMANCE

ENVIRONMENT POLICY
- Understand environmental impact (damage, legislation, market pressures)
- Assess risks and opportunities
- Identify required standards
- Establish policies and goals

ENVIRONMENTAL AUDIT
- Define basis for performance assessment (targets/standards)
- Identify damage drivers and assess
- Check-performance vs standards/targets
- Identify technical/ managerial solution options

ENVIRONMENT STRATEGY
Implement changes:
- technical
- management/ operations
- training
- marketing/PR
- market analysis
- internal care programme
- establish EMS

ENVIRONMENT MANAGEMENT SYSTEM

Achieving the goal of managing environmental performance requires environmental objectives to be fully integrated into business activities. An environment management system needs to be built into day-to-day management processes.

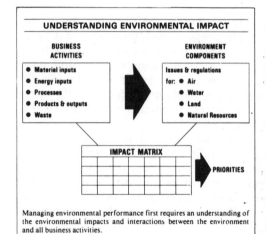

UNDERSTANDING ENVIRONMENTAL IMPACT

BUSINESS ACTIVITIES
- Material inputs
- Energy inputs
- Processes
- Products & outputs
- Waste

ENVIRONMENT COMPONENTS
Issues & regulations
for:
- Air
- Water
- Land
- Natural Resources

IMPACT MATRIX → **PRIORITIES**

Managing environmental performance first requires an understanding of the environmental impacts and interactions between the environment and all business activities.

COMPREHENSIVE PERFORMANCE REVIEW

MATERIALS AND ENERGY
- Renewable resources
- Sustainable extraction
- Secondary effects (eg deforestation)
- Energy use and source
- Transport
- Suppliers

PROCESSES
- Waste minimisation
- Pollution control
- Energy use
- Waste management
- Building and plant maintenance
- Transport

PRODUCTS AND OUTPUTS
- Impact during use
- Energy consumption
- Packaging
- Recyclability
- Disposal
- Potential for resource recovery

seek, in all dimensions, to be the best. This leads organizations to consider anything other than (for example) zero complaints, zero spills and accidents, zero pollution and zero waste as fundamentally unacceptable. As two medium-sized companies, making the same point, in different ways on different continents, put it:

We know we cannot achieve perfection in these things but this doesn't make mistakes and carelessness acceptable.

We are decent people. I don't soil my own home, I don't drop muck in the High Street, I don't think any of my colleagues do either. We have standards of personal behaviour. We try damned hard to make sure those standards apply to the business as well. I don't drop my crisps packet in my neighbour's garden; how can I look him in the eye if I've dropped our s..t in the river he goes fishing in? Answer me that!

This approach to environmental TQM/EQM leads IBM to apply the highest standards worldwide, and to be followed by companies such as ICI and BAT. It leads to the much vaunted initiatives such as Ciba-Geigy's six-point corporate principles, 3M's 3Ps (Pollution Prevention Pays) and Dow Chemicals' acknowledged leadership in standards of care in the chemical industry. And it finds one of its most interesting manifestations in Rhône Poulenc's Environmental Index.

Although not without its problems, Rhône-Poulenc's Environmental Index is calculated for aqueous effluent discharges by 'weighting the suspended solids, COD, dissolved salts, results of daphnia toxicity tests and the nitrogen and phosphorus produced by each plant by coefficients reflecting the environmental hazards posed by different components of the effluent stream and by production volumes for the period' (*ENDS*, November 1989, p. 16). Experimentation in the UK led to its introduction in 1990 and, in recent years, Rhône-Poulenc has developed additional indices for air and for wastes. Figure 5.11 reproduces a number of the different ways in which Rhône-Poulenc has shown the Water Index in recent publications.[23]

The company pronounces itself very pleased with the indices as a management tool for integrating the environment into all aspects of management and appraisal. As far as we are aware, other individual organizations have yet to take up this indexing notion,[24] the stated reason being doubt over its accuracy in that it allows trade-off between increases in some effluent against decreases in others. In other words, it loses too much information in the aggregation and is thus potentially misleading. In the absence of better suggestions,

---

[23] Chapters 11 and 12 cover the issues arising from disclosure.

[24] Although the Chemical Industries Association is moving firmly in this direction with its collation of industry data to produce environmental, distribution and energy indices.

Figure 5.11

RHÔNE-POULENC'S ENVIRONMENTAL INDEX

ENVIRONMENT INDEX
TO MEASURE PROGRESS

● Evaluating pollution created by plants throughout the world, both consistently and thoroughly, called for the creation of a new criterion. This is the "Environment Index," a first in the chemical industry. This index integrates all the major parameters for measuring water pollution: suspended matter, organic matter, toxicity, dissolved salts, nitrogen, phos-

phorus, etc., and is weighted to evaluate the actual potential damage to the environment. Begun experimentally on January 1, 1988 at several French plants, the Environment Index has already posted a 22% drop in aqueous waste.

The plan is to install it in all the Group's plants, worldwide.

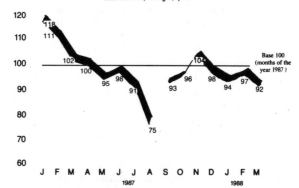

Base 100 (months of the year 1987)

Monthly trends in the Environment index: down 22% in fifteen months.

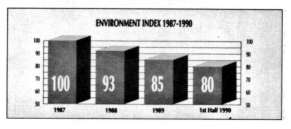

110

The Green Graph

To measure progress, Rhône-Poulenc recognized that it was essential to monitor all its efforts. In January 1988, the company set up an 'environmental index'. To good effect: it has already posted a 15% drop in aqueous waste.

however, we should have thought that Rhône-Poulenc's initiative was to be applauded and studied carefully.[25]

The irresistible advance in the penetration and sophistication of environmental auditing in all its forms and its inevitable link through to environmental management systems is now being enshrined in guidance and cajolery from the UK and the EC. It is to this that we now turn.

5.6 Eco-Audit, Eco-Labelling and BS7750

Two of the most significant environmental initiatives to emerge from Brussels in 1991 were the draft regulations for eco-audit and eco-labelling. Both are intended to be adopted on a 'voluntary' basis by member states and organizations – although the threat of their being made compulsory in the event of an insufficient response from industry is a real one. The hope is that 'the market' will favour organizations adopting the proposals and thus bring pressure to bear upon companies not adopting. A related development is from the British Standards Institution, which claims a 'first' in producing a new BSI standard on environmental management systems (BS7750). It is expected that all three will have a symbiotic relationship with BS5750 (ISO 9000) on quality.

The Eco-Labelling Regulation[26] takes a cradle-to-grave approach to products (see life-cycle assessment in Chapter 9) and should be fully operational during 1993. Based upon the German 'Blue Angel' programme, an eco-label will attach to a product in such a way as to ensure 'free' passage of the product throughout the countries of the EC.[27] The award of an eco-label will be taken to suggest that the total product meets the very highest standards of environmental care throughout its life – to be, in fact, the result of a total environmental quality management system. Hence the tie-in with the eco-audit. It has been mooted that an eco-label cannot be achieved without an organization first having qualified for the eco-audit.

As the EC struggles towards a standard environmental audit regime it still lags behind Northern America and parts of Scandinavia

[25] For more detail see *ENDS*, November 1989, Salamitou (1991) and various Rhône-Poulenc publications – most notably *Presence* (R-P house magazine), special issue on the environment, 1990.

[26] The Regulation was agreed in December 1991. For more detail, see, for example, *Integrated Environmental Management*, February 1992 (pp. 2–4), and May 1992 (pp. 17–18).

[27] The Netherlands has also developed its own system of eco-labelling – concerned that the EC standards will be too low and too late. There have also been a number of specific industry initiatives intended (it would seem) to forestall regulation. For example, a number of travel agents joined together in 1991 to establish a Green Flag System for 'sustainable tourism and conservation'. The CIA's Responsible Care Programme might also be seen as a variation on this theme.

Figure 5.12

```
                    The EC eco-audit proposals

    A company registering for the eco-audit will be committing itself to:

    •  define an environmental policy;
    •  set targets for achievement;
    •  develop environmental management systems;
    •  review/audit progress towards targets;
    •  make the information public;
    •  be subject to independent verification;
    •  set new targets as a continuing process.
```

to a significant degree.[28] The EC's eco-audit proposals had a rocky ride in the EC during their early stages. The Regulation had simplified the whole process required by the putative directive as well as reluctantly choosing to make the issue 'voluntary' as opposed to highly regulated.[29] The principal objectives of the proposals are to establish a Community-wide framework for:

(1) establishing internal environmental management systems;
(2) systematic, objective and periodic review of performance;
(3) public reporting (see Part C).

In its current form the Eco-Audit Regulation is designed so that any company may register and, if successful, will be awarded a certificate. This will not only enable the organization to use the eco-logo but should ease other matters like consent negotiation, impact assessments and cross-boundary movement of goods in the EC. The basic outline of the proposals is shown in Figure 5.12.

A major development in the EC proposals is the requirement for 'accredited external verification'. Not only may this make the eco-audit more demanding and, thus, more valuable, it has major implications for the market in 'independent verifiers'.[30] The formation of the AEC and the Institutes of Environmental Assessment and

[28] There are laws requiring environmental auditing in both Sweden and the Netherlands. Sweden's audits are strictly internal and are not independently verified. The Netherlands is typically acknowledged as the most experienced of the EC countries in this field. The system, although voluntary, involves both internal and external reporting. The Dutch government is considering making the requirements compulsory in the face of too little response to the voluntary initiative.

[29] However, the drafts do contain the facility for member states to draw up lists of prescribed industries who can be made compulsorily subject to the proposals. This would be the sort of function that might be expected of the national Environmental Protection Agency.

[30] The term 'independent verifier' was removed from later drafts to be replaced by the more general 'auditor', thus further weakening the power of the initial eco-audit proposals. The proposals, principally from the Institute of Environmental Assess-

Figure 5.13

BS7750: Environmental management systems

(1) like eco-audit, the BSI standard will be initially voluntary and adopts a similar structure and regime as employed in BS5750 on quality management systems;

(2) a preparatory environmental review including an inventory of emissions and wastes from each facility;

(3) assessment of environmental impacts and the setting of improvement targets;

(4) the establishment of the targets in managerial and centre performance appraisal, responsibility and accountability;

(5) the implication is that organizations will also need to have systems in place to review the supplies of materials (see below), their products in use as well as their financial investment procedures (see Chapters 13 and 14);

(6) detailed management plans and regular audits of performance (the audits undertaken by personnel independent of the facility audited who may be members of the organization or external auditors);

(7) the whole process must be auditable;

(8) once the award of BS7750 has been made it will be renewed by assessment of the organization's continuing commitment to the development of the systems in place and the review and audit of those systems.

---

of Audit (see note 7, above) owes a great deal to the prospect of the eco-audit becoming part of standard business practice. As yet, the professional accountancy bodies have shown little or no direct interest in these developments and there would seem to be every prospect of the environmental audit regime being developed from first principles and with little overt concern for the implications of independence. The issues are far from trivial. Not only is there the important matter of the professionalization of a trade association[31] but, in a business context, companies, banks, insurance companies and governments will be relying upon the attestation function. In a world where 'regulation' is considered morally and economically inferior to 'market solutions', one can only hope that the market may astonish us all and produce sensible, professional solutions.[32]

The operation of the eco-audit will be closely tied in practice to the BSI standard on environmental management systems – BS7750.

ment, for the development of a National Environmental Auditors Registration Board, which do not emphasize 'independence', are thus more practicable and easier to achieve but do not fill the market gap – as yet at least – for 'independent attestation', as will be required as eco-audit develops. The 'independence' element is more strongly emphasized by the smaller International Institute of Environmental Auditors.

[31] See, for example, Power (1991). In the USA there are now a variety of training courses, degree programmes and designatory 'certified' this and 'registered' that as the paraphernalia of professionalism come into being.

[32] *New Consumer* (Autumn 1991, p. 4) reports that its experience suggests a most high likelihood that insurance companies and large investment institutions will require an *independent* attestation of eco-audit and related environmental information. See Part C.

Claimed as a 'world-first' in June 1991 when the first set of guide-lines and proposals for standards on environmental management were published, BS7750 has the elements shown in Figure 5.13.

While organizations seeking registration under the eco-audit regulations may seek certification *ab initio*, it seems highly likely that achievement of BS7750 will be a useful (but not yet compulsory) first step. And, not only may eco-audit be a prerequisite for eco-labelling but it seems likely that achievement of BS5750 (ISO 9000) will help in the achievement of the environmental standards. This provides a demanding but substantive framework for the organization serious about its TQM/EQM for the 1990s – and one which must go beyond BS5750, BS7750, eco-audit and eco-labelling. And as every organization which has set about the achievement of BS5750 (ISO 9000) knows, these are not matters to be taken lightly. The amount of work and reorganization needed is significant and the earlier an organization begins on the long road the sooner it will begin to reap the real benefits expected from the process.

5.7   The Supplier Audits

The supplier audit is a relatively new phenomenon whose importance and popularity are growing. Not only do BS7750, eco-audit and eco-label move in this direction but a number of major companies and other organizations (such as local authorities) are developing these and a much larger number of major companies intend to set them in place when they have their own house in order.

The essence of the supplier audit is that products and services bought in by an organization should meet the standards applied within that organization. The reasons are various and fairly obvious: defensive (a green claim for a product, service or process can be undermined by the use of non-green inputs); ethical (making claims which are untrue, misleading or mischievous and/or for which the organization has no evidential basis does not enhance its ethical stance); environmentally active (whether seen as a proselytizing activity or as part of the (in the UK at least) initiatives by large companies to help the smaller, these audits advance the level of environmental awareness in organizations); strategic (establishing supply chains, employee and competitive advantage in advance of changing law and public perception).[33]

The supplier audits, being a recent phenomenon, have no established method. At their most effective they constitute an advanced form of green consumerism and rely on policy statements whereby an organization will not buy from (for example) a company which

[33] Such audits do not relate only to physical goods and services. Chapter 10 talks about the impact of ethical investment on the supplies of funds to companies and even established major investment institutions such as Norwich Union are establishing supplier audits for the supply of funds. This is somewhat different in emphasis – although similar in effect to the banks instituting audits as a prerequisite of loans.

Figure 5.14

Extract from IBM's policy on supplier audits

Recognizing the crucial role played by IBM UK's thousands of suppliers and sub-contractors in maintaining environmental standards, a task force was established within the purchasing organization in May 1990 to review and promote supplier awareness of key issues.

- Establish supplier self-assessment environmental guidelines;
- Issue guidelines to all suppliers;
- Establish detailed environmental questionnaire for major company suppliers;
- Pilot and issue questionnaire to major suppliers.

. . . and this continues through Transport, Distribution and Car Fleet!

does not have the eco-audit certification. Currently, we are finding that the supplier audit is driving green awareness back into organizations which had previously ignored it. This is generally achieved by the customer educating the supplier. By the early 1990s, companies like British Telecom, the DIY chain B&Q and the supermarket chains of Gateway and the Co-op were reported as having developed major analyses of their suppliers as a step towards much tighter environmental standards.[34] IBM (UK) has perhaps one of the longest established policies in this field and presents an especially good example. The extract from its *Environmental Programmes* shown in Figure 5.14 indicates the process.

There is an obvious tie-in with LCA (Chapter 9) and with concepts such as the duty of care and (what ICI calls) 'Product Stewardship'. That is, what are now considered to be the standards that a responsible organization must apply require that the organization be aware of both the 'upstream' and 'downstream' effects of its activities. All the evidence suggests that supplier audits will be a significant influence on corporate environmental activity in the years to come. Their influence is likely to be slow but, in the nature of so many environmental developments, will work with a ratchet effect, constantly raising standards until no organization will be able to ignore them if they wish to deal with those greener than themselves. A major group in this connection will be the local authorities.

5.8 Local Authorities and Environmental Audits

Local government in the UK is playing a leading role in the development of more environmentally sensitive organizations. Although

---

[34] See *ENDS*, February 1990, pp. 18–24, for more details.

they have not yet risen to the importance played by, for example, the federal authorities in Canada, UK local authorities are acting in regulatory, monitoring, enabling and supervisory roles, significantly improving their waste management function plus fulfilling other roles within integrated pollution control. Their functions within the broad term of environmental audit are considerable – both as agents of government and as organizations in their own right – stretching from monitoring pollution and their role within EIA, for example, to areas such as the far-reaching public register of contaminated land.[35]

Local government in the UK has also taken serious steps in the environmental auditing of its own activities. This is based largely around the Friends of the Earth *Environmental Charter for Local Government* (1989), which recommends a basic two-stage audit. The first is a State of the Environment Report in which the local authority attempts to construct a comprehensive picture of the current state of the local environment. Many authorities such as Grampian, Fife, Lancashire, and Kent have undertaken and published such reports.[36] The Report provides the structure and baseline against which all future analysis takes place. The second stage is then policy impact assessment – the analysis of the impacts that local authority policies have on the environment. From here local authorities can set targets and establish plans which can be monitored and reviewed on a regular basis.[37]

These stages in the environmental audit lead, as with companies, to the point where supplier audits have to be considered. A number of UK local authorities have, over the years, established social and environmental criteria in their development, investment, purchasing and planning policies. It thus comes as no surprise to hear that, for example, Barnsley MBC and West Sussex CC require BS5750 in all tendering applications and many authorities are intending to introduce a similar requirement with BS7750.

As local authorities overcome the initial disruption that inevitably arises from their increasing role within the development of national environmental policies and begin the process of taking a hard look at their own environmental activities, there seems little question that local government of whatever political hue will prove to be a most important factor in determining the environmental climate within which organizations operate. A major experience from our visits was that the sensible company has long taken steps to develop a

---

[35] See e.g. Pollock (1992) and Friends of the Earth (1990), pp. 107 *et seq.*

[36] A major problem for all organizations, not least local authorities, is the establishment of systems to collect (and then collate) the data. One authority, Lancashire, used the integration of environmental issues into the school curriculum as a source of data collection, setting schools to act as measuring and collection points for a variety of characteristics such as flora, noise and pollution. The implications this may have for the data are not discussed here.

[37] For a useful example, see Kent County Council's *Elements*, No. 3, Winter 1991.

good working relationship with its local authority, and nowhere is this more true than in relation to environmental matters (see also Chapter 13).

5.9 Concluding Remarks

Environmental audit is undoubtedly the one area of environmental awareness that any organization ignores at its peril. It is also a massive, complex, amorphous and rapidly developing area. Environmental audit touches many areas of current, proposed and possible future environmental regulation and serves, for all organizations, as a first step towards environmental sensitivity and as a regular and essential part of environmental management systems. And this still leaves two major areas: the role of independent attestation and that of the statutory financial auditor. Given the already dense nature of the material in this chapter, we have left those two topics until Part C, where we will discuss them in relation to the information to which such audits will relate – typically external reporting.

The parting remarks we would like to make are twofold. First, with the term 'audit' having been appropriated from accountants – as was the case with 'social audit' in the 1970s and 1980s – there is a great need to take care with terminology so that one is entirely clear about the objective of the activity undertaken. The review, the check against standards or the investigation of potential chemical hazards each require different approaches, different knowledge of law and other source disciplines and different personnel and experiences. Clarity in these matters can save lives, money, time and a great deal of disruption and heartache.[38]

The second point is more a general warning: environmental audit as whitewash will be counterproductive in the medium term. General evidence suggests that a significant minority of organizations which have undertaken an initial review have either not followed up on it or have set its parameters so loosely that the results are largely meaningless. The way in which the organizational climate is changing suggests that these sorts of approaches are not only a waste of time and money but can be seriously counterproductive. Relatedly, but more obscurely, there is the longer-term question which we raised in Chapter 2 concerning the extent to which the pressure of environmental change will require substantial alteration in organizational orthodoxy. This leads to questions of whether the relatively technical nature of environmental audit as currently constituted can and will genuinely address many of the fundamental dilemmas posed by the environmental crisis. Whilst a pragmatic stance is clearly in the current interests of organizations, this is not necessarily the only way forward or the most desirable route towards sustainability. These matters are covered in some of

---

[38] See e.g. Gray and Symon (1992a).

the further reading listed in this chapter and the issues are briefly re-examined in Part D.

Further Reading

Environmental Impact Assessment

Department of the Environment (1989) *Environmental Assessment: A Guide to Procedures*, HMSO, London.

Elkington, J. (1982) Industrial applications of environmental impact assessment, *Journal of General Management*, Vol. 7, no. 3, pp. 23–33.

Elkington, J., Knight, P. and Hailes, J. (1991) *The Green Business Guide*, Victor Gollancz, London.

Fuller, K. (1991) Reviewing UK's experience in EIA, *Integrated Environmental Management*, no. 1, August, pp. 12–14.

Local Government

Friends of the Earth (1989) *The Environmental Charter for Local Government*, FoE, London.

Which (1992) How green is your local authority?, *Which*, February, pp. 106–9.

Monitor the journals mentioned above plus, for example, *Public Finance and Accountancy* and *Local Economy*.

Widening the Debate

Gray, R. H. and Collison, D. J. (1991) The environmental audit: greengauge or whitewash? *Managerial Auditing*, Vol. 6, no. 5, pp. 17–25.

Gray, R. H. and Symon, I. W. (1992a) An environmental audit by any other name . . . , *Integrated Environmental Management*, no. 6, February, pp. 9–11.

Power, M. (1991) Auditing and environmental expertise: between protest and professionalisation, *Accounting, Auditing and Accountability*, Vol. 4, no. 3, pp. 30–42.

Environmental Audit, Eco-Audit, BSI

British Standards Institution (1991) *Draft British Standard: Environmental management systems (Parts 1–3)*, BSI, London.

Business-in-the-Environment (1991a) *Your Business and the Environment: A DIY Review for Companies*, BiE/Coopers & Lybrand Deloitte, London.

Confederation of British Industry (1990) *Narrowing the Gap: Environmental Auditing Guidelines for Business*, CBI, London.

Elkington, J. (1990) *The Environmental Audit*, SustainAbility/World Wide Fund for Nature, London.

Elkington, J., Knight, P. and Hailes, J. (1991) *The Green Business Guide*, Gollancz, London.

International Chamber of Commerce (1989) *Environmental Auditing*, ICC, Paris.

Moretz, S. (1989) Industrial hygiene auditing: Allied Signal takes the extra step, *Occupational Hazards*, May, pp. 73–6.

Special issues of a number of magazines, e.g.:

Industry and Environment (UNEP), Vol. 11, no. 4, 1988

Environment Business (Supplement), November 1991

Single Market News (DTI), no. 12, Autumn 1991

And for regular updates and insights see any of the leading journals and newsletters such as: *ENDS, Integrated Environmental Management,* KPMG Peat Marwick's *Environment Briefing Notes* and *European Environment Briefing Notes.*

APPENDIX 5
Examples of Guidance on the Conduct of Environmental Audits

Appendix 5.1   CEBIS Guide to Environmental Audit

THE ENVIRONMENTAL AUDIT

Environmental auditing is playing an increasingly important role in all sectors of industry and commerce. The CBI has called for every UK company to carry out an audit, the European Commission is drafting legislation to encourage the widespread use of auditing and a growing number of large companies are demanding that their suppliers and contractors undertake environmental audits.

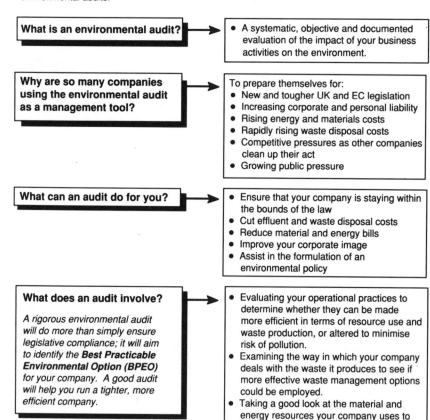

What is an environmental audit?

- A systematic, objective and documented evaluation of the impact of your business activities on the environment.

Why are so many companies using the environmental audit as a management tool?

To prepare themselves for:
- New and tougher UK and EC legislation
- Increasing corporate and personal liability
- Rising energy and materials costs
- Rapidly rising waste disposal costs
- Competitive pressures as other companies clean up their act
- Growing public pressure

What can an audit do for you?

- Ensure that your company is staying within the bounds of the law
- Cut effluent and waste disposal costs
- Reduce material and energy bills
- Improve your corporate image
- Assist in the formulation of an environmental policy

What does an audit involve?

A rigorous environmental audit will do more than simply ensure legislative compliance; it will aim to identify the **Best Practicable Environmental Option (BPEO)** *for your company. A good audit will help you run a tighter, more efficient company.*

- Evaluating your operational practices to determine whether they can be made more efficient in terms of resource use and waste production, or altered to minimise risk of pollution.
- Examining the way in which your company deals with the waste it produces to see if more effective waste management options could be employed.
- Taking a good look at the material and energy resources your company uses to see whether more environmentally sound alternatives could be substituted.
- Developing contingency plans for environmental mishaps.

Who should carry out the audit? 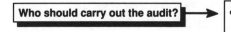 ➤
- If you have relevant expertise in-house, set up an internal audit team. You may wish to bring in external consultants to help.

And after the initial audit? ➤
- Define a set of corporate objectives based on the audit results and set them out in a formal **environmental policy**.
- Like a financial audit, an environmental audit is not a one-off event. Regular monitoring will be necessary to check that your company is moving satisfactorily towards its objectives.
- Incorporate an environmental component into both your training programme and communication strategy.

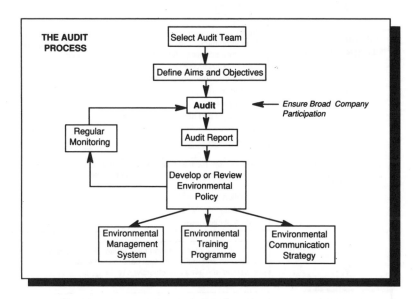

THE AUDIT PROCESS

Select Audit Team → Define Aims and Objectives → Audit ← *Ensure Broad Company Participation* → Audit Report → Develop or Review Environmental Policy; Regular Monitoring → Environmental Management System, Environmental Training Programme, Environmental Communication Strategy

Many companies have already reaped considerable benefits as a result of carrying out environmental audits. For example:

Sector	Action	Annual saving	Payback Period
Electronics	Recovery of copper	£27K	2 years
Metals	Recovery of foundry dust	£76K	3 months
Food	Improvement in the efficiency of water use and effluent treatment at a sugar factory	£200K	10 months
Public	Improved energy management introduced in local authority schools	£70K	2 years
Retail	Production of energy from waste	£32K	22 months

AUDIT CHECKLIST

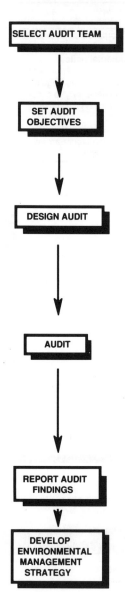

SELECT AUDIT TEAM

Team should include:
• Director or manager with access to the Board
• In-house personnel with skills in disciplines such as waste, energy, design etc
• External consultants to guide internal team, if necessary

SET AUDIT OBJECTIVES

Define what you want from the audit. Objectives may include:
• Compliance with legislation
• Financial savings
• Enhanced company image
• Increased efficiency
• Gaining a market advantage
• Protecting investment and insurance options

DESIGN AUDIT

Identify areas in which the company's activities may be impinging on the environment. These will vary according to the nature of the company's activities. A typical audit might evaluate:
• legal compliance
• waste management and emissions to air and water
• materials use
• energy use
• landscape and habitat disturbance
• transport
• noise and odour   *(see overleaf)*

AUDIT

Decide on the most effective way of gathering the necessary information to assess performance in the relevant areas.
You may wish to use:
• questionnaires
• site visits
• informal interviews

Gather all relevant information as planned. Encourage staff participation and make sure that personnel are aware of, and understand, the aims and objectives of the audit.

REPORT AUDIT FINDINGS

Analyse the company's environmental strengths and weaknesses in the light of audit findings. Where improvements are necessary, cost alternatives and identify BPEOs (**B**est **P**racticable **E**nvironmental **O**ptions). Produce written Audit Report.

DEVELOP ENVIRONMENTAL MANAGEMENT STRATEGY

Decide how the company will implement necessary improvements and set a time-scale for this. Develop a mechanism for monitoring progress towards the company's environmental objectives. Environmental excellence will not be achieved overnight - prioritise. Aim to incorporate sound environmental practices into day-to-day management. Encourage staff involvement at every level.

Scottish

MAIN AUDIT CATEGORIES

The following is not intended as a comprehensive checklist to be rigourously adhered to, but rather as a guide to the type of questions the audit team should be addressing.

LEGAL COMPLIANCE

- Do you know how UK and EC regulations and standards affect your business?
- Do your current practices comply with these?
- Do you take future environmental standards into consideration when planning new projects?
- Are you aware of, and where possible do you implement, the best available technology?
- Do you keep up with the latest regulatory requirements?

WASTE

- What waste does your company produce and how do you dispose of it?
- Could your waste be minimised, recycled or eliminated?
- Could you participate in waste-exchange schemes (ie. selling your waste to other businesses to use as raw materials or buying waste in for your own use)?
- Could you recycle office waste?
- Do you have adequate emergency procedures for accidental spillages and emissions?

TRANSPORT

- Do you transport your goods efficiently (eg avoid empty vehicles)?
- What special precautions do you take in the transport of dangerous goods and wastes?
- Do you regularly maintain vehicles and plant to minimise noxious emissions?
- Could you switch to vehicles with smaller engines?
- Could you develop a strategy that minimised use of staff transport? Could you encourage car pooling or offer a 'bicycle allowance', for example?

MATERIALS

- Could you cut down on use of materials? eg: Can products be reduced in size or reshaped to minimise materials and packaging? Is packaging excessive? Are you recycling materials within processes where possible?
- Could you use more environmentally friendly materials? eg: Do your materials come from renewable resources? Could you replace toxic materials with less toxic ones? Could you replace non-recyclable materials and components with recyclable ones?

ENERGY USE

- How much energy is used in each area of your business and do you regularly review energy use?
- Could waste energy be usefully redirected?
- Could you use combined heat and power?
- Is there potential for energy saving in your business? For example, could better insulation and heat controls, more energy-efficient lighting and plant, cut your fuel bills?

LANDSCAPES & HABITATS

- Do any of your activities (eg. the development of new sites) damage landscapes and habitats?
- Are your sites as tidy, quiet and dust-free as they could be?
- Are your sites landscaped to make them look attractive?
- Do you preserve natural habitats around your sites where possible?

                    April 1991

Appendix 5.2   Taken from ICC position paper on environmental auditing ICC Publication No. 468 Copyright © 1989 – International Chamber of Commerce (ICC) ISBN 92 · 842 · 1089 5. Published by ICC Publishing SA, Paris. Available from ICC Publishing SA, 38 Cours Albert Ier, 75008 Paris or ICC UK, 14/15 Belgrave Square, London SW1X 8PS.

Basic steps of an environmental audit

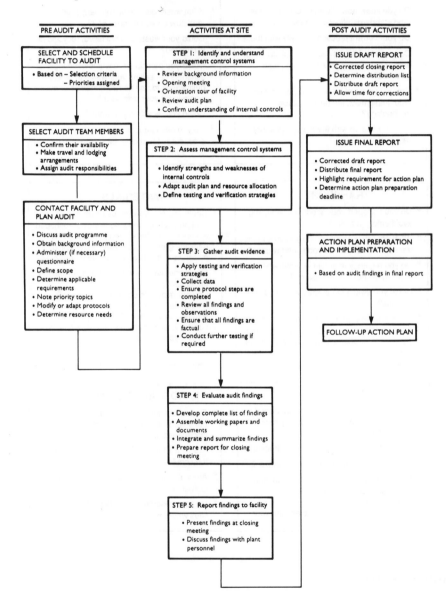

Appendix 5.3   KPMG diagrammatic summary of Eco-Audit and BS7750

EC PROPOSED ECO - AUDIT REGULATION
(1993)

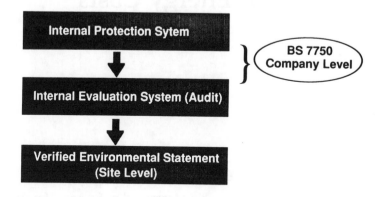

KPMG The National Environment Unit

BS 7750: THE SPECIFICATION

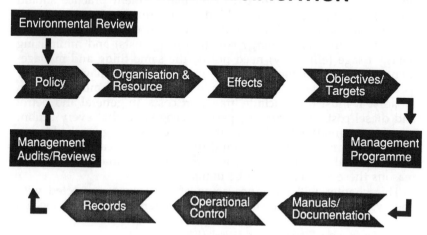

KPMG The National Environment Unit

6. Accounting and the Control of Energy Costs

6.1 Introduction

Energy is, to a considerable degree, the fulcrum for business/ environment relations. Whilst considered by many to be the most pressing environmental issue and certainly a critical factor in the pursuit of sustainability[1] (see Chapter 14), it is also the major area in which all parties are agreed that being environmentally sensitive can bring financial benefits. So much so, that approaches to energy management need have nothing whatsoever to do with environmental considerations directly. Good management practice should seek to minimize waste of all kinds and reduce unit costs, which means, *inter alia*, seeking out the minimum energy cost options. However, minimizing energy cost (reducing costs) and minimizing energy usage (efficiency) need not be the same thing and management who consider the former the more important may well prove to be short-sighted. 'Energy', as discussed here, must be seen broadly. It must thus include 'transport costs' in general and petrol and diesel costs in particular; permit recognition that every action, process, raw material and element of waste has energy embedded in it; as well as noting that heat (and thus energy) is carried away via water and other emissions.[2] For both environmental and financial reasons these elements must be minimized.

This chapter will introduce some of the issues connected with energy, the sorts of problems with which energy usage is connected

[1] See for example, Stevenson and Dowell (1990).

[2] This is a point made and developed in Winter (1988; pp. 128–30) in relation to (a) situations in which there are charges for water and therefore the financial and environmental desire to reduce usage makes water similar in nature to energy from the business point of view, (b) the fact that water is often raised in temperature for various reasons and thus becomes a major focus for energy recovery.

and where the savings – environmental and corporate financial – can come from and may be likely to come from in the future. We will then go on to look at ways of controlling energy usage before looking at the accounting implications and the role that accounting can play in energy minimization.

6.2   Energy: Some of the Wider Issues

The environmental issues associated with energy are complex and critical. Energy may be derived from non-renewable (coal, oil, gas, nuclear, geothermal) or renewable (wood, wind, sea, solar, hydro) sources. Western fuels are derived predominantly from the non-renewable sources.[3] Extraction not only depletes a scarce resource (which may have alternative, more sustainable uses – see Part D) and disrupts ecosystems but itself uses energy in the process. The extracted raw material is transported and processed, using further energy, before reaching the end-users – or arriving at power stations where it is further processed before reaching the consumers in the form of electricity. Energy creation is itself very energy-intensive and therefore not energy-efficient. Its use and processing produce waste heat, by-products and emissions of gases and are thereby directly linked to the creation of acid rain, global warming, air pollution and myriad other intrusions into the biosphere. The implications of these intrusions are still very much a matter for argument but the worst-case scenarios suggest devastation of the human species – developed and lesser developed countries alike – not to mention the impact on other species and the planet as a whole.[4] The implications of nuclear power are also far from straightforward[5] and geothermal and hydro schemes raise many difficult environmental problems themselves.[6] It would appear that no use of conventional energy in the West is entirely without its problems.[7]

[3] Ekins (1992, p. 91) suggests that in the developed countries outside Scandinavia and other countries with extensive hydro opportunities, the use of *renewable* energy is slight, viz: Denmark (1%), UK (2%), West Germany (5%), USA (5%), France (13%), Japan (14%), whereas Norway, for example, is 100% reliant on renewables.

[4] For more detail see e.g. Friends of the Earth, 1990, and Porritt, 1991.

[5] See, again, Friends of the Earth, 1990, for a summary.

[6] As anybody associated with energy and/or environmental issues in New Zealand will be glad to explain.

[7] Unfortunately, the debate is one which tends to generate more heat than light in many forums. In the UK, for example, reading the annual reports of the major energy producers would leave one with a warm, glowing feeling that each is absolutely safe and environmentally responsible. It is not clear that the principal critical issues are being honestly addressed by the energy producers or the politicians. There is a great deal of material on 'alternative' sources of energy but see Purkiss (1992) for a simple introduction to some of the options.

Energy is also a major factor in the G7/G77 debate. In the first place, *per capita* consumption of energy in the developed countries is approximately seven times higher than in the lesser developed countries, and when the most profligate (USA, Canada and Australia) are compared with the poorest, the figure is many times higher.[8] It is obvious that the West has far greater capacity for savings than does the developing world. For much of the developing world's population, energy use is directly geared to basic (often, less than basic) sustenance – warmth and cooking. These activities represent a small proportion of Western usage. The increasing pressure on energy for the developing world will continue to rise with the encouragement of industrialization whilst the rising demand for timber for fuel adds the final straw to devastated woodlands – with the attendant destruction of habitat, desertification, flooding, and so on.

Clearly, all sectors of the population are implicated in this process and the efforts of government, individuals, households and business will be necessary to mitigate the worst effects before the devastation starts to have more than marginal impacts on Western life. This will involve a major shift by business. For example, CO_2 is the principal 'greenhouse' gas contributing to global warming. In the UK about 70 per cent of all CO_2 is contributed by business and transport. The principal contributors to acid rain are SO_x and NO_x. The lion's share of these emanates from electricity generation, manufacturing and heating processes and road transport.[9]

The real irony is that the majority of the energy used in the developed world is wasted. Friends of the Earth estimates that the UK could, using present levels of technology, reduce its electricity consumption by 70 per cent. Figures such as this, while not making the very slow progress on non-renewable energy generation irrelevant, do put it into perspective. Furthermore, many developed countries – despite the scares during the 1970s 'energy crisis' – have shown little real commitment to major energy efficiency. With effective government subsidies to private road transport and very large inequalities between the different energy research initiatives, for example, the drastic change in emphasis which is needed in energy usage is still a thing of the future.[10]

6.3   Energy: Some of the Business Issues

The business climate is changing and the rate of change shows every sign of increasing. This, naturally, brings both threats and

[8] See e.g. Hutchinson (1991).

[9] For more detail of a calm and helpful kind on this see, for example, Business-in-the-Environment (1991b).

[10] For a general introduction to energy issues and a survey of the related data see, for example, Simpson (1990), chapter 7.

Figure 6.1

Carbon and energy taxes

Energy taxes and carbon taxes (which target the carbon content of fuels) in particular are part of a wider net of fiscal environmental incentives and penalties to harmonize good business and environmentally sensitive practices.

The EC proposals for an energy tax were initially resisted by business but they are gaining acceptance. The Netherlands favours a tax on energy of between 50 and 100 per cent. The USA continues to oppose such taxes.

The fear for countries and business alike is that of 'being first' and thereby suffering severe economic disadvantage. With a carefully thought-through scheme this need not happen.

For more detail see Footnote 12

---

opportunities. It is difficult to know where business stands at the moment in the different countries and, in particular, where the relative advantages will be found. The OECD countries have, it would seem, steadily improved energy efficiency. However, data are not always clear. In the UK there has been a 20 per cent reduction in energy usage per £1,000 of GNP during the 1980s as well as a per-unit-of-GNP reduction in energy costs. This apparently hopeful message is distorted by the very significant reduction in heavy industry over that period and significant reductions in unit energy costs by the energy suppliers to many of the bigger customers. Japan, on the other hand, has significantly reduced its energy per unit of production – a situation forced upon it by the need to import most energy.[11]

At the national and international levels there are the commitments to reduce greenhouse gases, and this must imply some reduction in energy usage. The probability of carbon taxes looks ever more likely while the related increase in controls over air pollution and the widely debated 'tradable pollution licences' will have significant impacts on all organizations. (Some information on these approaches is shown in Figure 6.1 and 6.2).[12]

The UK has already seen the impact of differential pricing in leaded and unleaded petrol and more countries are experimenting with developments of this sort. The one development that will make the critical difference will be if energy costs are raised against the general downward trend. In addition to any energy taxation system there has been a long debate as to whether or not energy currently

---

[11] See Elkington, Knight and Hailes (1991) for further detail.

[12] For a useful introduction to the issues see Ekins (1992a), and on the wider issues of economic environmental initiatives see Bryce (1990), Owens, Anderson and Brunskill (1990) and de Savornin Lohman (1991). The issues are widely discussed in the environmental economics literature – see, for example, the Pearce references in the bibliography and also Opschoor and Vos (1989).

Figure 6.2

Tradable pollution licences

Widely discussed in the environmental economics literature and entering the agenda in the EC and UK as well as in New Zealand (see, for example, Gilkinson, 1992), tradable pollution licences emerged first in the USA. The idea is that an imaginary bubble is put over the company and it is issued with a permit to fill that bubble with up to x amount of specified pollutants. The 'clean' company will not use all of its licence and may trade it to a 'dirty' company – thus transferring cash from the 'bad' to the 'good'.

The USA scheme is in two stages, intended first to bring the dirtier companies into line with basic requirements and then steadily to reduce the baseline. Futures in such permits were being traded by early 1992.

The scheme(s) is/are not without their problems but there is relative enthusiasm for them in business and politics where other forms of environmental control are hotly opposed.

For more detail see Footnote 13

---

represents its 'true' cost. National or international law which required, for example, higher standards of electricity generation emissions or energy efficiency; which was stricter on environmental impact assessment (see Chapter 5); which required accident-free oil movement and/or a cessation of oil-tanker flushing into the seas; which required tighter standards of remediation; and so on, will all reflect the environmental costs and add to the financial costs of energy.[13] There seems little question that such changes are coming throughout the world. It is only a question of when and how much.

At the industry level there is an increasing amount of leadership into energy efficiency. Some of these are not new: the 1970s energy crisis prompted a range of developments – in energy-saving technologies, in building design, in computer-controlled energy-monitoring systems, etc. – which are now available to industry. In the UK there is the government-based Energy Efficiency Office (for address see Appendix B) which offers advice, contacts and potential direction towards grants and other forms of help. In addition the Energy Efficiency Office funds the Energy Design Advisory Service, which can give energy-based guidance on the building or refurbishment of premises. The UK government continues its hands-off, cajolery approach in this field. In October 1991 the Department of Energy launched a campaign to encourage companies to sign a declaration of their intention to adopt an energy policy and to reduce energy usage. As with many of these 'voluntary' initiatives there is little evidence that it is having any real effect on the wider business community. Of more direct influence have been initiatives prompted by industry itself. These have included the British Gas

---

[13] For more detail see OECD (1989) and reports by Kehoe, *Financial Times*, 5 June 1991, p. 15, and by Durr, by Griffiths and by Hargreaves, *Financial Times*, 24 July 1991, p. 25.

initiative GEM (Gas Energy Management) and encouragement from, for example, the Chemical Industries Association and Business-in-the-Environment of the experimentation with and the development and use of performance indicators. These initiatives have typically included energy performance indicators of the 'energy-use-per-tonne-of-output' type. As we shall see below, approaches of this sort have proved very successful in many companies, with major financial savings reported by companies adopting these and other methods.[14]

At the company level a lot is happening. In large part, companies which learnt from the 1970s energy crisis have continued to install, develop and refine their energy-efficiency projects. For these companies, energy saving has become part of the normal way of life. For example, a medium-sized manufacturing company forecasts that the payback period on its energy-saving investments is set to reduce in the near future as energy costs rise. This has encouraged a complete rethink of its energy usage and investment strategy (see also Chapter 8). IBM has long recognized the importance of energy and, as part of its 'taking the longer view', has been adopting more energy-efficient investments. Sainsbury has been widely reported as having adopted sophisticated management of energy costs throughout its operations. Furthermore, especially for manufacturing companies, each saving in energy can lead to further savings elsewhere through, for example, a reduction in COSHH concerns, reductions in wastes and waste waters, reductions in emissions to air and water and attendant reductions in further treatment and consent costs (see Chapter 7). Energy is also a major issue in recycling and life-cycle assessment (see Chapters 7 and 9), where Norsk Hydro, for example, reports 'a small energy profit' in the recycling of aluminium. For other companies, rising energy concerns provide opportunities for their technology and products – whether control technology or an increased demand for insulation or double glazing. We look at how these things come about in the next section.

6.4   Controlling Energy

As we have seen, the surveys of business practice and intentions with respect to the environment have produced widely differing results. One 1990 survey suggested that over 60 per cent of companies had no formal energy-saving measures in place and had no intention of developing any.[15] Such a high proportion should be of concern given the very real environmental and financial savings to be made. However, three other surveys suggested that over 70 per cent of companies had some form of energy conservation

---

[14] See e.g. Burkitt (1990).

[15] Burkitt (1990) pp. 49 *et seq.*

Figure 6.3

Extract from IBM's energy policy

'Responsible use of energy is one of the cornerstones of the Corporate Environmental Policy which has required high priority to be given to energy efficiency and to the conservation of raw materials.'

1984–89 Energy Plan:
- Target 20%
- Achievement 25.6%
- Cost Savings £2.5M

(IBM UK Environmental Programmes, 1991)

---

measures in place.[16] All surveys agreed, however, that they experienced net benefits from the measures, often from very small initial outlays. As Winter[17] states it: 'if energy . . . [is] consistently well-managed, there are bound to be savings in costs and raw materials'.

IBM has been in the business of energy saving for many years (see Figure 6.3) and its plans set the targets for the following years in each functional area such as Products, Energy Supply, Energy Saving IT, Buildings. For a company with a well-established track record this is feasible. How, though, might an organization get started?

Organizations, if they do not ignore the matter altogether, seem to follow one of three routes: piecemeal, in-house initiatives; a comprehensive, top-down approach; or a combination of the two. For example, although energy saving is not an especially big issue in New Zealand, Milburn Cement established a piecemeal set of housekeeping initiatives to reduce office energy and encouraged its engineers to look for ways of saving energy. After twelve months of this, a full environmental audit (which included energy issues) was commissioned and this set in train more substantial, longer-term and systematic savings. Figure 6.4 illustrates some of the basic, initial steps that any organization can take to begin to save energy. Burkitt (1990) argues that lighting costs account for between 25 and 50 per cent of the average office electricity bill and energy-efficient lighting could save UK business up to £240 million ($384 million) per annum.[18] These are not trivial amounts. However, there is a limit to how far lay initiatives can take the organization's energy savings. A more systematic approach becomes necessary. If the organization has the talent in-house, it may well be able to undertake a systematic appraisal of its energy usage without outside help. Many guides to

[16] See Chapter 2, Figure 2.6, where these surveys are summarized.

[17] Winter (1988) pp. 128–30.

[18] Burkitt (1990).

Figure 6.4

Initial (simple and cheap) energy-saving steps

* Insulate walls and roofs
* Consider double-glazing
* Insulate boilers and lag hot-water pipes
* Check hot-water temperatures and reduce if possible
* Isolate heating systems and give local control
* Turn off lights and heat when not in use
* Use energy-efficient lighting
* Check for leaks in heating and water pipes
* Draught proofing
* Fit thermostats and time controls
* Step up maintenance of all energy-related equipment
* Maintain, upgrade, install, heat recovery and heat exchange equipment
* Appoint individuals responsible for energy savings in different areas of the organization
* Ask for suggestions from all staff but specialists (e.g. heating engineers) in particular

And begin to monitor usage.

---

aid this approach exist. Two – from CEBIS and the UK Energy Efficiency Office – are provided in Appendix 6 and others can be found in, for example CBI publications and the excellent Business-in-the-Environment guides.[19] Alternatively, expert advice – in either a specialist energy audit or as part of a fuller environmental audit – may be necessary. (See Chapter 5 for information about environmental audits.)

The first step towards any systematic approach to energy efficiency is a full assessment of what energy is used, where and how it is used, and what leakages occur. Is this changing over time? This will focus attention on the areas where maximum savings can be made. (One aspect of this – the financial and non-financial accounting for energy – is dealt with below.) As ICI noted, 'we have been monitoring for some time. Now it is time to start dusting off the old stuff from the 1970s and starting to introduce some of these things.' There is no need to reinvent the wheel. Considerable expertise was assembled during the energy crisis of the 1970s and organizations should exploit that wherever possible. For example, in 1982 CIMA (the Chartered Institute of Management Accountants) published three papers representing the state of the art in energy saving and accounting with detailed illustrations from Courtaulds and Pilkingtons. Although not the simplest of documents they contain a mine of experience and ideas for all organizations.[20]

---

[19] A further and useful checklist plus commentary can be found in Winter (1988), whilst Elkington, Knight and Hailes (1991) and Elkington (1987) are full of examples of energy-saving initiatives by organizations.

[20] CIMA *The Evaluation of Energy Use: Readings* (London: CIMA) 1982.

Fortunately, many companies are happy to share their experience.[21] For example, Business-in-the-Environment, in collaboration with KPMG, has encouraged a series of performance indicator projects. The resulting case studies are to be published and include examples of companies experimenting – and succeeding – with energy savings. British Gas and Sainsbury have been especially open about their experiences.

The Sainsbury example has been running since 1974 and claims to save well over £7 million per annum. Computer systems monitor all energy usage and associated costs in considerable detail. These are then compared with per capita and area usage data. From this, controls over heat and light can be established. All managers are shown the monthly usage costs against targets and are accountable for the difference. The benefit of a long experience in the field reflects in the company's involvement with building design, which allows efficiency to be built in so that, for example, heat is recycled and integrated systems use the heat generated by the fridges. Sainsbury claims that its stores now use only 60 per cent of the energy that would have been required ten years ago. Office space has similarly been considered. Motion-sensitive lighting and thermostatically controlled heating and air-conditioning all produce savings.

There is less evidence on the types of controls that have been successfully applied in the field of transport. Inevitably, price differentials on unleaded petrol and diesel will have effects on buying decisions by companies in a way which should reduce long-term expenditure. Furthermore, constant monitoring of transport costs – including energy – would be a normal part of any good management. This should have the effect of forcing transport miles and associated costs downwards. However, it is quite apparent that culture and financial subsidies in the West encourage private road transport over other methods and – as with energy usage – may actually lead to an increase in road miles. There seems little prospect of the majority of organizations switching to cycles and public transport[22] until there is a major switch in the financial and physical infrastructure of transport. Given the enormous effort and publicity which is pouring into energy savings in the 1990s, the absence of much sensible discussion of transport seems odd and very short-sighted.

---

[21] See also Elkington, Knight and Hailes (1991).

[22] Although both Ciba-Geigy and Body Shop announced initiatives to encourage staff use of bicycles and public transport in, respectively, 1991 and 1992. Many local authorities in the UK have a policy of positively encouraging bicycle and public transport.

Figure 6.5

Initial steps in accounting for energy costs

- Codes within the chart of accounts for each source of fuel.
- Separate posting of energy invoices to accounts for oil (different sorts as appropriate), petroleum, diesel, electricity, mains gas, bottled gas, coal, etc.
- A means of assessing direct usage for recharging processes, through product costs, ABC (Activity Based Costing), site costs or whatever the organization's cost allocation basis is.
- A means of realistically allocating 'non-traceable' costs to the cause of their creation.
- The usual holding to account of activity etc. centre management.
- A means of presenting trends in the energy costs (see below) – this may need some re-creation from previous invoices.
- Separate identification of these energy costs within costs reports, budgets and other control and performance information.
- Some consideration of intra-organizational transfers of energy (e.g. recycled heat) and whether the effort in accounting for this and recharging it is beneficial (in environmental and/or financial terms) as a result of potential changes in behaviour.
- Cost summary and other reports should be able to identify major users of which fuels (this then becomes the target area for senior management and the investment programme).
- In so far as the accountants are involved in investment appraisal and capital budgeting some means must be established to ensure that energy investment is considered alongside other investment proposals.

6.5   Accounting for Energy

One of the most straightforward ways in which accountants can contribute to the developing environmental sensitivity of organizations is accounting for energy. A prerequisite for control is knowing about the thing to be controlled. The first step is to separate out energy costs in the basic accounting and costing systems. This seems self-evident but if our survey is reliable (See Appendix C) fewer than 50 per cent of large companies have a system to account for energy separately and fewer still actually recharge the costs to activity centres, preferring, for reasons of simplicity, to treat them as part of general overhead.

Given the very wide range of accounting systems used in practice there can be no hard and fast rules for accounting for energy but any system must have a substantial proportion of the elements shown in Figure 6.5. These elements not only start the process of collecting data upon which the control of energy costs can be based but they also raise the profile of energy costs (at, for example, site, product or divisional level) in the minds of employees and management; and attempt to attribute the costs to those incurring them.

This alone will not, however, lead to reduction in energy usage. Not only must there be mechanisms for ensuring that energy costs are actively controlled – through energy-related investments, through ensuring that energy costs form part of performance appraisal (see, for example, Chapter 8), etc. – but there must be a separate accounting for energy *units* as opposed to just the costs. For example, declines in energy costs may arise through changes in the nature of the business, through changes in processes and, most importantly, either through switching between fuels or reductions in per unit costs of energy. This could easily disguise a failure to increase actual energy efficiency. As with any useful costing system, the units must also be recorded so that energy targets and volume variances, for example, can be assessed. It is this combination of separate identification of fuels by both cost and units that has led to the successful control of energy by IBM, ICI, Carron Phoenix, Marks and Spencer, Tesco, Sainsbury, etc. Other companies have chosen to control only for financial or unit measurement. This is potentially dangerous. Accounting for only the financial implications does not place the organization in a position to forecast changes in fuel costs and assess their impact. Most enlightened organizations realize that energy costs will rise substantially, and that now is the time to reduce exposure by reducing usage. It is this that will, in the longer term, reduce costs consistently. Accounting only in units, whilst it may be better environmentally, rarely produces the hard cash motivators for control and does not necessarily lead to minimizing energy costs.

6.6   Accounting in Energy Units

One of the more enlightened (or crazy) ideas that emerged during the energy crisis of the 1970s was the proposal to use energy units as the basic mechanism for bookkeeping. Although the idea suffered from a number of weaknesses it also had its advantages. The weaknesses derived from the lack of a relationship with cash in a world where financial control still predominates, and the focus upon only one element of an organization's environmental interaction. The benefit of the idea came principally from its identification of other forms of 'income', 'cost' and 'profit'; ones any organization seriously intent on pursuing sustainability would recognize.

The essence of the notion was that all bookkeeping entries currently denoted in £ or $ or whatever could be redesignated in terms of the units of energy contained in their production. A complete accounting based on the idea has never been developed and some of the practical issues are certainly far from simple. But the notion of tracing energy inputs to various options is far from stupid and a shadow accounting system based on therms, BTUs, tonnes of coal equivalent or whatever could begin to inform policy-making. Banks (1977) gives a couple of examples:[23] in 1970 the

---

[23] Banks (1977). For more detail on these matters generally, see Dick-Larkham & Stonestreet (1977); Hewgill (1977, 1979); Sellen (1980).

automobile accounted for 21 per cent of the USA's total energy consumption; and a wooden frame house contains less than a third of the energy input necessary to produce a brick house of the same dimensions and energy efficiency.[24] Whilst market and financial logic has accepted these situations, an energy account of the two exposes the bizarre results of our taken-for-granted assumptions. Serious restructuring of energy prices, when (or if) it comes, should have the effect of reducing the disparity and encouraging the challenge of energy accounting to be taken up once again.

In addition to the potential benefits in terms of efficiency and forecasting ability that can arise from attempts to account in energy units, other real and pragmatic possibilities exist. For example, energy accounting can be a mechanism by which waste energy might be successfully tracked. One international chemical company has been experimenting with this as part of its allocation of energy costs to activities. Identification of waste heat – from buildings, via smokestacks, in the waste water stream – has helped line management identify where 'their' energy costs are going and, given the high level of accountability, encouraged them to devise ways of minimizing the losses. Sainsbury has a well-developed system run on similar lines. Another possibility for accounting in energy units arose in a medium-sized extractive and building products company. Discussion on the desirability of measuring the environmental improvement arising from design and process changes led to the innovative use of 'energy units per cubic metre of buildings constructed' as an experimental performance measure. As energy was very closely correlated with the majority of the company's environmental impacts, this proved to be an especially helpful measure for which separate accounting was necessary. As with the experiments of the 1970s, we can realistically expect more imaginative developments in accounting for energy to emerge as the environmental crisis deepens.

6.7   Some Issues for the Future

Energy, like most other matters relating to protection/destruction of the environment, is experiencing very rapid change. In the UK we are beginning to see more substantial experimentation with other forms of fuels including biomass, wind and solar power. This is no longer the province of specialist centres like the National Centre for Alternative Technology (see addresses in Appendix B). Although the UK has been dedicated to its attachment to nuclear energy and slow in developing its non-fossil fuel obligation the options available to organizations are slowly growing. The EC continues to encourage a degree of innovation in fuel usage and throughout Europe there is,

---

[24] It is not clear whether this allows for longevity and maintenance.

at last, debate about placing restrictions upon the motor car, while in the USA companies as diverse as Xerox Corporation and CMS Energy are reported as experimenting with alternative fuels for motor vehicles.[25] No organization's energy policy is likely to remain untouched by these and the other changes in train.

Energy issues are also essential in the debates on recycling and life-cycle assessment (see Chapters 7 and 9) and the development of eco-labelling is bound to bring energy usage more to the fore of the political and business arenas. But nothing substantial will happen until a more serious recognition of the issues encourages government action. Current institutional and fiscal arrangements encourage, rather than discourage, energy usage, negotiations between suppliers and users of energy have forced prices down, not up, and blanket policies on energy will hurt the poor more than the rich. To finish by putting the matter in some sort of context, Friends of the Earth remarks that the 1990 UK housing standards are approximately equal to those adopted in Sweden – in 1930! With a will, better information, a slightly more proactive government and, most significantly, a slightly longer-term attitude to investment payback (see Chapter 8) there are significant financial savings to be made that can only benefit our badly mauled physical environment.

Further Reading

General Introductions to the Issues

Elkington, J., Knight, P. and Hailes, J. (1991) *The Green Business Guide*, Gollancz, London.
Friends of the Earth (1990) *How Green Is Britain?*, Hutchinson Radius, London.
Simpson, S. (1990) *The Times Guide to the Environment*, Times Books, London.

Energy, Business and Accounting

Burkitt, D. (1990) *The Costs to Industry of Adopting Environmentally Friendly Practices*, CIMA, London.
Chartered Institute of Management Accountants (1982) *The Evaluation of Energy Use: Readings*, CIMA, London.
The Cheriton Energy Management Accounting Scheme (1991) Cheriton Publications, Cambridge.
Price Waterhouse (1991) *Energy: containing the costs*, Energy Efficiency Office, London.
Winter, G. (1988) *Business and the Environment*, McGraw-Hill, Hamburg.

Other Sources of Information and Assistance

The Business-in-the-Environment publications are especially valuable and the Association of Energy Conservation and the Energy Efficiency Office are

---

[25] *Business and the Environment*, May 1992 Vol. 3 no. 5 p. 11.

helpful. British Gas has a number of useful and interesting publications which relate to the issues, and the more obvious sources such as the CBI, the Environment Council and CEBIS all have information and guidance on the issues. (Addresses given in Appendices A and B.)

APPENDIX 6.1
CEBIS environmental checklist: energy management

ENVIRONMENTAL CHECKLIST
ENERGY MANAGEMENT

QUESTIONS

- Has the potential for energy saving in the company been systematically evaluated?
- Have energy efficiency and conservation programmes been implemented?
- Has the potential for recovering energy from processes for re-use been evaluated?

ASSESSMENT

	A	B	C
Evaluation of potential for energy savings and Implementation of action programme (ES)	No evaluation	No systematic evaluation	Systematic evaluation and energy efficiency programmes in place

If ES = A or B then action strongly recommended

ACTION MAY INCLUDE

- Undertaking an 'energy audit' to identify how much, how and where in the company energy is being used.
- Evaluating audit findings and drawing up an energy efficiency action plan.
- Implementing the action plan, starting with the zero and low cost energy saving options.
- Setting energy use targets and monitoring energy use to ensure that efficiency measures are being effectively implemented and to identify further opportunities for energy savings.

SOURCES OF INFORMATION AND ADVICE

- The Energy Efficiency Office provides expert advice. It also produce excellent guides on energy efficiency.
- CEBIS Fact Files and Helpline

January 1992

APPENDIX 6.2
Energy Efficiency Office for Scotland checklist

HOW DOES YOUR FIRM MATCH UP?

Lowering energy costs is easy – if someone in the organisation will face up to rising bills and the waste of resources.

Anyone can start by ticking this checklist and seeing how many "No" answers appear.

Each "No" can be changed to a "Yes" with a call to the Energy Efficiency Office for some information and then a little effort to put the ideas into practice.

	YES	NO
1. Is energy efficiency on the agenda of your next Board meeting?	☐	☐
2. Does the board regularly see and review the energy figures?	☐	☐
3. Have you appointed an energy manager?	☐	☐
4. Is your energy manager in touch with the Energy Efficiency Office?	☐	☐
5. Have you carried out an energy survey?	☐	☐
6. Have you set up an energy efficiency programme?	☐	☐
7. Is it being implemented?	☐	☐
8. Have you instituted a "good housekeeping" programme?	☐	☐
9. Have you installed a monitoring and targeting system?	☐	☐
10. Have you invested in either low or high cost efficiency measures?	☐	☐
11. Are you carrying out staff training in energy efficiency?	☐	☐
12. Do you have copies of EEO publications relevant to your energy use?	☐	☐
13. Do you read "Energy Management"?	☐	☐

ENERGY EFFICIENCY OFFICE FOR SCOTLAND

For free advice on the creation of your own energy efficiency action plan, please contact us by letter, phone or fax.

We can help you to lower your fuel bills and reach higher profits with a simple cost effective self-help programme.

Energy Efficiency Office for Scotland
Room 6/57
New St Andrew's House
Edinburgh EH1 3TA

Tel: 031-244 1200   Fax: 031-244 4860

7.   Accounting and Controlling for the Costs of Waste, Packaging and Recycling

7.1   Introduction

The management and control of waste (together with packaging and recycling) form one of the two main areas (energy being the other) in which environmental and financial/economic considerations are often seen to be congruent. For this reason, it is one of the major areas in which corporate environmental initiatives have been undertaken. The financial benefits to be derived from an at least 'light green' management of waste can be immediate and obvious, which makes it an aspect of organization/environment interaction in which accountants can play – and are playing – a considerable role.

The concept of 'waste' has two, very distinct dimensions. We can think of these as 'wastefulness' and 'pollution'. The human/economic dimension (wastefulness) relates to using more than we need; the by-products of production; by-products in use; the disposal of the by-products; and what to do with the products when humans have stopped using them. The ecological dimension (which also includes mankind, of course) relates to the effect of this process on the capacity of the biosphere to continue functioning (pollution in its widest sense). There are intrinsic human/economic reasons for minimizing waste but these become critical when the biosphere can no longer handle the wastes we produce. This is what is now happening. The utopian dream of the greener industrialists consists of a 'closed loop' system in which *all* wastes (including all heat and emissions) are virtually eliminated and recycled back into an economic system which introduces 'new' material into the system only from truly sustainable and renewable sources. We are some considerable way from this (impossible?) dream at the moment, but it is this sort of thinking which largely underpins most approaches to waste minimization.

Figure 7.1

The ubiquity of 'waste'

Waste is everywhere:

* vehicle emissions;
* heat escape and loss;
* air emissions and greenhouse gases;
* air emissions and acid rain;
* emissions and dumping in fresh water;
* dumping and emissions to the sea;
* industrial by-products;
* packaging;
* products at the end of their use;
* leakages to air, water and land;
* domestic refuse and sewage;
* abandoned and decommissioned plant and buildings.

Figure 7.2

Waste disposal in the news

Perhaps one of the prevailing images of the 1980s involved the wanderings of waste-bearing vessels like the *Karin B*, the *Deep Sea Carrier*, the *Zanoobia* and the *Khain Sea* (the so called 'leper of the oceans'), which travelled the globe looking for places to dispose of their waste and found that the world was no longer large enough, or willing, to accommodate them. Crises like these come and go but the core issues remain – how can the wastes generated by the world be dealt with in an environmentally sound manner?

7.2   Some Aspects of the Wider Problem

Waste is a global problem. Figure 7.3 reports some data from OECD countries and Figure 7.4 indicates where some of the waste comes from in the UK. Untreated, it all has to go somewhere and the biosphere is the only place for it.

Although worldwide attempts to reach agreement on controlling the levels of wastes and associated pollution have not been especially successful, the institutional and regulatory framework of nations and trade groups (such as the EC) is developing very rapidly. Such developments include, *inter alia*: increasing specification of what constitute 'controlled substances'; fuller guidance on their use and disposal; greater concern over the place and the medium of disposal; tightening regulation of emissions and discharges; and, of course, a steadily rising cost associated with all forms of waste. This has spread inexorably to controls over packaging and initiatives on recycling. These will be considered later in this chapter.

Figure 7.3

Selected environmental indicators from OECD			
	Municipal waste pc. kgs	Energy use pc. tonnes oil eq.	CO_2 emiss pc.
Australia	681	5.0	4.3
Belgium	313	4.6	3.2
Canada	632	9.6	4.8
Denmark	469	3.7	3.4
France	304	3.7	1.8
W Germany	331	4.5	3.2
Ireland	311	2.7	2.2
Italy	301	2.6	1.9
Japan	394	3.3	2.2
Netherlands	467	4.4	3.4
New Zealand	662	4.3	2.0
Sweden	317	6.7	2.5
Switzerland	427	4.2	1.9
UK	353	3.7	2.9
USA	864	7.8	5.8
OECD average	1131	4.8	3.4

pc = per capita

Figure 7.4

Waste sources in the UK		
Sector	Million tonnes	%
Agriculture	250	49
Mining	107	21
Sewage	1	–
Dredgings	21	4
Household	20	4
Commercial	15	3
Construction	32	6
Industrial	69	14

Source: Digest of Environmental Protection Statistics 1991, Department of the Environment 1991 (p. 63).

The EC's strategy on waste management has three major strands that closely follow the principles of waste management at the corporate level.

(1) Prevention and minimization are to be encouraged throughout all processes. They are helped by eco-labelling, BS7750 and eco-audit (see Chapter 5), and the prospect of EC waste levies and taxes.

Figure 7.5

Some upward pressures on waste disposal costs

1. The sheer volume of waste generated: This must put pressure on disposal facilities, thereby forcing up costs.

2. Reduction in waste disposal facilities: Includes less available local landfill sites, increased control over the sites; control over incineration and incineration plants; greater restriction over exporting wastes to other, often Third World, countries.

3. Rising awareness of consequences: Even domestic and other non-toxic waste is now recognized as a potential hazard.

4. Increased transportation costs: These reflect, inter alia, increased control of transport quality on land and sea.

5. Insurance costs: Throughout the whole waste chain – and especially trans-portation.

6. Problems of safety in disposal: Particularly of increasingly toxic wastes and especially when mixed with other wastes to produce a 'cocktail' of unknown potency or effect.

7. Increasing 'waste aftercare': Needs to be incorporated into waste disposal methods and therefore waste disposal costs.

8. Increased legal costs: Especially associated with the waste disposal organizations, these have also helped to drive up waste disposal costs.

(2) Recycling and reuse: EC directives, especially regarding packaging and containers, are rapidly changing the economics of the different activities (but see below).
(3) Safety in disposal: this strand of EC policy has produced guidance on landfill, incineration and waste shipment as well as the civil liability for damage caused by waste.[1]

More clearly than for any other element of the organization's interaction with the environment, the 'terms of trade' on waste are undergoing significant change. Waste control and disposal costs are rising and will continue to do so (see Figure 7.5). In addition to these direct cost changes, legislation will introduce a wider range of penalties for infringements of waste regulations and alterations in the taxation regime can be expected to provide corporations with a steadily changing and increasing cost structure.[2]

Furthermore, as environmental issues have an impact on earlier stages in one's production chain, inputs to the organization will

[1] For more detail on the legal aspects see, for example, Ball and Bell (1991); and *Integrated Environmental Management, ENDS* and *KPMG Environment Briefing Note*, which all carry regular updates.

[2] See, also, for example, *Financial Times*, 26 November 1991, *ENDS Report* 202/ November 1991, Tinker (1985), Porritt (1990), Smith (1991).

Figure 7.6

> ## Why minimize waste?
>
> *Reduce:*
> * production costs;
> * on-site waste monitoring and treatment costs;
> * handling, transport and off-site disposal costs;
> * raw material costs;
> * energy and water costs;
> * long-term environmental liability and insurance costs
> * the risks of spills and accidents;
>
> *and improve*
> * income through the sale of reusable waste;
> * overall operating efficiency;
> * the safety of employees;
> * the company's image in the eyes of the shareholders, employees and the community.
>
> *Source:* DTI (1990)

become progressively more expensive – as a result of which all wastage will cost more. Increased water charges – especially given water's role in much waste disposal – are a particularly good example here.[3] Finally, experience in Europe suggests that corporations which are not in the vanguard of environmentally driven developments on waste, packaging and recycling will have entire national and international markets closed to them.[4] Such implications have the most considerable financial consequences of course.

In this chapter we must recognize that 'waste' and 'packaging' and 'recycling' are largely inseparable and little will be gained from distinguishing them. A number of issues specific to recycling and packaging do arise, however, and these will be picked up later.

7.3 Corporate Waste Management

What we refer to as waste (whether wastefulness or pollution) arises throughout the whole production and distribution process as well as in the use of product itself (see Figure 7.7). The essential aim, from an environmental point of view, is to *minimize* resources throughout that process. This minimization of resource use, and waste in particular, will be in keeping with the economic aims of the business – but only to a point. A considerable amount of 'waste' can be represented by the products themselves and this raises a fundamental problem for all businesses where *maximization* of throughput

---

[3] See, for example, Litterick (1991).

[4] And especially the implications of the ruling on the Danish returnable beverage containers – see, for example, *ENDS Report* 192/February 1991, p. 19.

Figure 7.7

Some elements in the process of waste production

Quality of input:
- appropriate specifications;
- technical quality;
- packaging of delivery;
- JIT considerations;
- quality decay.

Quality of processing:
- efficiency of conversion;
- hazards in use;
- heat, noise, emissions and discharges from the process;
- wastage and quality failures from the process;
- waste/by-products generated.

Quality of output:
- how important is the product?
- reliability and quality in use;
- length of life;
- repairability;
- disposability;
- transport and packaging to user.

---

is the more usual goal.[5] Within the current constraints in which businesses operate, the 'light green' response is the only one that many organizations can see as 'realistic'.

Most companies which have carefully addressed the issue of waste – throughout all aspects of their operations – have found significant financial savings. As the DTI suggests, there are many immediate, economic reasons (shown in Figure 7.6) for seeking these savings. The process will most typically begin as part of the general environmental review (see Chapter 5) and then progress to a specific waste audit. Figure 7.8 is an example of the sort of checklist with which any organization would begin this process.[6]

Anecdotes of corporate financial savings abound. Widely publicized experiences such as the 3Ms 3Ps (Pollution Prevention Pays) initiative and the Dow Chemicals WRAP (Waste Reduction Always Pays) project, whilst among the best-known and best-developed programmes, are no longer the rarity they were.[7] The key to all

[5] This is a major stumbling block in the environmental–business debate. The evidence strongly suggests that Western individuals must make and use *less* whilst corporate success normally depends on the production and use of *more*. It is an aspect that clearly distinguishes the 'light' and 'dark' green perspectives. This is not, however, a problem that corporations can solve – even if they wish to – without some profound change in the financial, economic, social and ethical framework within which they operate. See Chapters 14 and 15.

[6] Many other examples and sources of help exist. See e.g. BiE (1991a). Appendix 7.1 also contains a checklist from CEBIS.

[7] See, for example, Coopers and Lybrand Deloitte, *Industry briefing*, February 1992.

Figure 7.8

Waste management checklist

Initial review
*   Inventory of wastes generated to establish baseline information (environmental review/audit).
*   Sources, quantities, physical and chemical characteristics of wastes identified (see duty of care requirements).

Management responsibilities
*   Establish a policy regarding waste disposal.
*   Ensure a director or senior manager is responsible for wastes.
*   Allocate responsibility for wastes and packaging to the appropriate level of management.

Waste minimization
*   Waste considerations designed into products at the development stage.
*   Separation and treatment of wastes at the source of production.
*   Reuse or recycling of wastes within production process or elsewhere inside and outside the organization.
*   Consideration of the environmental impact of packaging.
*   Consideration of the post-consumer environmental impact of the product, that is, possibilities of taking back and recycling a product's components.

Waste management on site
*   Site survey identifying inefficiencies and hazards.
*   Review practice to ensure standards and practice established in policy are maintained.
*   Ensure reporting procedures are adequate to monitor compliance with legal standards and policy.
*   Keep appropriate records.
*   Ensure safe storage of wastes on site where necessary.
*   Develop emergency contingency plans where relevant, test and review these regularly.
*   Ensure appropriate insurance cover obtained.

Reporting
*   Internal reporting to ensure policy achieved.
*   Internal reporting for performance appraisal purposes.
*   External reporting of policy and performance.

Source: adapted from *Management Waste Guidelines for Business* (London: CBI) CBI (1992a) *Environment means business* series.

---

these programmes, though, has been that they have been tied both to a TQM culture *and* directly to the financial systems of the organization. And this has been helped by initiatives like the Duty of Care provisions in the UK,[8] related initiatives such as ICI's 'product

---

[8] The essence of the Duty of Care provisions is that the waste *producer* is responsible for ensuring that all waste generated is responsibly handled. This, in practice, means that the waste producer must vet and co-operate closely with the organization which will dispose, re-treat or recycle that waste. For more detail, see, for example, *ENDS Report* 204/January 1992 (pp. 29–30) and Irvine (1991).

Figure 7.9

When is waste not waste?

There are a number of incidents which have reinforced the ecologists' recognition that the 'natural' state of the biosphere is unknowable and somewhat academic. Pilkington's, for example, faced a fascinating and widely publicised conundrum. Keen to get rid of their waste spoil heaps for a variety of business, legal and aesthetic reasons they ran into opposition from environmentalists! The spoil heaps over time had developed a local ecology which now supported a number of species of wild orchid. What was originally 'waste' had now become part of 'biosphere'. Conundrums of this sort are more and more frequent.

---

stewardship'[9] and the increasing market opportunities that have arisen for the retreatment, recycling and more professional disposal of wastes. On top of which, organizations seeking either (or both of) market advantage or a more responsible attitude to their waste have undertaken original initiatives which provide some indication for the future. Examples of this include the UK's Business-in-the-Environment,[10] Volvo's initiative in labelling parts in manufacture for safe disposal (and for recycling; see below), company/local authority liaisons like the Furness Waste Consortium[11] as well as National Tyre Distributors' imaginative introduction of a nominal 'green fee' which they charged to customers to highlight the costs of disposing of worn tyres. The possibilities are endless and Figure 7.10 acts as reminder of the priorities that need to be borne in mind in devising strategies in the waste management field.

7.4   Accounting for Waste

There would appear to be three main ways in which organizations are accounting (in the widest sense) for waste. The first, simplest approach recognizes the total actual and potential costs of waste management on a company, activity or site basis, and adjusts policy accordingly. A large number of companies have followed this route – including one to which environmental issues were a matter of complete indifference but whose tight cost-control was a central element of the organizational culture. The second approach employs non-financial accounting as its driver and establishes a recording and communicating information system that captures physical quantities of waste. IBM's system of logging gross tonnage of waste into and out of sites and holding site management accountable for

---

[9] 'Product stewardship' is more widespread than ICI's well-publicized initiative; see, for example, Dollimore (1992).

[10] See Coopers & Lybrand Deloitte, *Industry briefing*, February 1992.

[11] For more detail see Hoggart (1992).

Figure 7.10 Waste management hierarchy

Preference	Waste management strategy
Most preferred ↑ ⋮ ↓ Least preferred	Prevention and minimization of wastes through use of cleaner technology, product and process redesign and better management techniques
	Reuse and recycle wastes either:
	• as used initially
	• in a secondary manner
	Incinerate/landfill in a manner that provides energy recovery (by heat recovery from incineration[12] or methane gas production from landfill[13]
	Incinerate/landfill without any energy recovery
	Uncontrolled disposal

Adapted from: Elkington, Knight and Hailes (1991) and KPMG Management Consulting Environmental Briefing Note 7/Spring 1991.

its control and reduction is of this sort. And of course the two approaches are not mutually exclusive and can be used together to good effect (as the Washington Department of Ecology Guidance Paper on pollution prevention demonstrates).

The third approach is normally the most sophisticated and the most directly related to conventional accounting. It is best illustrated by the experience of Rhône-Poulenc and Monsanto. Rhône-Poulenc is widely known for its Environmental Index (see Chapter 5), which was originally devised to monitor water quality coming off sites and later extended to all forms of waste.[14] From this, the company devised a comprehensive waste accounting system which charged all waste management costs (costs arising from disposal, insurance, gaining consents, emergency procedures, spillages, etc.) back to line management.[15] In effect, the 'Polluter Pays Principle' was operated for each and every facility – R&D and service units included. The motivational effects were clear: line management were recognizing the 'externalities' of their activities imposed on the rest of the company, would seek to reduce it – *and* being 'on the spot' could often devise cost-effective ways of simply reducing those costs.[16]

[12] Indeed within the cement industry proposals exist to burn waste in their kilns to reduce energy bills. See *ENDS Report* 200/September 1991, pp. 11–23.

[13] Shanks and McEwan are using methane gas produced by landfill sites to generate electricity. See *Financial Times*, 26 November 1991.

[14] See also the CIA's closely related initiative in this regard.

[15] In this the company was leaning towards the ABC principles, whose full potential in this field have yet to be fully explored.

[16] One simple example saved a great deal of money. Waste water leaving a site was a cocktail of many chemicals. The presence of traces of certain controlled substances in the water meant that *all* the water had to be specially treated. The waste accounting system encouraged the manager to identify the point at which the traces joined the

Monsanto has gone a stage further and imposed an 'internal tax' on all internally generated waste, thereby doubly penalizing – and doubly motivating – management responsible for waste production.[17]

These examples of the accounting system providing important data on environmentally related activities are mirrored in many organizations. In one medium-sized manufacturing company this had been achieved without any awareness of it as an environmental issue at all. All management were appraised on purely financial terms but the director responsible for COSHH and other environmental and safety issues had *carte blanche* from the board in his duties. (Again, this was principally for financial reasons based on the belief that falling foul of the regulators, the local community or the employees was simply bad, as well as unethical, business.) All identifiable costs were automatically charged back through the accounting system, whose primary goal was to allocate as high a proportion of organizational costs as possible. This was reinforced by the COSHH director's practice of demanding that spills, leakages, discharges and any waste materials on site were dealt with immediately by the responsible management. This might include the requirement that a process be closed down for a day or so while the problem was solved – with the obvious impact on the manager's financial performance. This led, interestingly, to very high pressure from line management to ensure that investment decisions were based on the highest health and safety standards and environmental considerations (see Chapter 8).

These illustrations are ideal examples of the way the accounting system, operating in conventional ways, can realistically contribute to the environmental sensitivity of the organization. In this sense, our findings that less than 30 per cent of accountants in large companies are operating a form of accounting for waste are disturbing (see Appendix C). But the accountant's role need not stop here. As we shall see, awareness of these matters can compel investment decisions to take account of waste in a way that may conflict with conventional investment appraisal criteria (see Chapter 8). The accountant's desire to minimize costs must not blind him or her to the fact that the waste *quantity* and the effects of that waste also need to be minimized (as we saw with energy, in Chapter 6). This needs both quantity and financial units to be accounted for. And last, but by no means least, minimizing total resource use – not just that which is identified as waste – is an almost inevitable consequence of environmental concerns which accountants, along with business management, will have to learn. It will be a painful lesson,

---

water stream and separate them out before they joined. The water then became simply 'grey water' and the volume of controlled substances needing treatment was infinitesimal compared to the total water volume. Simple, obvious and effective.

[17] See, for example, *ENDS Report* 189/October 1990, pp.14–18.

Figure 7.11

Some steps in accounting for waste

- Separate all waste management and disposal costs to identifiable cost headings.
- Expand the obvious to take account of other waste-related matters – e.g spillages, emergency and contingency facilities, insurance etc.
- Develop a non-financial accounting system that tracks all wastes on to and off the sites.
- Relate the costs to the organization's waste tracking and identification system.
- Take advice from the facilities, waste or environmental director and charge back the cost to the process creating the waste.
- Develop ABC thinking, if not a system, to refine and develop this process.
- Introduce these items to the lines of the budget-centre budgets.
- Recognize the strategic and investment implications (see Chapter 8).
- Consider an internal taxation of waste.
- Ensure that the performance appraisal and reward system recognizes these matters.
- Ensure that all forecasts take special notice of the rapidly changing 'terms of trade' on waste.

---

going against the ingrained instincts that led to success in the 'pre-environmental' era. Figure 7.11 lists some steps to be taken.

7.5 Packaging

Most of what we have said above can apply equally to the specific issue of packaging. However, a number of particular developments make elements of packaging something of a special case. Packaging has been an especially high-profile target for many consumer groups – not least because the majority of packing is single-trip and so visibly useless at the end of the trip. For the company the purposes of packaging are clear: protection in transport, stacking, enhancement of shelf-life, display, marketing and a means of communication with the purchaser. And as companies which have seriously tried to design a minimal packaging – such as Crighton's exploration of toothpaste containers – have discovered, the matter is far from simple. At the other end of the spectrum, however, Microsoft's recent experience of being ridiculed over the ludicrous redundancy built into its packaging has spread ripples through the computer software industry and is an experience which is becoming increasingly common for companies generally.[18]

Experience suggests that significant savings – both financial and environmental – can be made from careful examination of packaging. The Business-in-the-Environment initiative helped Start-Rite to save 6.5 per cent of its packaging costs; Pilkington has saved through redesigning the way glass is transported, and IBM's monitoring of incoming packaging led to productive discussions with suppliers.

[18] Reported in *Computer Weekly* Thursday, 11 June 1992 (p. 1).

Figure 7.12

Soap and detergent industry code of practice on packaging waste

- Reduce the amount of packaging per product use.
- Make maximum practicable use of recycled materials in packaging.
- Use materials which can ultimately be recovered from the waste stream for further productive use.
- Use materials which can be safely landfilled if no alternative handling is available.

Source: Integrated Environmental Management, no. 10, June 1992, p. 18.

Voluntary initiatives (shortly ahead of legislation it might be noted)[19] are increasing (see Figure 7.12). For example Marks and Spencer notes: 'we can no longer think of packaging as "rubbish" – our initiatives show how you can turn waste into valuable raw materials, saving both money and our precious environment'.[20]

But the real thrust for European companies is coming from the EC. Germany set the lead with tough packaging laws in 1991. They require minimal packaging with a high proportion of recyclability – by 1995, 80 per cent of all packaging must be collected. France and Holland were following suit late in 1991. The development is opposed by many companies, especially British ones which 'still put products in the biggest possible package to make them look larger'[21]. However, the EC has chosen to take the tough route and business can no longer ignore the environmental impact of its packaging. The EC targets are a very significant step towards reducing packaging waste (see Figures 7.13 and 7.14).

Given the determination of the EC in this matter it might be that very little accounting for packaging is necessary. That is, organizations are having to reduce their packaging or face a major proportion of their markets being closed to them. Minor details like the cost of packaging are largely irrelevant in those circumstances. In this light, the fact that less than 20 per cent of accountants with large UK firms had any involvement with accounting for packaging and returnable containers might not be a cause for concern (see Appendix C). This is probably short-sighted.

Redesigning of packaging, transport systems and the products themselves to take account of stricter EC regimes will be very costly. Furthermore, product costing will have to recognize the extra costs

---

[19] However, Friends of the Earth reports that proposals to the UK government from the packaging industry body, INCPEN, are indicative of a failure of industry to address the central issues and produce a hard commitment to reduce significantly the waste associated with packaging. See *Earth Matters*, Summer 1992, p. 3.

[20] Manager Jack Levene, quoted in 'Waste not, want not', *M&S Magazine*, 1991, p. 47.

[21] *The Economist*, 30 November 1991, (p. 97).

Figure 7.13

Elements of the EC packaging directive

- All packaging to be reusable or recoverable by the year 2000.
- Member state responsibility for providing for the return or collection of used packaging and packaging waste – this will fall on to the supplier in most cases.
- Specific requirements for packaging of hazardous material and hazardous waste.
- All packaging to bear markings to facilitate reuse and recovery.
- Removal of 90 per cent of packaging from the waste stream.
- Final disposal of packaging and packaging waste to be no greater than 10 per cent by weight of total packaging.

Figure 7.14

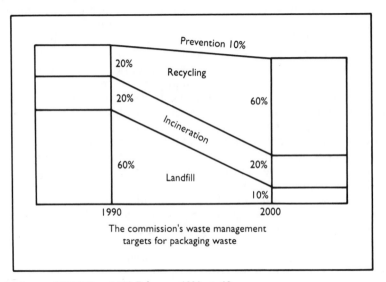

Source: ENDS Report 193 February 1991, p. 19.

involved in marking, recovering and reusing the packaging. This will lead to increased use of returnable containers, which, for many, will bring back the long-forgotten skill of accounting for them. The obverse of this scenario is also of interest to accountants – can one's organization accept goods which are not packaged adequately? Will there be a market in trade discounts if you accept the packaging? If any company is to respond sensibly to these developments it will have to begin its redesigning and rethinking as soon as possible. The accountant's potential contribution here is most significant as without careful budgeting of *all* costs associated with a changing packaging regime, the organization could be caught cold. But done

Figure 7.15

Low- and non-waste technology options	
Waste/Material	*Disposition*
Chemicals & toxic metals:	Reclaim, recycle, degrade, dispose.
Oily wastes:	Collect, recycle, dispose.
Construction materials:	Reclaim, re-use, reduce bulk.
Domestic wastes:	Biomass, Fuel/CHP, reduce bulk.
Paper, glass & plastics:	Collect, recycle.
Source: Simpson (1990), p. 83	

properly, the intelligent reduction, reuse and recycling of packaging should have very real financial and environmental benefits.

7.6   Recycling and Reuse

Despite the publicly expressed enthusiasm for recycling, it can be only a 'light green' response to the environmental crisis. Recycling is not a self-contained activity (it requires further energy and/or raw material input) and it is not the first resource-saving option (refusing to consume, reducing consumption and reusing resources all rank above recycling[22]).

Recycling comes in a number of forms, of varying complexity (Figure 7.16)[23] and raises its own individual new problems for industry to face.

A number of the industry-led initiatives have been widely publicized: IBM's collection of old machines for recovery of precious metals and components;[24] and the German and Swedish car industry initiatives to take back old vehicles for recovery of materials, for example, are not only reducing demands for virgin material but are forcing companies to 'design for disassembly'. In the words of one major manufacturer:

The recycling of . . . [product] is profitable and is encouraging designers to think about designing for recycling. For example, plastics used to have

[22] See *Integrated Environmental Management*, 3/October 1991, p. 25, where the UK government accepts that recycling ranks behind minimization and reuse. Interestingly, 'refuse' is not presented as an option, which broadly reflects the orientation of Western society towards unquestioned growth.

[23] For more detail on these issues see Landbank (1992), p. 26, *ENDS Report* 194/ March 1991, p. 11, 195/April 1991, p. 22, and 204/January 1992, p. 13, which notes a proposed German law would oblige retailers of electronic equipment to take back and dispose of items at their expense. The Netherlands looks likely to follow suit. Some of these issues relate particularly to local authorities – see below.

[24] See *ENDS Report* 192/January 1991, p. 23.

Figure 7.16

The variety of recycling

It is useful to distinguish three levels of recycling.

(1) *'Original recycling'*:   Recycling to the same quality as the virgin material, and reuse
of the recycled material in the same manner as before. This is the most preferred
option as only the energy taken to recycle the material is consumed. The success
of this relies on energy being cheap enough to allow recycling. Aluminium is a good
example of this – Norsk Hydro notes that recycling requires only 5 per cent of the
energy needed to produce the virgin aluminium from ore.

(2) *Recycling and reuse of material at a lower purity than originally*:   Less preferred
because extraction or production of the virgin material is still required. Further, it
is less likely to be profitable, and therefore less likely to occur because the resale
value at the lower level usage is likely to be minimal. This occurs where plastic
bottles are recycled into carpet pile, plastic cups into coat hangers and other non-
food contact applications, organic waste into compost, etc.

(3) *Recycle material into a form suitable for use as a fuel*:   The least preferred option but
does have the advantage of reducing the amount of waste going into landfill and
may be beneficial if energy is recovered from the process.

The complexity of the recycling task also varies, from recycling offcuts of raw materials
to recycling components from complete items such as electronic equipment or motor
vehicles or separating recyclable items from a mix of non-recyclable items.

---

*sticky labels on them but this gave problems when recycling with regard
to removing the label and glue and the contamination this caused of the
plastic. Now the information previously in a label is stamped on the
plastic along with detailed information concerning the composition of
the plastic.*

While recycling is widely recognized as 'environmentally
desirable', the proportion of wastes which are recycled remains
small.[25] One major reason for this is the low prices received for
recyclable materials – forced ever lower by increased demand for
recycling facilities. Although aluminium recycling is profitable,
for example, the margins on other materials make them a currently
unattractive investment.[26] Indeed the *WARM Report* claims, against
the predominant deregulation trend of recent years, that:

*Market forces are inadequate to deal with such pressures, since a value is
being placed by society on the recovered materials which cannot be justified
solely (or, in some cases, at all) in commercial terms. [It is therefore*

[25] See, for example, *The Economist*, 13 April 1991, p. 22, and 30 November 1991, p.
97.

[26] See, for example, Landbank (1992). It may well be that the raw materials prices
of a number of these materials do not reflect their full environmental cost: for
example, the prices for paper and board are unlikely to include the cost of replanting
forests; likewise, the cost of metals is unlikely to incorporate the cost of remediation of resource extraction sites. It is therefore unlikely that current cost and price
mechanisms will reflect a preference for recycling.

Figure 7.17

Typical energy savings in production from recycling

(As a percentage of energy for production from virgin raw material)

- Aluminium: 95%
- Steel tinplate: 74%
- Paper and Board: 40%
- Glass: 20%

NB These savings do not include consumer transport energy and this will diminish if not eliminate the savings.

Source: The WARM Report, p. 26.

Figure 7.18

Incentives to increase recycling to meet existing and future targets

1. Education.

2. Advertising.

or the use of economic incentives:

3. Levy on virgin materials: sufficient to fund the costs of recycling – the consumer pays for the imputed environmental cost of the product as the levy would be included in the product's price.

4. A deposit system: on, for example, refillable containers thereby providing the consumer with an incentive to return items.

5. Tax relief: on borrowings for investment in recycling technology is also a possibility.

6. Grants to aid investment.

7. Stimulate demand for recycled products: for example, subsidies may ensure that recycled materials are cheaper than virgin products, rather like the cost differentials that presently exist between leaded and lead-free petrol.

8. Recycling credit system: such a system has been introduced in the UK. (This mechanism is dealt with below as it arises within the context of domestic waste and local authorities.)

---

necessary] to remove the element of competition from recycling . . . these recycling targets will be achieved in the most cost-effective way by co-operation rather than competition. Cooperation makes even more sense in environmental terms, by conserving resources and reducing the energy expended in collecting and sorting waste materials.

Although voluntary (or at least, semi-voluntary) initiatives from industry are making some progress,[27] it certainly looks as though, if

[27] See, for example, BT's developments on the minimization and recycling front: Wynne-Davies (1992).

Figure 7.19

Some possible roles for the accountant in an organisation's recycling strategy

(1) Incorporating recycling costs into product cost (especially where recycling is mandatory). This requires identification of who is to bear the costs of recycling and determination of the effect of any fiscal measures on product costs. Such information would be necessary for the recycling levy proposal. Accountants would determine likely future collection and recycling costs, the volume likely to be recycled and therefore the amount of the levy needed.

(2) Separate identification of the costs and revenues arising from recycling activities is necessary to enable the assessment of the feasibility of recycling including product design for recycling.

(3) Establishing the cost of incorporating recycled materials into the manufacturing process. (E.g. Procter and Gamble has reduced the environmental impact of its packaging by incorporating recycled plastic. This also expands the market for recycled plastic.)

(4) Preparation of budgets and performance appraisal that include recycling targets, quantified in both financial and non-financial terms.

(5) The viability of recycling plans and investment in recycling technologies and the related investment appraisal. Hurdle rates of return may require modification to ensure recycling targets can be met.

---

the necessary targets for recycling and reuse are to be met, intervention in 'the marketplace' is necessary (see Figure 7.18). In the present situation, it will fall to accountants to seek out economic recycling and reuse options and to assess corporations' current recycling efforts financially.

Ways in which the accountant can positively contribute on the recycling front are shown in Figure 7.19.

However, it seems most likely that the range of *conventional* options that a successful organization can consider will close down somewhat as recycling begins to bite, but *imaginative* solutions and options will give the commercial advantage. The accountant's expertise will be essential here – not simply to avoid a reactionary accountant preventing imaginative options but also in thinking creatively about the financial implications of different options. This can perhaps be illustrated best with a particular example from the local authority experience.

7.7 Domestic Waste, Local Authorities and Other Operators

Households also produce large volumes of waste (see Figure 7.20) which must be handled, typically by, or through, a local government organization where the emphasis tends to be on recycling. This need not be the case though. Not only can local authorities take a positive role in encouraging waste minimization and reuse (as has happened to a degree in Canada, for example) but a more imagina-

Figure 7.20   UK household refuse composition

Material	Weight ('000 tonnes per annum)	Weight (%)	Volume (%)
Paper (paper, board, newspapers, etc)	4,890	30.5	35
Putrescibles (waste food, garden clippings)	4,480	28.0	28
Miscellaneous solid waste (rubble, cinders, etc)	2,240	14.0	14
Glass	1,520	9.5	4
Plastics	1,350	8.4	15
Ferrous metal (steel, tinplate)	1,120	7.0	1.8
Textiles (wool, linen, cotton, jute, synthetics)	300	1.9	2
Non-ferrous metals (aluminium, etc)	120	0.7	0.2
TOTAL	16,020	100.0	100.0

Source: *The WARM Report*, p. 1.

tive planning and financial regime can open up more productive options. Thus, our own calculations suggest that many local authorities could, economically, buy a composting system for every household with a garden. The reduction in the waste stream could be as high as 28 per cent (although it is most unlikely to meet this), and this reduces, among other costs, vehicle and incinerator repair. A major, and well-publicized, variation on this theme – the Ontario blue box scheme – has produced some interesting economics.[28] There is considerable opportunity for imaginative financial examination and scenario planning in this context.

Certainly local authorities[29] face a number of difficult logistical decisions that have financial implications for which are needed accurate costings of existing and proposed collection methods; recycling options; sorting and cleaning (decontamination) of the waste stream; final disposal options; recycling levies and recycling credits (see Figure 7.21) and other incentives,[30] and so on.

[28] See, for example, R. Laughlin and L. K. Varangu (1991).

[29] In the UK, domestic waste disposal has been conducted under the auspices of three organizations: waste collection authorities (WCAs), that is, local authorities; waste disposal authorities (WDAs), county councils in the shires; and waste regulation authorities (WRAs), usually counties or metropolitan district groupings. The future structure of domestic waste collection, disposal and regulation is uncertain with a number of private companies now participating in the market and arm's-length local authority waste disposal companies being formed.

[30] A market research report by Mintel found most consumers are willing to recycle but are restricted by lack of facilities to store recyclables in their homes, or access to recycling points either due to insufficient points nearby or lack of transport to get to the designated recycling points. See *ENDS Report* 204/January 1992, p. 12.

Figure 7.21

Recycling credits in the UK

The UK Environmental Protection Act 1990 provides for a system of recycling credits which provide economic incentives to ensure that components of the waste stream are recycled that otherwise would not be. The idea behind this system, implemented in April 1992, is that anyone removing material from the waste stream should receive the sum of money that the local authority otherwise would have had to spend to collect and dispose of it.

This requires the costs of waste disposal to be calculated on both a short- and long-term basis.

Whilst colleagues in industry worry about the costs of getting waste safely (and cheaply) off-site, the local authorities share with other (private) disposal site operators the concerns of managing and maintaining disposal facilities. Indeed, how should one account for landfill restoration and aftercare costs? Problems include the build up, migration and in some cases ignition of landfill gas; leaching into ground and surface water; and other (increasingly numerous) occurrences which can be considered life and health threatening. These, combined with provisions in section 74 of the Environmental Protection Act 1990 requiring financial provision adequate to discharge the obligations arising from landfill aftercare, result in potential, significant liabilities which may well give rise to future costs.[31]

Future costs that may be incurred include:

- monitoring costs necessary to identify any problems;
- remedial costs for damage already done;
- costs to prevent damage from existing and potential problems;
- litigation costs that may arise within this context[32].

Identifying future liabilities involves looking forward and backwards over many years. For example, in one landfill, currently undergoing remedial work, domestic waste had been accepted since 1963 and studies of the likely future effects estimate that maximum concentrations of leachate are expected in 2001[33].

Options to finance these future costs include:

(1) taking out insurance cover (this is unlikely to be viable);
(2) individual operators providing for costs by setting aside funds as waste is being placed in landfill. Responsibility for aftercare then rests with the individual operator;
(3) formation of a government-sponsored aftercare fund financed by a waste disposal levy on all operators. In this case final

---

[31] See, for example, Kemp and Gerrard, 1991.

[32] See *ENDS Report* 205/February 1991, p. 11.

[33] Ibid.

responsibility for sites would be transferred to government. Regardless of how such a scheme would be funded accounting issues would be raised concerning:

(a) the existence and valuation of contingent liabilities for restoration and aftercare costs;
(b) the valuation of waste disposal sites currently held – which would need to be revised in the light of these additional potential costs; and
(c) the appropriate treatment of providing for costs in terms of the effect on the income statement.

There would be concerns in industry and at the government level if profitability in the waste disposal industry were to fall dramatically or if the local authorities were unable to maintain standards through exceptional pressures on costs. Waste management and recycling goals probably require the stable provision of waste treatment and disposal facilities.[34]

7.8   Conclusions

In a literal sense, the management of waste, packaging and recycling should automatically follow from good environmental management linked with an active and sensible approach to the management of the business. However, experience suggests that careful management of waste does not follow so naturally, and certainly the speed of change in the regulation and the economics of waste, packaging and recycling means that no organization can afford to ignore it. The need for responsive accounting and financial information systems is just as important in this area as any other – and the ways in which the accountant can become involved are rather more obvious than in most other areas (with the probable exception of energy). But the level of accounting involvement in this area is still remarkably low, which helps neither the business nor the environment.

Further Reading

Department of the Environment (1991) *Waste Management – The Duty of Care: A Code of Practice*, DoE, London.
Department of Trade and Industry (1990) *Cutting Your Losses: A Business Guide to Waste Minimization*. Business and the Environment Initiative, DTI, London.
CEFIC (European Chemical Industry Federation) (1990) *Guidelines on Waste Minimization*, CEFIC, Paris.
The WARM System: A Proposal for a Model Waste Recovery and Recycling System for Britain. A Gateway Foodmarkets Report prepared by The Landbank Consultancy. 1992.

[34] For one insight into the waste industry, see, e.g. Skeel (1991).

Porritt, J. (1990) *How Green Is Britain? The Government's Environmental Record*, Hutchinson Radius, London.
Simpson, S. (1990) *The Times Guide to the Environment: A Comprehensive Handbook to Green Issues*, Times Books, London.
Winter, G. (1988) *Business and the Environment*, McGraw Hill, Hamburg.

APPENDIX 7.1
CEBIS environmental checklist: waste management

QUESTIONS

- Does your company keep a waste inventory and if not, how are the types and quantities of wastes you produce monitored?

- Have you checked whether you produce any special waste, and if so, do you know what action is required to ensure its safe disposal?

- Are you complying with the Environmental Protection Act's Duty of Care?

- Have staff been allocated clearly defined duties and are they adequately trained?

- Does the company have procedures to deal with accidental spillage of waste?

ASSESSMENT

	A	B	C
Waste Inventory (WI)	Little systematic evaluation of waste arisings	Informal evaluation of waste arisings	Detailed inventory of waste arisings
Waste Storage/Handling (WS)	No formal system in place	Informal system in place	Formal system with responsibility allocated to properly informed staff
Waste Disposal (WD)	No monitoring of waste disposal route	Monitoring not systematic	Full evaluation of compliance with Duty of Care

If WI, WS or WD = A or B then corrective action necessary and urgent

ACTION MAY INCLUDE

- Auditing all waste arisings and establishing a waste inventory.
- Checking if any special waste is produced and how it should be managed.
- Auditing waste management practices and establishing "best practice" systems for waste handling and storage.
- Defining clear responsibilities and training amongst staff.
- Checking compliance with the Duty of Care
- Setting up emergency procedures to deal with accidents or spillages.

SOURCES OF INFORMATION AND ADVICE

- CEBIS Fact Files and Helpline
- '*Control of Pollution (Special Wastes) Regulations 1980* '(available from HMSO)
- '*The Duty of Care: A Code of Practice* '(available from HMSO)
- Waste Management Papers (available from HMSO)
- District Council and/or Hazardous Waste Inspectorate Scotland

8. Investment, Budgeting and Appraisal:

Environment at the Heart of the Accounting and Financial Systems

8.1 Introduction

Accounting and financial systems are crucial to the operations of all organizations. They provide records of what has been done and measures of the success or failure of past activities; they provide the constraints on actions and estimates of, and constraints on resources necessary for the actions; they supply targets and measure and reward performance against those targets, and provide a substantial part of the analytical framework within which new activities are assessed and planned. Whilst it is overstating the case to say that accounting and financial systems are *the* most important information and control systems of an organization, certainly few organizational activities can take place without involving accounting and finance.

We have discussed the ways in which accounting and environment can be in fundamental conflict. It follows that unless environmental considerations are embedded into the core functions of the accounting and financial systems, those functions will not only be unsupportive of organizational change towards a 'greener' orientation, they will actually prevent it. This is the position the more 'environmentally advanced' have now reached. Having put environmental policy in place, undertaken and implemented environmental review/audit, undertaken training, become involved with the green agenda and taken imaginative steps in matters such as wastes, emissions, transport, packaging and energy control, they are facing the central problem of how to ensure that environmental considerations are central to the organization's every activity. (But see Figure 8.2.) An essential prerequisite for this is 'greener' management accounting and control systems.

But this is where the problems begin. Although the issue is clearly crucial, experience on *how* to incorporate environmental

Figure 8.1

> **Environmental considerations must be an integral element of the management accounting and control systems:**
>
> - The costing system;
> - The planning system;
> - The budgeting system;
> - Variance analysis;
> - Capital budgeting & expenditure;
> - Plant maintenance;
> - Investment appraisal & post-audit;
> - Performance measurement & appraisal;
> - Reporting & accountability systems;
> - Reward systems;
> - Forecasting;
> - Scenario assessment;
> - Options review;
> - Purchasing policy;
> - Research and development;
> - Business cases;
> - Business acquisition and development;
> - Treasury management;
> - Control of sub-contracting;
> - Risk assessment;
> - Insurance policy;
> - Financing decisions.

factors into the financial systems as they relate to, for example, investment appraisal, budgeting, design, R&D, is still fairly limited.[1] Our own survey suggested that less than 40 per cent of large UK companies have any environmental factors built into the financial investment appraisal process, less than 20 per cent have environment built into the budgeting systems, and in only a minority of large companies are the accountants and accounting systems closely involved with central environmental questions as they relate to the company. As with much of the material we have already discussed, until experimentation is more widespread and more open, one is necessarily limited in the guidance that can be offered. As Elkington (Elkington, Knight and Hailes, 1991, p. 81) states: 'The language of finance, in short, has not developed fast enough to keep pace with the changes being brought about by environmental pressures.'

Whilst individual organizations and industries are developing different forms of performance targets (see, for example, Figure 8.3), their integration with the traditional accounting systems is still rare.

---

[1] In the UK, Business-in-the-Environment and ACBE have both recognized the importance of the issues and the paucity of guidance available and are attempting, at the time of writing, to set up experimental projects in the area.

Figure 8.2

The Ciba-Geigy approach to environmental protection

Ciba-Geigy, widely considered to be an environmentally advanced company, has established the sort of 'multi-tiered, multi-stranded' approach which may be the only realistic response to environmental pressures without a fully developed environmental accounting and financial system. Such a system will *force* the accounting system to respond to the changing corporate emphasis. It runs through every facet of the company and consists of:

* corporate principles;
* corporate guidelines;
* central technical function;
* environmental officers;
* policy co-ordination;
* auditing.

Source: Adapted from *ENDS Report* 177/October 1989, pp. 16–18.

Figure 8.3

Voluntary performance indicators adopted by the UK chemical industry

Health and Safety
* fatalities;
* non-fatal major accidents;
* diseases;
* accidents in relation to man-hours.

Environment
* amount of 'special waste';
* discharges of 'red list' substances;
* site-specific data expressed in an 'environmental index'.

Distribution
* number of transport incidents in relation to million tonne miles.

Energy
* energy consumption per tonne of product.

Complaints
* number of complaints made by public and regulators.

Source: Adapted from *KPMG European Environment Briefing Note*, Winter 1991/2, p. 11.

In such circumstances without integration, the traditional performance criteria can always be expected to dominate. Indeed, one survey[2] found that while the accounting system might often identify – and, indeed, emphasize – the costs associated with environmental

---

[2] See Nikolai, Bazley and Brummett (1976).

initiatives, there was no corresponding emphasis on the benefits (environmental, financial or otherwise). This has the obvious effect of discouraging rather than encouraging environmental projects, performance and initiatives.

In this chapter we will briefly review the accounting and financial implications associated with embedding more fundamental environmental change into an organization. The focus will be upon a number of the functional areas in which accounting is highly involved – most especially investment and investment appraisal – but we shall also touch briefly upon performance appraisal, budgeting and R&D. The experience in this area and the information on this experience which companies are willing to release, as we have said, is still somewhat sketchy. So, in the rare situations where 'best practice' exists, experience of operating that practice is usually in short supply. Once again, until experimentation is more widespread, guidance will contain a large measure of speculation.

8.2   Investment Spending

Environmental pressures are forcing up corporate spending – and especially investment spending. The ICC estimated that corporate environmental spending was around 2.1 per cent of sales in 1991 and expected to rise to 3.3 per cent by the year 2000 – an increase of around 50 per cent. For the chemicals industry as well as for other 'frontline' industries such as food and metal manufacturing, the figures will be much greater. And these are estimates based only on current anticipated environmental demands. Of particular relevance, nearly half of these expenditures[3] were for capital items.

However, there is a potential conflict in the story coming from industry on this matter. On the one hand, it is clear that costs of environmental protection will rise as 'the additional cost of doing business' which is unlikely 'to diminish in future years'.[4] On the other hand, the dominant message from and to industry is that environmental protection and, in particular, environmental investment bring financial benefits to the organization. For example, controlling pollution costs in the quarrying and cement and in the paper and pulp industries is reported as saving at least 7 per cent of gross costs.[5] Indeed Coopers and Lybrand report[6] that initial experiments conducted under the Business-in-the-Environment initiative were showing rapid financial returns in savings in packag-

---

[3] At least expenditures classified as 'pollution control'. For more detail see *ENDS Report* 180/January 1990, pp. 6–7, the report by Mary Fagan, *Independent*, 13 April 1991, p. 17, and Thompson (1991).

[4] Clive Thompson (1991).

[5] *Industry costs of pollution control*, EcoTec, Birmingham, 1991.

[6] Coopers & Lybrand, Deloitte *Industry Briefing* February 1992.

Figure 8.4

The CBI's checklist of areas of environmental importance (with financial consequences)

- Procurement, preparation & transport of raw materials;
- All manufacturing processes;
- Maintenance, efficiency and replacement;
- Use of products and one's products in use;
- Disposal of waste;
- Recycling of used products and packaging;
- Research and development;
- Planning of product or output;
- Design of manufacturing;
- Design of residuals and re-use of products;
- Design of central waste-handling facilities;
- Design of a system to minimize waste;
- Development and planning controls;
- Local building controls;
- Aesthetic elements in design and layout;
- Local emission and effluent control;
- Quality control and product liability;
- Control of storage;
- Decommissioning and abandonment.

Source: Adapted from *Clean up – It's good business* (London: CBI) 1986

---

ing, fuel and water supply costs, while environmentally driven investments of amounts varying from £16,000 to £200,000 ($25,600 to $320,000) were showing paybacks anywhere between eighteen days and two years. So, although costs are rising as a result of environmental pressures, there are significant benefits to be obtained. Naturally enough, these benefits cannot be achieved by all organizations:

> *Although there are many other pressures at the moment on businesses of all sizes, those companies which take the trouble to investigate their environmental performance, and then start to make improvements, will gain a significant long-term advantage over their less-aware competitors. Businesses which are slow off the mark are likely to find it increasingly difficult to market their products, dispose of waste, obtain insurance, attract finance, keep within a new and much enhanced legal framework and recruit and retain the best staff.*
>
> (Coopers & Lybrand Deloitte, ibid, p. 7)

Of more immediate concern is why companies are not exploiting these potential advantages without prompting from organizations like Business-in-the-Environment, the CBI or the ICC. In part, it must be because there *are* so many other pressures on business that the time and energy do not seem to be available to explore the available opportunities. Recognizing that, any organization – perhaps

Figure 8.5

Criteria involved when selecting from existing technologies

* Low cost (recognizing that location affects cost)
* Low energy use (again influenced by location)
* Availability of raw materials
* Availability of external markets
* Materials balance for the site as a whole
* Cleanliness of the process (waste quantity and type, disposal opportunities)
* Opportunity (availability of the technology, recognition of the need for the technology)
* Improved labour productivity
* Safety of operation
* High material yield

Source: Adapted from Lawrence (1991)

---

using some of the suggestions from earlier on in the book (see, for example, Chapter 3) – should be able to take steps to find the time. But that is not the whole story. First, it is quite apparent that many organizations are still ignorant of the growing environmental pressures and the extent of environmentally led opportunities. Books such as this may go some way towards alleviating that. Second, the organizational structure, and in particular size in pursuit of economies of scale, may well tend to restrict imaginative initiatives by, for example, reducing staff identification with the project or simply breeding slower, more tiring bureaucratic processes.[7] Third, evaluating the BAT element of BATNEEC (Best Available Techniques Not Entailing Excessive Cost) is not a simple matter (See Figure 8.5). And fourth, as we have discussed, the accounting and financial systems are making the NEEC dominate in BATNEEC.

8.3   Investment Appraisal

Just as there is no single method of evaluating investment opportunities, so can there be no single way of incorporating environmental considerations into investment decisions.[8] The traditional investment appraisal techniques – typically, discounted cash flow (DCF), payback and, more recently, contribution to profit or EPS

[7] See Davis (1991), p. 62, who is especially eloquent and persuasive on this point. The point is widely discussed in the management literature but rarely put into practice. The experiences of 3M, Volvo and others show that small can be beautiful. For more detail see, for example, Dauncey (1988), Hutchinson (1991).

[8] Investment, in this context, is intended widely, to include not only new capital investment and projects and processes but also R&D as well as land and new businesses (with the potential remediation and other liability issues).

Figure 8.6

An environmental investment checklist

Do you take account of environmental requirements and implications in all areas of budgeting and investment? In particular:

* Have you taken account of environmental spend in your budget plan (both short and long term)?
* Do those lending money stipulate environmental requirements?
* Do you carry out a due diligence review of any site or business you may be acquiring, assessing possible financial or legal liabilities relating to environmental issues?
* Do you take account of environmental issues when considering new investment – e.g. in land, technology, new business areas? Is environmental performance one of your investment criteria?
* If you invest in other businesses, do you check or specify the environmental performance standards which they should meet?
* Do you invest in R&D into more environmentally sound processes and products?
* If you operate a company pension scheme have you considered how this money is invested? You may choose to invest only in companies which manage their environmental performance effectively.
* Have you considered sponsoring a particular environmental organization or programme?

Source: Adapted from BiE (1991a), pp. 28–9

(earnings per share) – have a very real tendency to narrow the range of issues considered and encourage short-term, less risky options. Indeed, the widely acknowledged 'short-termism' of the Western capital markets can now be seen to be driving investment through reference to EPS criteria. The freedom for environmental initiative in such circumstances is limited. 'Payback' clearly and explicitly emphasizes the short-term. Furthermore, DCF, which should encourage a longer-term perspective, tends to discourage large projects with an expected life of more than about ten years[9] and, most importantly in an environmental context, inevitably places less emphasis on events later in the project's life. Thus, for example, a conventional DCF calculation would take little account of a plant's reduced efficiency towards the end of its life (with potential increases in emissions and spills) and would, literally, discount abandonment and decommissioning costs or any other environmentally related problems (e.g. land contamination) which might then become apparent. So, in general, a longer-term *and* more environmentally sensitive attitude to investment is required (see Figure 8.6) but traditional investment appraisal discourages this.

The real irony, however, is that in a business climate changing rapidly as a result of environmental pressures (law, technology, attitudes, regulations, etc.), management *must* be seeking the

---

[9] See Elkington et al. (1991) p. 81.

shortest of returns in order to stay flexible in response to those changes and to avoid the risk of being locked into obsolete, environmentally malign technology and processes. The only investment appraisal regimes we met which seemed able to cope with this problem were in one medium and one very large company where a TQM/EQM culture discouraged conventional investment appraisal altogether. That is, quality was defined in terms of 'being the best at what we do' and incorporated a 'zero incidents' requirement in health, safety and environmental factors. The investments we discussed were of the 'Must we have it? Can we afford it? Buy it' type and appeared to be very successful in maintaining the highest economic *and* environmental standards. For other situations though, some changes to the investment regime are necessary.

An example of the most complete response to this conflict within the investment appraisal process comes from Alcan. The company says that its environmental policy – adopted in 1978 – drives all investment (and R&D, see below) expenditure. That is: capital spend is clearly strategic in nature; strategy requires actions to meet corporate policy; therefore investment must be undertaken to meet the environmental policy. This takes two forms: first, strategic, identifiably environmental, expenditure is specifically undertaken to meet legal, forthcoming and/or corporate environmental standards; and second, *all* capital spend proposals must include an environmental statement. Thus, all investments are screened to meet environmental standards (in exactly the same way as any sensible organization screens its investments for health, safety and COSHH considerations). This sort of approach is increasingly common among the larger, more environmentally aware corporations. IBM seeks to undertake EIA (see Chapter 5) on all major projects – whether required to or not – and an increasing number of organizations are requiring a detailed environmental statement with all business cases.

Two observations: first, it is perhaps surprising that in a BATNEEC/BPEO-regulated world such additional processes should either be necessary or worth making a fuss about (see Figure 8.7). It would appear that the regulatory frameworks are not biting as hard or as widely as is needed. Second, the *ex ante* control outlined above does not guarantee success. That is, the *ex post* audit and evaluation must take explicit cognizance of the environmental criteria. This is especially difficult in highly decentralized organizations. For example, Albright and Wilson's early environmental response was to set internal BATNEEC across all its sites. Managers soon learned, however, that if they failed to meet *financial* targets as opposed to environmental, BATNEEC, considerations they were penalized. This critical problem of performance assessment has bedevilled many environmental initiatives, and is considered below.

Accountants have a potentially important role to play here. First, if every investment must meet fixed, immutable, economic criteria

Figure 8.7

> ### The selection of a best practicable environment option (BPEO)
>
> 1. Define the objectives of the project.
> 2. Identify all feasible options.
> 3. Qualitative and quantitative analysis of the options' environmental impact.
> 4. Clear, objective presentation of the information relevant to the choice.
> 5. Select BPEO.
> 6. Have choice scrutinized by individuals independent of the initial choice.
> 7. Implement and monitor performance against expected/desired criteria.
> 8. Maintain an audit trail of all steps, information and individuals involved in the process for post-audit.
>
> *Source:* Cmnd 310 (1988) *Best Practicable Environment Option* Royal Commission on Environmental Pollution, (London: HMSO)

under all circumstances then environmental considerations will continue to be marginalized and included by chance rather than by choice. So often, we were told, it was the accountants who applied and maintained such criteria and thus prevented wider ones from being applied. The first step, therefore, is for the accountant to bring this issue to the board's attention and have the guidelines changed in line with environmental policy. There is not much intrinsic (as opposed to PR) value in a policy which cannot be achieved because of conflict with other, more traditional criteria.

The second step is to be more imaginative in assessing the relative merits and demerits of investment proposals. In addition to the basic screening of all investments as discussed above, a number of factors can be brought into this. These are considered in the following sections.

Costs

Assessing the costs of an investment proposal is usually the least contentious element. However, a more realistic approach to cost recognition will often make the conventional 'non-environmental' projects look less attractive. When considering 'environmental' projects, or those with a strong environmentally driven content, one must be sure to compare like with like. For example, a conventional 'non-environmental' project may well have ignored or played down factors that a more environmentally centred project would incorporate. Have all the likely regulatory costs (e.g. fines, clean-up, insurance) been included? Is there an adequate allowance for waste disposal and for remediation and abandonment costs? And are there issues which a 'non-environmental' project might legitimately ignore but which the organization will have to fund in some other way (for example, emission control or landscaping)? In addition, are there any aesthetic or environmental (non-financial) 'costs' which a 'non-environmental' project will incur? What are the ethical implications of this and, to be 'hard-nosed' about it, how will they affect the business, its image and reputation?

Benefits

Traditionally, any investment proposal will identify the income streams deriving from the project. Research into post-audit suggests that these (as well as the costs) are frequently incorrectly estimated[10] and a realistic investment proposal will test the sensitivity of the income streams. As the world becomes more environmentally aware and the regulatory framework hardens, non-environmentally sensitive income streams will grow harder to obtain, leading to either early abandonment of the project or the need to incur extra (environmental) costs to maintain them. Such recognition will help support the environmentally driven investment. Of more substance, however, are the non-financial benefits of environmental investment – or at least those benefits which either have no direct *financial* value (e.g. protection of habitat) or where the potential financial benefits are almost impossible to assess (e.g. effects on morale, image, reputation, status with the regulators, etc.). It is a short-sighted (as well as a potentially unethical) policy to ignore such benefits.

Criteria applied

Is the criterion being applied to the investment proposal the most appropriate one? We already know that conventional investment appraisal techniques encourage shorter-term projects. It is also widely accepted that criteria related to short-term accounting profit measurement are unlikely to be to the benefit of the long-term economic health of the organization. But are there other criteria, specifically related to your industry and to the particular advantages of your organization, more sympathetic to environmental matters? What organizations are striving for is a more subtle and sophisticated use of performance indicators that are either integrated, or at least in harmony, with the traditional financial indicators. (In the present climate, of course, it is the rare organization that can ignore entirely the short-term financial and accounting measurements. In the long term, if there is one, it will be the rare organization that will be permitted to let short-term financial and accounting measures dominate environmental targets – see, for example, Chapters 14 and 15.)

Possible options considered

A traditional scenario in investment appraisal involves a review of possible options and then selection from a short-list. Although this

---

[10] See e.g. Scapens and Sale (1981) and Neale (1989).

will be too 'textbook' a scenario for many organizations it does have elements of realism. What is important is whether the investment proposers *have* considered other – often more imaginative – options. This is clearly a difficult task for an organization whose staff are fully stretched and which needs a rapid decision. But everybody is learning about environmental matters and, as we saw above, creative approaches to investment can bring unexpected financial as well as environmental benefits. For example, the potential changes in energy prices offer a range of new investment possibilities – as well as potentially reducing the payback period on energy-efficient investments. We have also seen and discussed investments which became more financially *and* environmentally interesting through the application of different energy sources, softer (alternative) technology, imaginative end-of-pipe waste treatment possibilities and through looking for a site-wide input from all functional areas and specialists.

Opportunity costs

At long last it is becoming more widely recognized that there are many investments an organization cannot afford *not* to undertake. These may be strategic, they may be related to TQM, but increasingly the opportunity costs of not investing on environmentally sound criteria will be considerable. One of the best illustrations of this is the plant-closure threat. Instances of a plant being closed in the UK due to environmental transgressions are rare indeed and the extent of the transgression must usually be enormous. This is not so in many other countries where the threat of closure is real and considerable. The costs associated with closure are obviously significant. In such a regulatory climate, an investment appraisal must take account of such opportunity costs which can make the environmental investment not only more attractive but inescapable.

Time horizon

Are the time horizons employed in the investment appraisal realistic? Given the climate of environmental concern, should the organization be using longer (or shorter) horizons? Does this affect the investment judgement? It should be remembered that environmental costs are certain to carry on rising. Whilst one may be able to avoid supplier audits, clean-up costs, duty of care liability and so on for one or two years, can one realistically expect such matters to be (financially) irrelevant in three or more? The forecasting element in the investment proposal becomes a critical factor (see below).

Discount rate

Apart from the well-known problems with the discount rate in NPV calculations, discounting literally discounts the future. The whole

Figure 8.8

> **Suggestions for more environmentally sensitive investment appraisal**
>
> 1. Recognize that many environmentally driven investments will have financial pay-offs under conventional criteria.
> 2. Recognize that conventional investment appraisal criteria act *against* environmental criteria.
> 3. Environmental policy should drive strategic investments.
> 4. All investment proposals should be accompanied by the environmental case (a mini-EIA).
> 5. All investments must be screened against environmental criteria.
> 6. The accountant should speak with the board and have the relationship between the environmental policy of the organization and its investment criteria clarified.
> 7. A more imaginative approach to investment appraisal should be adopted via the 10-point checklist:

environmental debate is about the present generation's moral failure to provide for the future. Continued use of discount rates encourages that. This is a central issue in sustainability and must be addressed by all organizations seeking to be sustainable (see Chapter 14).

'Valuation of externalities'

By this we do not mean 'placing a value on nature' – an activity we oppose[11] – but recognizing that, first, taxation changes which reflect environmental matters will force organizations to internalize some of the costs that were previously external (e.g. an energy tax); and, second, there is a serious moral 'cost' in ignoring the effect of an investment's externalities on communities and on the planet. The investing organization will have to recognize the potentially changing price structures *as well as* the significant ethical choice that is made in ignoring the consequences of actions.

Sustainable costs

Chapter 14 will introduce this notion in more detail but the basic idea is that we might consider that each organization, each cost centre, each investment, should be required to leave the biosphere no worse off at the end of each accounting period. An investment proposal which incorporated the costs of repairing damage to the biosphere[12] might look a very different financial proposition.

---

[11] See, for example, Gray (1992).

[12] Recognizing that a great deal of the damage to the biosphere is irreparable and therefore the costs of repair are infinite.

Figure 8.9

10-Point checklist for more environmentally-sensitive investment appraisal

1. Environmentally screen all investments.
2. Reconsider costs.
3. Reconsider benefits.
4. Reconsider the criteria applied.
5. Reconsider the possible options considered.
6. Consider the opportunity costs.
7. Reconsider the time horizon.
8. Reconsider the discount rate.
9. Consider the 'valuation of externalities'.
10. Consider sustainable costs.

Even this brief analysis indicates that there is clearly a long way to go before investment appraisal can fully incorporate environmental criteria. The experience of companies and other organizations is that attempting to do so is a slow and painful process which runs counter to the culture and values that management have strived so hard to acquire. In many regards, it will seem very frustrating indeed for a sprinter to be tapped on the shoulder and told that he or she should really be (what must look like) leapfrogging backwards. The suggestions here may assist accountants to begin to help their organizations through this painful but brutally essential transition.

8.4   Performance Appraisal

As we saw above, all the environmental *ex ante* control in the world will be useless unless the *ex post* control also reflects environmental criteria. In a closely related context the following observation sums up a dilemma well known throughout management accounting[13]:

> *When managers see that their execution of socially responsible policies and programs is evaluated in promotion and compensation decisions, along with performance in meeting familiar profit, cost and productivity goals, they will believe and they will be motivated. For obvious and valid reasons middle managers concentrate their attention and skill on the accomplishment of performance objectives for which they know they are held responsible. They appraise responsibility in terms of two familiar criteria. The first is what is measured and the second is what is rewarded.*
>
> (Ashen (1980) quoted in Chechile and Carlisle (1991), p. 254)

---

[13] See e.g. Prakash and Rappaport (1977).

So, not only must the environmental criteria be seen to be explicitly recognized in post-evaluation but they must also be part of the reward system. In the UK, whilst there are now moves in this direction, few appraisal and reward systems we encountered paid more than lip-service to this principle. Perhaps it is early days yet. However, those companies (in the UK and elsewhere) which had embedded environmental criteria into the performance appraisal process suffered severe teething problems until the organizational culture swung sufficiently behind the principles. The essence of the problem was predictable: what happens when financial and environmental criteria conflict? There is no simple solution to this but explicit incorporation into the reward system appears to be the most effective. By contrast, three organizations we visited made no reference to environmental criteria in appraisal and reward systems and, when conflict was faced, the traditional financial measures always dominated the environmental.

As with the investment appraisal considerations, there are both environmentally ethical and financial reasons for paying special attention to this area. Having raised environmental expectations, a reward system which then encourages environmentally malign behaviour is both unethical and extremely bad for morale. As with staff attraction and retention so with motivation – an environmentally malign organization which does not fulfil its promises to its staff cannot expect much loyalty or motivation. This has obvious ethical implications and it is also quite apparent that a demotivated workforce will be less cost effective and innovative – with the obvious financial implications.

8.5 R&D and Design

Alcan's experience is that, if the environmental policy is to have any real significance, it must drive not only the investment policy, but also the R&D effort and, ultimately product and process design. This clearly makes strategic sense[14] but the short-term pressures on business plus accountants' traditional evaluation criteria have generally tended to discourage R&D, design and innovation initiatives.[15] And the matters are not trivial. Alan Hayes, Chairman of ICI Agrochemicals, is reported as estimating that the green issue has added 10–15 per cent to the cost of developing a new compound. He says: 'I regret that this has been done at the expense of fundamental work' and when a new molecule in the agrochemical industry can take up to thirteen years to develop and patents last for only

[14] See, for example, Nixon (1991).

[15] See, for example, Nixon & Lonie (1990), Gray, (1986).

Figure 8.10

Some environmentally related design desiderata
• Minimum resource use in production and end-use • Minimum waste in production and in end-use • Minimum emissions and discharges from production and in end-use • Minimum use of packaging and transport • Recyclability of product and of production residues • Disassembly at end of use • Repairability of product in use • Longer life of process and product (noting the conflict here with responsiveness to the changing green agenda).

sixteen, business has some hard rethinking to do – or the framework in which business operates needs amending.[16]

It is quite clear that R&D falls into the class of things that business cannot afford *not* to do. This is equally true for environmentally related R&D,[17] which will determine whether an organization has the products, processes and services the markets want – and which society will permit – in the near future. The 'D' of R&D closely and inevitably links with design considerations. We have already touched upon the design issues related to packaging and other waste (see Chapter 7) and it is quite apparent that design will increasingly have to incorporate a wider range of environmentally related considerations (see Figure 8.10). Indeed, US corporations are increasingly making explicit the way in which both competition and regulation are driving developments in design for environment (DFE).[18] Techniques such as EPS (environment priority strategies) in product design (closely related to life-cycle assessment – see Chapter 9) are emerging and being developed to assist organizations with these difficulties.[19]

For the accounting and financial systems the considerations are largely the same as for investment and performance appraisal (see above). In particular, accountants must guard against any tendency for the workings of their systems to prevent environmental initiatives. Strategic concerns must dominate and to the extent that the accountant is fully involved in that process in a positive and productive way accounting will be serving its paymasters adequately.

[16] See the report by Theobald in *Management Today*, March 1990, p. 63.

[17] For more detail see Davis (1991), pp. 110–12 and Winter (1988), pp. 131–3, who provides a useful checklist for product development. Elkington, Knight and Hailes (1991), chapter 8 is especially helpful here.

[18] *Business and the Environment*, July 1992 Vol. 3 no. 8 pp. 2–4.

[19] See, for example, Ryding (1991).

We have not yet found, nor have we any particular suggestions for, accounting and financial systems working in a proactive fashion to aid environmentally benign R&D and design.

8.6 Budgeting and Forecasting

It is apparent that a considerable element of an organization's response to the environmental agenda depends upon its estimate of how the environmental climate is changing and will change in both the short and long term. That estimate must then be backed up by financial and other resources. This inevitably involves forecasting and budgeting. Apart from the basic bookkeeping and costing activities of accounting, the accountant's role involves constant forecasting (although often implicitly). Everything from depreciation policy, stock valuation and the calculation of debtors provisions through to the processes of budgeting and setting (and evaluating) performance targets involves a forecast of future conditions. We have already seen aspects of the way in which environmental issues will influence forecasting in, for example, investment and performance appraisal, waste and energy management and environmental auditing; similarly, the organization's management of its external relations (see Part C) depends to a great extent on how the company expects environmental issues to affect and be perceived by

Figure 8.11

Some environmental factors that will be reflected in an organization's budget

- Environmental capital spending
- Allowance for trade-off between environmental and financial criteria in investment and project appraisal
- Provision for EIAs and environmental business cases
- Provision for bringing all sites up to best practice standards
- Provision for design of new information systems
- Spending on waste management and disposal
- Spending on energy
- Packaging and returnable containers
- Spending on environmental review
- Costs associated with environmental purchasing policy and supplier audits
- Landscaping, remediation, decommissioning, abandonment costs
- Recognition of the associated contingent liabilities
- Provision for emergency and spillage procedures
- Provision for fines, insurance and other legally related costs
- Provision for specialist review and advice
- Provision for (temporary) plant closure
- Transport spending
- Environmental projects whether on-site, in-house, or in conjunction with external groups

its external constituents. Environmental factors must now become an explicit and central part of all organizational forecasting. We have seen that this will affect the accountant in many ways – but the most important will probably be through the budgeting process (see Figure 8.11). At its most basic, this is no more than an extension of conventional budgeting practice – slightly redesigned to make explicit a 'new' business issue. However, our survey (see Appendix C) suggested that less than 15 per cent of accountants in large UK companies had any explicitly environmental factors built into the budgeting process and only a further 4 per cent had any plans to do so. Major steps need to be taken by the accounting and financial functions in this area if organizations are to be able to respond sensibly to the environmental pressures.

8.7   Conclusions

The companies which are leading the world in the development of more environmentally sensitive systems and modes of operation are themselves discovering that going further than a 'light green' gloss is difficult indeed. But they also recognize that go further they must. One major indicator of progress – and, if absent, in preventing further development – is the extent to which the accounting and financial systems incorporate environmental criteria. Those systems which lie at the heart of the organization – the budgeting and investment and performance appraisal systems, for example – have remained largely untouched by the changing environmental agenda. Until they do develop in this way, organizations will face conflicts between environmental and conventional financial factors – and in those circumstances the financial will always win over the environmental.

Further Reading

Chechile, R. A. and Carlisle, S. (eds) (1991) *Environmental Decision Making: A Multidisciplinary Perspective*, Van Nostrand Reinhold, New York.
Davis, J. (1991) *Greening Business*, Blackwell, Oxford.
Elkington, J., Knight, P. and Hailes, J. (1991) *The Green Business Guide*, Gollancz, London.
Owen, D. (1992) *Green Reporting: Accountancy and the Challenge of the Nineties*, Chapman & Hall, London.
Winter, G. (1988) *Business and the Environment*, McGraw-Hill, Hamburg.

9. Life Cycle Analysis and Assessment

9.1 Introduction

Life cycle assessment (LCA), although it has been in existence for a couple of decades, sprang to prominence in the 1990s as the potential Holy Grail of environmental decision-making. Its aims and claims were not modest:

> *LCA is an* objective *process used to evaluate the environmental burdens associated with a product, process or activity. This is accomplished by identifying and quantifying energy and material usage and environmental releases. The data are then used to assess the impact of those energy and material releases on the environment, and to evaluate and implement opportunities to achieve environmental improvements. The LCA includes* the *entire lifecycle of the product, process or activity, encompassing: extracting and processing of raw materials; manufacturing, transportation and distribution; use/re-use/maintenance; recycling; and final disposal.*
> (Fava, 1991, p. 19, emphasis added)

It is essential to recognize from the outset that life cycle analysis/ assessment – under whatever name it appears[1] – is no magic wand; is usually driven by the goals of the organization conducting it and will not automatically mean an improvement in environmental performance unless conducted with that goal explicitly in mind; and it is, in effect, no more than functional application of systems theory and systems thinking.[2] Nevertheless, the prominence of LCA

---

[1] In addition to the variations of life cycle 'analysis' and 'assessment', other names meaning the same or similar things include: cradle to grave analysis/assessment; eco-balance assessment; resource analysis; environmental impact assessment (noting the potential for confusion with EIA; see Chapter 5).

[2] See Chapter 1, which contains some references as an introduction to systems theory and systems thinking. It should be noted that LCA also bears more than a passing relationship to the approach to environmental review discussed in Chapter 5.

Figure 9.1   A simplified LCA for a pencil (with other LCA interconnections)

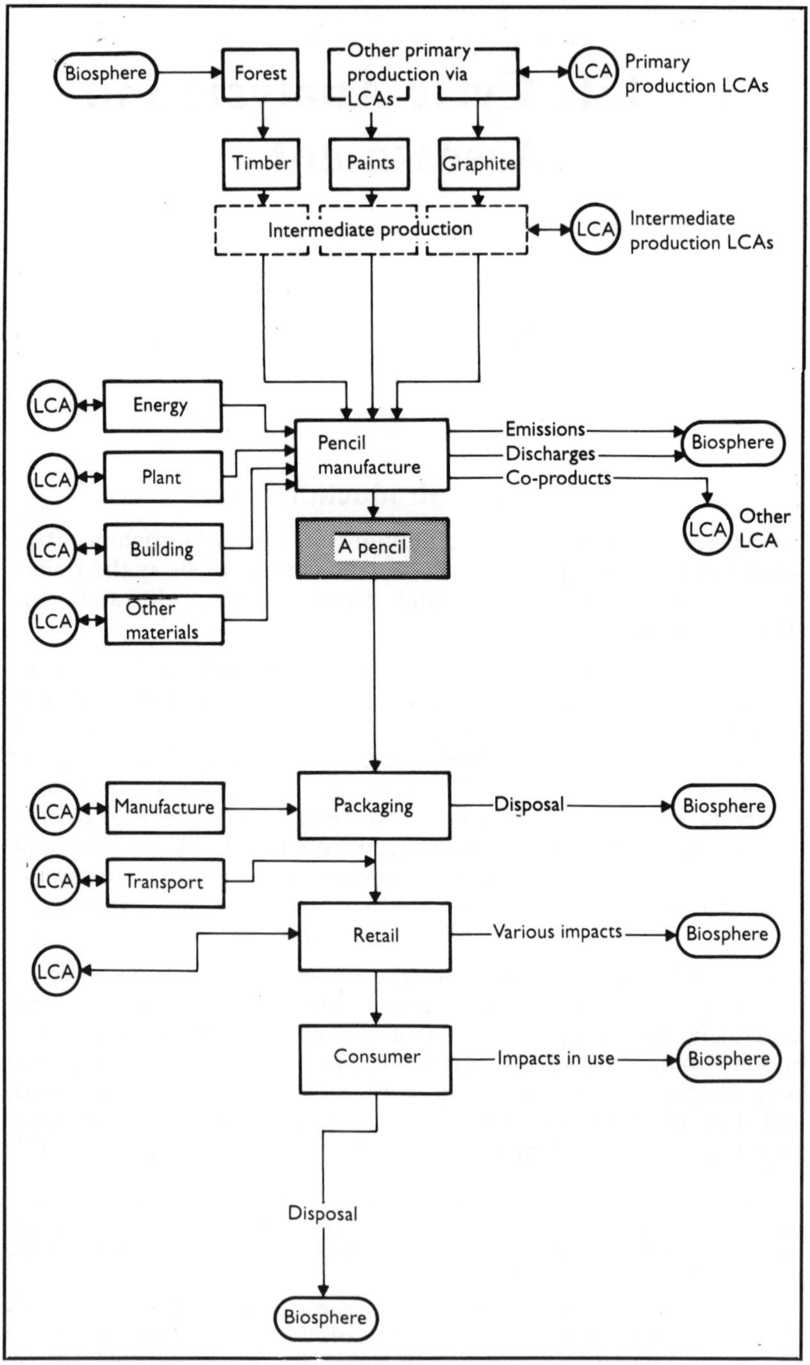

means that we could not ignore it and, *as a process*, it has considerable value. Even if it only leads one to the conclusion that there can be no such thing as an 'environmentally friendly company', LCA does encourage an explicit acknowledgement and recognition of the full life cycle of any product or activity and this is a major contribution.

9.2 Considering the Life Cycle

The principle of considering the life cycle of any activity is essentially elementary. For illustration, consider a particularly simple product like a pencil. Without knowing anything of the technical issues involved in the production of pencils we can illustrate the scope of an LCA. (The addition of technical knowledge will improve the LCA – and increase the complexity – whilst more complex products will produce more complex life cycles.)

One starts from the product itself – the pencil – and then traces the life cycle forwards and backwards. An initial outline of the life cycle of the pencil is shown in Figure 9.1. A number of immediate observations are possible:

(1) One must trace all raw materials (wood, graphite, paints, etc.) back, through earlier production phases, to extraction from the biosphere and recognize: (a) the ecological effects of that extraction (e.g. impact on forest habitat, oxygen/carbon dioxide balance, etc.); (b) the energy used in the extraction and transportation; and (c) the energy, machines, etc. which were used to produce the means of extraction.
(2) The same process must be undertaken for all intermediate production processes.
(3) One must trace the product forward to its packaging (and *its* manufacture and disposal), transport and eventual use in the hands of the consumer.
(4) The product must then be traced to the biospheric interactions it has in use and in disposal.
(5) All inputs and outputs from each stage in the life cycle must be captured.

What becomes apparent is that, first, any life cycle will interrelate with many other life cycles (e.g. the paint manufacturers, the plant and machinery manufacturers, etc.) and potentially arbitrary lines will have to be drawn around systems of life cycles – the *LCA system must be bounded*; and, second, each LCA will involve an *infinite regress* – the wood came from a tree; the tree housed insects, was an essential element of the local soil ecology and played its part in oxygen/carbon dioxide balance; this affects bird life, the growth in the soil and global warming which in turn affects . . . and so on.

Thus, the life cycle of any product is inevitably exceptionally complicated and so no LCA *can* be complete and comprehensive. It

Figure 9.2 An overview of LCA

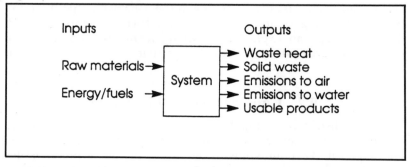

Figure 9.3

Summary of the three stages in LCA methodology

Life Cycle Inventory   Review of the product, identification and description of all resources, emissions, discharges and disposals throughout the cradle to grave of the product.

Life Cycle Impact Analysis   Identification, possible quantification and assessment of the human and other ecological impacts of the elements identified in the inventory stage.

Life Cycle Improvement Analysis   Attempts to reduce, ameliorate or eliminate the impacts identified through various means including redesign of products and processes.

is unlikely to catch the majority of the biosphere–product interactions and, as a result, it will rarely have much claim to objectivity. With this in mind we can consider the stages in LCA.

9.3   The Methodology of LCA

The overall view of LCA is summarized in Figure 9.2, which clearly echoes the environmental review of Chapter 5. LCA is then seen as having three major stages, shown in Figure 9.3, and these are popularly summarized using Figure 9.4. The stages are relatively self-explanatory (although that is not to suggest that they are in any way simple or uncontroversial).

Life cycle inventory is usually guided by the stages shown in Figure 9.5 and it should be noted that, already, the system has been very closely bounded to exclude the infinite regress and the more troublesome ecological interactions such as habitat. The results from this phase are then collated into an assessment matrix which forms the basis for the life cycle impact analysis. (An example of a matrix is shown in Figure 9.6, which is taken from the EC eco-label process with which LCA bears a close relationship – see also Chapter 14.)

Figure 9.4 The popular form of summarizing the three stages in LCA methodology

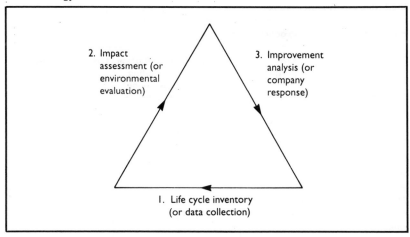

Figure 9.5 LCA inventory analysis: a simplified framework

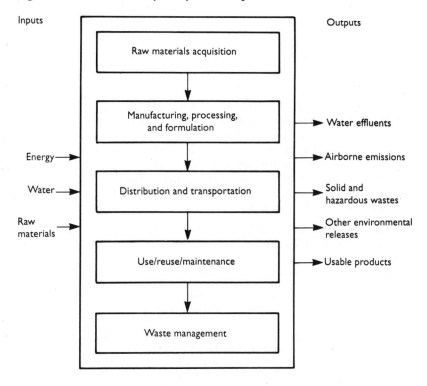

Source: Blumenfeld, Earle and Shopley, in *Prism*, 3rd Quarter (1991), p. 50.

Figure 9.6 Summarizing the LCA inventory for impact assessment

Indicative assessment matrix					
Environmental fields	**Product life cycle**				
	Pre-production	**Production**	**Distribution (including packaging)**	**Utilization**	**Disposal**
Waste relevance					
Soil pollution and degradation					
Water contamination					
Air contamination					
Noise					
Consumption of energy					
Consumption of natural resources					
Effects on eco-systems					

Source: Annex 1, *Official Journal of the European Communities*, No. L 99/6 (11.4.92).

The matrix is completed,[3] first, by simply identifying those cells in the matrix which are considered relevant and then attempting some quantitative or qualitative description of the impacts.[4] This is, obviously a far from simple task. There are usually widely divergent views as to the impact of various elements and these different viewpoints are often strongly held. Therefore, the results are often controversial.[5] Landbank Consultancy Ltd's approach to this task has been to assemble

> *independent panels of scientific and environmental experts . . . whose task it will be to make informed and authoritative judgements about each of the*

[3] Each environmental medium where impact is felt should be further divided; for example, air contamination may involve a number of different pollutants – CO_2, NO_x, SO_2, NH_3, etc. Energy consumption may be further divided into source of production – non-renewable, renewable or internally generated (for example, by the incineration of wastes).

[4] The use of a quantitative method results in a table of what are sometimes called eco-balances. Within this context the word eco-balances refers to a product's energy and material inputs and its impact in use and disposal. In other contexts the word is used to denote carrying capacity of an ecological system.

[5] See e.g. Hunt (1991) and the Procter and Gamble example discussed below.

main pollutants or environmentally damaging activities. These judgements will take the form of an environmental points system, reflecting the relative significance of each pollutant.[6]

In this way a range of 'expert' opinion is obtained and 'averaged'. An alternative, but related (and far simpler) approach is to take a series of focused impacts and assess those by reference to specific tests. The Rhône-Poulenc and CIA 'environmental index' is of this sort (see Chapter 5).

In life cycle improvement analysis, the final step of LCA, the information gathered at the two earlier stages is assimilated into the redesign of systems to improve the environmental performance of products. The previous information should provide a prioritized list of goals for environmental improvement and, from this, a range of associated improvement options can be derived. Specific implementation of improvements would then follow and may involve, for example, increasing energy efficiency, reducing raw material usage, cleaner production technologies, reducing emissions, as well as recycling schemes and less packaging.[7]

There are considerable interdependencies between the three stages of LCA. For example, knowledge of the impact of the production process should drive the factors included in the life cycle inventory phase.[8] Likewise, given that LCA is a very time-consuming activity the products investigated will in part be determined by the severity of their environmental impacts – naturally, the most environmentally malign areas should be tackled first. Further, LCA should not be a static exercise but an iterative, dynamic one whose development mirrors the development in our understanding regarding the impacts of activities. Improvements in environmental impacts under LCA are likely to be incremental, with each LCA building on the next – LCA is not a one-off exercise to cure all environmental ills.

9.4   The Use of LCA

LCA is still in the development phase but companies have found it useful. Norsk Hydro has undertaken LCA of fertilizers, polymers and aluminium the results of which have been published (see

---

[6] See Carol Charlton, 'Life Cycle Assessment – making sense of environmental complexities' in *CBI Environment newsletter* No. 6/November 1991 (pp. 13/14).

[7] See also Chapter 6 on energy and Chapter 7 on waste, packaging and recycling.

[8] This is influenced by the limits set on the upstream and downstream effects. For example, the discharge of a very toxic substance in minute amounts warrants inclusion in LCA; however, the incorporation of this discharge in the life cycle inventory phase is dictated by the toxicity of the substance which is in fact determined in the life cycle impact analysis.

Figure 9.7

Some inherent limitations of LCA are:

- Bounding the system: identifying the 'cradles' and the 'graves'. It is inevitable that the system must be bounded but too often it is done far too closely.
- Identification and measurement of impacts: the correct things must be measured and the uncertainty absorption inherent in quantification treated carefully. For example, is it more appropriate to measure a volume of discharge or the toxicity of it?
- Difficulties of information: particularly the difficulty of obtaining the information and the problems of handling so much. The drinks container LCAs involved many thousands of data points which all must be collected on comparable bases.
- Scientific ignorance and uncertainty: means that all data are conditional and incomplete.
- Difficulty in prioritizing: given constraints and uncertainty – how should one identify the most immediate aspects to examine?
- Difficulties in choosing the preferred environmental/financial options.

Chapter 12);[9] BSO/Origin's 'environmental accounts' involve LCA methodology (see Chapter 12);[10] and IBM ties LCA methodology to its EIAs (see Chapter 5) in an attempt to assess the financial and environmental trade-offs in material and product use. But in each case, the system of the LCA has been very closely bounded. On a wider scale, the investigations for the development of the EC eco-labelling scheme have required LCA and demonstrated the difficulty of the analysis. The widely reported investigations of washing machines,[11] soft-drink containers,[12] glass versus aluminium recycling

[9] See, for example, Norsk Hydro UK's environmental report which provides an analysis of the environmental effects of its products at some stages of their life cycle; principally manufacture, use and disposal. Further, R. A. Willett, Chief Executive of Gateway Foodmarkets Limited, notes that Gateway 'have been applying life cycle assessment principles' in their work towards achieving their environmental goals.

[10] See BSO/Origin accounts. Even though they state this to be the case, in fact they incorporate one upstream effect, the direct environmental impact caused by power stations (see p. 11). This suggests that their limit imposed on upstream effects serves to preserve the simplicity of their analysis, rather than to prevent double counting.

[11] See an article in *Integrated Environmental Management*, No. 2/September 1991 (pp. 17–19), which looks at the UK pilot study for an eco-label for washing machines. A 'broad brush approach' to LCA was adopted to 'work through the issues rather than produce . . . [a] definitive assessment of the environmental impact of washing machines'. The study also recognized that a number of issues need to be resolved, including 'the importance of subjective judgements and the need to incorporate them into the process in a structured way; and the many competing factors which need to be balanced when setting the qualifying levels in the criteria' and, finally, recognized that these issues need to be addressed in a 'consistent and transparent way'.

[12] Franklin and Associates adopted the rule that 'the sum of all natural resource requirements and environmental effluent of all excluded processes should be no more than 5% of the total for that particular container system'. See *Integrated Environmental Management*, No. 4/November 1991 (p. 20). They also note that the danger of this rule is that important secondary or tertiary effects may be excluded.

and petrol versus diesel fuel for motor vehicles[13] have been valuable – principally as a means of identifying the complexity involved in making environmental choices.

Indeed, companies have not met with particular success when using LCA results in their advertising.[14] The Procter & Gamble (P&G) experience with LCA and disposable nappies is salutary. P&G held approximately 80 per cent of the disposable nappy market and in 1989 claimed in promotional material:

> We have carried out environmental impact assessments of products and processes for many years. Now we are developing new techniques which will help us make more complete and helpful assessments of the environmental profile of products, packaging options etc. We do these assessments 'from cradle to grave', taking account of all factors from raw material production to disposal of the end product. One early use of these new techniques has been to study the comparative environmental impact of Pampers versus traditional towelling nappies. The results showed nothing to choose between the two types of nappy in terms of overall environmental impact when all factors are taken into account (including the need to sterilise and wash towelling nappies)[15] [emphasis added].

This claim was supported by two LCAs, one by P&G itself and the other sponsored by it. The claim did not go unchallenged, with the Women's Environmental Network (WEN) and the National Association of Diaper Services (NADS) criticizing P&G's LCA, claiming that it contained errors and omissions which obscured the conclusion that reusable nappies are less damaging than disposables. These two organizations used alternative LCAs to support their criticisms; however, they differ from the P&G LCA in areas of contention over systems boundaries involving questions such as:

- Are the components of disposable nappies such as packaging and bindings, etc. relevant?
- Are cotton-growing and the manufacture of reusable nappies relevant?
- How many reusable nappies should be included per nappy change?
- What pollutants are relevant to this analysis?

Until such issues are resolved it is difficult to see how alternative LCAs will arrive at other than contradictory results.

[13] See for more information ENDS Report 205/February 1992 (pp. 13–15).

[14] ENDS Report 201/October 1991 (p. 25) reviews the claims made by Spillers Foods regarding the environmental responsibleness of its plastic and aluminium laminate can in marketing literature on the basis of LCA. The claims were found to be misleading and based on assumptions that did not hold in reality. This issue is widely recognized in the USA where initiatives are underway to try and make the process more reliable – see e.g. Business and the Environment (May 1992, Vol. 3. no. 5 p. 2).

[15] Procter and Gamble Limited Environmental Review 1990. See also Hindle (1992).

Figure 9.8

Uses of life cycle analysis

Information to external parties
- shareholders, re impact of their investments;
- consumers to assess products;
- pressure groups regarding a product's and organization's environmental impact;
- policy makers concerning environmental impacts of products;
- other interested parties, for example: ethical investors, eco-label regulatory bodies, eco-audit regulatory bodies.

Information for internal parties
- establish comprehensive baseline information on a product's overall resource requirements and emissions;
- help determine priorities for environmental care action;
- provide managers with information to set targets and measure environment-related performance;
- guide product development;
- provide a basis for advertising claims and public relations exercises;
- BS7750;
- as part of the supplier audit process;
- aid in the selection of the 'best' practical environmental operation (BPEO).

Adapted from SETAC *A Technical Framework for Life-cycle Assessments* (1991).

A further point illustrates the particular problem of defining the limits of LCA. P&G obtains the majority of the wood pulp for Pampers from Sweden, and its supplier, Stora, is embroiled in legal battle with the last indigenous people of Europe, the Sami, over land use rights.[16] The following quotations, from the two sides of the controversy illustrate how far apart the parties are, expressed in the context of LCA.

> *How can a product be ethically or environmentally sound if it's displacing indigenous peoples from their traditional lands for the sake of continued profits? Surely this sort of impact must be considered in the life cycle analysis of Pampers.*[17]

> *Stora do supply us with the pulp fluff for the Pampers range but we were not aware of the legal action to which you refer. Our life cycle analysis would not take this sort of action by our suppliers into account because it is not the kind of area you can define in life cycle analysis. The boundaries only stretch to the logging process.*[18]

While P&G's experience provides a caution for the use of LCA in making advertising claims, it raises more serious questions about the

[16] See *Green Magazine*, December 1991 (pp. 11–15) for more details of the issue.

[17] Bernadette Vallely, Director of WEN. See *Green Magazine* December 1991 (p. 12).

[18] David Hammon, P&G's environmental affairs manager, see *Green Magazine* December 1991 (p. 12).

Figure 9.9   Accountants and LCA

LCA Checklist for accountants	Accountants' involvement
Pre-LCA	
• establish goals of LCA	
• identify constraints to LCA (time, cost, etc.)	✓
LCA – Inventory	
• determine extent of products' effects (upstream and downstream)	
• define limits of analysis and assumptions	
• design systems to gather relevant information	✓
• gather information	
• audit information collected	✓
LCA – Impact analysis	
• define impacts to be considered	
• determine risk assessment to be adopted	
• convert LCA inventory items into relevant impacts	
• audit impact information	✓
• assess impacts	
LCA – Improvement analysis	
• establish budget available	✓
• establish environmental priorities	
• identify areas where significant improvements exist	
• canvass alternatives	
• cost and assess alternatives	✓
• implement improvements	
• monitor results of improvements and react where necessary	
• audit outcomes	✓
Post-LCA	
• assess goal achievement	✓
• make information available to a wider consistency	✓
• make new goals	

validity of conclusions drawn from LCAs in general. It would seem that at present LCA has not evolved to the stage of being reliable, and much work needs to be done to develop it; indeed because of the subjective judgements that are inherent in the process it may never provide the type of information required for many of the possible uses proposed (see Figure 9.8).

9.5   A Role for Accountants?

Whilst LCA has been, predominantly, the domain of scientific and technical expertise, the principles of the process can be easily understood – and contributed to – by management and others with a business systems perspective. This clearly applies to accountants, whose skills and experience in evidence collection and evaluation, systems design and evaluation, and audit have a potentially important role to play in the development of LCA. Furthermore, whilst the environmental options may be seen as technical issues, the financial implications of existing activities and potential options are clearly the domain of the accountant and an essential practical step in the life cycle improvement analysis (see Chapter 8).

Our own survey (see Appendix C) suggested while almost 30 per cent of large UK companies employ some form of LCA, virtually no accountants were involved in the process itself. Figure 9.9 is therefore provided as a potential guide for accountants.

9.6 Conclusions

Accountants should really know better than anyone the dangers of accepting the claims of a technique and, even more so, accepting numbers and answers that come from little-understood techniques. LCA is an essentially simple and sensible process but one which cannot fulfil its claims and aims. Like budgeting and cost–benefit analysis, the principal benefit lies in the process of undertaking the exercise rather than in believing the answers that come out of that process. The final word perhaps should be left to Dennis Postlethwaite, Unilever scientist and member of SETAC's Europe's LCA task force: 'The more you know about LCA the more cautious you become... To say "my product is better than yours" is a little dangerous. In Scandinavia six studies on milk containers have been published, all of which come to different conclusions.'[19]

Further Reading

Society of Environmental Toxicology and Chemistry (SETAC) (1991) *A Technical Framework for Lifecycle Assessments*, SETAC, London.

Department of the Environment (1991) *Giving Guidance to the Green Consumer – Progress on an Eco-labelling Scheme for the UK*, a report by the National Advisory Group on Eco-labelling, DoE, London.

Boustead, I. and Hancock, G. F. (1981) *Energy and Packaging*, Ellis Horwood, London.

Blumenfeld, K., Earle, R. and Shopley, J. B. (1991) Identifying strategic environmental opportunities: a life cycle approach, *Prism*, 3rd Quarter, pp. 45–57.

See also *ENDS Report* and *Integrated Environmental Management*, which carry regular pieces and updates on LCA.

[19] See *ENDS Report* 198/July 1991 (p. 24). These comments are supported by other experts in the field.

PART C

EXTERNAL RELATIONS

Part C: External Relations – an Overview

by Martin Houldin, KPMG, National Environment Unit

We started by saying that accountants have a role to play in environmental management because of the potential business implications of environmental issues. For example, the contamination of land will affect assets and liabilities, as well as incurring cost through possible breach of consents and/or the requirement to clean up. Also, we have suggested that companies can benefit financially either through opportunities to increase market share and/or market new products, or through greater cost efficiency in areas such as waste treatment and disposal. Clearly, these are subjects that should be of direct interest to accountants.

The accountant's role may therefore depend on his or her responsibilities, take a number of forms, ranging from being involved in environmental audits through the internal audit programme, to appraising investment proposals with an eye to the environmental benefits, to the analysis of waste and energy costs in order to encourage their reduction, and to the provision of information to support environmental management.

There are two other key areas that need attention from accountants, particularly those in senior positions: the interest in environmental issues from the financial services sector; and the trend towards more corporate environmental reporting. Both are currently leading to quite a lot of activity with some major companies.

Financial Services

Relationships with different parts of the financial services sector are important to all companies. Here we are talking about banks and other commercial lenders, insurance companies, fund managers and investment companies (such as merchant banks, venture capitalists). We need to cover each of these, although all have a broadly common interest in how environmental issues will affect the company's financial position.

Banks are interested both from the point of view of their credit risk and any potential liability falling to them. Risk is primarily a question of whether the assets are worth enough to provide adequate collateral, and whether the business is a going concern. Two important environmental issues have a direct effect on these aspects. First, the need to meet higher regulatory standards will require investment in plant and equipment, and possible write-off of existing plant. This, as well as the possibility of markets being affected, is a key going-concern issue. Second, potentially contaminated land can lead at best to asset devaluation and at worst to major clear-up operations and liability for other damage caused (this could lead to annual charges).

Banks are therefore looking at the effect of environmental issues on a business, and questioning whether land assets provide adequate security in existing loan agreements. Clearly, these issues are equally important for new business. Banks and any lender must also face the prospect of the liability for damage being passed to them in the event of liquidation and foreclosure.

Insurance companies are also involved in risk but from a different perspective. There is perhaps more focus on the possibility of major contamination or pollution incidents, especially those which could affect human health. General insurance cover is now almost completely unavailable, and companies need to seek specific environmental cover. Where this can be obtained, the cost will be high and companies will need to meet stringent standards before insurers will grant it.

All investors will be interested in these questions of going concern, risk and potential liability. Fund managers, with their eyes more on share price and profit forecasts, are beginning to raise detailed and searching questions about the financial implications of environmental issues, whether revenue or cost. Companies are still finding it difficult to answer these questions, partly because plans are not yet in place (but perhaps should be) and partly because their financial systems are not geared up to providing this kind of analysis. They will need to be in the not-too-distant future.

Investment companies which aim to acquire a major equity stake are taking steps to ensure that all these issues have been thoroughly investigated and provided for where necessary. Of particular interest to them is the extent to which the company's management have adequate procedures and systems for managing environmental risk and performance. These are therefore issues for senior accountants in the company seeking finance.

Merchant banks advising companies involved in mergers and acquisitions, management buy-outs and similar transactions are now advising their clients on the appropriate due diligence steps to take prior to completing the transaction at a given price. Accountants on both sides of these corporate transactions will need to be involved and on top of the issues.

Companies in all these financial services sectors are already actively involved with addressing each of these issues. Whether they call them credit reviews, risk management assessments, investigations, valuations, or due diligence reviews – they are essentially dealing with the same set of questions. Senior accountants need to be prepared to tackle these issues, and may see the benefits of planning ahead.

Disclosure in accounts
will fall into a number of areas:

* contingent liabilities
* extraordinary or exceptional charges against profit
* operating and financial review comments
* profit and capital expenditure forecast for shareholders' circular.

External Reporting

We are witnessing significant growth in the extent of external reporting of environmental performance and/or attributes. This Part deals, quite rightly, with the questions concerning how environmental issues will affect the financial reporting aspects of the annual reports as well as with the reporting on non-financial information.

While we are unlikely to see much in the way of introduction of specific environmental disclosure requirements outside North America, existing Accounting Standards, together with current Exposure Drafts, are considered adequate for the short term. The European Commission's interest in public access to information may, however, change this in the longer term. Meanwhile it is becoming a more important issue for accountants.

Non-financial reporting, in the shape of separate sections in the annual report, or in special environmental reports, is very much on the increase. There is tremendous variety, however, starting with a simple statement of intent or mission (which could barely be termed a policy), to full statements of policy and objectives, and moving towards (in stages) reports on performance with statistical back-up. The direction of developments in this field is undoubtedly to report on performance and achievement rather than intent.

What role there is for accountants remains to be seen, and perhaps depends on different company situations. Accountants will, however, need to be alert to any financial information contained in the environmental sections, and to ensure consistency. And the stick is that if companies do not voluntarily disclose environmental information, external parties – the 'social audits' – will.

There is no doubt that there are many external issues in which accountants need not only to become involved but, in some cases, to play a leading role. It is true that at the time of going to press, the external relationships, and their implications for accounting and financial information, are *probably the more important, and certainly more visible* where there is most activity.

10. The Greening of Finance:

Bank Lending, Insurance and Ethical/Environmental Investment

10.1 Introduction

As with the supply and purchase of goods and services (see Chapters 3, 6 and 7), the supply and purchase of funds are also influenced by the developing environmental agenda. For the banks, there is increasing concern over the security of loans and the potential for lender liability, for insurers increasing concern over what is and is not commercially insurable, and, for the investment community, there is increasing evidence both of a concern to exercise some environmental criteria in decisions to buy shares and of environmental criteria playing a crucial part in mergers, acquisitions and management buy-outs.[1] The implications for companies and other organizations are considerable. Not only are there the problems of (*inter alia*) an increasingly restrictive short-termism and difficulties in attracting funds for environmental initiatives which may not offer conventionally attractive rates of return (see Chapter 8) but such funds as can be attracted are more and more likely to have demanding environmental conditions attached. Broadly speaking, in addition to having to meet increasing environmental standards and struggling to persuade financiers to take a broader view of environmental initiatives, enterprises are being faced with two further – and somewhat different – sets of pressures. First, there is the purely commercial pressure from banks and insurers concerned about their own exposures and, second, there is a growing awareness among investors of the importance of ethical and environmental matters – a development led by the major green investment funds. The whole pattern of funding to and from enterprises is in the process of changing.

---

[1] This is also touched upon in Chapter 11.

This chapter will attempt to provide a brief introduction to these issues. We will begin with a résumé of the issues facing lenders and borrowers. This will raise further questions about insurance issues. The bulk of the chapter will then review the experiences of the developing and increasingly important ethical/environmental investment funds.

10.2   Bank Lending and Environmental Liability

A report in 1992[2] outlined the serious difficulties a number of established businesses were having in persuading banks to grant loan finance – due not to doubts about the core business or normal business exposure risk but to environmental considerations. The banks eventually granted the loans but the costs to the enterprises – in environmental audits and legal costs, for example – significantly increased the price of the finance.

From the banks' point of view the problem has three elements.

(1) Is the business to which the bank is lending likely to find itself involved in serious environmental problems which will increase its costs and make its servicing of the loan problematic?
(2) If the business goes into liquidation and the bank becomes the owner of the property of the company (actual or *de facto*) what are the possibilities of environmental liabilities attaching to that property – especially land – for which the bank will be liable?
(3) Can the 'polluter pays' principle require the bank – as *business associate* – to take part in any business clean-up costs – even if the business is not in liquidation and the bank has not foreclosed?

The issue first emerged in North America over the clean-up of contaminated land. Under the 'Superfund' legislation (see Chapter 11) organizations owning contaminated land could be held liable for it being cleaned up – a potentially massive liability. Banks whose loans were secured on such land began to find themselves the owners of significant liabilities: the US environmental authorities could come after them for the clean-up costs. This extended to Canada and has also gone beyond contaminated land to such things as hazardous products, toxic spills and failures to comply with environmental legislation. The development of EC legislation on contaminated land, on civil liability caused by waste and the polluter pays principle have moved the issues into Europe.[3]

At a minimum, such developments are encouraging lenders to

---

[2] David Lascelles, Only clean and green borrowers need apply, *Financial Times*, 27 March 1992, p. 19.

[3] See Chapter 11 for more detail on this and references which develop the ideas. For an introduction to the banking view see, for example, Rowley and Witmer (1988/89) and Singh (1989).

audit potential borrowers[4] but much more significant is the change in bank lending policies. A survey of American banks[5] showed that:

- 16.7 per cent had abandoned property rather than taking title because of environmental concerns;
- 62.5 per cent had rejected loan applications based upon the possibility of environmental liability;
- 88.1 per cent had changed lending procedures to avoid environmental liability;
- 13.5 per cent had incurred clean-up costs on property held as collateral;
- 45.8 per cent had discontinued loans to certain businesses because of fear of environmental liability.

The situation in the USA became more critical still in 1990 with the decision in the *Fleet Factors* case, in which the lender was held responsible because it participated 'in the financial management of a facility to a degree indicating a capacity to influence the corporation's treatment of hazardous wastes'. A bank did not have to exercise that capacity to be liable.[6] With the similarities in USA and UK interpretations of liability the fear is that the UK banks could find themselves in a similar situation. Although the North American financial community has succeeded in getting Congress and the EPA to reconsider the liability issues, and it is still unclear exactly how the EC legislation will eventually operate in this area, it is clear that bank lending on a worldwide basis is having to address some fairly critical matters.

The UK response from the banks has been led by the National Westminster Bank, where an environmental management unit has been established. This has led to guidelines being issued to branch management and enabled the bank to monitor carefully the changing legislative environment. At a minimum, it seems certain that issues such as these (plus developments in the UK like the register of contaminated land) will push land prices further downwards.[7] In order to mitigate the worst scenarios, there has been much talk of

[4] Chapter 5 dealt with some of the environmental audit implications arising from this. A critical point, however, is that the major moves in the UK, at least, are not designed to deal with the independent attestation which banks (and as we shall see, insurers) will need in order to establish their assessment of risk in lending. It is in this field that the smaller Institute of Environmental Auditors is directing its attentions.

[5] American Banks Association survey 1991 based upon 1,741 community banks, reported in Bernard Simon, Sharks in the water, *Financial Times*, 27 November 1991, p. 16.

[6] See Lascelles (note 1, above), Simon (ibid) and Neil Bennet, Clean-up costs force banks to rethink lending, *The Times*, 14 January 1992.

[7] By 1992 the collapse of property prices was already presenting a most serious financial crisis in the UK. These developments threatened to worsen an already critical position.

trying to establish a 'secured lender exemption', by which banks would limit their potential liability and so try to halt the very real trend of lenders refusing to lend for potentially hazardous environmental projects[8]. *In extremis*, a significant proportion of industry could find itself without access to loans, and the implications for national levels of economic activity are significant.[9]

The environmental agenda is threatening significant change to the banks' *modus operandi*. Not only are there the direct and potential financial problems but the environment raises important ethical questions that financiers cannot dodge for much longer:

> *The business of moving money is inextricably linked to the movement of raw materials, finished goods, labor, and ultimately, to the quality of our environment . . . the movement of dollars, pounds, and yen may also involve the creation of toxic wastes, ozone depleting chemicals, global warming gases, and other environmental disruptions . . . Banks that do not take an active stance on environmental issues may instead find themselves reacting defensively to a host of societal, financial and regulatory pressures.*

> (Sarokin and Schulkin, 1991, p. 7)

The banks' traditional reluctance to respond to environmental issues is directly under pressure with the launch of the UNEP 'Statement by Banks on the Environment and Sustainable Development' for the 1992 Earth Summit (see Chapter 15). Banks, particularly in the US and Japan, proved to be especially reluctant to sign[10] but this UNEP initiative is very much the writing on the wall. So, banks – like companies – that take a stance on the environment early on in the process will gain considerably. In the UK National Westminster and the Co-operative Bank (see Figure 10.1) have made the running.

10.3   Risk and Insurance

At its crudest, this growing concern of the banks can be seen as the development of a new kind of risk, one the financial community must manage if it is to continue operating. As a form of risk,[11] environmentally related liabilities are extremely far-reaching, potentially very expensive and largely unpredictable – if for no other reason than that the law is changing so fast as to make future liability an unknown quantity. But companies (and banks) turning to

[8] See, for example, Thompson (1992).

[9] There is an especially interesting case study which examines various elements of the liability, lending decision and financial institutions relationship. See Napier (1992).

[10] For more detail see *ENDS Report* 208/May 1992, p. 3.

[11] No distinction is drawn here between risk and uncertainty.

Figure 10.1   An example of a bank ethical policy

The Co-operative Bank
Ethical Policy.

"Can a bank exert a positive influence on the future of the World? Can you? Together we can at least try. We can stand up and let our views be known. We can show that behaviour that is unacceptable to society should not be acceptable in business. We can act as a force for a change."

Terry Thomas, MD Co-operative Bank

1. **We will not** loan. invest or supply financial services to countries governed by oppressive regimes.

2. **We will not** help finance companies that manufacture and export arms and weapons to countries that oppress their people.

3. **We will not** invest in any business involved in testing cosmetics on animals.

4. **We will not** support any person or company that causes animal suffering through intensive factory farming.

5. **We will not** offer financial support to a business. farm or other organisation engaged in the production of animal fur.

6. **We will not** support any organisation involved in blood sports.

7. **We will not** invest in or loan to manufacturers of tobacco products.

8. **We will** try to ensure that none of our services are exploited for the purposes of money laundering. drug trafficking or tax evasion.

9. **We will** help and encourage all our business customers to adopt a pro-active stance on the environmental impact of their own activities.

10. **We will** actively seek out individuals. commercial enterprises and non-commercial organisations that have a complementary ethical attitude.

11. **We will** extend and strengthen our Customer Charter in order to maintain our high standards of customer confidentiality.

12. **We will** continuously re-appraise our customers' views on all of these and other issues and develop our ethical stance accordingly.

The **CO)PERATIVE BANK**

081406

their insurance companies are facing problems. Again the UK and EC are learning from North America, where the writing of environment impairment liability policies was a major loss-maker by the early 1980s and pollution cover virtually disappeared in the mid-1980s as the Superfund developments seemed to try to shift liability from corporations to insurers as 'the last deep pocket' upon which the EPA could draw.[12] The situation continues to develop rapidly in North America and whilst that in the UK and the EC does not yet appear to have become critical the danger that it might do so is ever present. There promises to be a great deal of uncertainty in this area for some time to come.

The major problems seem to centre around the insurers' unwillingness and/or inability to cover all possible risks. Whilst it may be possible to insure for future events, those relating to past activity are often uninsurable. Sudden and accidental pollution can be covered but gradual pollution cannot. Injury, damage, compensation costs may well be insurable but it is unlikely that an insurance company will want to look at clean-up costs. Increasingly, insurers will insure only sites that have been inspected/environmentally audited and will provide strict exclusion clauses governing activities and standards. And so many potential environmental problems are unforeseeable whether due to legal changes, general ignorance, unexpected results of the chemistry cocktail one is working with and so on. One can therefore expect a continually changing situation in insurance markets.

In the meantime, organizations must look much more closely at the insurance cover they have and undertake some reassessment exercises. (A helpful checklist from CEBIS is included in Appendix 10.1). The environmental insurance an organization does have is likely to cost more because:

(1) although the insurance companies are learning to separate out various risks, the overall risk is rising and this will increase the cost to the customer;
(2) this insurance cover is likely to be for a smaller proportion of the total risks of the corporation; and
(3) the prerequisites for acquiring environmental risk insurance will be environmental audits and high standards of environmental management throughout the facility to be insured.

It would seem that enterprises must[13] recognize too that insurance is not the best way in which to manage environmental liability – it is too costly, too partial, does not cover all current areas of potential environmental risk and is not capable of covering the wide range

[12] For more detail see, for example, Hester (1991).

[13] Such advice was provided, for example, at the Environment Council meeting, Insuring for Environmental Risks, 1 February 1990.

of possible situations that could arise. High insurance costs will actually encourage corporations to improve their environmental management, using risk cover as the final safety net.[14]

10.4   The Environmental Influence of Financial Institutions

There seems little question that the banks and insurance companies are driven by conventional business motives – an improving risk/return trade-off, with steady growth or, at least, no contraction. The motivation would seem to owe nothing to ethics or to concern for the environment in any intrinsic sense. Nevertheless, the general impact on organizations of financial institutions exercising the gravest caution over environmental matters has been enormous, and shows every sign of growing. That is, because of banks' and insurance companies' fears over profit and risk, other organizations will, of necessity, have to undertake environmental audits, set in place rigorous environmental management systems and, perhaps most significantly, move away from the more environmentally risky activities. Self-interest is driving a significant rise in environmental sensitivity. It is this sort of observation that, quite justly, is used to bolster the case for a 'market' and 'voluntary' approach to the environmental sensitivity of organizations. However, not all in the garden is completely organic and uncontaminated.

The developed economies[15] are already facing situations, as we have seen, in which the environmental and profit criteria appear to be in conflict. As we saw in Chapters 5 and 8, environmental management requires a proactive and creative approach to investment. This is possible only when the providers of the funds are willing to recognize other, non-financial criteria and/or take a longer-term view of the investment, loan or whatever. There is not yet much evidence of this. In fact, it has been argued that financial institutions in general, and banks in particular, see themselves as 'amoral' – as environmentally neutral. This is clearly not the case.[16] Ultimately, financial institutions have the greatest power over organizations, can greatly influence them in positive ways and pro-

[14] Two major forms of development in Europe have been undertaken to try to overcome the most damaging elements (to the insurers and industry, that is) of this situation. The Chemical Industries Environmental Impairment Liability Insurance Facility is a good example of a trade association providing the wherewithal to protect the risk of the industry. In France, Italy and the Netherlands pools have been established against which insured claimants can draw.

[15] And this begs questions about the relationship with G77 countries. This is addressed briefly in Chapter 15.

[16] See Sarokin and Schulkin (1991) for the case with respect to banking. In general terms this view can be supported by the wider case made against economics and accounting – which is summarized in Appendix 1.

foundly hinder them in negative ways. This is critical because it largely determines the extent to which organizations can become more 'ethical' and more environmentally sensitive. Thus, can the board adopt a path towards sustainable development if this is likely to reduce profits and dividends? It seems likely that the capital markets in general, and the banks and institutional and individual shareholders in particular, at the very least offer a constraint upon managerial discretion and, at a maximum, encourage the pursuit of profit, dividends and interest to dominate other ethical or environmental objectives.[17]

The development of environmental sensitivity will frequently be costly and limit an organization's options, and the capital markets, shareholders and other providers of funds will have to recognize this. They become crucial to any discussion of how organizations may become more environmentally sensitive.

These issues also raise ethical questions of the justice of investors (perhaps alongside other providers of funds, material and labour) taking a return from an organization which has caused environmental degradation.[18] It raises questions as to the rights of capital's objectives to (perhaps) dominate all others, which – in turn – leads to a questioning of liberal economics.[19] It also leads to practical questions as to whether our present institutional arrangements will actually permit managers to undertake anything other than the most superficial greening of their organizations – even if they wished to. Perhaps most importantly, however, in recent years there has been a tendency in the West to reinforce the idea that the financial community is self-interested and greedy – in fact to suggest that investors had a *duty* to put profit above all else.[20] We believe we have shown that such a dominance by profit may ensure environmental crisis and risk the end of the species.

It is these matters that we wish to concentrate upon for the remainder of this chapter – to introduce the role of the shareholder to our discussions of environmental sensitivity, to review the extent to which we might expect shareholders to take stands on ethical and

[17] See also, on a related theme, Buzby and Falk (1978, 1979), of which more in later sections of this chapter.

[18] This issue is returned to in Part D, when the question of sustainability is examined. This concept suggests that it is possible to conceive that shareholders' dividends are currently paid out of *natural* capital.

[19] See Parts A and D; but see also Gray (1989, 1990d, e, f) and Gray and Morrison (1991).

[20] Typically see Friedman (1962) but see also Benston (1982a; 1982b), Walton (1983). The majority of financial accounting textbooks reinforce this idea, usually implicitly; textbooks on business finance reinforce the idea explicitly. It is little wonder therefore that accountants, in general, might see accounting profit as a God-given goal and anything which conflicts with it, such as the physical environment, as the stuff of heresy. See Gray et al. (1992).

Figure 10.2 Social responsibility and shareholders

Characteristic	Social Performance	Social Disclosure	Accounting Profit	Stock Market Performance
Social Performance		No relationship	Slight relationship	Slight relationship
Social Disclosure			Slight relationship	Possible relationship
Accounting Profit				Positive relationship
Stock Market Performance				

environmental matters and thereby to lead organizational management and, finally, to outline the way in which ethical and environmental investment is developing.

10.5 Do Shareholders Care About Ethics and the Environment?

For nearly twenty years, researchers have attempted to assess whether social responsibility (including ethical standards and environmental issues), social disclosures, economic and accounting performance and the performance of share prices were related. This attempt consisted of a number of strands which, in the particular context of this chapter, were directed towards assessing whether shareholders rewarded, penalized or were indifferent to companies with a better than average social performance. The elements are reflected in Figure 10.2.[21] In broad terms the research is inconclusive but seems to suggest that investors *do* care about social disclosure and social performance *only* when it will affect financial performance, and to the extent that investors care about the intrinsic ethical positions of organizations, they care very little. Attempts to isolate the 'environmental' element of 'social' have produced broadly similar results.

These are depressing, if unsurprising, results. Depressing in that they suggest that the most environmentally sensitive management will be excessively limited in the environmental options available to them and no lead on environmental matters can be expected from

---

[21] The results in the figure are distilled from many studies. These are summarized in Ullmann (1985), Mathews (1987) and Belkaoui and Karpik (1989). See also Brooks (1986), Gray, Owen and Maunders (1987), Cowen, Ferreri and Parker (1987), Guthrie and Parker (1990), Gray (1990b).

shareholders unless it repays them financially: '[an overwhelming number of chief executives] would like to invest in improved technology for environmental reasons . . . but they could not persuade their institutional shareholders and other City stakeholders that investment was justified'.[22]

The profound ethical question this raises is among the most important that accounting, finance, economics, business and the environmental agenda must face up to but although we have touched upon the matters (see Parts A and D) we must leave this to others to discuss and move on to the more direct issues.[23] This leaves us with two broad questions: is it in the financial self-interest of shareholders to respond to environmental sensitivity? and are shareholders really so very selfish and greedy? In response to the first question, we saw in Part A that although some organizations would make financial gains from the environmental agenda, this was likely to be fairly short term and involve being only 'light green'. Substantial greening was likely to incur financial costs in the short term, at least for most organizations. However, far more likely is that those organizations which *do not* respond to the environmental agenda will face very substantial costs – up to and including liquidation.

The more interesting question at this stage is the extent of the self-interest exhibited by investors. The emergence of the ethical and green funds represents an intriguing phenomenon in this connection.

10.6   The Emergence of Ethical and Environmental Investment

Socially responsible, or ethical investment, funds were first launched in the USA in the early 1970s, and by the late 1980s controlled $50 billion in assets.[24] In the UK, such ethical funds came to prominence with the launch of the Friends Provident Stewardship Trust in 1984. By 1988 the UK ethical funds controlled about £120 million in assets.[25] The upsurge in green awareness in the late 1980s gave the ethical investment market a considerable boost. In the USA this followed the *Exxon Valdez* Alaskan oil spill and the launch of the Valdez Principles (see Chapter 4) by the CERES[26] project of the US

[22] Quoted by Mark Campanale, Merlin Ecology Fund, at Environmental Council Seminar, July 1991, based on an August 1990 survey by PA Consulting.

[23] See e.g. Owen, Gray and Maunders, 1987; Lehman, 1988; Owen, 1990; Reilly and Kyj, 1990; Jacobson, 1991.

[24] The Dreyfus Third Century Fund was established in 1972 (see, for example, Chastain, 1973).

[25] See, for example, Dunham (1988).

[26] The Coalition for Environmentally Responsible Economies.

Figure 10.3

UK ethical and environmental investment funds

Merlin Jupiter Ecology Fund
Clerical Medical Evergreen
HFS Green Chip Fund
TSB Environmental Investor Fund
CIS Environmental Trust
Eagle Star Environmental Opportunities
Abbey (Life) Ethical
All Churches Amity Fund
NM Schroder Conscience Fund
Acorn Ethical Fund
Friends Provident Stewardship Income Trust
Friends Provident Stewardship Unit Trust
Friends Provident Stewardship North American Trust
Scottish Equitable Ethical Unit Trust
Target Global Opportunities
Sovereign Ethical Fund
Buckmaster Fellowship Trust
Fidelity Famous Names

Adapted from Perks, Rawlinson and Ingram (1992).

Social Investment Forum.[27] The impact of the funds is not related just to the amounts that they invest – their influence has encouraged local government funds, pension funds and others to adopt ethical or environmental criteria in their investment decisions. In the USA the funds now invested in a way which involves some ethical or environmental criteria are estimated variously at 10 per cent of total Wall Street funds[28] or at around $400 billion.[29]

In the UK, the 'green' ethical funds were led by the formation of the Merlin Ecology Fund in 1988. By the early 1990s estimates are that the total UK ethical investment market involves £6 billion in assets[30]. Figure 10.3 lists the ethical funds active in the UK by the early 1990s in the approximate order of their emphasis on environmental issues.[31]

The foregoing shows that there is a small but significant and growing proportion of the capital markets which is willing to under-

[27] See also Edgerton (1989).

[28] See Lander (1989).

[29] Bromige and Partners (1989) referred to by Harte, Lewis and Owen (1991), p. 229.

[30] For more detail see Dunham, 1990; Mitchell, Sams and White, 1990; Owen, 1990; Harte, Lewis and Owen, 1991; Perks, Rawlinson and Ingram, 1992.

[31] New funds are coming into the market all the time: early 1992 saw one from Commercial Union, for example. This list must not be taken as definitive.

Figure 10.4

Negative criteria operated by UK ethical/environmental funds

Poor environmental record
Poor working environment
Repressive regimes
Tobacco
Alcohol
Armaments
Gambling
Animal exploitation, experimentation and furs
Nuclear
Sexually explicit or violent media
Complaints upheld by the Advertising Standards Authority
Drugs
Political donations

Adapted from Harte, Lewis and Owen (1991) and Perks, Rawlinson and Ingram (1992)

---

take investment on other than purely financial grounds.[32] Furthermore, the evidence is mixed about the extent to which 'ethical
investors' actually do sacrifice financial returns. Reports have
suggested that the stronger the definitions and criteria used by the
fund, the more likely it is to 'underperform' against a non-ethical/
environmental portfolio. The ethical/environmental funds are still,
however, a relatively new phenomenon and it would be too early to
jump to definite conclusions. Certainly any fund looking for 'totally
socially responsible' companies or 'totally environmentally friendly'
companies will have a very small portfolio indeed. At a minimum,
therefore, it is possible to conclude that an investor may be 'slightly
ethical/environmental' to no financial detriment. Stronger views are
likely to be costly.[33] Indeed, the Body Shop – the darling of the
UK green funds – notes that there is no such thing as an environmentally friendly company – only more or less environmentally
sensitive.

[32] It is possible to hypothesize that the inconclusive nature of the studies on the
relationships between social disclosure and performance, and accounting and
economic performance, which we referred to earlier could have arisen from two
'capital markets' – one wholly geared to financial return and one geared to a mix of
financial and ethical considerations which introduced 'noise' into the markets.

[33] For more detail see Perks, Rawlinson and Ingram (1992), Harte, Lewis and
Owen (1991), Dunham (1988, 1990), Burman (1990), Dobie (1990) and, in particular,
the report in *The Independent on Sunday*, 23 February 1992 ('The best and the worst of
ethical funds'), in which the strictness of ethical criteria is identified as a financially
detrimental factor – to be solved by being less ethical! A report by John Davis,
Observer, 2 February 1992, notes that more focused green funds are having trouble
performing at or near market rates. Other evidence makes this conclusion more
doubtful.

Figure 10.5

Positive criteria operated by UK ethical/environmental funds

High standards of environmental awareness
Promotion of employee welfare
Equal employment opportunities
Useful contribution to community welfare
Provides environmentally beneficial goods or services
Provides socially beneficial goods or services
Has good customer relations record
Makes substantial charitable donations
Involvement in specific sectors (e.g. medical and health care; education)

Adapted from Harte, Lewis and Owen (1991) and Perks, Rawlinson and Ingram (1992).

10.7   Criteria and Information for Ethical/ Environmental Investment

The ethical/environmental funds operate both 'positive' and 'negative' criteria in selecting companies in which to invest. The negative criteria are easier to operate and involve avoiding companies active in certain sectors or involved with countries, incidents or activities selected by either the investor or the fund managers as inappropriate. Figure 10.4 lists the negative criteria of UK funds – in approximate rank order of emphasis given by the funds. As Perks, Rawlinson and Ingram (1992) point out, these negative criteria need to be refined in order to make them operable – for example, 'alcohol' may be avoided altogether but this will exclude all major grocery retail chains, companies which make and supply home brewing kits, etc. The firmness with which the criteria are applied varies considerably.

Positive criteria raise more difficult problems, not least because information is difficult to obtain. Figure 10.5 lists the positive criteria operated by the UK funds – again in approximate order of emphasis. Once again, Perks, Rawlinson and Ingram (1992) identify the lack of precision with which these characteristics are defined and the variable manner in which different funds apply them.

There are two immediate implications arising from these studies of the ethical and/or environmental investment movement. First, it is very difficult to assess the extent to which the trusts actually comply with their own standards – just how green are the green trusts? The answer obviously varies from trust to trust but the list of those companies more popular with the ethical/environmental investment funds indicates that finding green companies has proved a difficult issue for some funds and the best that one can hope for is 'greener' companies – those that tend to be in the forefront

Figure 10.6

The most popular 'green' UK companies for investment trusts and reasons for selection	
British Gas	(greenhouse effect)
Halma	(pollution control)
Body Shop	(animal and habitat welfare)
Powerscreen	(recycling)
Tesco	(recycling, ozone layer, transport, healthy eating)
Argyll Group	(healthy eating, recycling)
Simon Engineering	(pollution control, recycling)
Ocean Group	(energy conservation, pollution control, sensitive land use)
Sutcliffe Speakman	(pollution control, recycling)
Allied Colloids	(pollution control)
Attwoods	(pollution control)
Bespak	(ozone layer, pollution)
Freeman Group	(energy conservation)
Marks and Spencer	(healthy eating, energy conservation, recycling)
Sainsbury	(healthy eating, energy, land use, recycling, community care)
Shanks & McEwan	(pollution control, recycling)
Whatman Reeve	(recycling)

Adapted from Perks, Rawlinson and Ingram (1992)

of environmental (and/or ethical) standards rather than those that represent ideal types. Figure 10.6 lists the companies which Perks, Rawlinson and Ingram identified as the most popular with UK environmental funds – in approximate order of popularity. By way of comparison, Figure 10.7 also shows the companies listed in the Merlin Jupiter Ecology Fund portfolio for spring 1992.[34] The predominance of companies in environmentally related activity and 'cleaner' energy systems may not be a great revelation but it does indicate the difficulty that some ethical/environmental funds have in finding 'mainstream' industrial and commercial activity which meets even relatively mild environmental criteria. Put more forcibly, few conventional organizations can meet even embryonic environmental standards – an observation which has potentially critical implications for the future of the environment and business (see Part D).

However, to see the green funds only in terms of their actual investments is to underestimate their impact. For example, the Merlin Jupiter Ecology Fund has been a major force in campaigning for a raising of the environmental agenda and has been instrumental

[34] The Merlin Research Unit's growing experience is reflected in a changing emphasis in the portfolio, where companies which lead a sector on environmental criteria or are a developing force in the 'better' environmental sectors are increasingly recognized as worthy of inclusion. It is worth noting that of the fifty-six spring 1992 companies in the portfolio, less than half were in the portfolio two years earlier, suggesting fine and shifting criteria.

Figure 10.7

Merlin Jupiter Ecology Fund portfolio (Spring 1992)

- Cosmetics: Body Shop, Creightons
- Retail: Argyll, Tesco
- Manufacturing general: British Polythene, Eurotherm, Microfilm Reprographics, Powerscreen, Reckitt & Colman, Rotork, Stewart and Stevenson, Vitaulic, Technocell
- Energy and energy saving: British Gas, Calor, London Electricity, Manweb, Molynx, Servomex, Sheffield Insulations, Brooklyn Union, Burlington Resources, California Energy, Groundwater Technology, New Jersey Resources, North American Gas, Washington Gas Light
- Environmental management products and services: Halma, Headway, Freeman, Ocean, RPS, Whatman, FuelTech, Handex, Imco, Nalco Chemicals, Simon Engineering, Wellman, Tetra Technologies, Tomra Systems, Vetropak Holdings
- Water and water management: Protean, Wessex Water, Yorkshire Water, George Kent, Memtec, Générale des Eaux
- Agricultural and food: Cranswick Mills, Heinz
- Information/communication: British Telecom, Cable & Wireless, Reuters, Alcatel
- Financial services: Abbey National, National Westminster

Adapted from *Merlin Research Bulletin* 8, Spring 1992

in raising issues on a far wider platform than simply those companies in which it invests. Many environmental funds have been driven by a more developmental and campaigning role beyond simply advising investors[35] and, in the UK, the news in 1992 that Norwich Union (not especially known as an explicitly ethical/environmental investor) was issuing a questionnaire to companies in order to assess their state of environmental sensitivity suggests that environmental criteria are spreading beyond the activities of the dedicated environmental funds. Unfortunately, few of the trusts yet try to exercise direct influence upon the companies although there is evidence to suggest that this is beginning to change.[36]

The second of the questions that arose from the studies of environmental investment relates to the information available to the investment managers and the implications that this has for the external reporting regime. Both Harte, Lewis and Owen (1991) and Perks, Rawlinson and Ingram (1992) found that the annual report was the most frequently used source of information for the investment decision but that this document gave negligible guidance on the ethical/environmental matters by which final selection was to be made. Whilst the funds use other sources of information – including direct contact with the companies – this does not remove the crucial

[35] This is especially true of the Ethical Investment Research Service (EIRIS). Also, for example, the Ethical Investors Group pledge to give 50 per cent of their profits to designated charities or groups.

[36] EIRIS (1989) and see any of the Merlin Research Unit publications.

question as to whether or not annual reports *should* provide usable data about an organization's ethical/environmental performance – after all, a major justification for annual reports is that they guide investment decisions. When ethical/environmental issues are introduced to a decision made without regard to ethical considerations, the annual report fails to fulfil its purpose[37]. This issue is addressed further in the following chapters.

The reluctance of organizations to develop transparent and reliable environmental reporting systems is, however, looking increasingly short-sighted. As we shall see in Chapter 13, if the companies do not self-report, some other body will do it for them. This already happens in the ethical/environmental investment world. An example from EIRIS (1992) illustrates the principle. Employing information from the public registers which had been opened up under the UK's Environmental Protection Act 1990, EIRIS identified failures by UK companies to meet their water pollution consent levels.[38] Although there are problems with the analysis and its presentation,[39] the EIRIS report identifies, *inter alia*, that: 26 of the UK top 50 companies were water polluters; major companies such as Shell, ICI, Allied-Lyons, Hanson and Grand Metropolitan breached their discharge consents more than 35 times during 1991; and that ICI and GEC breached consents for red-list substances. As information becomes more freely available, this sort of data will flow more easily and the ethical/environmental investor will become more informed. It would seem therefore that not only do current reporting frameworks not facilitate ethical/environmental investment – they positively discourage it. Until external reporting demonstrates a healthier balance between the financial and the ethical/environmental (where these are in conflict) it will be the activities of the 'social audit movement' (see Chapter 13) that will fill the gap.

10.8   The Future for Ethical/Environmental Investment?

There have been a number of major factors which have restricted the development of ethical/environmental investment – the willingness of the investor and the lack of information are only two of them. Of equal, or even greater, importance has been the law's restriction on how investment bodies invest their funds. At its simplest, investments which fall under the Trustee Investments Act 1961 or similar place the investor under a fiduciary duty to pursue maximum financial return. More especially, it is *illegal* for the trustees to forgo

---

[37] For more detail see Harte, 1988; Rockness and Williams, 1988; Harte, Lewis and Owen, 1991; and Perks, Rawlinson and Ingram, 1992.

[38] *Water Pollution: a briefing for the environmental investor* (London: EIRIS) 1992.

[39] See, for example, *ENDS Report* 205/February 1992, p. 9.

a higher return on ethical grounds.[40] As a result, a significant proportion of potentially ethical/environmental investment is apparently closed off to the major funds in the capital markets. (*However*, this situation does not prevent the fund from exercising ethical influence over the 'owned' company – a rare but, happily, growing practice.) The situation facing charities in the UK was less draconian but still restrictive. However, a judgement handed down in 1992 does appear to have loosened the restraints for charity trustees.[41] All the evidence seems to suggest that ethical/environmental investment will continue to grow. It was no longer a fringe activity by the early 1990s but there still remained a massive counterweight of inertia, law, financial self-interest and thoughtless ignorance (this last predominantly perpetuated through education and textbooks) against which the ethical or environmental investor had to struggle. At times this has forced individuals or groups to side-step the whole process entirely.

The UK, like other countries,[42] has seen a small but steady development in structures designed to enable investors to put money directly to work in ways which meet their personal ethical/environmental criteria. The most widely noticeable of these has perhaps been the exceptionally influential Traidcraft, but other organizations such as the Centre for Alternative Technology, Shared Interest and the Ecology Building Society have also achieved a considerable amount. The first three, for example, undertook share flotations in the late 1980s and early 1990s; all three were reasonably successful *despite the fact that none of the three could realistically promise either capital growth or income*. Although small organizations, these three do point to the fact that direct and serious ethical/environmental investment does and can exist and they demonstrate that there is nothing immutable, god-given, morally superior, legally established or inevitable about the widespread, modern and amoral belief that investors are – and *should be* – rich people growing richer, and that the job of accounting is to serve them in this pursuit. Traidcraft, Shared Interest and the Centre for Alternative Technology, plus myriad organizations outside the UK, demonstrate that any conflict between economic value and ethical and environmental value can be resolved if humanity is put before greed.[43] The ethical/environmental investment trusts are also attempting to demonstrate this painful but critical lesson.

---

[40] For more detail see Ward, 1991.

[41] Reported in *New Economics* 21, Spring 1992, p. 3. For more detail contact EIRIS.

[42] See e.g. the illustrations and proposals for 'alternative economic systems' in Plant and Plant, 1991; Robertson, 1985, 1990; Ekins, 1986, 1992; Dauncey, 1988; Weston, 1991.

[43] For example, see e.g. Robertson, 1985, 1990; Ekins, 1986, 1992b; Plant and Plant, 1991.

10.9 Conclusions

The providers of funds exercise a critical amount of power over organizations. Whilst much of this can be restrictive upon any management attempting to develop an organization's environmental sensitivity beyond the lightest tinge of green, there are signs of environmentally positive actions flowing both from the self-interest of banks and insurance companies and from the rather more altruistic motivations of the ethical and environmental investor. However, as long as the providers of funds are seen, and see themselves, either as amoral or as duty-bound to seek the maximum profit over all other considerations, the full response that any organization could make to the environmental agenda must remain a muted one.

Further Reading

Banking and Insurance

This is an area in which keeping abreast of the very rapid changes is essential. The following references can provide no more than an introduction to some of the issues.

Hester, Edward, J. (1991) Environmental issues for insurers and risk managers, *Integrated Environmental Management*, no. 2, September, pp. 21–2.

Rowley, D. A. and Witmer, T. L. (1988/89) Assessing environmental risks before booking a loan, *Commercial Lending Review*, vol. 4, no. 1, pp. 53–64.

Sarokin, D. and Schulkin, J. (1991) Environmental concerns and the business of banking, *Journal of Commercial Bank Lending*, February, pp. 6–19.

Singh, J. (1989) Pollution risks may hamper acquisitions, *National Underwriter*, vol. 93, no. 15, pp. 31–3.

Ethical/Environmental Investment

For an excellent and thorough basic introduction to the field see:

Miller, Allan (1992) Green Investment, chapter 11 in D. L. Owen (ed.) *Green Reporting: Accountancy and the Challenge of the Nineties*, Chapman Hall, London.

For an outline of what it is in the UK and how to go about it see:

Ward, Sue (1991) *Socially Responsible Investment*, 2nd edition, Directory of Social Change, London.

The two research studies quoted from extensively in this chapter are:

Harte, G., Lewis, L. and Owen, D. (1991) Ethical investment and the corporate reporting function, *Critical Perspectives on Accounting*, vol. 2, no. 3, pp. 227–54.

Perks, R. W., Rawlinson, D. and Ingram, L. (1992) An exploration of ethical investment in the UK, *British Accounting Review*, vol. 24, no. 1.

Research articles which explore the matters further include:

Owen, D. (1990) Towards a theory of social investment: a review essay, *Accounting, Organizations and Society*, vol. 15, no. 3, pp. 249–66.

Rockness, J. and Williams, P. F. (1988) A descriptive study of social responsibility mutual funds, *Accounting, Organizations and Society*, vol. 13, no. 4, pp. 397–411.

Further information about EIRIS, Jupiter Tarbutt Marlin, Traidcraft, Shared Interest, the Ecology Building Society and the Centre for Alternative Technology can be found by writing to the organizations whose addresses are given in the appendix to this book. The Traidcraft story is reported in:

Adams, R. (1989) *Who Profits?*, Lion, Oxford.

APPENDIX 10.1
CEBIS environmental insurance checklist

ENVIRONMENTAL INSURANCE

As environmental legislation tightens and environmental liabilities grow, companies are increasingly turning to their insurers to cover environmental risks. The insurance industry's previous experience, however, is making it cautious, and any company hoping to buy comprehensive pollution insurance cover is likely to be disappointed. Almost all insurance policies now contain a clause specifically excluding liability for gradual pollution and cover "sudden and accidental" incidents only.

CURRENT POLLUTION INSURANCE

Insurance cover for damage caused by pollution is distinguished according to whether damage was a result of a single incident or gradual pollution. Two types of policy, both limited in their coverage, are currently available in the UK.

'Sudden and Accidental'
Nearly all standard public liability policies now restrict coverage to 'sudden and accidental' incidents and exclude all claims for damage caused by gradual pollution. A 'Single Event Pollution Triggered Incident Clause' (SEPTIC) is often written into standard liability policies, but even then, the cover this offers is limited. Cover is restricted to third party liability and is effectively on a 'claims made' basis. Claims made policies require that the incident is caused, discovered and filed as a claim within the same, one year, policy term.

'Gradual Pollution'
Liability cover for gradual contamination and leakage is available through 'Environmental Impairment Liability' (EIL) policies. However, cover is on a 'claims made' basis only and the excess payable by the claimant is often substantial (currently £25,000 - £100,000). Applicants must provide a detailed description of the history of the site and processes operated on it, and may need to undertake a full environmental audit at their expense. Many EIL policies specifically exclude coverage for pollution liability resulting from non-compliance with environmental legislation.

NB Some companies and trade associations are assessing their pollution liability risks and developing their own contingency funds to cope with this. The Chemical Industries Association, for example, has developed its own EIL policy, and a limited liability scheme is available to members of the National Association of Waste Disposal Contractors.

POLLUTION INSURANCE TRENDS

In response to possible compulsory pollution insurance resulting from proposed European Community legislation on civil liability and waste management, the Association of British Insurers is considering a scheme of "pollution ratings" as a means of assessing risk before issuing environmental impairment liability insurance. Assessment for the ratings is likely to include the applicant's potential for pollution, including the size of the operation and any previous claims records; the level of pollution control in place, including the installation of pollution abatement equipment and management and workforce attitudes to environmental safety; and the value of the environment that may be polluted.

LIMITING YOUR LIABILITY

For most companies, insurance cover for 'gradual pollution' is likely to be prohibitively expensive. If this is the case, the most sensible precaution you can take is to minimise risk at source. Even those companies applying for pollution liability cover will have to satisfy the insurers that they are taking comprehensive steps to keep their environmental risks to a minimum.

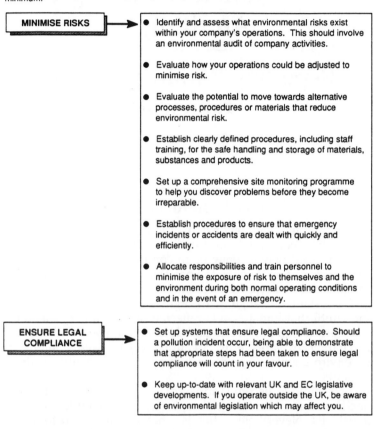

MINIMISE RISKS

- Identify and assess what environmental risks exist within your company's operations. This should involve an environmental audit of company activities.

- Evaluate how your operations could be adjusted to minimise risk.

- Evaluate the potential to move towards alternative processes, procedures or materials that reduce environmental risk.

- Establish clearly defined procedures, including staff training, for the safe handling and storage of materials, substances and products.

- Set up a comprehensive site monitoring programme to help you discover problems before they become irreparable.

- Establish procedures to ensure that emergency incidents or accidents are dealt with quickly and efficiently.

- Allocate responsibilities and train personnel to minimise the exposure of risk to themselves and the environment during both normal operating conditions and in the event of an emergency.

ENSURE LEGAL COMPLIANCE

- Set up systems that ensure legal compliance. Should a pollution incident occur, being able to demonstrate that appropriate steps had been taken to ensure legal compliance will count in your favour.

- Keep up-to-date with relevant UK and EC legislative developments. If you operate outside the UK, be aware of environmental legislation which may affect you.

SET UP MANAGEMENT SYSTEMS

- Establish and maintain effective environmental management systems. This might include setting up procedures to monitor, document and review all aspects of the company's operations from 'cradle to grave' including resource use, process emissions, and waste management.

11. External Reporting and Auditing I:

Reporting Within a Financial Framework

11.1 Introduction

Except to the very slightest extent, the physical environment is not reflected in a company's bottom line. The environment and the pursuit of profit may actually be in conflict, as we saw in Part A. If companies continue to make the health of the bottom line a (perhaps even *the*) primary objective, we cannot seriously expect much in the way of substantial change in an organization's environmental interactions until that interaction is reflected in the primary statements – the scorecards of the profit and loss account and balance sheet. This chapter explores how, if at all, organizations might introduce environmental financial numbers into the statutory financial statements.

It will rapidly become apparent that trying to separate the financial and the non-financial reporting, for example, is awkward and artificial. Nevertheless, this is what we have tried to do in the light of the amount of material that needs to be covered. This chapter will examine the conventional financial accounting framework and associated statutory audit; Chapter 12 will look at a wider definition of 'accounting' and consider non-financial reporting and accountability. Chapter 13 will then step outside the normal assumption that an organization should self-report and examine some of the information disclosure initiatives by bodies independent of the reporting organization.

Currently, the vast majority of examples of environmental accounting are the result of voluntary disclosure – the initiative of the reporting entity, perhaps encouraged by codes of practice or the prospect of developments lying just over the horizon. There is virtually no regulation anywhere in the world which requires environmental disclosure to the public domain. Even the more general requirements to disclose accounting policies have not, as yet, brought forth disclosure of *environmental* accounting policies.

The only country in Europe currently requiring any disclosure of environmental matters is Norway – and this generally results in only the most imprecise statements to the effect that all relevant law has been complied with.[1] Indeed, it does seem that unless disclosure requirements are very strict, rather empty disclosure is what results (see the next section). The USA is somewhat more advanced[2] but it also has found that disclosure standards have to be tight. This has led the SEC to expand their environmental disclosure requirements to include specific disclosure of contingent liabilities in the financial statements (see below: contingent liabilities, remediation etc.). In Canada, it is again the Securities Commission that has started the environmental disclosure ball rolling[3] although, more recently the Canadian Institute of Chartered Accountants approved an accounting standard on remediation costs and this has now been passed by the Canadian Standards Committee (see below, Sections 11.4 and 11.5).[4]

Thus, with the occasional exception (e.g. the German chemical industry code for defining and disclosing specific environmental costs[5]), the institutional framework for environmental reporting is virtually non-existent. Hence the current importance of voluntary disclosure.

---

[1] See Roberts (1992) for more detail and discussion in this area. The amended Enterprises Act of Norway 1989 actually requires the board of directors' report to include physical information about emissions and contaminants and information about plans to clean up activities.

[2] The SEC S-K Regulation Item 101 requires enterprises to disclose the material effects that compliance with environmental laws may have on capital expenditure, earnings and competitive position. Item 102 requires disclosure of certain existing estimates of current and future environmental expenditures. Item 103 requires disclosure of any significant environmental, administrative or judicial proceedings that will have an impact on the enterprise. The Superfund Amendments and Reauthorization Act 1986 also requires disclosure of environmental risks arising from activities. For more detail see Newell, Kreuze and Newell (1990). For more detail on the USA climate in general see, for example, Dirks (1991) and Rabinowitz and Murphy (1991).

[3] The Ontario and Quebec Securities Commission require listed companies to include the financial or operational effects of environmental protection requirements on the capital expenditure, earnings and competitive position of the company for the current year and a forecast of impact for future years.

[4] In 1992 the Society of Management Accountants in Canada (CMA) issued its analysis and recommendations on environmental accounting, which are far reaching but cautious about recommending that developments take place immediately; see CMA (1992).

[5] These are the Recommendations from the Business Economics Division of the German Chemical Industry Association (Verband der Chemischen Industrie e.V) which have been in place since 1973 and are currently under revision.

Figure 11.1

Themes in voluntary corporate reporting

1. First, and perhaps most important, the *proportion* of companies disclosing and the *extent* of that disclosure are small and the *quality* (in terms of, for example, the verifiability or specificity of the data) is low. These statements are true for virtually all social disclosure and especially true for environmental disclosure before about 1988.

2. There is some variety in disclosure – over time, between countries and between industries. Social disclosure in general and environmental disclosure in particular reflect the changing business climate and the social, economic and political environment in which they occur. However, the *total* amount of voluntary disclosure stays fairly constant over time; what changes is the subject addressed in that disclosure.

3. There is a very definite size effect in that larger companies are more likely to disclose than smaller companies.

4. Very little disclosure would qualify as information under any normal criteria and very little of it indeed will contain numbers, financial or otherwise. The emphasis is on PR rather than transparency.

11.2   Environmental Disclosure within the Conventional Financial Accounting Framework

Research studies[6] have examined the extent to which companies produce social information – of which environmental information would be a part. A number of the general themes that emerge from this are summarized in Figure 11.1.[7]

As might be expected, the recent upsurge in concern for environmental issues has brought an attendant increase – albeit slight – in the emphasis on environmental disclosure. Three recent surveys give us a picture of environmental disclosure among the larger companies in the world.[8] The UN survey related to financial state-

---

[6] For reviews of this material which provide a basis for what follows see Maxwell and Mason (1976), Lessem (1977), Preston, Rey and Dierkes (1978), Schreuder (1979), Trotman and Bradley (1981), Brooks (1986), Cowen, Ferreri and Parker (1987), Gray, Owen and Maunders (1987), Gray (1990d), Harte and Owen (1992), Owen (1992), Roberts (1992).

[7] See also Guthrie and Parker (1989, 1990) and Guthrie and Mathews (1985), who argue, in an Australian context, for three (relatively modest) peaks in environmental disclosure in 1970–74, 1979–1984 and post-1989 in response to changing public concern with such issues. They also show differences in the proportion disclosing *any* environmental data among the top 50 companies in USA (53 per cent), Australia (21 per cent) and UK (14 per cent). However, on an international basis, it proves difficult to conclude anything about the pattern of disclosure by industry. The disclosure figures given by Guthrie and Parker are based on the largest companies and therefore overemphasize the overall level of disclosure. For companies as a whole the proportion will be much lower. See also Gray (1990d).

[8] The following data are taken from Roberts (1991), *Company Reporting 1991* and UNCTC papers E/C.10/AC.3/1992/3. But see also *Financial Reporting* 1990/91 and 1991/92 for more detail on the UK situation.

Figure 11.2 Environmental reporting by companies

Country	World-wide	France	Germany	N'lands	Sweden	Switz'd	Total Europe	UK
Survey	UNCTC			Roberts (1991)				Coy Report
Sample Size	222	25	40	15	15	15	110	670
% age Disclose	86%	52%	80%	60%	80%	60%	68%	10%

ments ending in 1989 or 1990 and the companies surveyed were drawn primarily from the Fortune Global 500 with emphasis on specific manufacturing and extractive industries. This sample was dominated by USA and Japanese companies. Roberts's survey was aimed at large companies and, on the basis of practicality, the sample was restricted in size and to English-language reports. The *Company Reporting* survey took in a much wider range of companies than did either of the others (see Figure 11.2).

Despite the probable national differences in disclosure rates[9] the overall levels of reporting might encourage one to be bullish about the success of voluntary disclosure. However, the UK figures not only demonstrate that any success there might be cannot be taken to be universal but also counsel caution. Although the UK *may very well* be the lowest disclosing nation among the developed countries, the UK sample takes in more than the country's largest companies and thus we may be sensible to infer that a size effect (referred to above) is present.[10]

A further factor which should caution any celebration of voluntary reporting arises from the content of the 'disclosure'. In the great majority of cases, disclosure tended to be descriptive. Only about 40 per cent of the worldwide survey gave financially quantified information, less than 40 per cent for Europe and, for the UK, the figure was nearer 1 per cent. In addition, those financial numbers which *were* disclosed tended to be provided on an *ad hoc* basis. Typically, one will find selected numbers reported within a more

[9] Which, with most other factors, must be treated with care due to the crudeness of the reported data and the incomparability of the samples.

[10] Further recent surveys confirm that disclosure is both a rather patchy and a big-corporation phenomenon. Kirkman's study of UK reporting (P. Kirkman and C. Hope *Environmental disclosure in UK Company Annual Reports* Cambridge University, 1992) shows that UK disclosure is really only the province of the largest companies, whilst a 1992 KPMG survey shows the same phenomenon in Canada and the USA. The KPMG survey also shows the effect of the regulative environment in North America is to successfully encourage more quantitative and financial disclosure than in Europe, but it also appears to have encouraged less experimentation and voluntary efforts.

wide-ranging discussion on the organization's environmental inter-actions. There are exceptions to this (see, for example, Ciba-Geigy's 1989 annual report in Figure 11.3) but there does not appear much prospect of systematic reporting until standards are agreed and regulations established.[11]

11.3   Why Disclose Environmental Data Voluntarily?

Industry will be expected to make more information on its operations and performance available to the public, either voluntarily or by regulation. The European Directive on the Freedom of Access to Information on the Environment has been published and accepted by industry and the Green Bill has reinforced the concept of public registers . . . The CIA agrees that the public has a proper right to know details of environmental perfor-mance of chemical plants . . . However, we will continue to resist the publication of information on process technologies which would give important information to competitors and add unnecessary costs and resources.

(C Thompson, VP, ARCO Chemical Europe, 1991)

An organization might voluntarily report financial information to develop corporate image; to legitimize current activity; to distract attention from other areas; and to forestall legislation. There is also some evidence to suggest that some organizations find it to their advantage to develop their reporting ahead of regulation in order to give themselves time to create the necessary information systems and to build up the expertise necessary in a new area of reporting. Gray, Radebaugh and Roberts[12] take a more systematic approach to the problem and suggest that any organization considering voluntary disclosure will assess the relative costs and benefits. Their study found that benefits were a function of: the information's positive impact on share price; the effect of any reduction in per-ceived risk arising from the information; and 'political' benefit arising from changed perceptions of government, employees, shareholders, etc. The costs were both direct and indirect. The former were those arising principally from data collection and processing, and attendant auditing costs.[13] The latter arose primarily from any loss of competitive advantage plus any negative impacts

---

[11] These data should come as no surprise. Research evidence for many years has consistently shown that voluntary reporting by organizations tends to be very partial, very patchy, descriptive and non-comparable. See, for example, Bierman and Dukes (1975); Benjamin and Stanga (1977); Perks and Butler (1977); Firth (1984); Burchell *et al.* (1985); Gray, Owen and Maunders (1987); Gray (1990d); Gray, Radebaugh and Roberts (1990).

[12] Gray *et al.* (1990).

[13] Wright and Kaposi (1992) suggest that an average plc will spend over £100,000 on design fees and production costs alone.

Figure 11.3   Extract from Ciba-Geigy Annual Report 1989

Our Responsibility for the Environment
Protection of the environment is the third pillar of our overall entrepreneurial responsibility, the first two being economic success and social obligations. This fact is expressed in what we spend on the principal activities:

- Product safety
- Process safety
- Environmental protection in production

Current and Capital Expenditure for Safety and Environmental Protection
in 1989

In millions of Swiss francs	Switzerland	Group companies	Total
Current expenditure			
Product safety	130	110	240
Process safety	90	140	230
Environmental protection (production)	200	260	460
Total	420	510	930
Capital expenditure			
Product safety	20	5	25
Process safety	40	70	110
Environmental protection (production)	180	85	265
Total	240	160	400

We also wish to go on making constant qualitative and quantitative progress, in other words to lower the consumption of natural resources and to reduce risks and the emission of wastes. We see in this, too, a contribution to qualitative growth. Product and process safety and environmental protection form part of the training of everyone at Ciba-Geigy right up to top management. The results are collected and assessed increasingly systematically by material and energy balance-sheets and by audits carried out regularly at all sites by technically qualified internal auditors.

on share prices and 'political' perceptions. Interestingly, their study showed that environmental disclosure was perceived by companies to have a very slight net cost but there was no loss of competitive advantage.

Motives for voluntary disclosure are unlikely to be simple. Our own experience suggested that disclosure depended, principally, upon the culture of the company as reflected in statements such as 'the company discloses because shareholders and other stakeholders have a right to the information' or 'we wish to demonstrate stewardship and a responsible management'. More pragmatically, one major chemical company said:

A statement of the financial spend is a sign of the company's commitment. It is increasingly realistic to recognize the need for environmental disclosure. The political climate is changing and it will become impossible to resist it. We also want to take our medicine early and to go through the pain barrier early in the process. We also want to tell people what we have done!

Whereas another of Britain's biggest companies recognized that: 'If customers and shareholders are going to have to pay the costs of more environmentally friendly activity then the figures will have to go into the accounts in order to demonstrate that one is serious.' Our own survey (see Appendix C) again met a general resistance to disclosure, but where disclosure *was* considered a positive move by companies the dominant reasons were stated as the shareholders' and/or the public's right to information.

In general, however, given the low level of disclosure, the more interesting questions concern why a company *does not* disclose more. Answers to this question varied during our visits and interviews:

- 'In the end, why should industry put its head above the parapet and disclose levels of organizational activity? What are the advantages? Where do you stop? Why not call for reporting of health and safety as well? It is only one part of the organization's mission' (a major energy, company).
- 'Not all the data is available and the company is getting used to collecting it. We will then disclose it a bit at a time to lessen the trauma' (a major chemical company).
- 'Our holding company are obsessively secretive and very keen to minimize the information in the accounts' (a medium-sized manufacturing company).
- 'We are just waiting to see what happens. There is no point in jumping the gun' (a major extractive company).
- 'We are a low key company and it [environmental activity] was something we were doing anyway. We never thought to make much fuss about it. It is the nature of the company not to make too much fuss about things' (a major electronic company).
- 'It is proving difficult to identify and isolate the figures' (a major consumer products company).
- 'It gets pushed out by the accountants. I don't suppose we have ever seen it as that important really' (a medium-sized engineering company).
- 'I don't know really. I hadn't thought about it' (a small electronics company).

Our own survey added something to this. The clearly dominant reasons given for non-disclosure were (in rank order): the absence of any demand for the information; the absence of a legal requirement; that the costs would outweigh the benefits; and, somewhat less

Figure 11.4

```
┌─────────────────────────────────────────────────────────────────┐
│                                                                   │
│        Reasons for voluntary disclosure or non-disclosure         │
│                                                                   │
│   Disclosure:                                                     │
│   •  If not done voluntarily it will become mandatory             │
│   •  To legitimize current activities                             │
│   •  To distract attention from other areas                       │
│   •  To develop corporate image                                   │
│   •  To build up expertise in advance of regulation               │
│   •  Positive impact on share price                               │
│   •  Reduction in perceived (company and information) risk         │
│   •  Political benefits                                           │
│   •  Competitive advantage                                        │
│   •  Shareholders' and other stakeholders' right to know          │
│   •  To explain expenditure patterns                              │
│   •  The desire to tell people what the company has done/achieved │
│   •  Forestall disclosure by other parties                        │
│                                                                   │
│   Non-disclosure:                                                 │
│   •  Obverse of the above                                         │
│   •  No need/motivation to do so                                  │
│   •  Wait and see                                                 │
│   •  Cost                                                         │
│   •  Data availability (and related costs)                        │
│   •  Secrecy                                                      │
│   •  Absence of demand for the information                        │
│   •  Absence of a legal requirement                               │
│   •  Never thought about it                                       │
│   •  Prioritizing areas for disclosure                            │
│                                                                   │
└─────────────────────────────────────────────────────────────────┘
```

important, that the organization had never considered it. (See Figure 11.4 and Appendix C.)

11.4   Proposals and Developments

In the last three years, there has been a growing number of corporations including their environmental efforts with their economic efforts as reported in their annual reports to shareholders. The vehicle that shareholders count on for accountability and the management of their investments, that is, the annual report, seems the logical place to demonstrate accountability for environmental stewardship on behalf of these same investors.

Certain companies have published annual environmental reports for shareholders and a broader community of external stakeholders. At present there is quite a bit of diversity in the way these reports are being developed. But I believe that it is only a matter of time before the stand alone environment report to shareholders will be an annual duty of the corporation. *It is a tool with potential profound impact. It can be part of the tool kit with which we rebuild public trust. We, at Alcan, are in the process of reviewing if we should move environmental reporting from the annual report to a stand alone.* Whatever is decided, it will be in keeping with the saying 'don't just trust us – track us'. (Dr R. Brouzes, Director Environmental Affairs, Alcan Aluminium Ltd, Canada. Given at the Canada–UK Colloquium on Environmental Issues, Glasgow, November 1991; emphasis added)

There is a growing concern in many countries that initiatives in environmental accounting and reporting must be grasped.[14] The initiatives may come from almost any source, but, in the market-knows-best world of the early 1990s, pre-eminent is pressure for voluntary action by corporations.

Voluntary Reporting Initiatives

The UK, for example, remains wedded to cajolery and the voluntary initiative. For instance, in May 1991 the Secretary of State for the Environment urged companies to set targets and publish accounts of their performance against those targets[15] and subsequently set up the Advisory Committee on Business and the Environment (ACBE) designed to derive an action plan for business and allow business to have a direct input to government policy. Other 'voluntary' efforts in the UK include Business-in-the-Environment, the CBI's Environment Business Forum, the Hundred Group of Finance Directors[16] and the Responsible Care Programme in the chemical industry. All these initiatives have some element of reporting built into them[17].

This voluntary emphasis is popular throughout Europe. Eco-audit and BS7750, for example (see Chapter 5), are intended to be adopted voluntarily by companies. Both of these initiatives have a requirement to report publicly. On a wider scale, the adoption of many of the international environmental charters such as Valdez and the ICC Charter for Sustainable Business (see Chapter 4) is voluntary and although the charters require a reporting commitment, there is no evidence of audit to ensure that this happens.

In general, the touching faith in the likely ubiquity of voluntary environmental reporting initiatives is entirely misplaced. As we saw above, there are really no grounds for believing anything of signi-

[14] For example from USA, Canada, Australia, New Zealand, Eire and the UK see, for example, Kestigan (1991); Rubenstein (1989); Molinaro (1991); Owen (1992); Bebbington and Gray (1990).

[15] The 1991 Shell Lecture at the Royal Society of Arts, as reported in the *Guardian*, 17 May 1991.

[16] The 100 Group released its 'Statement of Good Practice: Environmental Reporting in Annual Reports' in June 1992.

[17] For example the CBI Environment Business Forum requires that members subscribe to a set of environmental commitments and publish an annual report covering environmental disclosure; continued membership depends upon this performance.

ficance will happen in the voluntary domain. It will take leadership
of a less tentative kind to ensure that a substantial proportion of
enterprises report the effects of their environmental interactions.

The Accounting Profession

*First we [accountants] can encourage companies to develop innovative
environmental policies, to disclose them in the financial statements and to
keep them regularly updated . . . We must measure up to the environmental challenge if we are to fulfil our duty as a profession to promote the
public interest. We forget at our peril that we do not own our natural
assets, we merely hold them in trust for future generations.*

(Lickiss, 1991, p. 6)

The accounting profession's experience with social accounting in the
1970s suggests that, if history repeats itself, we can expect a lot of
interested speculation, warm words and controlled debate but very
little action or commitment. However, a significant proportion of the
accounting profession is concerned that an important initiative was
let slip in the 1970s and intends to avoid letting this happen again.
We may not get a third chance.[18] In the UK most of the major bodies
have established environmental initiatives. The ACCA has a major
research programme under way (of which this book is a product)
and has initiated the widely reported Environmental Report Awards
(of which more in the next chapter). The ACCA has also provided
initial funding for the establishment of a long-term initiative in
the form of the Centre for Social and Environmental Accounting
Research. CIMA has a standing committee on environmental matters
and has produced useful publications on energy (see Chapter 6) and
the costs of environmental sensitivity (see Chapter 3). The ICAEW
has established a major research fund to encourage research into
environmental accounting matters, and the research committee
overseeing the initiative reported its findings in 1992 and made
recommendations for consideration by the Accounting Standards
Board. CIPFA is engrossed in helping local government handle the
rather immediate and practical implications of Britain's growing
legislation whilst ICAS was reported to be considering the issues in
early 1992. Only the ACCA and ICAEW initiatives appear to be
attempting seriously to change corporate practice.[19]

In Canada, the CMA has offered guidelines on good practice
for the management accountant[20] whilst the CICA initiative[21] is

---

[18] See Owen (1992).

[19] Despite the significant initiative taken by the then President of the ICAEW, Mike
Lickiss, in recognizing the crucial challenge that environmental issues have for
accounting and the accounting profession (Lickiss, 1991) it has not spread further.

[20] CMA (1992).

[21] Reported in *The CICA Newsletter Dialogue*, November 1990, p. 2, the project is
'Accounting for and reporting on environmental issues within the existing financial

specifically designed to present information for consideration by the Accounting Standards Steering Committee. The CICA project will cover disclosure issues and consider matters such as accounting policies, costs charged to operations, environmental costs capitalized, liabilities and provisions (including contingent liabilities), tax implications and the potential legal implications of disclosure/non-disclosure.[22] Such an approach, whilst not having the force of law, will place recommendations and guidelines in a rather more forceful framework than the general levels of cajolery that the UK has tended to adopt.

It would seem that the accounting professions of the world are, as yet, reluctant to take the firm lead in environmental accounting that is needed. Indeed our own survey of UK accountants (see Appendix C) confirmed that although accountants may see their role as requiring that they contribute to innovation, very few were doing so in the environmental domain. This seemed to be for two dominant reasons: they had not seen this as part of their role and they did not know how accounting might contribute to the development of organizational environmental sensitivity.

The United Nations

What is probably the most significant and longest-standing initiative in the development of environmental reporting within a conventional financial accounting framework has come from the United Nations Centre for TransNational Corporations InterGovernmental Working Group of Experts on International Standards of Accounting and Reporting (UN CTC ISAR). The Ninth Session of UN CTC ISAR (1991) made detailed recommendations as to the types of environmental disclosure that corporations should undertake.[23] The intention of the UN CTC ISAR is that these recommendations should be adopted by sovereign governments. To date this has not happened. The Recommendations from the Ninth Session are summarized in Figure 11.5.

The report of the Tenth Session in March 1992 contained the results of the UN survey referred to above and interpreted these results as confirming the need for substantial guidance and the regulation of disclosure. Despite this, and without presenting *any* contrary evidence, it is apparent that many of the leading industrial nations continue to resist the UN's initiative and, in particular, any

---

reporting framework' and was approved by the Accounting Standards Steering Committee on 16 October 1990.

[22] This echoes USA experience in many ways. For more detail on the North American experience see, for example, Dirks (1991).

[23] See papers E/C.10/AC.3/1991/5.

Figure 11.5

Recommendations for environmental financial reporting from UN CTC ISAR 9th session

In the directors' report
- environmental issues pertinent to the company and industry;
- environmental policy adopted;
- improvements made since adopting the policy;
- enterprise's environmental emission targets and performance against these;
- response to government legislation;
- material environmental legal issues in which the enterprise is involved;
- effect of environmental protection measures on capital investment and earnings;
- material costs charged to current operations;
- material amounts capitalized in the period.

In the notes to the financial statements
- the accounting policies for recording liabilities and provisions, for setting up catastrophe reserves and for disclosing contingent liabilities;
- $/£ amount of liabilities, provisions and reserves established in the period;
- $/£ amount of contingent liabilities;
- tax effects;
- government grants received in the period.

---

possible disclosure requirements.[24] Major reasons employed in opposition to disclosure include the difficulty of collating the data and the dangers of providing price-sensitive information. The UN CTC Tenth Session survey (taken with a smaller survey conducted for the Ninth Session) seems to offer evidence which disputes this.

The survey for the Ninth Session examined German and Swiss companies' reporting. The sample of twenty companies was predominantly from the chemical and pharmaceutical and the metal and mining industries. It found a high level of specific (both financial and non-financial quantified) disclosure – sufficient to suggest that the problems with disclosure were far from insurmountable. The question arose as to why German and Swiss companies should have such a much higher level of disclosure, and concluded:

> ... since environmental expenditures were a large and growing share of their total expenditures, they felt they needed to keep track of them. Once having the information, they also claimed that the publication of this information was valuable. They received fewer questions on the environmental performance in shareholders meetings and local governments were

[24] This apparent assertion can be inferred from UN CTC ISAR papers E/C.10/AC.3/1992/3 and would be supported by anybody who has attended these sessions. It is widely recognized in UN CTC ISAR that the leading industrial countries *do not want any imposition of environmental disclosure.*

*more likely to grant approvals for their projects based upon their reputa-
tion for being 'open' about information disclosure.*[25]

The survey went on to look at developing countries and examined
the reporting by subsidiaries of German and Swiss companies in
Brazil. Here again the information was collected and used but,
importantly, disclosure was at a much lower level.

The Tenth Session survey built upon this but, in reporting the
results, concentrated upon industries rather than countries. The
survey attempted to assess the extent to which the world's largest
companies were disclosing the matters recommended in Figure 11.5.
Whilst 86 per cent disclosed some environmental data only 40 per
cent gave any financial data, 19 per cent provided quantitative
information on emissions and only 3 per cent (all from the USA)
gave information on contingent liabilities.[26] The reporting was not
systematic and exhibited significant industry differences, with
pharmaceuticals and motor industry companies disclosing significantly less qualitative, financial and non-financial quantitative
information than the forestry, metals, petrochemical and chemical
industries.

These surveys and similar studies consistently demonstrate a
marked reluctance by companies to disclose voluntarily. This leads
to a patchy and inconsistent set of disclosures. Little, if any, of
the information which might be disclosed presents insurmountable
barriers to companies, and those in some countries and some
industries are far more willing to disclose than the majority. Whilst
there is much to be learnt from the voluntary disclosure practices
of companies, if one is serious about the need for environmental
disclosure, voluntary codes will not achieve it.

The Business Council for Sustainable Development (BCSD)

The BCSD was established in Geneva by leading industrialists in the
run-up to the 'Earth Summit' in Rio de Janiero in July 1992.[27] The
Council commissioned a number of studies, one of which, in conjunction with the Canadian International Institute of Sustainable
Development (IISD), asked Deloitte & Touche/DRT International
(1991) to examine a framework for corporate reporting on sustainable development.[28] Ignoring, for the moment, the questions raised
by the term 'sustainable development' (these are considered in

[25] UN CTC ISAR Papers E/C.10/AC.3/1991/5, pp. 13–14.

[26] The exclusion of Canada from these figures for the disclosure of contingent
liabilities is difficult to explain in the light of Canadian disclosure. See, for example,
Hawkshaw (1991).

[27] See Chapter 15 and Schmidheiny, 1992.

[28] DRT International *Framework for Corporate Reporting on Sustainable Development*
(Toronto: DRT/BCSD/IISD) August 1991.

some detail in Chapter 14), the DRT International report was a relatively uncontentious review of accepted wisdom on developing environmental reporting. Despite its genesis, from an international accounting firm, its use of conventional accounting analysis (e.g. the relevance, understandability, verifiability, etc.) and its recognition of the failure of present accounting systems to deal with environmental matters, the report's interaction with the conventional accounting framework was negligible. Although there are recommendations for disclosure they are muted in a way that one might more usually associate with a UK accounting profession publication. Its recommendations rely principally upon selective reporting of physical targets and their achievement. There is little here that deserves attention, especially in a financial accounting context. The non-financial reporting material will be examined in some more detail in Chapter 12.

Changing Laws

As we have seen, beyond the relatively little information required by law in Norway, the USA and Canada, there appears to be a significant resistance to the development of legally required financial accounting and reporting about the environment. It is difficult to see how this attitude can be sustained for much longer – not just because the matters are crucial to environmental accountability and transparency (see Chapter 14) but because of the developments already in progress. In addition to the contingent liability and audit issues (dealt with in the next two sections), the roller-coaster of concern, awareness and knowledge of environmental issues must eventually bring about reporting regulation. This is especially likely in the EC. Chapter 5 noted the reporting requirements which are embedded into the eco-audit and BSI initiatives. In addition, the EC Directive on the Freedom of Access to Environmental Information[29] will place the increasing amount of information collected by regulatory bodies into the public domain – effectively the regulation of environmental reporting by another route. The days of environmental transparency are almost upon us.

It was therefore especially sad to see the demise of a UK initiative in the form of a private member's bill read in the House of Commons in January 1992.[30] The Corporate Safety and Environmental Information Bill would have required disclosure of (inter alia) enforcement notices and environmental convictions as well as health and safety data relating to employees. The bill predictably failed in the deregulation-is-next-to-godliness atmosphere of early 1990s

---

[29] European Directive 90/313 *Freedom of Access to Information*. See Chapter 10 for some discussion about how this is already bringing information into the ethical investment domain.

[30] Reported in *Accountancy*, March 1992, p. 48.

Britain but sparked more than a little interest and provided a fore-taste for the future.[31]

In the area of conventional financial accounting for the environment, the most likely pressures will come from the issues of the contingent liabilities and those arising through the statutory audit.

11.5   Contingent Liabilities, Remediation and Contaminated Land

In 1980 the United States issued the Comprehensive Environmental Response Compensation and Liability Act (CERCLA)[32] and ushered in a new era of environmental management with very specific accounting implications. CERCLA was designed to force 'responsible parties' to clean up land contaminated through dumping, waste storage, leakages, etc. To enable this to happen where the 'responsible party' was unable to find the costs of clean-up (remediation), CERCLA established a 'superfund' – 88 per cent of which came from industry – to pay for the process (hence the more common reference to this Act and similar proposals as 'Superfund'). By 1988, the USA Environmental Protection Agency had identified 27,000 potential sites for clean-up at an estimated $25 million per site. Of the 27,000, only 10,000 had been inspected, a little over 1,000 were on the National Priority List, 124 sites had remediation processes in operation and 43 had been cleaned up.[33] The potential of Superfund is immense but due to technical and legal difficulties[34] progress is slow. However the matter is clearly far from trivial and Wheatley[35] says of the situation: 'The situation in the United States is so serious that it threatens the solvency of the whole insurance industry as well as the solvency of many major corporations in the US. The EPA has estimated the cost of cleaning up the 27,000 waste disposal sites in the US would approach one trillion dollars.'

The accounting issues that arise from Superfund are fairly direct and cover the making of provisions for remediation, contingent liabilities and how to account for a fixed asset which suddenly acquires a negative value.[36] The matter has focused the mind of

[31] See the report by Andrew Jack, Green tinge to the company books, *Financial Times*, 15 January 1992, p. 16.

[32] As amended by the Superfund Amendments and Reauthorization Act of 1986 (SARA).

[33] See EPA Superfund Advisory, US EPA OS-110 (Washington DC: Office of Solid Waste and Emergency Response), Summer/Fall 1988. See also, for example, Arthur Andersen (1990), Wheatley (1991).

[34] It is said that the only people cleaning up under Superfund are the lawyers.

[35] Wheatley (1991) p. 208.

[36] See. for example, Newell, Kreuze and Newell (1990). However, the issue also spread further than accounting and corporations. Banks with loans secured on land

accountants on environmentally related matters like never before.[37]

The issue spread first to Canada, where in 1990 the Accounting Standards Steering Committee approved 'Capital Assets',[38] which requires that provisions be made for removal and site restoration costs. The issue is now growing in Europe. The EC Draft Directive on Civil Liability for Damage Caused by Waste is expected to be functional by 1993. Although not retrospective like Superfund, the financial implications for companies, insurers and bankers are considerable. The process of compiling the registers of contaminated land has already begun, in the UK under the provisions of the Environmental Protection Act 1990.[39]

This does not yet seem to have led to any noticeable response in accounting practice. The UN CTC ISAR survey found no contingent liabilities disclosed outside the USA, and in the UK, for example, the only such liabilities that do appear relate to US land.[40] There has been an increasing discussion in the UN CTC and elsewhere as to whether these environmental liabilities are in any sense different from 'ordinary' contingent liabilities which could fall within existing accounting rules on such matters[41] or, at a more general level, within the accrual concept of providing for future estimated expenditures. In this case, the oil and gas companies offer examples of possible practice where provision for site abandonment/remediation costs and contingent liabilities for site remediation would not be uncommon.[42]

A major spillover from these issues has been in the mergers and acquisitions market. An acquiring company which has not undertaken environmental audit to ascertain the potential environmental

---

found themselves identified as liable 'responsible parties' and insurance companies would find themselves having insured, effectively, uninsurable losses. For more detail see Rowley and Witmer (1988/89), Singh (1989), Sarokin and Schulkin (1991). See also Chapter 10.

[37] For detail on the US experience and the accounting implications see, for example, Surma and Vondra (1992), and Zyber and Berry (1992).

[38] CICA Handbook Section 3060 and for more detail see Hawkshaw (1991).

[39] For more detail see Humphreys (1991), Wheatley (1991) and Pollock (1992); although ENDS February/1992, p. 24 reports delays and problems with implementing the registers.

[40] This matter was discussed with two companies – both connected with extraction – during our visits. One company considered that they made very little impact on the environment and what little remediation they did have would be covered by the sale proceeds from breaking down the plant on the site. The other company recognized the issue and its potential size but being in a regulated industry it would need to apply for permission to increase its price to cover the subsequent provisions.

[41] For example SFAS 5 (FASB); IAS10 (IASC); SSAP18 (ASC/ASB).

[42] See, for example, KPMG Peat Marwick McLintock *Oil and Gas: A Survey of Published Accounts* (London: PMM) 1989, where information on the UK SORP (Accounting for Abandonment Costs) is outlined and examples of disclosure on abandonment and illustrations of contingent liabilities are provided.

liabilities of its target can find itself in the most serious financial problems. This has had the effect, already, of instilling some much-needed caution into the market – caution also extending into management buy-outs.[43] All deals in this area are thus affected by environmental factors in the alteration of prices and costs in these markets. In effect the whole of corporate finance is beginning to feel the wind of this change – with attendant effects on the financial director's role.

If these issues are half as serious as is suggested then the complete absence of such matters from the financial statements should give rise to concern. It is difficult to imagine how the absence of major contingent liabilities and the lack of provision for remediation costs can leave a set of accounts with a 'true and fair' view. It is an issue which is beginning to exercise the auditors.[44]

11.6   Statutory Audit of Financial Statements

The 'truth and fairness' of the financial statements – an elusive quality at the best of times – are not made easier to assess by the contingent liability and remediation provision issues. Furthermore, there are other elements of the accounting system which are driven by environmental matters and which may have a direct impact on the financial statements.[45] These include:

(1) *Obsolete stock* – through, for example, changing tastes or developments in legislation or other standards. Costs of storage and/or disposal of certain chemicals, for example, may also rise, with attendant implications for assessments of net realizable values.

(2) *Production assets* Changing legislation may make existing processes illegal or require additional costs, the life of assets may be shortened under BATNEEC, or changes in demands and/or standards relating to the product may decline. All of these will reduce the life and terminal value of the asset.

(3) *Depreciation policy* – to reflect changing conditions of life of productive assets.

(4) *Viability of product lines* – may be put into question through changing taste, standards or legislation. This may raise going-concern issues.

(5) *Additional costs of production or processes* – ranging from increasing upstream cost (through, say, changing standards on extractive

---

[43] See, for example, Buying trouble, *KPMG Dealwatch*, Vol. 91, no. 2, 1991, pp. 3–7.

[44] For an especially useful introduction to the issues for accounting in a European context see Ball and Maltby (1992).

[45] This is a message widely publicized by David Pimm of Coopers and Lybrand Deloitte, and published in *The Environment and the Auditor*, a discussion paper from C&LD, 1990.

Figure 11.6

Some areas in which the statutory financial statements and audit will need to reflect environmental considerations

- Contingent Liabilities: especially on contaminated land but also spills and unauthorised emissions;
- Provisions: especially for remediation, abandonment and decommissioning costs (cf the oil and gas company practice) but also waste disposal and recycling commitments as well as potential catch-up, insurance and legal costs;
- Reserves: especially for catastrophes;
- Valuation of Fixed Assets: especially land and buildings;
- Depreciation Policy: to recognise, for example, shorter life of productive assets under rising BATNEEC considerations;
- Additional Capital Costs Associated with Productive Assets: especially the need to incur additional costs to bring existing plant within current standards;
- Obsolete Inventory and Inventory Costs: including stock made obsolete through environmental concerns, storage and disposal costs of environmentally-malign materials and recycling commitments.

---

industries or an energy tax) through to costs of pollution abatement equipment and the costs of waste disposal. These must be anticipated, perhaps provided for and questions of capitalization of certain expenditures considered.

(6) *Catch-up and potential legal costs* How should significant costs incurred or, more difficult, major potential liabilities arising from legislation be considered? This clearly relates to the remediation, abandonment and contingent liability issues discussed above. What, however, is an auditor to do when a company will not disclose these things and thereby impairs what little truth and fairness the financial statements might claim?

These matters will spill over into the illegal acts of an auditor's clients. The problem, however, is that until either the organization has the sense to undertake an environmental audit (see Chapter 5) or the HMIP or other regulator turns up on the doorstep, how is the auditor to assess the risks associated with environmental issues?

These matters are clearly far from trivial but, to date, the accounting profession has not chosen to give any serious lead in this area. The Big Six firms are taking the matters seriously – as witnessed by the publicity granted to the Coopers and Lybrand decision to train their students in the environmental implications in the statutory audit. Some of the Big Six, however, also have the environmental expertise they need sitting on the other side of the Chinese Wall in their management consultancy departments. For firms without this facility, the matter probably deserves immediate and serious attention.

Finally, should a company or other organization produce a set of environmental accounts and ask for an auditors' report, how can, how should the auditor act? This is likely to become a more common problem.[46]

11.7   Further Experiments

As the need for environmental reporting increases so will the experimentation with various approaches to incorporating environmental factors within the financial framework. These will probably be of three broad types: further developments within conventional financial accounting (of which the BSO/Origin experiment is the most notable recent attempt – see below); approaches from the direction of sustainability (which is examined in more detail in Chapter 14); and attempts to learn from – and link to – experimentation with national accounting systems. As long as there is a desire to remain within conventional financial measurement it seems most likely that much can be learnt from the years of experimentation with adjusting national income accounts and the United Nations' System of National Accounts (SNA) to correct for the more outrageous failures of the SNA and to incorporate environmental factors into measurements of a nation's well-being. As yet, experiments at the corporate reporting level have not fully explored these possibilities. Recent attempts, for example, in France and Norway to link corporate accounts to national accounts through environmental 'satellite' accounts have generated a lot of interest but have, so far, produced nothing workable and the approach appears to have been (temporarily) abandoned. Nevertheless this remains an area of great potential for future research.[47]

At the same time, it would be a mistake to forget that the environment was not 'invented' in the late 1980s. As a result there are experiments from the past that deserve attention. Two notable such attempts are those from Dierkes and Preston (1977) and Ullmann (1976). Ullmann, for example, sought to define, based on case-study work, a corporate environmental accounting system (CEAS). By trying to tie together the economic and the environmental, he produced what he called 'CEAS units'. These he defined as:

> *First, the company measures its environmentally relevant inputs and outputs in physical units (tons, kWh, cbft etc). Second, by multiplying these amounts with the corresponding [Equivalent Factors – defined by*

[46] To date, the independently attested environmental reports – for example, Norsk Hydro, British Airways and Body Shop – have used environmental consultants rather than accountants to act as auditor. More obviously *financial* environmental accounts – for example BSO/Origin, see below – have not requested attestation of their reports.

[47] See, for example, Peskin, Portney and Kneese (1981), Ahmad, El-Serafy and Lutz (1989), Daly (1989), The Economist (1989), Peskin (1989), Ruckelhaus (1989), Wright (1989), Lutz, Munasinghe and Chander (1990), Peskin and Lutz (1990), Repetto (1990), Anderson (1991), and see also Christophe (1989) and Christophe and Bebbington (1992).

reference to scarcity and impact] and by adding up the resulting CEAS-units, a sum is obtained which reflects the total environmental impact produced by the company's business activities during one year.[48]

The model and its principles, although somewhat naive and underdeveloped, offer a different approach to incorporating the physical environment into the accounting system of an organization.

There were other, earlier, experiments in the USA – most notably by Linowes, Eastern Gas and Fuel Associates, Philips Screw, First National Bank of Minneapolis and Clark C. Abt and Associates.[49] All have lessons for the development of forms of environmental reporting and from which companies such as BSO/Origin could learn to avoid reinventing wheels and thereby save money and resources.

11.8   BSO/Origin[50]

BSO/Origin is a Dutch company whose experimental environmental accounts are especially notable in that they attempt to link the economic and environmental activities through financial numbers reported in an amended value added statement. The previous, most remarkable experiment in this direction of reporting information which attempted to link the economic and the 'non-economic' was the social accounts produced by management consultants Clark C. Abt in the USA in the early to mid-1970s. These accounts from Abt attempted to show a fully integrated set of financial and social accounts through both a profit and loss account and balance sheet. The experiment was one from which a great deal was learnt but much more experimentation is necessary to determine whether or not the idea could be fully operationable. The impression gained from the Abt experiment was that whilst much could be done, the resultant numbers were so confusing as to verge on the meaning-less. Nevertheless, the Cement Corporation of India did produce and publish a set of Abt-based social financial statements in 1981. This demonstrated that you could do this – even if you could not be entirely sure what it was you had done when you finished.[51]

The BSO/Origin company, again a management consultancy like Abt, has continued the experiment but has cleverly avoided a number of the Abt pitfalls by focusing on the value added statement (VAS). The VAS is both a more focused statement than the con-

---

[48] Ullmann (1976) p. 74 and see also Dierkes and Preston (1977).

[49] For more detail see e.g. Estes, 1976; Belkaoui, 1984; Gray, Owen and Maunders, 1987.

[50] The following is adapted from Gray and Symon (1992b) but see also Huizing and Dekker (1992), who review the 1990 accounts, and *ENDS Report* 210/July 1992, pp. 19–21, which also reviews the 1991 accounts.

[51] For more detail see Gray, Owen and Maunders, 1987.

stantly debated profit and loss account and balance sheet and, in addition, has the advantage of explicitly recognizing that share-holders are neither the only participants in, nor the only contri-butors to, organizational activity. The VAS was originally devised as either (depending upon one's point of view) a labour-centred attempt to demonstrate the contribution of labour to the financial success of the organization, or as a business-centred attempt to indicate the share of the organization's financial success that the employees received. BSO/Origin places the environment in the position of labour and, most notably, takes the business-centred, rather than environment-centred position. In fact, it comes as no surprise to learn that, by reference to its own calculations, BSO/Origin still shows a net value added (as opposed to value lost) after allowing for environmental factors.

In addition to the statutory financial statements and the usual review of operations, BSO/Origin's rather splendidly designed 1990 annual report contains a seven-page (13-page if the pictures are included) essay entitled 'Pulling our planet out of the red' plus three pages of environmental accounts together with five pages of explanatory notes. The essay is among the most coherent, brief expositions of a mid- to deep-green position one is likely to find as well as being (as far as we are aware) the most direct and honest assessment of the corporate/environmental relationship from a company. It is well worth reading for this alone.[52] However, the essay's principal purpose is to explain the thinking behind the environmental accounts.

BSO/Origin's starting point is that environmental crisis requires that we begin to recognize that economic value added has been achieved only at the cost of environmental degradation. If we are to know the real value added (*sic*) then we must deduct the ecological value lost (*sic*). The company then goes on to argue that ecological impact can occur at three stages: direct from the company, down-stream from the company (i.e. via the consumer) and upstream from the company (i.e. the supplier). But what should be included? BSO argues that it is essential for all companies to produce environmental accounts if any real progress is to be made. This is because only then can we avoid the double-counting of, for example, impacts that arise from the products the company purchases for use. Very clear rules are needed to establish which ecological impacts can be determined as falling to which organization – that is, to allocate carefully the ecological impact of activities between the organizations and in-dividuals involved in (say) the extraction of the raw materials, the processing, the manufacture and the use of the end product.[53] An

[52] The 1991 report is introduced by an invited essay on anthropology and the devastation of ethnocentrism.

[53] The issues discussed here are also apparent in the concerns in life cycle assessment – see Chapter 9.

important point is made in this context: any company can reduce its apparent direct impact by (for example) switching from fuel oil heating to electric heating and thereby handing the responsibility for the emissions back to the supplier.

BSO is very clear that its decisions as to what to include and value and what to exclude are largely arbitrary. This clarity is very valuable to future experimenters as well as to users of these accounts, who are therefore able to add in or deduct items at their discretion. The company assumes that it causes little downstream negative impact and, given the nature of its business, suspects that the downstream effects will, on balance, be ecologically positive. The downstream effects are thus ignored. The upstream effects (suppliers) are ignored because those matters should be dealt with in the supplier's environmental accounts and there is too little information for BSO to establish impact. The company does, however, make two exceptions: in the use of energy supplied to the company and in the supply of waste-processing facilities which the company purchases. The essay then concludes with some explanation as to how the different ecological impacts were valued – the impacts are imaginatively derived but all impacts are not valued on the same bases. The calculations are shown in more detail in the explanatory notes accompanying the environmental accounts.

The accounts themselves provide a detailed breakdown of the ecological value lost. This is shown as 'Cost of environmental effects' (itemized between various emissions and wastes) less 'environmental expenditure' (being the net expenditure undertaken by the company). The net value lost is then shown against the conventional economic value added by the company to produce a net value added. (This is summarized, based on the 1990 accounts, in Figure 11.7)

BSO/Origin, wisely, claims little for these accounts (which are not audited). On the down-side, the company recognizes that the accounts are partial, subjective and, in effect, add possible apples to approximate pears and subtract the result from hypothetical oranges. One would be ill-advised to place any weight on these accounts. However, with very good reason it *does* claim that experiments such as these are essential if business is to contribute to sustainability and that some experimentation is preferable to inaction. BSO further suggests that there is much value in the process itself of undertaking this kind of analysis. It is for these reasons that we believe that the BSO/Origin experiment deserves wide attention and the company deserves significant applause for the attempt. These environmental accounts are not the end of the journey but one step along the way – along which BSO/Origin intends to continue. (An extract from the BSO/Origin 1990 Accounts is included in Appendix 11.1)

Figure 11.7

Valuing ecological impact with BSO/Origin

Putting financial numbers to ecological impact must choose between, typically: the cost of preventing the ecological impact; the cost of repairing the ecological damage; the value lost to society from the ecological impact. BSO/Origin, in common with most experiments, mixes the three. Consider the following:

NO_x and SO_2 emissions
NO_x emissions are 'valued' at Dfl.10 per kg NO_x. This appears to be a reasonable assessment of the *costs of reducing* NO_x emissions. This does not measure 'ecological impact'. SO_2 on the other hand is 'valued' using a hybrid method, viz. 'the impact of both NO_x and SO_2 ... is essentially associated with acid rain ... Since 1kg SO_2 contains 1.44 times the acid equivalent of 1kg NOx its environmental impact can be calculated on a proportional basis, giving a costing of (1.44 x Dfl.10 = Dfl.14 per kg SO_2). This is the value we have used for SO_2.' Thus an estimate of its ecological impact is derived by taking a figure for the cost of prevention and multiplying it by a factor of its impact. The resultant number means little if anything at all. It *does not* capture ecological impact.

Waste water
The 'value' of the ecological impact is taken to be an estimate of the cost of returning the waste water to drinking water. (The calculation is not a full ecological impact calculation because it makes no attempt to account for ecological impact – e.g. destruction of habitat, health hazard, etc.). The calculations are based upon domestic water cleansing costs, noting the special nature of the company's effluent (e.g. heavy metals) and measured in terms of Dutch 'inhabitant equivalents'. BSO/Origin estimates its water waste costs twice this figure, namely 48Dfl per inhabitant equivalent.

These calculations employ three different bases to produce financial numbers. They are not comparable. For the accounts to have more meaning the calculations will have to be performed on a consistent basis.

11.9   Practical Ways Forward?

For a company seeking to develop its environmental reporting within the conventional financial accounting system there are a number of strands that can be woven together. First, the backbone must be the proposals from the UN CTC ISAR. These represent current interpretations of best practice, fall comfortably within the current financial reporting framework and, importantly, have been shown to be practicable and unlikely to be price-sensitive. This amounts, in effect, to disclosure of accounting policies and identification of income, expenditure, investment and (actual and contingent) liabilities related to environmental matters.[54] The second stage is to consider the material in the earlier sections on contingent liabilities etc. and statutory audit. That is, to expand on the UN's proposals to take account of wider remediation and abandonment issues (and the provisions related thereto) and to recognize explicitly

---

[54] For more detail see Gray (1990d) and the relevant UN papers.

Figure 11.8

Suggested practical approach to financial environmental accounting and reporting

The United Nations recommendations
* disclosure of accounting policies;
* cost of current environmental expenditure;
* environmental expenditure capitalized in the period;
* liabilities, provisions and reserves;
* contingent liabilities;
* tax effects;
* grants received.

Develop disclosure with the auditor in mind
* reconsider provisions for remediation and abandonment;
* provisions for inventory, accelerated depreciation, new investments, etc.;
* actual and provided-for legal costs.

Make the environment more visible
* disclose energy (including transport) costs;
* disclose waste handling and disposal costs;
* disclose legal compliance costs;
* consider packaging costs;
* consider the disclosure of environmental fines.

---

the concerns that a statutory auditor may have. The third stage is to recognize that a major effect of accounting and reporting is to make things *visible*[55] – and by so doing, to make other things *invisible*.[56] The disclosure of, for example, energy costs, waste disposal costs, legal compliance costs, costs of packaging, fines for breaking (e.g.) consents, etc., represents a simple and cheap way of reflecting some of the environmental aspects of the organization within the financial statements.

These proposals are summarized in Figure 11.8. To take them further, the organization will need to undertake its own experimentation, learn from previous experiments (e.g. the BSO/Origin approach) and/or try to address the issue of accounting for sustainability (see Chapter 14).

Ultimately, however, reporting and accounting for the environment cannot be entirely satisfactory within a conventional financial

[55] See e.g. Hopwood, 1986; Gray, 1992; Laughlin, 1991.

[56] Thus, for example, the flurry in the UK over the disclosure of R&D expenditure came down to whether or not companies were willing to emphasize this number and, thus, emphasize the activity. The presence of R&D in a set of financial statements draws attention to the issue. It is the same with labour-related expenditure. The UK has a fairly healthy level of disclosure of labour-related expenditure and this has the effect of raising the importance of that issue and, one hopes, of recognizing the importance of labour itself. So it can be with environmentally related expenditures and income.

accounting framework – other forms of non-financial accounting and reporting become necessary. This is the purpose of Chapter 12.

Further Reading

Capitalization of costs to treat environmental contamination (1990) Emerging Issues Task Force Report 90–8 (Norwalk CT: FASB).

Company Reporting, no. 13, July 1991.

Environment Research Group (1992) *Business, Accountancy and the Environment: A policy and research agenda*, ICAEW, London.

Financial Reporting, published by ICAEW, surveys British environmental reporting in the 1991 and the 1992 edition.

Gray, R. H. (1990) *The Greening of Accountancy: The Profession after Pearce*, ACCA, London.

Gray, R. H., Owen, D. L. and Maunders, K. T. (1987) *Corporate Social Reporting: Accounting and Accountability*, Prentice-Hall International, Hemel Hempstead.

Owen, D. L. (1992) *Green Reporting: The Challenge of the Nineties*, Chapman Hall, London.

Roberts, C. B. (1990) *International Trends in Social and Employee Reporting*, ACCA, London.

Rubenstein, D. (1991) The lessons of love, *CA Magazine* (Canada), March, pp. 35–41.

Society of Management Accountants of Canada (1992) *Accounting for the Environment: Management Accounting Issues Paper 1*, CMA, Hamilton.

Surma, J. P. and Vondra, A. A. (1992) Accounting for environmental costs *Journal of Accountancy* (USA) March, pp. 51–55.

United Nations Centre for Transnational Corporations (1992) *International Accounting and Reporting*, United Nations, New York.

White, M. A. (1992) 'SEC disclosures of environmental matters' in *The Greening of Environmental Business*, Sacha Millstone (ed.), Government Institutes, Washington DC.

In addition to the references provided throughout the text it is necessary to try to stay in touch with the very rapidly developing environmental agenda through, for example, *The ENDS Report, KPMG Environmental Briefing Note, KPMG European Environment Briefing Note, Integrated Environmental Management, CBI Environment Newsletter* or any of the other newsletters in the field.

APPENDIX 11.1
Extract from the BSO/Origin 1990
Annual Report

Cost of environmental effects in thousands of guilders

Atmospheric emissions

	Emission	Unit cost		Total
			Dfl.	
Natural gas for heating purposes				
NO_x	456 kg	10 Dfl./kg	5	
CO_2	483 t.	100 Dfl./t.	48	
Total				53
Electricity consumption				
SO_2	7,934 kg	14 Dfl./kg	111	
NO_x	6,202 kg	10 Dfl./kg	62	
Particulate emissions	667 kg	10 Dfl./kg	7	
CO_2	2,515 t.	100 Dfl./t.	252	
Total				432
Road traffic				
NO_x	20,585 kg	40 Dfl./kg	823	
HC	14,948 kg			
CO	55,452 kg			
CO_2	7,232 t.	100 Dfl./t.	723	
Total				1546
Air traffic				
NO_x	1,160 kg	10 Dfl./kg	12	
CO_2	317 ton	100 Dfl./t.	32	
Total				44
Waste incineration				
SO_2	300 kg	14 Dfl./kg	4	
NO_x	369 kg	10 Dfl./kg	4	
Particulate emissions	254 kg	10 Dfl./kg	3	
HCl	692 kg	13 Dfl./kg	9	
CO_2	277 t.	0 Dfl./kg	0	
Total				20
Subtotal				2,095

	Emission	Unit cost		Total
			Dfl.	
Atmospheric emissions (subtotal)				2,095
Waste water				
Water treatment	277 inh.eq.	48 Dfl./i.e.	13	
Transport	277 inh.eq.	12 Dfl./i.e.	3	
Residual water pollution			27	
Total waste water				43
Waste				
Company waste production				
Quantity	377 t.			
Recycled paper	− 146 t.			
Net waste	231 t.			
Collection	377 t.	80 Dfl./t.	30	
Incineration	231 t.	100 Dfl./t.	23	
Residual waste after incineration				
Bottom ash	23 t.	100 Dfl./t.	2	
Fly ash	7 t.	200 Dfl./t.	1	
Subtotal			56	
Power station waste production				
Fly ash	64 t.	200 Dfl./t.	13	
Water treatment waste production				
Sludge	4 t. dry matter	500 Dfl./t. dry matter	2	
Total waste				71
Grand total				2,209

Environmental expenditure in thousands of guilders

	Dfl.
Fuel levies (Netherlands)	
Natural gas (heating)	1
LPG (cars)	18
Power station fuel	8
Total	27
Water treatment and refuse collection charges, sewerage charges and other environmental taxes	138
Private-sector waste processors	51
Total	216

Value lost
in thousands of guilders

	Dfl.
Cost of environmental effects	2,209
Environmental expenditure	− 216
Value lost	1,993

Net value added
in thousands of guilders

	Dfl.
Value added	255,614
Value lost	− 1,993
Net value added	253,621

The Environmental Accounts form part of BSO/Origin 1990 Annual Report. For more information please write to BSO/Origin, P.O. Box 8348, 3503 RH Utrecht, The Netherlands.

12.   External Reporting and Auditing II:

Non-Financial Reporting

12.1   Introduction

As we have already seen in Chapter 11, the separation of financial and non-financial environmental reporting is somewhat artificial. But non-financial forms of disclosure are often the easiest – and cheapest – for an organization to undertake initially. It is no surprise therefore to learn that non-financial reporting is by far the more common.[1] Sadly, however, much of this 'disclosure' is largely empty of content. On a worldwide basis, the majority of such 'disclosure' can be categorized as statements of good intentions and selective self-congratulatory assertions owing more to image and advertising than to information communication, accountability and transparency. We will pay little attention to such 'disclosure' in this chapter but try to concentrate on the more constructive forms of non-financial disclosure – that might actually pass as informative.

More specifically, Chapter 1[2] demonstrated that an essential factor in environmental degradation arises from conventional accounting's restriction to only money measurement and the consequent exclusion of environmental matters from the accounting systems. As a result, non-financial environmental reporting, when undertaken in a serious spirit, is likely to be the more relevant to the matter in hand – the physical environment – and be potentially more informative. Ultimately, 'good' non-financial disclosure is likely to be the more powerful means of discharging environmental accountability (see Chapter 14 for more detail).

---

[1] As all the surveys of both environmental reporting – and the wider social reporting – have shown. See, for example, the UN CTC survey (referred to in Chapter 11) and other surveys summarized in Owen (1992), Gray, Owen and Maunders (1987), Gray (1990c), Owen (1991), Roberts (1991).

[2] See also Gray (1990d); (1992).

Figure 12.1

Examples of influences on organizational disclosure of non-financial data (with a UK emphasis)

Self-generating
* 'Market' pressure (1–3, 5)*
* Peer pressure (1–4)
* Employee considerations (1–4)
* Environmental policies (4, 5)
* Public relations (1–4, 13)

Industry initiatives (2–4, 12)
* ACBE
* Business-in-the-Environment
* UK Environment Business Forum
* Chemical Industries Association

Voluntary 'regulations'
* Eco-audit and the verification of information (5, 11)
* BS7750 (5)
* Eco-labelling (5, 9)
* Signing up to charters (4)
* UN CTC ISAR proposals (11)

Compulsory regulations
* Freedom of access to information (2, 3, 11)
* Environmental impact assessments (5)
* Environmental Protection Act (2, 3)
* EC and the single market (2, 3)

*Note: the numerals indicate chapters where further detail can be found.

Non-financial disclosure is also the area in which, in Europe at least, cajolery, industry initiatives and regulation are having (and will have) their greatest impact. That is, the types of information required under codes of conduct, charters, BS7750, eco-labelling, eco-audit, the Freedom of Access to Information Directive, etc.; all emphasize the presentation of information related to activity rather than finance, impact rather than costs, environmental targets rather than investment.

12.2   The Pressures to Disclose

Most of what we outlined in Chapter 11 – in terms of developments, reasons for disclosure/non-disclosure, etc. – applies equally to the disclosure of non-financial data. The pressures on organizations to disclose are considerable and growing (see Figure 12.1, which also refers to the chapters in which further detail can be found). The essential implication of Figure 12.1 is that all organizations will find themselves subject to an increasing amount of transparency regarding their dealings with the environment. If, then, for no other reason than to forestall criticism, avoid legal wrangles or to minimize the possibility of being caught in either embarrassing ignorance or an apparent state of disregard for the biosphere,[3] organizations are beginning to acknowledge that some pre-emptive environmental disclosure starts to make sense.

However, there are no limits to the way in which an organization might chose to report and, whereas there is some sort of framework placing limits and structures on financial accounting,[4] no such structure exists for non-financial reporting. Recognizing this, we have established the steps outlined in Figure 12.2 as a guide to building up an organization's approach to environmental reporting. These steps – which whilst they may appear discrete, clearly are rarely so in practice – will provide the broad framework for this chapter.

12.3   Disclosing Policy

The first step in Elkington's 'Ten Steps to Environmental Excellence' (1987) reviewed in Chapter 3 was the establishment of an environmental policy (see Chapter 4). This is the first necessary (but not sufficient) condition for any organization serious about increasing its environmental sensitivity. The next logical step is to communicate that policy to constituents and stakeholders.

An organization may establish an environmental policy either by subscribing to one of the public charters or by deriving its own (see Chapter 4). A few companies may do both, many have done neither. There is, however, a slow but steady increase in the adoption of policies. One survey of major UK companies suggested that 60 per cent had such a policy but only 60 per cent *of those* disclosed them.[5]

Disclosure of policy has a number of identifiable stages. First, an organization may simply state that it has an environmental policy. Next, that policy, or a summary of it may be disclosed – within the annual report or elsewhere. Figure 12.3 presents one such example from Alcan Ltd (Canada).[6] In the UK the 1990 reports of GEC and Delta went somewhat further and presented selected items of activity; other companies (for example, United Biscuits and Vickers) seemed content merely to recognize that the environment presented issues for the business. Figure 12.4, from British Gas and Petro-

---

[3] Witness, for example, recent problems for Exxon, Shell, British Petroleum, Imperial Chemicals Industries, Albright and Wilson, etc.

[4] Albeit a somewhat rickety one; see, for example, Laughlin and Gray (1988) for an introduction.

[5] This compares favourably (if somewhat surprisingly) with the *Company Reporting* survey of 1991 which found only 5 per cent of companies in the UK disclosed environmental policy. See Hillary (1992) and for more detail see Chapters 2 and 4.

[6] Note that this was a 1988 report and things have moved on – for Alcan, if not for other companies – since then.

Figure 12.2

Steps in environmental accounting and reporting

POLICY
(i) Statement of environmental policy (or steps being taken). The Valdez Principles or ICC are the current state of the art.
(ii) Steps taken to monitor compliance with policy statement.
(iii) Statement of compliance with policy statement.

PLANS AND STRUCTURE
(i) Structural and responsibility changes undertaken in the organization to develop environmental sensitivity (e.g. VP of environment; committees; performance appraisal of line managers).
(ii) Plans for environmental activities – introduction of Environmental Impact Assessment; Environmental Audit; Projects; Investment Appraisal criteria; etc.
(iii) Talks with local green groups; plans to work with community etc.

FINANCIAL (see Chapter 11)
(i) Amount spent on environmental protection – capital/revenue; reaction to/anticipation of legislation; voluntary/mandated; damage limitation/proactive (enhancement) initiatives.
(ii) Anticipated pattern of future environmental spend – to meet legislation, as voluntary; capital/revenue.
(iii) Assessment of actual and contingent liabilities (e.g. 'Superfund' type problems); impact on financial audit; impact on financial results.

ACTIVITY
(i) Compliance with standards audits, procedures for, results of and issue of compliance with standards report.
(ii) Environmental audit and issue of summary/results.
(iii) Physical units analysis on (e.g.) materials, waste and energy.
(iv) Analysis of dealings with regulatory bodies/fines/complaints.
(v) Awards/commendations received.
(vi) Analysis of investment/operating activity influenced by environmental considerations.
(vii) Analysis/description of voluntary projects undertaken (e.g. tree planting; schools liaison).

SUSTAINABLE MANAGEMENT (see Chapter 14)
(i) Identification of critical, natural sustainable/substitutable, and man-made capital under the influence of (not necessarily 'owned' by) the organization.
(ii) Statement of transfers between categories.
(iii) Estimates of sustainable activities.
(iv) Estimates of 'sustainable costs' which would have to be incurred to 'return the organization (and thus future generations) to same position as they were in before the activity'.
(v) Assessment and statement of input/output resource-flows and changes therein.

An alternative or complementary reporting form might recognize the different dimensions of environmental impact – such as resources used; emissions; waste; energy; products; transport; packaging; health and safety; toxic hazards; biosphere; built environment; visual environment; community interaction.

Figure 12.3

> ### Extract from Alcan Aluminium annual report 1988
>
> '... *take all practical steps to prevent or abate all forms of pollution which result from our operations...*'
>
> From Alcan: *Its Purposes, Objectives and Policies* June 1978
>
> Alcan has a continuing commitment to good environmental performance and plays an active role in supporting the Brundtland concept of 'sustainable development'. It is responding to the challenge of rising environmental standards in many ways, from total plant replacement to land reclamation. Concern for all stakeholders, including the local community, is the corporate and personal guideline. Environmental controls, both inside plants and in their surroundings, are an integral part of our operations. Over the last 10 years, more than $480 million has been spent on environmental improvement measures.

Canada, represents what might be considered 'standard' disclosures of environmental policy.

Policies are, by the nature of things, typically general documents. The next stage for an organization is to turn the policy into specific objectives, then to disclose this and, eventually, to report upon the level to which those objectives have been met. Two UK examples, from ICI and IBM, are good illustrations of this. ICI published a general environmental policy in 1989;[7] published specific targets in the 1990 annual report (see Figure 12.5) and, in 1991, published an analysis of progress towards those targets.[8] IBM went further, and offered hostages to fortune in the form of specified dates for the achievement of objectives (see Figure 12.6).[9]

In a tidy, textbook, world policies should translate neatly to plans, goals and objectives against which reports of activity should be disclosed. However, these neat distinctions between policies, activities, objectives, plans, etc. are frequently blurred in practice.[10]

12.4   Plans and Structures

Having disclosed an environmental policy, an organization then needs to decide how (if at all) it intends to meet this policy. That will

[7] This policy was available separately, published in April 1989. It is fairly general, even as policy statements go. ICI has also signed the ICC Charter but makes no obvious reference to this.

[8] See ICI *Progress Towards Environmental Objectives 1991* for more detail and a good illustration of reporting practice.

[9] The company also includes a mini-endorsement from John Elkington – one of Britain's leading environmental auditors. For more detail see *IBM UK Environmental Programmes* 1990.

[10] A major chemicals company stated that their reporting policy was clearly *ad hoc* in that they were reporting (and intend to continue reporting) as information and data on elements of their environmental strategy became available.

Figure 12.4A

BRITISH GAS
AND THE ENVIRONMENT

**British Gas is responsible for providing
gas safely, efficiently and economically to
over 17 million customers. Its operations
include: exploring for, producing, storing, and
transporting natural gas and oil, both in the UK
and internationally; the sale and servicing of
equipment and appliances for the use of gas; and
world-wide technical and consultancy services.**

**It is Company policy to take full account of the environ-
mental, health and safety implications of its operations,
and to protect the natural environment. Specifically,
British Gas aims:**

● **to comply with the spirit as well as the letter of environmental, health and safety legislation and approved codes
of practice, co-operating fully with relevant statutory and
non-statutory bodies;**

● **to assess the likely environmental effects of planned
projects and operations, and to maintain throughout its
operations standards of environmental protection reflecting best industry practice in comparable situations,
improving on such standards where reasonably
practical and economic;**

● **to foster among staff, suppliers, customers, shareholders, and communities local to British Gas
operations, an understanding of environmental issues
in the context of the business, and to report publicly
on the Company's environmental performance.**

**The Company has always paid particular attention
to environmental issues relevant to its activities,
and in recent years has won Environmental
Management Awards in the UK and in Europe.**

British Gas

Source: British Gas plc, 1990

Figure 12.4B Petro-Canada's Environmental Policy

P E T R O - C A N A D A
POLICIES

ENVIRONMENTAL PROTECTION

Environmental protection is a fundamental Petro-Canada value. The Corporation recognizes that every employee has a vital role to play in achieving environmental protection. Senior management will lead in the implementation of this policy. Petro-Canada's commitment will be incorporated into business activities through the following guiding principles. Petro-Canada will:

- ensure our operations comply with government legislation, corporate policy and applicable industry standards concerning the protection of the environment and the public

- determine, evaluate and mitigate the environmental impacts of our business during project planning, implementation, operation and decommissioning

- ensure that appropriate waste and emissions management programs are developed and implemented

- respond to emergencies in a prompt and effective manner

- ensure that all employees and others engaged on our behalf are aware of the need, informed of the requirements and trained to protect the environment

- use energy and other resources efficiently in our operations

- support research on the environmental effects of our products, processes and waste materials

- deal openly and fairly with members of the public regarding our activities

- support its employees, involved in legal proceedings which result from their employment, to the full extent it considers reasonable

Divisional presidents and vice-presidents are responsible for developing specific operational procedures and standards which are consistent with this policy. Petro-Canada expects its suppliers, partners and business associates to have compatible environmental procedures and values.

Corporate status reports will be presented regularly to Executive Council and the Board of Directors.

The President and Chief Operating Officer is accountable for the maintenance, regular review and interpretation of this policy.

W.H. Hopper
Chairman and Chief Executive Officer

February, 1992
Date

J.M. Stanford
President and Chief Operating Officer

Figure 12.5

ICI Statement of Environmental Objectives

1. All new ICI plants will be built to standards capable of meeting all regulations that might reasonably be expected in the most environmentally demanding country in which ICI will operate that process.

2. ICI will reduce waste from its operations by 50 per cent by 1995, paying special attention to that which is hazardous.

3. To establish an even more rigorous programme for conserving energy and re- sources, paying particular attention to actions to safeguard the environment.

4. To set up waste-recycling programmes in-house and also in collaboration with customers.

Source: ICI plc Annual Report 1990.

---

require some degree of organizational and structural change. On the face of it, disclosure of plans and structures is a popular area for voluntary disclosure in organizations' external reporting. However, on closer inspection, it is rare to find consistent, systematic report- ing of much that could be construed as other than public rela- tions 'puff'. Referring again to Elkington's Steps to Environmental Excellence, we find that the organization seriously pursuing environ- mental sensitivity will prepare an action programme, arrange adequate staffing (including training and representation at board level), allocate adequate resources and invest appropriately (this was explored in Chapters 3 and 4). What is needed, next, is some dis- closure about this.

This is the type of disclosure most usually associated in the UK with companies of the stature of BP and ICI, which have regularly reported – in rather general terms anyway – the structural steps they have taken towards whichever social or environmental policy goal was under consideration at the time. In the UK the lead was taken by Body Shop, whose *Another Year in Our Lives* booklet published with the 1990 annual report details the actions, activities and steps undertaken by the company to maintain its status as the 'consuming greenies' favourite plc. This was then followed by the publication of the Body Shop *Green Book* in 1992, which provided a 'comprehensive report of our environmental performance' which, with an in- dependent attestation from Arthur D. Little, provided evidence on the extent to which the company could be considered to be achiev- ing the aims of the 1990 booklet. This approach (of reporting aims and targets and then reporting achievement of these) taken by ICI and Body Shop, for example, represents an important strand of current 'best practice' in voluntary initiatives in environmental disclosure.

Less dramatic, but rather more typical among disclosing com-

Figure 12.6   Example of Disclosure of Environmental Objectives

---

ENVIRONMENTAL PROTECTION

Ozone depleting chemicals

Against a background of mounting evidence that Chlorofluorocarbons (CFCs) can damage the ozone layer, the IBM Corporation has moved from being one of the largest CFC-users – mainly as cleaning solvents – in the mid-1980s to a challenging commitment to early CFC elimination.

Its world-wide target for elimination of CFCs and Methyl Chloroform from products and processes is well ahead of EC regulations – CFC withdrawal by 1997 – and 2004 for Methyl Chloroform withdrawal.

Halons – used minimally by IBM in some specialised fire protection systems – must also be eliminated by 1999 under EC regulations.

Products and Processes

- Corporate world-wide goal to eliminate use of:
  CFCs   YE 1993
  Methyl Chloroform   YE 1995
- Greenock Site eliminated CFCs   1Q90
- Hursley Laboratory eliminated CFCs   1Q91
- Havant Site on target for corporate goal

Insulants and Refrigerants

- Replace existing refrigerants in air-conditioning systems with low ozone depleting chemicals, dependent upon availability of suitable alternatives   Ongoing
- Add clause in construction contract guidelines to ensure only CFC-free insulation materials are used in new construction or refurbishment projects   4Q90

Office Supplies

- CFC-free office supplies introduced   4Q90

Fire Protection Systems – Halon

- Replace Halon-based specialised fire protection equipment as appropriate alternatives are developed.   Ongoing

Environmental Master Plans

- The use and elimination of ozone depleting chemicals to be monitored through location EMPs   1992

Source: Extract from *IBM UK Environmental Programmes – 20 years of commitment* (with target years, quarters and year-ends given after each objective)

panies, are the forms of environmental disclosure consisting of hesitant reports on progress made towards (or with) environmental audits; the expectations of environmental pressures on production; investment and sales; and the appointment of a director in charge of environmental matters. Examples in this area abound and there is really no limit on the forms the disclosure might take. However, so we do not lose sight of the context and purpose of disclosure in this section we finish with a most useful illustration from CEFIC, shown in Figure 12.7.

CEFIC (Conseil Européen des Fédérations de l'Industrie Chimique) published their *Guidelines for the Protection of the Environment* in 1987 and published a subsequent explanatory and support booklet in 1989 'to help responsible managers to establish good procedures for voluntary communication of environmental information'.[11] It provides a most useful template for organizations moving beyond policy disclosure and into the communication of more significant environmental data.

It is when we turn to the reporting of activity, however, that external environmental reporting of non-financial data really begins to show its possibilities.

12.5 The Reporting of Activity

It has long been argued[12] that the discharge of social and environmental accountability requires certain minimum conditions related to current regulations, independent attestation[13] and understandability.[14]

Examples of practice predictably refuse to fall into tidy predefined categories, however, so we shall restrict ourselves to some of the more interesting examples, namely Norsk Hydro, British Airways, Caird, ICI, British Gas and British Nuclear Fuels (BNFL) – all from the UK – Rhône-Poulenc (France), Noranda (Canada) and the State Electricity Commission (SEC) of Victoria (Australia). On a worldwide basis there are many more interesting examples. In the USA Monsanto's 1990 Report is an especially thorough and clear example of environmental reporting. Between them, they point some of the way towards best practice (see section 12.6 below).

Reporting of activity with no context, explanation or analysis is

[11] *CEFIC guidelines for the communication of environmental information to the public* (Brussels: CEFIC) 1989, p. 8.

[12] See e.g. Gray, Owen and Maunders, 1986, 1987, 1988, 1991, and Gray, 1992, Owen, 1992.

[13] One particularly interesting approach to the 'third party' question was undertaken by Atlantic Richfield in the 1970s. For more detail see McComb (1978) and Gray, Owen and Maunders (1987). The 'third party' role is especially crucial in the 'social audit' approach discussed in Chapter 13.

[14] See Gray, Gray et al., and Owen *op cit.*

Figure 12.7 Extract from Conseil Européen des Fédérations de l'Industrie Chimique *CEFIC Guidelines for the Communication of Environmental Information to the Public* (Brussels: CEFIC) 1989, pp. 6–7.

CEFIC GUIDELINES FOR THE PROTECTION OF THE ENVIRONMENT

All human activity, including that of the chemical industry, affects the environment. CEFIC believes that the protection of the environment is an integral part of good business practice and that the industry has a duty to satisfy itself that its products are manufactured, handled, transported, used and disposed of safely and without unacceptable risks for the environment. This requires that companies not only comply with the law, but also take independent and responsible actions.

In order to assist in translating these principles into management practices, CEFIC, in the context of the Environmental Guidelines for the World Industry established by the International Chamber of Commerce, has prepared the following guidelines for chemical companies:

1 *Prepare and regularly review at the highest management level company environmental policies and establish procedures for their implementation;*

2 *Foster among employees at all levels an individual sense of responsibility for the environment and the need to be alert to potential sources of pollution associated with the operations;*

3 *Assess in advance the environmental implications of new processes, products and other activities, and monitor the effects of current operations on the local environment;*

4 *Minimize adverse environmental effects of all activities and take steps to minimize waste and to conserve resources;*

5 *Take the necessary measures to prevent accidental releases;*

6 *In cooperation with public authorities, establish and maintain contingency procedures to minimize the effect of accidents that may nevertheless occur;*

7 **Provide the public with the information necessary to enable them to understand the potential environmental effects of the companies' operations and be prepared to respond positively to expressions of public concern;**

8 *Provide the public authorities with relevant information and assist them in establishing well-founded environmental regulations;*

9 *Provide appropriate advice to customers on safe handling, use and disposal of the companies' products;*

10 *Ensure that contractors working on the companies' behalf apply environmental standards equivalent to their own;*

11 *In transferring technology to another party, provide the information necessary to ensure that the environment can be adequatly protected;*

12 *Promote research into the development of environmentally sound processes and products.*

Figure 12.8

Minimum disclosure conditions for the discharge of social and environmental accountability

(1) Organizations must disclose, at a minimum, the extent to which they are meeting current regulations (were playing by the 'rules of the game' – see also Chapter 14) – the Compliance-with-Standard Report (see below).

(2) Further, in order to provide reliability and credence to the information, there must be third-party involvement – either as the reporter or as an auditor.

(3) Finally, for the information to be understandable it must be possible for a reader to assess its completeness and to relate the data to the experience of the non-expert layperson.

Adapted from Gray, Owen and Maunders (1986), (1987), (1988), (1991).

---

unlikely to qualify as 'good' information – whatever the criteria and however successful the public relations exercise. The first way in which context can be provided is by a comparison through time. We saw this with Rhône-Poulenc's environmental index in Chapter 5. A similar approach is shown in Figure 12.9 in extracts from the ICI and Noranda reports.

The ICI extract is part of what could be interpreted as a large company reporting as it finds out. The reported data on phosphates, cyanides and heavy metals are immediately persuasive, encouraging and impressive and the accompanying discussion (not shown here) is earnest and, seemingly, honest and guileless. However, the scales are not labelled and explained, no further context is given and the discussion and the data are unrelated. The Noranda Minerals example reports on the number of environmental and other audits the company has performed in recent years. Again it is reassuring and impressive at first sight. It does, however, lose context without targets or further explanation or analysis. This is significantly ameliorated by the consistent standard of data that pervades the whole of the environmental report from which this extract comes.

The next stage beyond presenting data in a time-series is to show it against target or, better still, against standards – legal or otherwise.[15] The examples in Figures 12.10 and 12.11 have these elements.

The SEC extract (Figure 12.10) comes from the 140-page annual report, which contains a scattering of environmental data and discussion but no comprehensive, systematic reporting. Reported alongside other non-financial performance indicators, the environmental data can perhaps be seen as an integrated part of the organ-

---

[15] One of the many lessons learnt by the Social Audit Ltd experience in the UK in the early 1970s is that the standards also begin to make more sense if they are related to commonly understood phenomena – for example, if levels of BOD (Biological Oxygen Demand) are related to aquatic life support.

Figure 12.9 Two Examples of Reporting Activity

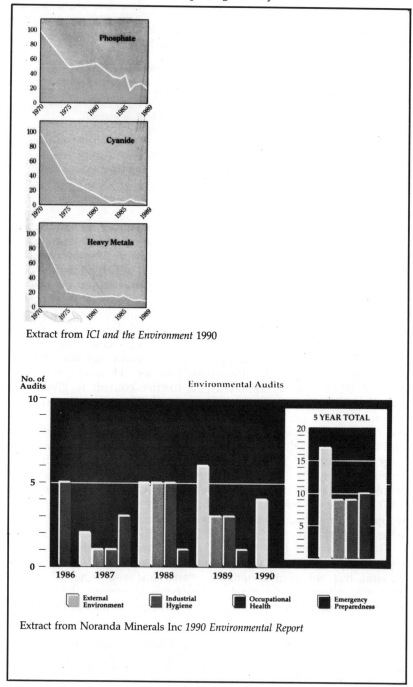

Extract from *ICI and the Environment* 1990

Extract from Noranda Minerals Inc *1990 Environmental Report*

Figure 12.10

Extract from SEC's aims and performance				
Environment:	Target 1990/1	Actual 1990/1	Target 1991/2	Target 1994/5
Dust (g/cuM)	<0.11	0.10	0.10	0.09
Water intake from Latrobe catchment (Ml/GWh)	3.8	2.9	3	3
Salt discharge in Latrobe river (t/GWh)	0.95	0.092	0.92	0.85
CO_2 emissions (Mt/annum)	42	43.3	42	42

Source: State Electricity Commission of Victoria *Annual Report 1990/91*

ization's operations. Given the targets and previous actual data, one is also potentially informed about the (apparently unambitious) progress and aims of the company. The incompleteness of the information, however, is rather startling and, given the public awareness of electricity generation and its attendant environmental issues, the chosen indicators and the partial context given in the attendant text make the report seem oddly selective.[16] This contrasts, at least initially, with the report from Noranda Forest in Figure 12.11.[17] The standards against which performance is judged in these cases are the legal compliance standards. Some explanation, together with statements about missing data, is provided and, once again, within the broader context of the full Noranda environmental reports a significant picture is provided. The Noranda reports must be among the best examples of environmental reporting in the early 1990s. They are not, however, without their problems: the absence of any explanation as to the quality of the legal standards and the notable absence of the external verifier/'third party'.

Two British companies, Caird Group and British Airways, went

[16] This issue of selective reporting is important and a major reason why some indicator of 'completeness' is necessary. In the 1970s, a leading reporting initiative from Eastern Gas and Fuel Associates in the USA reported on a range of social issues but omitted any environmental issues arising from their activities – even though this was the area in which their major impact would be felt.

[17] Noranda Minerals adopts a similar reporting format.

Figure 12.11   Reporting Activity against Standards

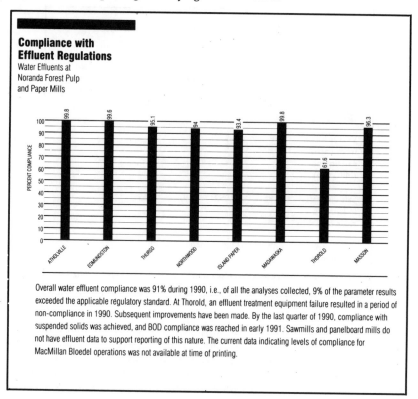

**Compliance with
Effluent Regulations**
Water Effluents at
Noranda Forest Pulp
and Paper Mills

Overall water effluent compliance was 91% during 1990, i.e., of all the analyses collected, 9% of the parameter results exceeded the applicable regulatory standard. At Thorold, an effluent treatment equipment failure resulted in a period of non-compliance in 1990. Subsequent improvements have been made. By the last quarter of 1990, compliance with suspended solids was achieved, and BOD compliance was reached in early 1991. Sawmills and panelboard mills do not have effluent data to support reporting of this nature. The current data indicating levels of compliance for MacMillan Bloedel operations was not available at time of printing.

Extract from *Noranda Forest 1990 Environmental Report*

directly to the heart of the 'independence' issue and published summaries from the environmental audits undertaken on their behalf by independent consultants. Caird published the summaries of both the first and their second environmental audits by environmental consultants, Mott MacDonald. These were published separately from the annual report but were widely available; the annual report carried a shortened version of the environmental auditor's report immediately before the directors' report.[18] British Airways went a stage further, publishing a full environmental review performed by consultants Technica. A further summary booklet was prepared and published by BA in which the principal matters were reviewed. These are direct, hard-hitting and (as far as one can assess) honest. The extract shown in Figure 12.12 illustrates

[18] The published reports were not entirely glowing either. For more detail see Owen (1992a), chapter 8.

Figure 12.12   Independent Reporting

The WAY FORWARD

By
Dr HUGH SOMERVILLE
Head of Environment

The aim of the review was to assist the airline's environmental management team in identifying areas, within the airline's operations at Heathrow and in its worldwide flying programme, that require either remedial action, further study, or perhaps a combination of both.

Each of the Technica recommendations has been prioritised from those warranting implementation within six months to low priority items to be actioned at the discretion of the airline.

As mentioned in the foreword by David Hyde, Director of Safety, Security and Environment, British Airways has a record of environmental action. A number of actions have also been initiated before and during the Technica review.

Examples of the actions in hand, including some arising from the Technica review, are given below. The list is not comprehensive and forms only part of the environmental programme developed by the airline as part of its commitment to the environmental goal:

✔ **Commit at Board level to a corporate goal:** *To be a good neighbour concerned for the community and the environment.*

✔ **Prepare an inventory of aircraft emissions, including CO_2, CO, NOx, and UHC.**

✔ **Reduce and eliminate the use of CFCs in our operations:**
1) reductions of 20 per cent already achieved in cleaning of electronic parts,
2) substitute methods identified and being introduced for aerosol applications;
3) investigation of regulatory constraints that require use of CFCs;
4) release of CFCs in mandatory fire training.

✔ **Convert the majority of the road transport fleet, where relevant, to lead free petrol.**

✔ **Reduce the numbers of Chapter 2 aircraft in advance of regulatory requirements.**

✔ **Order, US$ 5,731 million worth of new technology aircraft and Rolls-Royce engines.**

✔ **Initiate an annual environmental report which will act as a measurement of the airline's performance.**

✔ **Survey our waste generation and disposal at Heathrow.**

✔ **Establish the quantity and quality of our aqueous effluents.**

✔ **Extend Energy Management schemes which have already achieved savings in energy consumption of value £6 million.**

✔ **Establish cross-functional working groups to address a range of topics, including waste, recycling and aqueous effluents.**

✔ **Increase staff awareness on environmental issues.**

✔ **Initiate "Greenwaves", an environmental suggestion scheme, and "Greenseal", an award for excellence for staff contributing to environmental conservation.**

✔ **Continue the conservation of species at risk through our "Assisting Nature Conservation Scheme" programme, which has already aided the survival of more than 50 species worldwide.**

✔ **Continue a long-term programme of re-using, selling on and recycling many items that may have otherwise gone to waste.**

✔ **Establish at Director level an Environmental Council to review environmental issues.**

Despite these initiatives, and others not listed here, British Airways is not complacent. We will continue to examine our operations, in the United Kingdom and throughout the world, where they interact with the environment.

Extract from *British Airways Environmental Review 1991*

the style. The apparent honesty shown in Figure 12.12 is rather startling to a British audience. For example, the extract suggests – and the report confirms – that BA is lagging behind best practice on the efficiency and emissions from aircraft, is not controlling CFCs sufficiently, does not have information on aqueous effluents, etc. Furthermore, Figure 12.12 shows that the company is now publicly committed to a wide range of non-trivial environmental actions. The disclosure by BA is significant and worthy of attention in a number of ways (see next, section 12.6). A not-unrelated approach is taken by British Nuclear Fuels (BNFL), for example. The reports issued by the company are backed up by independent attestation, concentrate on the core of the business – radiation – and have provided system-atic reporting for some years. The BNFL approach differs from BA, however, in two important regards: first, it is self-justifying rather than self-critical (thus structural change could perhaps be expected at BA but not BNFL); and second, the inevitable omissions which are remarked upon in the BA report are skated over in silence in BNFL – that impression of earnest honesty is missing.

Finally, as an example of how to start to pull these different approaches together *and* score considerable public relations kudos from the exercise, the Norsk Hydro Environmental Report, in 1990, set the standard for others to beat.

12.6   Norsk Hydro (UK) Environmental Report

Norsk Hydro is Norway's biggest industrial group. In an environ-mentally conscious country like Norway, the company was sensitive to its environmental record and believed itself to be an environ-mentally responsible organization. A spate of bad publicity in 1987 following from the actions of environmental activists caused the company to take a long hard look at its environmental interactions. The results were not good. Initially the company was understand-ably defensive about this but, in 1989, as part of its strategy to reclaim its reputation, it published a fairly comprehensive report of its Norwegian activities. In 1990 Norsk Hydro published a further report covering all the group's activities, worldwide, and in the same year Norsk Hydro (UK) became the first of the overseas sub-sidiaries to follow suit – to considerable public attention.[19]

The UK report provides an introduction to the UK group (Norsk Hydro (UK) is not an especially high-profile company in the UK) and then goes on to review environmental interaction in each of the company's business sectors. For each sector, background data on the company are provided, together with information about environmentally sensitive elements – e.g. emissions and discharges, raw materials and hazardous substances. Further data are provided

---

[19] See, for example, D. Thomas, 'Turning over a new green leaf', *Financial Times*, 24 October, 1990. For more detail see *ENDS Report* 185/June 1990, pp. 13–15.

on the regulatory framework within which the company operates,[20] the standards it must meet (where appropriate) and data on levels of activity. Figure 12.13 is an extract from the section on polymers and gives an indication of the style of the report.

Of course, the report can be faulted. Most notably, it is patchy and not consistent between sectors. However, as the company remarked, this is due to data not being collected, collated and reported on a consistent basis at that time plus a degree of selectivity as to what was thought important. However, any quibbles are far outweighed by the strengths of the report. It gives both 'good' and 'bad' news because 'people do not believe squeaky clean' and, *most significantly of all*, the report was subject to an independent 'audit' which was published as part of the environmental report – 'because journalists are a cynical bunch'. The complete audit report from Lloyd's Register is shown in Figure 12.14.

The publication of the environmental report was a gamble by Norsk Hydro (UK) – one undertaken principally on the grounds of improving the company's PR profile. The gamble has paid off. There has been none of the environmentalist backlash that was feared and the estimated cost of $50,000[21] has more than repaid itself in terms of PR and publicity, awareness of the company, attitudes of the employees and a raised awareness among management of the environmental factors involved in the company – especially those requiring attention. The relatively low cost to the company arises because the data were virtually costless. The company – as part of its TQM culture – already emphasized health and safety reporting, particularly as part of an initiative to reduce accidents, and had already developed some environmental reporting within the organization.

We can now say, having put our head above the parapet and not had it shot off, that the importance and value of openness and transparency in the way it leads to increased understanding, better public relations and reduced antagonism greatly outweighs the costs – which owe more to industry's fears than to reality.

(John Speirs, Norsk Hydro (UK), in interview, May 1991)

It is the need for this spirit of experimentation which led to the Chartered Association of Certified Accountants' (ACCA) Environmental Reporting Awards initiative in 1991 as a means of encourag-

---

[20] These are the UK regulatory agencies and legal frameworks and include: the National Rivers Authority and the Scottish River Purification Boards; Her Majesty's Inspectorate of Pollution; the Health & Safety Executive (HSE) and the Health & Safety at Work Act 1974; the Control of Substances Hazardous to Health (COSHH) Regulations 1988; the Control of Industrial Major Accident Hazard (CIMAH) Regulations 1984 and the Notification of Installations Handling Hazardous Substances Regulations 1982.

[21] This excludes staff time. The print run was 10,500.

Figure 12.13   Extract from Norsk Hydro (UK) 1990 Environmental Report

P O L Y M E R S

Dust levels in the resin and compounds plants are checked regularly with personal monitoring systems and during 1989 the programme was considerably enlarged. This increased programme has revealed minor plant and sampling faults which led to questionably high figures in some cases. Remedial projects to improve operational and sampling procedures will bring much improved results in the future.

The personal monitoring programme also includes checks on exposure to heavy metal compounds in appropriate areas.

Compounds Plant Monitoring for Heavy Metals

Measurement	Occupational Exposure Limit	Plant Area	1988	1989
Mean Cadmium Level (mg/m³)	0.05	Compounds	0.005	0.002
Mean Lead Level (mg/m³)	0.15	Compounds	0.174	0.004

The comprehensive personal monitoring system, which uses samplers worn by the workforce, is backed by a biological examination service, supervised by the works doctor. He assesses the results obtained from regular blood and urine samples, which are processed by an independent laboratory, and advises the company and the workforce about the optimisation of working practices to maintain good health. Under the COSHH regulations, workers' medical records will be kept for at least 30 years. During 1989 these biological monitoring procedures revealed no abnormal results.

Safety

HPL encourages the development of high individual and collective safety standards and the provision at all times of a safe, healthy, accident-free working environment. Corporate goals have been set for a reduction in the number of lost-time injuries (LTI) and recent performance is as follows:

	1986	1987	1988	1989
LTI per million hours worked	24	9	8	7

To achieve and consolidate excellence in the field of personal safety involves major changes to procedures and attitudes developed over the years.

HPL has engaged independent Safety Management Consultants to:

a) evaluate the present safety management system and help management understand how they can modify and strengthen their approach so as to reduce injuries further.

b) provide training in the techniques of creating and sustaining a successful management safety audit system.

The quality of the Safety Management System at Aycliffe has been recognised by the award in 1987 of a Sword of Honour by the British Safety Council.

Hazard

HPL is a top-tier CIMAH site (see page 7), because its business is polymerisation and it keeps liquefied VCM under pressure on the premises at Aycliffe.

The regulations require that HPL prepare a 'safety case' which analyses, identifies and minimises the hazards in operations. Such a case has been prepared and lodged with the HSE. It sets out HPL's plans for dealing with emergencies as they may affect the site and the surrounding area, and must be reviewed every three years.

These plans have been developed in close co-operation with the local authority, the police and the fire brigade. Local residents within a designated area have been kept fully informed of all HPL's plans and are well briefed on what to do in the unlikely event that an emergency occurs. In accordance with HPL's policy of openness, the company has arranged open days for the families of staff and for the public.

Her Majesty's Inspectorate of Pollution (HMIP)

The responsibility for monitoring the effect of HPL's operations on the earth, air and water within and around the site is shared between HMIP and Northumbrian Water. Air pollution is the prime concern of HMIP and HPL works closely with them.

The vent stacks from the PVC resin plants have to be monitored regularly for both VCM and dust, and all three plants perform well inside the consent levels:

P   O   L   Y   M   E   R   S

	Consent Levels	Performance	
		1988	1989
Mean VCM Emission (kg VCM/tonne PVC)	0.25	0.03	0.013
Mean Dust Emission (mg/m³)	0.115	0.01	0.004

In addition to the monitoring of dryer plant stacks there is a comprehensive programme of fence line monitoring for VCM agreed with HMIP. During 1989, 75 measurements were made with the following results:

Range of VCM Levels (ppm)	N.D.*–1.43
Mean Value (ppm Time Weighted Average)	0.084

*Not Detected

Northumbrian Water

This body is concerned with possible contaminations of ground water and of water leaving the site. HPL has every reason to avoid the contamination of ground water since use is made of water from a bore-hole on site. Regular checks are made on the quality of the water taken from the bore-hole. The liquid effluent leaving the site is governed by a 'Consent to Discharge Trade Effluent' given by the Northumbrian Water Authority. Additional legislation is presently coming into force including the Water Act 1989 and new Statutory Instruments arising from EEC directives. The 1989 performance is summarised below:

	Maximum Consent Level	Performance	
		Mean	Maximum
Suspended Solids (ppm)	400	110	394
Sulphate (ppm)	1200	114	600
Sulphide (ppm)	1	0.10	0.75
Chromium (ppm)	5	0.44	2.5

While these values are within the existing consent levels, HPL is planning continuous improvement so as to yield much lower levels. Attention has been concentrated upon reducing the level of suspended solids and the 1990 levels are already proving to be substantially better.

The Role of PVC

PVC has characteristics which make it superior to many competing materials. This section describes these attributes, relating them both to PVC production and to the impact of PVC production on the environment. The essential raw materials are oil and common salt, both basic commodities available in bulk supply. Catalytic 'cracking' of crude oil yields ethylene which is reacted with chlorine from salt to form vinyl chloride monomer. This in turn is polymerised to form PVC.

The production of PVC and its processing into end products require substantially lower energy inputs than are needed for competing materials such as glass, steel and concrete. In use PVC is non toxic, of long life and lightweight. There are many applications where these attributes provide economic advantages to users: in sewage and water pipes (where only one-sixth of the energy used to produce and lay cast iron pipe is needed for PVC pipe); as a bottling material (mineral water packed in PVC bottles takes 40% less fuel to transport than water transported in glass bottles); and in PVC packaging (in which food has a longer shelf life than in paper, a material which uses more energy in its production).

PVC bottles used for food and toiletries.

Figure 12.14   Norsk Hydro – Audit Report

L L O Y D ' S   R E G I S T E R

Scope

This assessment results from Norsk Hydro (UK) Ltd requesting Lloyd's Register to review and independently comment on its environmental practices and performances with specific reference to:–

Legislation compliance.

A check on figures presented in this report to ensure that they give a true and fair view.

The environmental monitoring and operating procedures at the sites visited, namely Hydro Polymers at Newton Aycliffe, Hydro Fertilizers at Immingham, Golden Sea Produce at Oban, Scotland, and Hydro Aluminium Metals and Alupres at Bedwas, Wales.

The method used for assessing the monitoring and operating procedures is Lloyd's Register's Environmental Assurance scheme, which sets guidelines for environmentally excellent companies (see box on page 28).

Summary of findings

The following are Lloyd's Register's findings based on the material submitted, the appearance of the sites visited and opinions formed during the visits:–

The sites visited all comply with existing legislation and consents where these exist. The compliance is better than the minimum legal requirement in most cases.

The figures in this report were found to give a true and fair view of existing environmental monitoring data.

Hydro's performance in the UK, based on the criteria laid down in Environmental Assurance, is good. Their actions and investments are consistent with a company whose aim is to reduce the environmental impact of its operations. Half the business units have an environmental policy and the rest are developing one. Consideration of environmental impact forms part of operations, and of assessments for plant expansions, on all the sites visited. The management of environmental improvements is a continuously evolving process, a fact of which Hydro is fully aware.

Commentary

Hydro operates in a wide range of industries in the UK from chemical and mechanical engineering through to food production. The sites visited span the total spectrum of operation.

The objective of this section is to support the finding that Hydro companies in the UK are well aware of the impact of their operations on the environment and to demonstrate their commitment through positive action and innovation to meet the challenge of solving existing and future environmental problems. This will be done by highlighting the strengths and weaknesses with examples of areas of good practice and areas where improvements are being instigated. Areas where certain of the Hydro operations do not completely meet the Environmental Assurance guidelines for excellent behaviour will then be identified.

Examples of good practice include:–

The central environmental policy found at Hydro Polymers and Hydro Fertilizers. In addition Hydro Polymers has a mission statement which covers behaviour towards the environment.

The regular environmental reports on all sites, both to site management (monthly) and to business unit HQ in Norway (quarterly).

The achievement of doing substantially better than the maximum level set for Best Practical Means (BPM) on vinyl chloride monomer (VCM) and dust emissions from the PVC resin plant.

The design of the ammonium nitrate plant to produce nearly zero emissions at Hydro Fertilizers. This involves the use of modern dust extraction technology.

The effluent treatment plant at Golden Sea Produce. This plant biologically cleans process water. The site also has a plant producing animal food and saleable fish oil from all other waste.

The complaint handling on all sites. The procedure and policy are clear, and any complaint is investigated. The complaint is followed up if the complainant has identified himself/herself.

The strong involvement in the local community exemplified by the open days at Hydro Polymers, the environmental liaison committee with local councillors at Hydro Fertilizers, the involvement with local schools at Golden Sea Produce.

L L O Y D ' S   R E G I S T E R

Examples of areas where improvements are being implemented include:–

The effluent treatment plant at Alupres. The plant neutralises the anodising chemicals and filters out solids prior to discharge to sewer. The plant is in operation, but there are some teething problems.

The development of a new settling tank design for Hydro Polymers' PVC resin plant. The aim is to reduce further the suspended solids in the effluent stream and to recover product.

The extensive internal and external noise surveys at both Hydro Aluminium Metals and Alupres. These resulted in action to reduce the noise level where current plant layout permitted. Further improvements are being considered.

The trials on the use of the small fish, wrasse, to combat the problem of the salmon louse. Success would result in the use of dichlorvos being substantially reduced.

The survey of air emissions at Hydro Aluminium Metals. This has led to the stack height being increased to its structural maximum to try to reduce the risk of the stack plume impacting on the nearby footpath. The problem is not completely solved, so other means of minimising the impact are being investigated. In addition, a stack emission monitoring programme is to be conducted.

The aim of initiating regular internal environmental audits. These would be in addition to the existing safety and house keeping audits. For certain plants there will in addition be corporate environmental audits in the near future.

The above are all examples of positive practices and actions. Lloyd's Register's Environmental Assurance standards are set as guidelines for excellent companies. There are a limited number of areas where Hydro in the UK does not fully meet these standards. In all these areas Hydro does comply with existing legal requirements and the recommended actions are not company wide but site specific. The following actions are suggested by Lloyd's Register to improve these areas:–

An investigation into options for waste minimisation at Hydro Fertilizers, Hydro Polymers, Alupres and Hydro Aluminium Metals.

A monitoring survey of liquid effluent at Alupres; this will allow confirmation of management's expectation of content and will improve their understanding of the operations' environmental impact.

A monitoring survey of air emissions at Hydro Polymers' PVC compounding plant; there should also be a survey of surface drains in relation to drum handling and storage to ensure that the potential for an incident, whereby a spill is washed to the local river, is minimised.

Investigation of other disposal options for the small quantity of fullers earth/talc with traces of ammonium nitrate from Hydro Fertilizers' plant.

Long term investigation by Hydro Fertilizers into the continued reduction and/or alternative disposal of the contaminant in the liquid effluent, which discharges under an existing consent into the Humber.

Conclusions

Lloyd's Register found that Hydro's UK sites understand well the environmental impact of their operations. There were clear signs of the effort expended to limit the environmental impact of the operations. Overall Hydro appears to be ahead of individual industry standards.

Environmental Assurance and Lloyd's Register

Lloyd's Register is a significant technical, inspection and advisory organisation as well as the world's premier ship classification Society. We have over 200 years of experience at providing independent advice and technical services to industry. Our engineers and specialists are recognised throughout the world for their integrity. The Society operates with no financial, political or commercial constraint and can therefore offer an independent, preventative auditing and validation service. Environmental Assurance is a scheme that has as its main focus a comprehensive technical and management audit, which is derived from guidelines for environmentally excellent behaviour.

Lloyd's Register carries out environmental assessments on all kinds of plant.

ing development in environmental reporting and identifying advances in 'best practice'.

12.7   The ACCA's Environmental Reporting Awards

As part of its continuing commitment to help develop the role that accounting might play in increasing an organization's environmental sensitivity,[22] the ACCA launched the Environmental Reporting Awards (ERA) initiative in 1991. The aim of the scheme was 'to identify and reward innovative attempts to communicate environmental performance', with a view to extrapolating, developing and encouraging best practice in environmental reporting. The scheme was initially open to only UK companies and state-owned enterprises but the 'environmental report' could be either separate or in the annual report. The judging panel was drawn from a wide cross-section, with representation from the UK Departments of Trade and Environment, the European Community's DG XI, the CBI, ethical investment, the TUC, environmental consultancy, environmental research, the Accounting Standards Board and the universities. The 1991 awards received 18 nominations or submissions, the 1992 received 30. Although this may seem a small number it did rather reflect the state of environmental reporting in the UK at that time (see Chapter 11 for more detail). The short-list of six led to two eventual joint winners: the award was presented to British Airways and Norsk Hydro (UK) by David Bellamy in March 1992.

In establishing criteria for judging environmental reporting, the panel used a combination of the research results from the ACCA projects, their experience with preparers, their needs as users plus an inductive approach to the reports submitted to derive a checklist of characteristics that environmental reports might be expected to possess. (See Appendix 12 and Figure 12.15.) The awards will continue for as long as it seems necessary to encourage voluntary reporting and to provide guidance through the identification of best practice. In this the ACCA ERA follows other reporting award schemes which have helped to develop, *inter alia*, employee reporting, simplified reporting and reporting by public sector organizations.

12.8   Experimentation, the Future and the Absence of Conclusions

Despite the longevity of the social reporting debate and the relative intensity of the recent explorations of environmental reporting, the

[22] The ACCA has demonstrated its commitment in its funding of one major research project in 1989, a further project in 1990 (of which this report is part – see Gray, 1990e) and its funding support of the Centre for Social and Environmental Accounting Research in 1992. (Further details about the Centre can be obtained from the address shown in Appendix B.)

Figure 12.15

The ACCA Environmental Reporting Award Criteria

The criteria are a largely predictable mixture of the prerequisite characteristics of:

- 'information' and 'communication' (e.g. reliability, understandability);
- accessibility through the annual report;
- practicability (especially with respect to what appears to be currently achievable with, for example, financial data);
- desirability for the future (e.g. sustainability).

---

number of fully developed examples of *actual* (and thus practicable) reporting are relatively few and far between. Until minimum standards are set and agreed, environmental reporting will remain experimental. Examples from which organizations may borrow ideas are numerous – some have been reviewed in this chapter[23] – but the possibilities are infinite. There are, however, some elements within an environmental report that can be considered the 'minimum' (see Figure 12.8). One element of this was that each report must identify the extent to which the organization has 'played by the rules' – the extent to which it has complied with standards. A simple indication of how reporting in this way might be approached is given in Figure 12.16.[24]

It is the combination of this compliance-with-standard approach plus the UN CTC ISAR financial and non-financial reporting recommendations that currently represent best 'target' practice in environmental reporting. *Actual* practice continues to fall somewhat short of this but one might come close on the non-financial environmental reporting through a combination of the Norsk Hydro (UK and Norway) reports alongside the Noranda reports from Canada together with the ICI and Body Shop (for example) reporting of objectives and their achievement. But practice is, as we have seen, isolated and has some way to go before environmental accountability and transparency are a reality.

But developments beyond this will always be possible. For example, in France, Bernard Christophe[25] has recommended that the French experience with the *bilan social* ('social balance sheet')[26] could form a basis for environmental reporting. Under this proposal, organizations would report on year-by-year improvements in a

---

[23] For more detail see, for example, Gray, Owen and Maunders (1987) and Owen (1992).

[24] More detail and the arguments in support of the compliance-with-standard approach are given in Gray, Owen and Maunders, (1986, 1987, 1988, 1991).

[25] See Christophe and Bebbington (1992).

[26] For explanation of the *bilan social*, for example, Gray *et al.* (1987), Hussey (1978).

Figure 12.16 An example of an environmental compliance-with-standard report summary

Area of std	1990 level	1990 std	1991 level	1991 std	Source of std	Description
Ground Water: Disch'ge 1 　Charact a: 　Charact b: Disch'ge 2	 w x	 a b	 y z	 c d	NRA Consent levels	(e.g.) X dies when BOD exceeds Y
Discharges to Mains: etc....						
Discharges to Air: etc....						
Disposal of Wastes: etc....						
Discharges to Sea: etc....						

way which combined elements of the compliance-with-standard approach and the Rhône-Poulenc environmental index (see Chapter 5) in manner reminiscent of variance analysis in costing. At the time of writing, however, this remained a proposal only and there are, as yet, no indications that France will take the lead in environmental reporting that it did in 1977 with the *bilan social*.

Encouragingly, other, substantive experiments are in progress. One of the most ambitious is that from the IISD.[27] This reviews the current accounting framework and goes on to develop the sorts of reporting which will be necessary if organizations are to move towards sustainable development.[28] The report includes a call to accounting policy-makers to take environmental reporting on board and finishes with a detailed – although predominantly non-financial – proposal for reporting environmental interactions. The report promises to be a major factor in the environmental reporting debate for some time to come.

[27] *Business Strategy for Sustainable Development: Leadership and accountability for the 90s* (Winnipeg: IISD/Deloitte and Touche) 1991.

[28] Unfortunately, the report does not attempt to show how its proposals are linked to sustainability. For more along these lines see Chapter 14.

Whilst we may not expect quite such substantive initiatives on a regular basis, we might reasonably expect new approaches and experiments from organizations (see Appendix 12.2 for just such an example) at a steady trickle over the coming years – until, that is, there is sensible agreement about regulation of environmental reporting. We would finish this review of non-financial environmental reporting with a word of caution from the start of the chapter. With very few exceptions, the vast majority of voluntary disclosure – perhaps especially in environmental reporting – owes more to advertising, public relations[29] and image construction than it does to information, accountability and transparency. All the evidence suggests that this is likely to remain the case without regulation. Environmental reporting may prove to be the major exception to this rule – and we certainly would be pleased if this was so. We wouldn't bet on it though.

Further Reading

Company Reporting, no. 13, July 1991.

Gray, R. H. (1990) *The Greening of Accountancy: The Profession after Pearce*, ACCA, London.

Gray, R. H., Owen, D. L. and Maunders, K. T. (1987) *Corporate Social Reporting: Accounting and Accountability*, Prentice-Hall International, Hemel Hempstead.

Owen, D. L. (1992) *Green Reporting: The Challenge of the Nineties*, Chapman Hall, London.

Roberts, C. B. (1990) *International Trends in Social and Employee Reporting*, ACCA, London.

United Nations Centre for Transnational Corporations *International Accounting and Reporting* (1992), United Nations, New York.

In addition, *Integrated Environmental Management* has a regular environmental reporting section which is intended to keep readers up to date with developments and experiments in environmental reporting. Monitoring any of the other newsletters in the field is also strongly advised.

---

[29] This and previous uses of the term 'public relations' have largely been pejorative and, strictly speaking, should have been accompanied by the term 'empty' or 'bad' as qualifiers. Public relations at its best must work with truthful, honest and complete conceptions of the organizations' activities and is a clearly essential part of the transparency, accountability and communication. Good public relations is a necessary prerequisite for any sort of organization–community partnership and for a resolution of conflict between the different stakeholders in the environment and economy. Too often, however, PR has come to mean the painting of soothing gloss on a situation regardless of any relationship with truth, integrity, honesty or public interest. It is in this sense that the pejorative use of PR is intended.

APPENDIX 12.1
ACCA Environmental Reporting Awards 1991 judging criteria

Environmental Reporting Awards 1991

COMPANY NAME	DOCUMENT		YEAR
	Annual Report		
ATTRIBUTE	None	Some	Good
1. Independence of Report/Audit			
2. Emphasis on core business			
3. Systematic approach			
4. Data: (a) is presented;			
(b) is understandable;			
(c) is comparable;			
(d) compliance-with-standard;			
(e) specific/potentially auditable.			
5. Summary: (a) does cover main issues;			
(b) does reflect fuller reports.			
6. Additional data can be obtained			
7. Annual Report: (a) does the reporting;			
or (b) refers to available information;			
or (c) is automatically accompanied by env report.			
8. Statement of policy/mission:			
– in auditable form:			
9. Statement of future actions:			
– in auditable form:			
10. Financial data on 'Superfund' liability.			
11. Financial data on environmental investment.			
12. Data on environmental audit/review.			
13. Assessment of sustainability.			

APPENDIX 12.2
The 'Green Accounts' from Danish Steel Works Ltd, Annual Report 1991

Green Accounts˙

As the first steel manufacturer, Det Danske Stålvalseværk A/S has prepared »Green Accounts«. These green accounts describe which materials are supplied to the Company's production plant, and which materials are turned into finished goods or to emissions, waste products to be recycled or waste. At the same time is stated in main groups the content of these materials of heavy metal, iron etc. The description is set up as a mass-balance sheet specified upon elements.

The green accounts are meant as a basis for an objective discussion about further reductions of the strain on the environment in connection with the Company's activities, as all materials which may be detrimental to the environment is being supplied to the Company through raw materials, alloys, energy etc. Thus it is important to involve other interested parties in the discussion, including the Company's suppliers and not least the manufacturers of the products which form part of the circulation of steel for recycling.

Only by viewing the entire life cycle of steel and each individual step in the use of steel to many of the products on which modern society is based, is it possible to continue the recycling of steel with the lowest possible strain on the environment as a consequence.

It is the objective of Det Danske Stålvalseværk A/S to show openness in questions relating to the environment, so that the uncertainty that might exist in connection with the Company's influence on the environment may be eliminated, and instead may give room for a discussion on how to obtain improvements.

The green accounts may thus be used as a basis for setting goals for improvements, e.g. through increased recycling of waste products, just as they may be used to show at which rate the improvements take place.

The Company is actively involved in formulating new environmental goals so that the next green accounts may reflect a positive development.

The green accounts presented are unique for Det Danske Stålvalseværk A/S. Neither in Denmark nor abroad is found any comparable material. There are no guidelines or standards for »Green Accounts«. Det Danske Stålvalseværk A/S has thus ventured into a totally new area and looks forward to the inspiration which a debate about the green accounts may result in.

The green accounts statements can be documented based on quantities from the year 1991 and from analyses, which a.o. are included in the Company's application for voluntary environmental approval. The aim is that independent auditors should be able to audit and sign also the green accounts, an objective that will be pursued in the coming year.

No conclusions may be drawn at this stage as to whether the green accounts are good or bad, but it is an expression of the fact that Det Danske Stålvalseværk A/S knows in detail which materials are being supplied and which are leaving the Company's production plant. This is in itself a major prerequisite to create improvements.

The green accounts are also an expression of the fact that Det Danske Stålvalseværk A/S' production plant works as a giant recycling filter. Materials that are detrimental to the environment and which come in with raw materials etc. are either tied in finished goods or steered towards recycling or depots so that the effect on the environment is minimized.

MASS BALANCE (TONNES)

GREEN

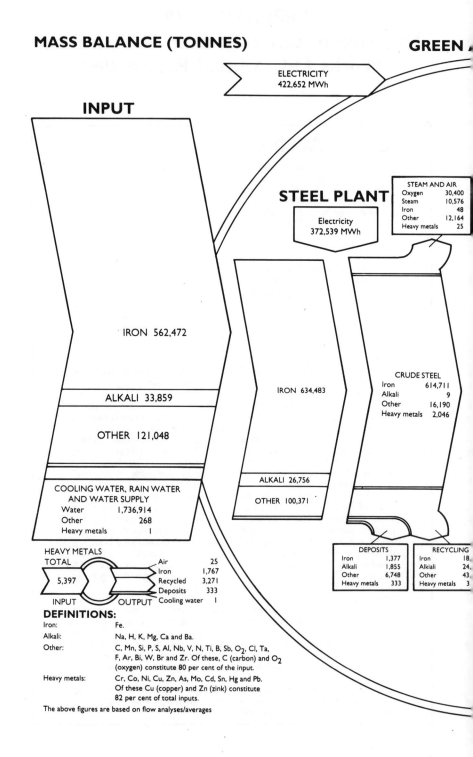

INPUT

ELECTRICITY
422,652 MWh

STEEL PLANT

Electricity
372,539 MWh

STEAM AND AIR	
Oxygen	30,400
Steam	10,576
Iron	48
Other	12,164
Heavy metals	25

IRON 562,472

IRON 634,483

CRUDE STEEL	
Iron	614,711
Alkali	9
Other	16,190
Heavy metals	2,046

ALKALI 33,859

OTHER 121,048

ALKALI 26,756

OTHER 100,371

COOLING WATER, RAIN WATER AND WATER SUPPLY	
Water	1,736,914
Other	268
Heavy metals	1

DEPOSITS	
Iron	1,377
Alkali	1,855
Other	6,748
Heavy metals	333

RECYCLING	
Iron	18
Alkiali	24
Other	43
Heavy metals	3

HEAVY METALS
TOTAL

5,397

INPUT — OUTPUT

Air	25
Iron	1,767
Recycled	3,271
Deposits	333
Cooling water	1

DEFINITIONS:

Iron:	Fe.
Alkali:	Na, H, K, Mg, Ca and Ba.
Other:	C, Mn, Si, P, S, Al, Nb, V, N, Ti, B, Sb, O_2, Cl, Ta, F, Ar, Bi, W, Br and Zr. Of these, C (carbon) and O_2 (oxygen) constitute 80 per cent of the input.
Heavy metals:	Cr, Co, Ni, Cu, Zn, As, Mo, Cd, Sn, Hg and Pb. Of these Cu (copper) and Zn (zink) constitute 82 per cent of total inputs.

The above figures are based on flow analyses/averages

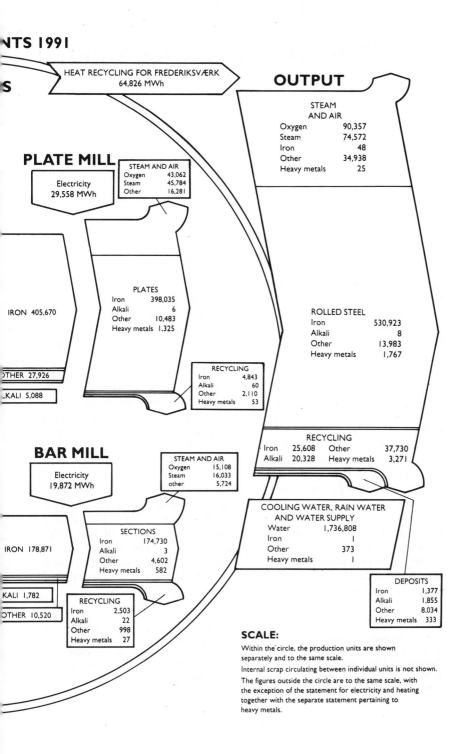

13. The External 'Social Audits'

13.1 Introduction

A major feature of any society with claims to be a democracy is the flow of information which should educate and inform the *demos*. However, access to information, rights to information and willingness to part with or share information are far from equal in any but the most mythically egalitarian society. Therefore, a related feature of those nations which we would normally consider to be democracies is the 'external social audit'. This is a broad and imprecise term which we will use here to refer to the preparation *and publication* of information about one organization by a body independent of that organization.[1] And in this context it can be seen variously as an independent demonstration of concern about the lack of information in a particular area; a healthy manifestation of a democracy seeking to balance up the information asymmetry; and/or a means of extending the current boundaries of accountability.

Whatever the purpose one might ascribe to them, they exist and succeed in presenting information about organizational activity in a very different way from that in which an organization might choose to speak of itself. Within the context of this section of the book they may best be seen as (i) an indication of the limitations of current external self-reporting practice by organizations and (ii) as a mechanism which will increase an organization's accountability whether it wants it or not.

---

[1] This may be seen as too limiting a definition; see, for example, Geddes (1992). As with 'environmental audit' the term audit is widely and confusingly used. Geddes, for example, prefers to use it in the context of a wide sense of any collecting and collating of information for use in a campaigning context. He thus includes 'needs' auditing, for example. We shall remain with our slightly more restrictive use of the term here.

13.2 A Brief Background and History of the Social Audit

The principal reason for considering the history of the social audits is the rich mine of experience that it represents – both for the 'social auditors' (to avoid the reinvention of wheels) and for the 'audited' organization (which can assess the extent of the challenge, threat or opportunity offered by these things).

The genesis of external social audits is typically attributed to the late 1960s and early 1970s in the USA (for example, Ralph Nader and the consumer movement; the Council on Economic Priorities) and the UK (for example, the Consumers Association, Social Audit Ltd and Counter Information Services). These were very different sorts of organization but they all succeeded in increasing the information in the public domain – in the words of Stephenson, a member of the Council on Economic Priorities:

> it appears that government cannot effectively evaluate and regulate big business. And it seems unwise to place the burden of corporate conscience on executives who are responsible for maximising profit, or on the stockholders who are normally motivated even more singularly by profits. The best place to start correcting this situation is in making more information available to the public.[2]

The UK's experience derives, initially, from that of the USA in that the early example of Ralph Nader (and Nader's Raiders) provided a model for consumer and related activism which influenced the founders of the UK's Consumers Association and Social Audit Ltd (and its research arm the Public Interest Research Centre[3]).

The Consumers Association was (and to some extent remains[4]) a campaigning consumer-based organization concerned with assessing quality, value for money and the ethical basis of the supply of goods and services to the end-consumer market through its magazine *Which?*. Concerned with more than just the 'best buys' in consumer products the Association sought (fairly successfully) to empower the consumer and to widen the scope of the accountability of organizations to the users of their services and products. It was an important early example of the social audit as a mechanism for challenging the passivity of the individual in the face of the growing power of organizations and their capacity to exploit advertising and the nature of choice.[5]

---

[2] Stephenson (1973, p. 69).

[3] This 'PIRC' should not be confused with 'PIRC' established in 1986 – the Pensions Investment Resource Centre.

[4] See, for example, Geddes (1992) p. 224.

[5] Commercial pressures in the late 1980s reduced the campaigning dimension of the Consumers Association, leading it to a narrower focus upon product cost and efficiency.

Figure 13.1

Some areas covered by Social Audit Ltd's *Social Audit Quarterly*

* Tube Investments Ltd (including an exercise in trying to encourage social action by the shareholders of the company)
* The Alkali Inspectorate (as was)
* Cable and Wireless
* Coalite and Chemical
* Avon Rubber Company Ltd

plus general reports on matters such as:
* armaments and industry;
* social costs of advertising;
* company law reform.

Social Audit Ltd was a more complex organization[6] originally established to demonstrate that a full social audit was a feasible proposition. The intention was to publish data covering an organization's interactions with employees, consumers, community and the environment in the interests of a wider accountability and the presentation of a 'balancing view'. The essential reasoning behind this was that organizations in general – and companies and government departments in particular – are successful at presenting their own point of view to the public at large. What was needed was a mechanism for presenting an alternative – hence 'balancing' – view. The first fruits of Social Audit's endeavours were published in the early 1970s in the *Social Audit Quarterly*, which, whilst not quite fulfilling the ambitions of the authors, remains a particularly good source of information (see Figure 13.1) on both the ways of collecting and presenting information and the difficulties of collating reliable and comprehensive data without the co-operation of the organization concerned.[7] Commercial exigencies were largely responsible for the cessation of the full, formal, social audits and the last manifestations of Social Audit Ltd's wider social role were a series of books and pamphlets in the late 1970s and early 1980s – which remain, although dated, a continuing source of direction on the collection and use of information for employees and consumers.[8]

Counter Information Services were a much more radical outfit[9] concerned more with the 'good story' and the empowering of labour

---

[6] By the late 1980s Social Audit was a much smaller and lower-profile organization and one which was much more focused in its attentions. It now concentrates primarily on the activities of drug companies and, in particular, the use, control and marketing of drugs in the lesser developed countries.

[7] For more detail, see Medawar, 1976 and Gray, Owen and Maunders, 1987.

[8] See Medawar, 1978; Frankel, 1978, 1981, 1982.

[9] They described themselves as a Marxist Collective of journalists. For more information see, for example, Gray, Owen and Maunders (1987) and Ridgers (1979).

Figure 13.2

**Some areas covered
By Counter Information Services
and the 'Anti-reports'**

- Rio Tinto Zinc
- Courtaulds
- Consolidated Gold Fields
- British Leyland
- Ford Motor Company
- GEC
- Unilever
- Lucas
- National Health Service

and reports on, for example:
- South Africa
- nuclear technology
- the Queen's Jubilee
- women in society.

---

than with anything that might conventionally pass for accountability and dialogue. Nevertheless, they represented a thorn in the side of industry for many years – particularly during the 1970s (see Figure 13.2).

The particular relevance in the present context of these bodies was that each covered environmental issues in its data gathering and publication. Social Audit's and CIS's reporting often contained a very significant element. For example, the CIS report on Rio Tinto Zinc contained a number of serious observations – usually drawn from *The Ecologist* magazine – about the environmental performance of RTZ in general and one of their sites in particular. Social Audit pioneered both the use of local authority pollution data and the reporting of emissions against consent levels – with explanations as to the biological implications of the consent levels themselves. These are innovations in data use and reporting to which we are only now returning and it is wise to remember that the emergence of environmental emissions data into the public domain is not a new phenomenon.

Apart from Social Audit and CIS, environmental issues played little role in the social audit movement throughout the 1970s and into the early 1980s in the UK. The emphasis in this period tended to be on the social consequences of the worst excesses of Thatcherism and, in particular, on the shadowing of plant-closure decisions.[10] In general, the 'social audit movement' is, was and remains a diffuse

---

[10] For more detail see Gray, Owen and Maunders, (1987), Harte and Owen, (1987), Geddes, (1988), (1992), Haughton, (1988).

and intermittent activity. The campaigning role is often best served by the combination of investigative journalism and the pressure groups – in the environmental domain this typically means Friends of the Earth and Greenpeace, of whom more later.

Meanwhile in the USA, the existence of the Council for Economic Priorities (CEP) has provided a consistency and regularity to the social auditing process. The CEP has been actively campaigning for over twenty years. Its purpose is to research, collate and publicize information about organizational activity as it affects society[11] across a wide spectrum of social issues – including the environment – and has produced over 100 reports on such matters as waste disposal, nuclear energy, air and water pollution, military spending, occupational safety. The long life of the CEP has enabled it to build up reputation, experience and a reliable methodology in the collection and reporting of data. One major effect of this has been to produce streams of data about such matters as pollution which other researchers have employed in the assessment of the social and environmental performance of corporate America. This had the effect of encouraging researchers – especially in accounting and finance – to keep alive the debate about the social, environmental and economic consequences of corporate activity in a way that is simply not possible in the UK and elsewhere. Whilst it is not clear where the funding for such an arrangement could come from (but see below), there is little question that other countries need this consistent and reliable source of data if sensible debate – other than simply controlled by the corporations themselves – is to be possible.[12]

13.3   The Environmental Social Audit: Present and Future

The diffuse nature of activities falling within the term 'social audit' should be apparent by now. This situation seems likely to continue and the plurality may in fact be a healthy phenomenon reflecting a vital and changing area of public concern. However, the very patchy and intermittent nature of the efforts to bring information into the public domain do tend to undermine its effectiveness. There are some signs that this state of affairs is changing. Not only are there now established campaigning information sources such as ENDS, EIRIS and PIRC but the environmental organizations and the ethical/environmental investment movement themselves are becoming much better established.

[11] See, for example, Miller (1992).

[12] For more information see Council for Economic Priorities (1973), Shane and Spicer (1983). The CEP have also played an important role in the ethical/environmental investment movement (see Chapter 10) and, to an extent, we can see organizations like EIRIS in the UK taking on the CEP role.

Figure 13.3

Friends of the Earth Right to Know Campaign

The USA Environmental Protection Agency requires reports of companies' releases of 322 identified chemicals under the Toxic Release Inventory (TRI). The TRI is published. Whilst the American public may know about the companies' emissions, the UK public do not. FoE have released data relating to major polluting chemical companies which also operate sites in the UK. ENDS report the FoE's release of the following data on discharges to land, air and water in 1988.

- BP 68,670 tonnes
- Dow Chemicals 15,745 tonnes
- Du Pont 145,085 tonnes
- ICI 9,990 tonnes
- Monsanto 91,640 tonnes
- Shell 77,550 tonnes
- Tenneco 3,935 tonnes

Adapted from *ENDS Report* 194/March 1991, p. 18

Such issues are important. With many of the organizations with which we have worked or have visited, it is often the 'external shock' that has prompted them to take a serious and hard look at their environmental activity. For example, one major company was concerned by the pressure from the ethical/environmental investment movement, three had been stung by Friends of the Earth and one mentioned Greenpeace's campaigns as the principal stimulus. There can be little doubt of the increasing efficacy (or irritant depending upon one's point of view) represented by such organizations and their 'social auditing' activities. Other organizations have set up consultation procedures with elements of the broad 'social audit' movement – whether prompted by a past conflict, fear of a future conflict or genuine desire to develop environmental sensitivity is not clear. But the very presence of a body – including some of the more campaigning environmental consultancies – has a substantive effect on the level of environmental awareness and avoids onset of complacency. Figure 13.3 is adapted from an ENDS report and indicates how the 'social audit' can succeed in forcing accountability upon organizations which may be keen to avoid it. This action is similar to that of EIRIS (see Chapter 10) and with a widely established and reliable information service like ENDS anxious to publicize such data, there is a sense that the UK, at least, is beginning to move towards a greater (if reluctant) transparency.

This process is encouraged and reinforced by other developments. In the UK the developing role of the local authorities is significant and the newer campaigning publications – notably *Ethical Consumer* and *The New Consumer* – are having a significant impact on organizational transparency. It is to this that we now turn.

13.4   Local Government and the Social Audits

During the 1980s in the UK, local authorities played an active role in
the conduct of social audits primarily directed towards what were
seen as the excesses of private development and the social impact of
decisions by private companies.[13] As we saw briefly in Chapter 5,
the rise in environmental awareness is placing a significant burden
on local government – not just in their role in controlling pollution[14]
and through their activities in such matters as waste disposal and
the putative register of contaminated land, but also in more proactive roles such as the State of the Environment Audits which many
local authorities are undertaking.[15] This seems to be providing a
baseline from which authorities can develop. Given the wide powers
that authorities have and their wide responsibilities for a substantial
proportion of the urban and rural environment in the UK, it is not
surprising to find authorities taking serious initiatives in the control
of transport,[16] planning applications, and a whole range of environmentally positive and environmentally negative activities. Furthermore, given the active role that many authorities undertook in the
1980s on the wider social agenda, plus their increasingly strong
position in respect of their information collection activities we can
reasonably expect authorities to become much more influential in
the collation and dissemination of information about organization–
environment interaction. Already, many local authorities are working closely with environmental groups as well as with industry
in order to advance the environmental agenda. However, what is
far from clear as yet, is how the potentially conflicting roles of
'development' – meaning economic growth and expansion of traditional forms of employment – and enhancement of the environment will be reconciled.[17] Already, local enterprise companies,[18]
established to regenerate business development throughout the UK,
are facing, with the appropriate local authorities, the tensions
about jobs and growth versus environment. At the present time,
unfortunately, the tension looks a real one and one in which,

[13] For further detail see e.g., Geddes, 1988, 1992, and Harte and Owen, 1987.

[14] Through their role in integrated pollution control, see, for example, the CBI
publications on *Local authority air pollution control*, CBI (1991).

[15] Kirklees Metropolitan Council in Yorkshire was the first to undertake such an
audit in 1989, and they have become state of the art since then with many local
authorities undertaking and publishing the result of their audits.

[16] For example, in 1991 Edinburgh City Council had actively monitored car use and
its effects in the city centre and were seeking powers to control or even ban the
private car from the city centre.

[17] See, for example, Gray and Morrison (1992).

[18] Effectively a series of arm's-length quangos. In Scotland, for example, these are
established on a regional basis in co-operation with Scottish Enterprise (formerly the
Scottish Development Office).

typically, we can expect the conventional economic criteria to win over environmental concerns.

13.5 The Campaigning Green Consumer

The 'green consumer' has probably been a major force on the process of organizational environmental sensitivity. Consumer boycotts and related activism have a long (and, at times, successful) history.[19] The late 1980s in the UK saw the arrival of this new breed of consumer. Whilst the notion of 'green' and 'consumer' are probably contradictions and the effect they can achieve (and have achieved) must be relatively superficial in the short term, the movement has certainly raised awareness, brought new products to the market and set in train effects of a far wider influence than the recycling of toilet rolls and the phosphate-freeness of washing powders.

In the UK a consumer movement specifically targeted at environmental issues can probably be dated from Elkington and Hailes's *The Green Consumer Guide* in 1988.[20] The upsurge of interest in the late 1980s brought a steadily growing interest in environmental and related issues as represented in consumer choice and products and, with it, came a rapid increase in demand for new information which the campaigning bodies and the journalists were pleased to supply. The rise in the number of campaigning bodies also rose steadily – which in itself increases the information-demand and the related pressure on organizations to disclose such information. Perhaps the most interesting 'social audit' manifestation in this regard was the development of new, campaigning journals such as *The Ethical Consumer, The Green Magazine* and *New Consumer. The Ethical Consumer* provides an assessment of companies and products based upon a wide set of criteria (see Figure 13.4) – far wider than just 'green' issues – that are a serious attempt to link the consumer with the people, countries, processes and effects that produced the product now being purchased and consumed. If environmental (and related) issues are to be sensibly addressed this recognition of the connection between all forms of consuming and the social and environmental impacts is essential. *The Ethical Consumer* is a particularly powerful indicator of the potential for social auditing both to educate and to develop accountability.

New Consumer operates in a similar way although its dissemination throughout the UK has probably been more pronounced as a result of the publication of *Changing Corporate Values* in 1991.[21]

---

[19] The consumer boycotts related to apartheid in South Africa are perhaps the best known and claimed as the most successful. Other major successes have focused around 'natural' foods, 'natural' beers and the cruelty to animals campaigns.

[20] Elkington and Hailes (1988) and see also Elkington and Hailes (1989).

[21] Adams, Carruthers and Hamil (1991) and see also Adams, Carruthers and Fisher (1991), which acts as a product-orientated version of the same research.

Figure 13.4

**The *Ethical Consumer* criteria
for evaluation of products
and companies**

Animal testing
Armaments
Environment
Irresponsible marketing
Land rights
Nuclear power
Oppressive regimes
South Africa
Trade union relations
Wages and conditions

This text represents a really significant piece of research, collating information about 128 companies (only 79 of which are British). The information was drawn together from a variety of sources – including, most significantly, a questionnaire to the companies themselves. (Their willingness or otherwise to respond to the questionnaire is noted in the text.) Figure 13.5 provides an illustration of the range of material and its presentation. The text alone represents a major data source just crying out for further research to assess its impacts.

13.6   Some Concluding Remarks

The wide 'social audit' movement in the UK has been exceptionally fragmented. It has had its successes and has certainly provided a collective wealth of experience about the research, collection, collation and publication of information about organizations and their social and environmental activities. However, the fragmentation might well explain why it is only in the early 1990s, under severe encouragement from the EC, that Britain is beginning to take more than one-off steps towards transparency and thus accountability and democracy. The development in the late 1980s of the campaigning green consumer bodies plus the increasing organization of the environmental bodies – typically Friends of the Earth and Greenpeace – together with EIRIS and the growing ethical/environmental investment movement suggest that, in the UK at least, the makings of a substantial influence in the social audit domain now exists.

This is crucial for companies and other organizations because it means, at its simplest, that if the company does not develop its own accountability, there is a growing and increasingly able body of expertise 'out there' that will be happy to do it for them. If there are

Figure 13.5 Extract from Adams, Carruthers and Hamill (1991) *Changing Corporate Values*

Disclosure

This rating indicates whether the company completed the New Consumer or CEP questionnaires, whether the company provided New Consumer with information over and above that in its annual report, to what extent the company went beyond minimum statutory disclosure requirements in its annual report and other material, and whether the company provided comments on its draft profile or entered into a dialogue with New Consumer concerning the issues covered.

✓✓✓	Well above average
✓✓	Above average
✓	Average
✗	Below average
✗✗	Well below average

Ethnic

This rating indicates to what extent the company encourages the placement and existence of some form of ethnic monitoring to evaluate policy is one factor taken into account as is a detailed equal opportunities policy. Support for Fullemploy, specific initiatives, recruitment and the number of ethnic minorities in senior positions particularly at board level, are all represented in the rating. No allowance has been made for cultural or immigration factors in different nations determining the level of minorities in the general population of the country of the advancement of members of ethnic minority communities within its organisation. The parent company.

✓✓	Above average
✓	Average
*	Inadequate information/ below average

Women

This rating indicates to what extent the company encourages the advancement of women within its organisation. This assessment includes aspects of personnel policy such as maternity leave, career breaks, creche provision, job share and specific training, as well as recruitment and promotion policy and the number of women in senior positions, particularly at board level. No allowance has been made for cultural factors in different countries determining the role of women in management.

✓✓✓	Well above average
✓✓	Above average
✓	Average
*	Inadequate information/ below average

Community

This rating is not based purely on the extent of the company's cash charitable giving in relation to profit. Secondment of staff, gifts in kind, facilities provided for staff to engage in community service are all taken into account. Membership of Business in the Community and the Per Cent Club in the UK are regarded as indicators. A general assessment of the percentage of charitable giving in relation to pre-tax profit comprises an element of the rating, though there is no allowance for traditions of corporate giving in different countries. There is, for example, a quite different perception between North American and many European countries on the place of corporate charitable giving.

✓✓	Above average
✓	Average
*	Inadequate information/ below average

Environmental impact

This rating indicates to what extent the company's activities have a significant effect on the environment. Those companies involved in the production of biomass, together with the extractive and manufacturing industries, are more likely to feature in this category.

 Major environmental impact (chemical, oil and mining companies)

xx Significant environmental impact (clothing, pesticides, electrical goods, pharmaceuticals, agricultural goods and motor car manufacturers)

x Above average impact (tobacco, fast food, soft drinks and brewing)

Environmental action

This rating indicates particular initiatives the company is undertaking to reduce environmental impact or improve its environmental performance or sensitivity. Significant indicators here are the existence of a written environmental policy or an environmental office or officer.

✓✓ Concerted environmental action

✓ Some environmental action

* Inadequate information

South Africa

Here an indication is made of the degree of a company's involvement, if any, in South Africa.

Y The company has a significant operating subsidiary in South Africa

Y The company has some type of licensing agreement or trading activity/sales office in South Africa

y A retailer offering South African products for sale in the UK

Other countries

This rating indicates whether the company has operating subsidiaries in developing countries.

Y Significant operating units in the Third World

Y Some operating units or major licensing agreements in the Third World

y Purchases a significant volume of products or raw materials from Third World countries

Respect for people

This rating indicates whether the company produces or retails alcohol or tobacco or is involved in the provision or promotion of gambling.

A	Manufactures alcoholic drinks
A	A significant retailer of alcoholic drinks
a	Some alcohol sales
T	Manufactures tobacco products
T	A significant retailer of tobacco products
t	Some tobacco sales
G	Provides substantial gambling services
g	Provides limited gambling services

Respect for life

This rating indicates to what extent a manufacturing company uses animals in testing its products.

✓✓✓	Products have not been tested on animals in the last five years, but ingredients have
✓✓	Products have been tested on animals in the last five years, but the company is funding or carrying out research into alternative methods of testing
✓	Has not used animal testing either in-house or through outside contractors for products or their ingredients in the last five years
*	Insufficient information to rate
✗✗	Products are currently tested on animals, but only pharmaceutical or medical products
✗✗✗	Non-medical products are currently tested on animals

Military

This rating indicates whether the company produces a significant volume of military equipment or provides essential goods or services to the military in the UK or elsewhere.

M	Has significant military sales (above £25m)
m	Has some military sales (between £5m and £25m)

Politics

This rating indicates whether the company has contributed financially in the period 1986-90 (many companies only make political donations in the period running up to a general election) to support political purposes within the United Kingdom as defined by Schedule 7 of the *Companies Act*.

C	Recent donations to the Conservative party or free enterprise support organisations
L	Recent donations to the Labour party or associates
E	Currently subscribes to, or has not confirmed a lapse of recent subscription to, the Economic League.

Please note that the ratings are applied, unless specified otherwise, to the whole company group. Because of the very large number of acquisitions by major companies and the growth of conglomerates over the last twenty years, many brands listed in the product group section will be found to have unexpected affiliations. These ratings are intended as a very approximate guide; for further detail about how they have been compiled please refer to Appendix A.

THE BODY SHOP INTERNATIONAL PLC

The Body Shop Group produces and sells natural-ingredient skin and hair care products and related items, both through its own shops and through franchised outlets. It has grown from its first retail shop, opened in Britain in 1976, to nearly 500 outlets in 37 countries. The company was founded by its current managing director, Anita Roddick. She opened the first shop in Brighton, selling a handful of natural toiletries adapted from materials she had seen used in less-developed countries.

Of the 151 shops in the UK, 115 are franchises, as are 320 of the 338 overseas outlets. Franchises are owned and run by the franchisee on a five-year renewable agreement. Franchisee credentials and motives are thoroughly assessed on ethical as well as financial grounds; however, the company makes no stipulations as to the pay and conditions of the staff in the franchised shops.

The Body Shop vigorously promotes a 'green' and 'ethical' image, and would seem to back this up in practice. Now truly a worldwide company, the USA is The Body Shop's youngest market and is operated by a subsidiary — The Body Shop Inc. Other subsidiaries include Eastwick Trading BV in the Netherlands, Colorings Ltd (a make-up and beauty range) in the UK, Jacaranda Productions Ltd (producing corporate, educational and training programmes for both The Body Shop and a wide range of external clients), and Soapworks Ltd.

The company sets out its mission statement as follows: 'The Body Shop cares about humanising the business community: we will con-

tinue to show that success and profit can go hand in hand with ideals and values. Profit is the lubricant to make things happen and the vehicle to help people — hence our philosophy of "profits with responsibility". We believe that a successful business has an obligation to educate and to inspire — we want to help initiate a new age of compassion and humanity. This is not hyperbole; it can, and already has been, translated into action.'

Financial data for the year ending 28 February 1990

Turnover	£94m
Profit before tax	£15m
Turnover by region:	
UK and Eire	£57m
Other EC	£7m
Rest of Europe	£4m
Australasia	£3m
Asia	£2m
USA	£6m
Rest of North America	£6m

Major shareholders: I.B. McGlinn has 30% of the ordinary shares. T.G. Roddick (chairman) and A.L. Roddick hold approximately 30.2% of the ordinary shares.

The Body Shop's annual report provides a substantial amount of information

about the social initiatives, personnel and purchasing policies of the company, and the group also completed the New Consumer questionnaire. The company has made social responsibility its unique selling proposition, and in this context it was felt appropriate to ask some supplementary questions about the effectiveness of its 'social' policies; these questions were answered in some detail. The overall level of disclosure by the Body Shop was amongst the highest of all the companies in the survey, which accounts for the detail given in this profile in comparison with the company's relatively small size.

In the twelve-month period to the end of February 1990 the average number of employees was 1,265. This figure does not include employees in franchised shops. Some 200 part-time staff are employed in the UK, and their benefits are harmonised pro-rata with their full-time counterparts. The company states that it operates a harmonised-benefits system across all grades of employees.

The Body Shop stresses its commitment to a high level of training, much of which is sales and customer-service driven, but which also seeks to inculcate 'Body Shop values'. These are set out in a ten-point Charter, and emphasise honesty, integrity, concern for individuals, animals and the environment. It states that 'Our policies and our products are geared to meet the real needs of real people both inside and outside the company'.

In the year ending 28 February 1990 the chairman and highest paid director were paid £110,000 and £172,000 respectively, representing 8% increases on the previous year. The company states that the entry level salaries of office/clerical and manual staff are £8,000 and £7,500 respectively. The company awarded basic pay increases of 10% and 8% in the last two years.

A private health insurance scheme, formerly for directors only, has been extended to a much broader selection of staff, and all staff have the opportunity to join the scheme if they wish to contribute themselves. There is disability insurance, a subsidised crèche (for which, for example, staff on £10,000 per annum

pay £30 per week), and a staff discount scheme. In 1989 the company introduced a pension scheme for employees with one years' service, and it has also introduced 'bonus schemes for staff relating to effort'. According to the company the rate of staff turnover for its directly-owned shops is 7.5%, extremely low for the retail sector.

Staff are encouraged to maintain the principles of the company's Charter, and employee involvement is encouraged. The company currently developing an 'initial document on employee involvement'. None of the company's staff is represented by trades unions or staff associations. The company commented that it 'does not have a policy of discouraging unions among its staff, but the necessity has so far not arisen.'

There is a limited share option scheme which is open to all staff after one year's service (this is currently being reviewed): eligible employees are granted options to purchase shares in the company through its share option scheme. At 5 April 1990 287 employees held shares in the company through its share option scheme. The company does not operate any form of direct profit-sharing scheme.

There are two women, the managing director and the communications director, on the board, but no members of ethnic minority communities. Of the fifteen highest-paid employees who are not directors, at least one is a woman. The company does not make a written equal opportunities statement but says that it does operate an equal opportunities policy. There is no discrimination on the grounds of age, race, religion, or sex. Men and women are employed in the same jobs in shops, offices warehouse and production sites. The company does not appear to operate any equal opportunities monitoring procedures. It offers paternity leave at the rate of ten working days after one year's service, and supports the work of the Fullemploy Group.

In the year ending 28 February 1990 the company made cash charitable donations of £163,000. The Body Shop Foundation

carrots for environmental and related disclosure (see Chapters 11 and 12), here is the stick.

Further Reading

Adams, R., Carruthers, J. and Hamil, S. (1991) *Changing Corporate Values*, Kogan Page, London.

Geddes, M. (1992) The social audit movement, chapter 10 in D. Owen (ed.) *Green Reporting*, Chapman Hall, London.

Gray, R. H., Owen, D. L. and Maunders, K. T. (1987) *Corporate Social Reporting: Accounting and Accountability*, Prentice-Hall, Hemel Hempstead.

Medawar, C. (1976) The social audit: a political view, *Accounting, Organizations and Society*, Vol. 1, no. 4, pp. 389–94.

Miller, A. (1992) Green investment, chapter 11 in D. Owen (ed.) *Green Reporting*, Chapman Hall, London.

Stead W. E. and Stead J. G. (1992) *Management for a Small Planet*, Sage, Newbury Park, CA; especially Chs. 7 and 9.

Plus other references throughout the chapter which either highlight the experiments in the past or provide more analytical assessment of the social audit and its implications.

PART D

FUTURE DIRECTIONS

Part D: Future Directions – an Overview

The law doth punish man or woman,
That steals the goose from off the common,
But lets the greater felon loose
That steals the common from the goose.
(Anon)

This book has been written with a very specific eye on not just what is practicable but also what business and politicians currently consider to be achievable. If, however, the deeper green view (to which we subscribe) proves to be the more accurate perception of the state of the planet and the causes of that state then humanity faces a stark choice between allowing current business and political views to prevail *or* seeking a sustainable future. The two are almost certainly not compatible. This section begins the process of examining the reasoning behind such a view and the implications it has for micro-economic activity.

14.   Accounting and Reporting for a Future:

Sustainability, Accountability and Transparency[1]

14.1   Introduction

Sustainability: Treating the world as if we intended to stay.

Throughout the book, we have tried to review the recent history, identify current practice, highlight best practice and estimate some of the major influences which can be expected in the near future. In this chapter, we take a harder look at the direction in which future developments *must* move if the environmental crisis is to stand any chance of mitigation. In particular, we focus upon sustainability as the key concept guiding mankind's future interactions with the environment. Whilst the essence of the concept – and the related notion of sustainable development – may appear simple, it is a profoundly difficult concept either to understand or operationalize. In fact, it may be that sustainability *cannot* be either understood or put into practice within our current economic and philosophical frameworks. If this is so then the challenge of sustainability really will (to use a sadly overworked cliché) become one of the greatest challenges the West could possibly face.

This chapter will introduce the concept of sustainability and some of its basic implications before going on to try to operationalize the term – first within an economic framework and then within an accounting one. It will be argued that moves such as this make sense only in a framework of accountability and transparency, which are then explored.

---

[1] Much of the work which appears in this chapter was originally prepared for the International Institute for Sustainable Development. The work and ideas of Tony Clayton and Paul Ekins have also influenced the development of our ideas. Their support and encouragement is gratefully acknowledged.

14.2   What is Sustainability?

The concept of 'sustainability' rose to prominence following the Brundtland report in 1987.[2] It became, very rapidly, the core concept in any discussion of human interaction with the physical environment. Further, on the face of it, it is a concept that is universally accepted as a desirable, even essential, yardstick by which to assess human actions. However, there is considerable disagreement over its precise meaning, over the actual operationalization of the concept and over its implications for the way in which human life is ordered.

The general definition of sustainability is *not* in dispute, namely that humanity must: 'ensure that [development] meets the needs of the present without compromising the ability of future generations to meet their own needs' (WCED, 1987, p. 8). However:

a large selection of quotations from recent writing on sustainability shows that there is no general agreement on exactly what sustainability means. This fuzziness is useful in forging a consensus to promote sustainable development but it also obscures the political, philosophical and technical issues that still remain unresolved from the 'environment versus growth' debate of the early 1970s.

(Pezzey, 1989, p. 1).

Whilst the basic idea of sustainability is self-evidently good sense and one with which few would wish (publicly) to disagree, identifying and assessing the detail of the concept has proved immensely difficult. Part of the problem is the very newness of the concept to Western man[3] with the result that Western intellectual tradition has little reliable experience or equipment with which to address and examine the term. The profundity of its implications is only just becoming apparent and these are not, generally, widely appreciated. Where they are understood, the likely impact they would have on Western lifestyle often makes the practical implementation of sustainability ideologically unacceptable. Thus, Pezzey (1989) arrives at his conclusion that there are broadly three levels of problems in addressing 'sustainability': what does the term mean? what is ideologically and politically acceptable? how do we put it into practice? We shall attempt to cast some light on these questions.

It is essential, however, that we be perfectly clear from the outset: whichever way we choose to define sustainability, we can never know whether or not we have reached it. That is, the point at which the planet achieves sustainability and whether that point has been

---

[2] World Commission on Environment and Development (1987).

[3] Evidence suggests that the so-called First Nations had the concept of sustainability embedded into their very culture. Western 'enlightenment' separated humans from the implicit acceptance of the notion but put nothing explicit in its place. It is the very obviousness of the concept that has led to its acceptance but which has also caught Western thought unprepared to incorporate it in any substantive way.

passed or has yet to be reached is simply *un-knowable*. Given any particular definition of sustainability (see below), at any given time, the planet has some maximum carrying capacity. The planet may be able to sustain that definition for some element of the life on it, for some period of time; it might be able to sustain into the foreseeable future; or it may be unable to sustain the way of life desired in the definition. That is, given some predetermined acceptable level of life on the planet Earth we cannot know to what extent that level is (a) achievable and (b) maintainable – i.e. sustainable. It is also unlikely that humanity – with its present science anyhow – can ever know that point. This does not stop us trying to define the area into which it might fall. After all, the human species alone may be well past the carrying capacity of the planet and if we can infer any data about this it seems sensible to try.

14.3 Trying to Identify Sustainability

One simple way of attempting to conceptualize the dilemma of sustainability is shown in Figure 14.1. The wavy horizontal lines purport to capture the range of long-term carrying capacities under differing assumptions, levels of economic activity, population, etc. In the crudest terms, the straight lines represent the economic growth patterns of the different nations of the world – with some nations (e.g. Australian Aborigines in their original natural environment) barely rising off the zero economic activity line. The diagram is clearly dangerously simple but enables us to highlight a number of important points. First, we have only circumstantial evidence as to whereabouts on the 'average global economic growth' line we currently sit. The most widely held assumption is that we are somewhere *above* point a. If this is so, humanity's way of life is currently unsustainable. Second, the point at which the G7 nations passed the point of sustainable activity, point b, was sometime in the past. Third, although contestable, most commentators suggest that it is the Western ways of life which are the least sustainable – left to their own devices, many LDCs would still be within the point of sustainability. Fourth, and crucially, there is not a single point of sustainability – it is a band depending on a wide range of assumptions and beliefs.

Sustainable for what?

Who or what do we wish to sustain? All existing species or just humans? All existing species but *not* humans? We are clearly failing to sustain all existing species when the rate of species extinction is accelerating.[4] For a 'deep green', sustainability must mean that species other than humans are sustained. When the problems of

---

[4] Which, of course it must logically do given the principles of ecology.

Figure 14.1   Where is the point of sustainability?

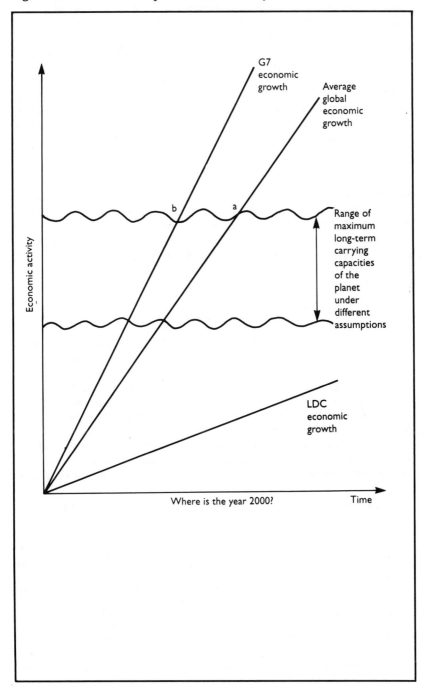

whether or not other species have ethical rights under concepts of justice[5] (for example) we find ourselves faced with an ethical (rather than instrumental)[6] dilemma as to the relative rights of humanity *vis-à-vis* other species and the planet itself. For many commentators, the fact that it is humanity that is desecrating the planet and causing the species extinction places the moral burden on to human beings. Many would argue that, even if humanity has any choice in the matter, the human species has no right to continued existence. The case is far from trivial and, in conscience, one which humanity must consider. However, we shall maintain the more usual anthropocentric approach to sustainability for the rest of this chapter.[7]

Sustainable for whom?

Which humans do we wish to sustain? It is apparent that humanity as a whole is not sustaining itself when so many die from famine, drought, floods and other environmentally related disasters. If Western leaders mean to sustain only Westerners, it should be made explicit. Further, we have the problem of population – do we wish to sustain (e.g.) 80, 100, 150 per cent of the present population? Who is it that we wish to sustain?

Sustainable in what way?

Most Western commentators consider that 'sustainability' *must* mean the sustenance of Western civilization at an economically more developed stage than at present. This has two elements: that more economic growth, higher consumption, etc. are essential because without them the wealth and technology for sustainability cannot be achieved[8]; and because anything other than more economic growth is unthinkable. Of course, this is fundamentally unjust unless the rest of humanity are encouraged to reach and be sustained at the same point of economic development as achieved by the 'advanced' Western economies. This is justified on the grounds that economic

[5] See, for example, the issue as discussed in Rawls (1972) and developed in, for example, the *Journal of Ecological Ethics*.

[6] See Gray (1992) on this issue.

[7] We do this for a number of reasons. First, we recognize that, for many readers, the concepts of anthropocentricism and its alternatives will be new. We do not wish to alienate readership at this stage. Second, the issue of human versus other species is complex and although critically important (we tend to think we fall only *just* to the side of giving humans certain, but very restricted, rights over the planet – we are (just) anthropocentric) we are not sure that this is the place to hold the debate. Third, the issues of sustainability from an anthropocentric point of view are quite complex enough to illustrate the range of problems that must be forcibly addressed if it is to be approached.

[8] For illustrations of this kind of 'thinking' see e.g. Burke, Robins and Trisoglio, 1991, and Schmidheiny, 1992.

wealth is needed to fund the remediation and investment necessary to achieve 'green' economic activity. We reject this. Not only is this hopelessly ethnocentric[9] but it is without foundation. There is *no* evidence to suggest that by increasing the very process which caused the environmental degradation (economic growth as currently measured) humanity will reduce the degradation, whereas cases to the contrary abound.[10] At its most brutal and simple, the pursuit of economic growth as currently conceived in the hope that it *might* solve the problems seems to us too high–risk a gamble.

Sustainable for how long?

It is also fairly obvious that life (as we currently understand it) on Earth cannot last indefinitely. It is also clear that virtually *any* use of finite raw materials is ultimately unsustainable. Furthermore, it is apparent that there is no fixed, steady state in nature and in ecology – species become extinct regardless of what humanity does and natural 'disasters' occur and change (e.g.) climatic conditions independent of human interference. Decisions, in any definition about sustainability, need to be made about what 'reasonable' future we might envisage for the race.

Sustainable at what level of resolution?

Whilst, for the species and life as a whole, sustainability is a global concept this does not necessarily provide an excuse for nations, regions and even corporations to ignore the concept. It is looking increasingly likely that international governmental agreement of any substance on sustainability will not be forthcoming. This means any moves towards sustainability will be achieved by the unilateral actions of nations, regions, corporations, individuals and action groups.[11] At the level of the corporation, accounting can play a major part.

These are obviously not easy questions and are further complicated by the wide disparity of views on:

(a) the nature and the extent of the environmental crisis;
(b) the degree to which environmental problems are systemic rather than isolated phenomena;

[9] That is, it assumes that advanced Western capitalism is the only reasonable and desirable form of existence. There might be some serious doubts about this assertion.

[10] See, for example, Ekins, 1992b; Goldsmith *et al.*, 1972; Robertson, 1978b; Daly, 1980; Goldsmith, 1988; Daly and Cobb, 1990; Anderson, 1991.

[11] In Scotland, for example, WWF commissioned a study from Dr Tony Clayton of IPAD to examine the meaning and implications of sustainability at the level of the Scottish nation. Scottish Natural Heritage, a quango charged with maintaining the country's natural heritage, is also required to act in a manner which will enhance the sustainability of the nation.

Figure 14.2

Some examples of current environmental pressures

Most environmental pressures are increasing exponentially. Thus mankind is faced with an accelerating:

* rate of ozone depletion;
* rate of species extinction;
* rate of habitat depletion;
* rate of increase in technological catastrophe and scientific ignorance;
* desertification;
* deforestation;
* incidence of acid rain;
* depletion of fishing stocks;
* decline in the planet's waste-sink-absorption capacity;
* erosion of soil;
* pressure on water resources;
* rates of poverty and starvation;
* rate of usage of non-renewable resources; etc. etc.

(c) the causes of the crisis; and, as a result;

(d) the level of effort which must be directed towards environmental issues; and

(e) the form that effort must take.

These are scientific and psychological problems – scientific, in that our knowledge is woefully inadequate[12] and psychological, in that differing world-views seem to predispose people to different interpretations of the same data.[13]

Then we have the problem of political or ideological differences: 'Whose problem is it?' This may take many forms at many different levels. For example, where we sit on the markets-versus-regulation debate; our attachments to growth and non-growth; the fears that electorates may be displeased by promises of *reductions* in material well-being as currently measured; and, in particular, the conflicting perspectives of the G7 and G77 countries all add heat and steam, but little clarity or light, to the resolution of critical debates.

If we could resolve these issues, we still have the question: 'Which problem are we addressing?' That is, the predispositions we bring and the intellectual frameworks we employ have considerable

[12] And is likely to remain so. It can be argued that whilst scientific knowledge is increasing, so is scientific ignorance. This latter arises from, for example, the rapidly increasing number of new compounds. Such new compounds are created faster than it is possible to examine all possible effects of the compound's introduction to other chemical, biological or physical environments. Hence the increasing ignorance.

[13] A less generous interpretation might be that we are observing two manifestations of collective psychosis in which pro-ecology views reflect other dissatisfactions with industrial life whilst the anti-ecology views are motivated by a deep reluctance to consider uncomfortable conclusions.

influence on how we define a problem and, therefore, on the problem we attempt to solve. Consciously and unconsciously, most approaches to environmental issues are greatly influenced by economic thought. Whilst environmental economics has provided a vast literature and contributed greatly to our understanding of the relationship between the global economy and the environment, environmental economics does not speak with a single voice. Furthermore, it is far from clear that economics, *by itself*, can offer complete insights and thus coherent solutions. Economics with (*inter alia*) its conventional attachment to particular ethical positions and particular assumptions about human nature, its focus upon prices, its preference for markets over regulation, its relatively narrow conception of what constitutes 'efficiency' and its assumptions about wealth distribution and (usually) the necessity for economic growth must, by definition, give us only partial insights into complex social and political problems raised by the environmental crisis.[14] So whilst economic reasoning can take us a long way in understanding the issues at stake[15] it cannot necessarily offer either complete truths or especially direct and practicable solutions.

At the corporate level, although there are many layers to this complex issue, two points are apparent: corporate uncertainty as to how far to take the environmental issues and really how to respond to the above confusion seems perfectly understandable; and corporations control a dominant proportion of world economic activity as well as being the major mechanism through which technological change comes about, exercising a major influence over society's range of choice, holding much of the international power, controlling much of the world's resources and representing a significant element in employment – with all the influences that entails. Therefore any discussion about solutions to environmental crisis and of progress towards sustainability must include the corporations. It is here that accounting, reporting, auditing and related matters have to make their contribution.

14.4   Caveats, Cautions and Environmental Management

One further way of articulating the 'what is sustainability?' question is shown in Figure 14.3. Its principal value at this point is that it focuses upon *unsustainability* as that is the most effective and practical way of moving towards sustainability. We might identify all actions as falling into one of the following categories:

[14] For more detail see, for example, Daly (1980); Tinker (1984); McKee (1986); Raines and Jung (1986); Gorz (1989); Daly and Cobb (1990); Reilly and Kyj (1990); Turner and Pearce (1990); Pearce (1991b); Gray (1992).

[15] See especially Pearce, Markandya and Barbier (1989) and Pearce (1991) and for a more 'radical' view see, for example, Ekins (1992a, 1992b); Anderson (1991).

Figure 14.3

Ekins/Hueting conception of sustainability

Unsustainability arises from the activities of production and consumption which rise beyond the point where there is no competition for the different functions of the environment – e.g. habitat, food provider, space, etc. Thus, sustainability may be of three types:

* Qualitative: when excessive emissions/wastes lead to excessive concentrations which lead to unsustainable effects.
* Quantitative: when excessive extraction/use leads to excessive depletion which leads to unsustainable effects.
* Spatial: when excessive occupation leads to congestion which leads to unsustainable effects.

Source: taken from a working paper by Paul Ekins based upon Hueting (1980).

---

(1) clearly sustainable;
(2) unclear but *potentially* unsustainable;
(3) clearly unsustainable.

The majority of the actions that are generally deemed 'economic' will normally fall into the last two categories.[16] If this is so, and the absolute point of 'sustainability' cannot be known, attempting to identify and develop activities which are both 'economic' and entirely environmentally benign is virtually impossible. The best one can hope for without a major paradigm shift and a revolution in how humanity orders its activities is to seek out activities which *are less unsustainable*. Most forms of personal transport are unsustainable, but transport by rail will normally be less so than by private car. Most economic production and consumption is ultimately unsustainable but energy- and materials-efficient manufacturing based upon the 'reduce, reuse, recycle' principles will be likely to be less unsustainable. And so on.

If this analysis is correct – or even broadly realistic – then there is one, quite crucial conclusion to be drawn from this. The general concern in the West to develop 'greener' organizations is quite unlikely to come close to achieving sustainability except under the most restrictive and optimistic of assumptions. More especially, the admirable and difficult progress made by organizations towards the development and integration of environmental management systems (see Chapter 5) *may* be a necessary condition for sustain-

---

[16] Appendix 1.1 makes this point; the material later in the chapter will also. For further development see, for example, Gray and Morrison (1991, 1992), Gray (1992) and the publications from Daly (1980, 1985, 1989), Daly and Cobb (1990), Dauncey (1988), Ekins (1986, 1992a,b), Goldsmith (1988), Goldsmith *et al.* (1972), and Robertson (1978a,b, 1984, 1985, 1990).

> We challenge the notion that any business can ever be 'environmentally friendly'. This is just *not* possible. All business involves some environmental damage. The best we can do is clear up our own mess while searching hard for ways to reduce our impact on the environment.
>
> *Source:* Body Shop's *Green Book* 1992.

ability *but it is most certainly not a sufficient condition.*[17] Only under the most optimistic of assumptions about technological change and planet carrying capacity and/or the most brutal assumptions about the rights of non-Western peoples and non-human species are we likely to come even close to any sort of sustainable future.

We can illustrate this point by trying to operationalize the concept of sustainability. To do so, we will come back into *relatively* conventional economic and accounting frameworks. This will necessarily involve some significantly heroic assumptions. The point we would make is that if sustainability is the daunting concept we will illustrate, with heroic assumptions, how daunting will it be if the central environmental criticisms of economics and accounting were also taken into account?

14.5   Operationalizing Sustainability

If we are concerned with practicable action as a way forward we must try to find some realistic exposition of sustainability that can be articulated in ways that enable real-world policy to be derived from it. There are a group of environmental economists – including Daly, Pearce and Turner – who have sought to do just this.[18] It is their views of sustainability which will be used here to enable us to move forward.[19]

Pearce *et al.* have produced what is probably the most widely quoted and accepted principle of sustainable development:

> *the necessary conditions as 'constancy of natural capital stock'. More strictly, the requirement as for non-negative changes in the stock of*

[17] For illustration see IISD (1992), which represents a brave and thorough examination of the development of environmental management systems and reporting but which purports to be a treatise on sustainability without any examination of why the one should lead to the other. Such lacunae should be highly disturbing if one has any doubts about the optimism of the basic assumption. We would wish to adopt such optimism but see no grounds for doing so. For further illumination see Elkington and Dimmock (1991).

[18] Examples of their work are included in the bibliography.

[19] We should be honest here and mention that although the work of Daly, Pearce and Turner is excellent and very important in many ways we have some profound hesitations about some of its bases; see, for example, Gray (1990f, 1992).

natural resources such as soil and soil quality, ground surface waters and their quality, land biomass, water biomass, and the waste assimilation capacity of receiving environment.

(Pearce *et al.*, 1988; quoted in Pearce *et al.*, 1989).

Pearce *et al.* and then Turner further developed this by employing the concepts of 'capital' and we can relate this to Daly's work using the concept of 'income'.

The 'capital' available to humanity can be thought of as falling into three categories.[20]

(1) *Critical natural capital*: those elements of the biosphere that are essential for life and which, for sustainability, must remain inviolate (examples include the ozone layer, a critical mass of trees, etc.).

(2) *Other (sustainable, substitutable or renewable) natural capital*: those elements of the biosphere which are renewable (e.g. non-extinct species, woodlands) or for which reasonable (however defined) substitutes can be found (perhaps, for example, energy from fossil fuels versus energy from renewable sources, given the right capital investment).

(3) *Artificial capital*:[21] those elements created from the biosphere which are no longer part of the harmony of the natural ecology, which includes such things as machines, buildings, roads, products, wastes, human know-how and so on.

The general point is that artificial capital (which is largely covered by priced transactions and thus is dealt with and measured in conventional economics and accounting) is created and expanded at the expense of the natural capitals. It is artificial capitals that are measured by GNP and by profit and which Western capitalism has been excessively successful at creating and expanding. But, as artificial capital expands so it becomes almost inevitable that the natural capital *must* decline – unless some way of managing sustainably can be found. It then follows that for sustainability to be achieved, the critical capital *must* not be touched and all diminutions in other natural capital must be replaced, renewed or substituted

---

[20] Sustainability is a concept rather wider than just the physical environment. It refers to ways of life, societies and communities and the general quality of life of humanity. Included in what follows there should also be, therefore, reference to 'social' capital – qualities of lives, education, culture, built environment, etc. The analysis without these things is difficult enough and we, in following Turner and Daly, have also left them out. Most 'deep greens' see sustainability as embracing these wider social (and it must be said, spiritual) concepts through a realigning of Western values and the pursuit of smaller community levels of activity.

[21] The more common term is 'man-made' capital. In deference to the gender implications of this we have used the word 'artificial' – other terms include 'constructed' or just 'made' capital.

for.[22] Under current economics and accounting that cannot happen. Further, Daly's point (which can be added to this analysis) is the commonly accepted notion in economics, business and accounting that prudent behaviour suggests we take as income only that which is left over after maintaining our capital intact – capital maintenance. What we currently measure as 'income' does *not* leave our *natural* capital intact – it leaves it depleted. It must follow, therefore, that our measure of income is wrong and the level of consumption that we have enjoyed has been paid for out of capital. Sustainability requires that we maintain our capital and only spend the income that allows us to do so.[23]

The operationalization of a concept as complex as sustainability is bound to oversimplify the concept and, in the process, perhaps lose some of the essential ingredients. As societies show no inclination to revert to a level of peasant existence where sustainability is much easier to achieve it is necessary to devise some method that can be seen to approximate the concept of sustainability in a practical way within our current institutional and structural arrangements. This is what Pearce, Turner and Daly achieve. The concepts can then be translated to a corporate level. This is where *accounting and reporting for sustainability* can perhaps help and to which the next section of this chapter is directed.

14.6   Accounting for Sustainability

Ultimately, reporting for sustainability must consist of statements about the extent to which corporations are reducing (or increasing) the options available to future generations. This is a profoundly complex, if not impossible, task. However, there do appear to be three major ways in which any organization could try to approximate this in a fairly practicable and systematic way which would potentially lend itself to reporting. These are the *'inventory approach'* and the *'sustainable cost approach'* – which are both based around

---

[22] One point of departure from the economists' approach would be the notion that one *can* substitute for natural capital. Whilst, for example, the energy use in coal (non-renewable natural capital) could be substituted by the energy use of solar panels (artificial capital) there is no way in which the total 'use-value' that future generations may derive from coal can be known. Until that is known, future generations cannot be compensated for our use of their coal. Other aspects of natural capital, species for example, cannot be substituted for. Attempts to put a financial value on all of the natural capital lead to arguments about how that valuation should be done, whether it is ethical and whether we really want to be in a position to trade *n* Mutant Ninja turtle toys for *m* golden eagles. Finally, there is a critical problem of deciding what is really critical capital. For the 'deep green' observer, a considerable major proportion, if not all, of the biosphere is critical capital.

[23] For more detail see Daly (1980, 1985, 1989), Daly and Cobb (1990), Pearce, Markandya and Barbier (1989), Turner (1987, 1988, 1989, 1990), Turner and Pearce (1990). See also Gray (1990e,f, 1991a and 1992).

the categorization of artificial and natural capital discussed earlier – and the *'resource flow-through/input–output approach'*, which is more general. (In a broad sense, one might bear in mind that the first two are attempts to report *about* sustainability and the last an attempt to move towards reporting *for* sustainability.) These will be briefly examined in turn *but* it must be stressed that each is still highly experimental.[24] Until corporations are willing to work alongside researchers with these exploratory models, it is inevitable that they will remain so. It should also be recalled that no reporting can take place until it has a related accounting/information system to back it up and supply the data. Finally, it should be recalled that the thinking behind the reporting we have discussed in this book is related to providing information to which society has a right and which will enable society – in the broadest sense – to make judgements about the activities of its organizations. It is, thus, an utterly *democratic* approach which sees accountability in general and sustainability reporting in particular as part of the dialogue between a society and its organizations. (This is discussed in the penultimate section of this chapter.)

The *inventory approach* is concerned with identifying, recording, monitoring and then reporting, probably in non-financial quantities, the different categories of natural capital and their depletion and/or enhancement.[25] The different elements of critical, non-renewable/non-substitutable, non-renewable/substitutable, and renewable natural capital which could be thought of as being under the control of the organization would first be identified by the corporation. These would then be reported with changes therein. In addition, likely impacts of those changes upon the categories of capital, the steps taken to mitigate those effects and/or any action to replace/renew/substitute the elements involved could then also be reported. Figure 14.4 provides a tentative illustration of the way this might look.

As with the compliance-with-standards (CWS) report discussed in Chapter 12, there may well be a need for some means of providing summaries but with detailed back-up data available to serious inquirers. Also, as with the CWS report, there is a critical need for corporations to engage with researchers in experimenting about the feasibility of the approach and working out methodologies.

The second of the approaches to *accounting for sustainability* mentioned above is the *sustainable cost approach*. This is easier to explain but may well prove to be exceptionally difficult in practice. Its attractions, though, are that it can fit within current report-

[24] And there are other experiments going on in, for example, Canada and New Zealand, which have yet to produce anything that looks like a corporate reporting approach. These are yet early days though.

[25] The only experiment in this area so far (of which we are aware) is that undertaken in New Zealand with regard to local authority reporting.

Figure 14.4

Inventory of X Corporation's sustainability interactions

CRITICAL NATURAL CAPITAL
Ozone depletion: The level of CFC use/emission for 1991 was XXX (1990, YYY). The corporation is committed to total elimination of CFCs by 1995 and HCFCs by 1997.
Tropical hardwood: The corporation has eliminated all use of tropical hardwood in its own processes (1990, YYY used). Supplier audits have established that all hardwood use by suppliers is from sustainably managed sources as accredited by ABC&Co.
Greenhouse gases: .... (See also Compliance-with-standards report on emissions)
Critical habitats/species:..............
    etc.

NON-RENEWABLE/NON-SUBSTITUTABLE NATURAL CAPITAL
Oil and petroleum products:
Product 1 – use, comparative figures, plans for reduction or substitution, funds or
    efforts expended to provide substitutes;
Product 2 – ditto, etc.
Other minerals and mineral products:
    etc.

NON-RENEWABLE/SUBSTITUTABLE NATURAL CAPITAL
Energy usage: Use details, changes in usage, plans to change, efforts towards renewable sources.
Disposal of wastes: Levels of wastes produced and types, changes and plans.
Efforts towards (a) discovery and access to new sources of resources (typically minerals) and (b) extending longevity of use, repairability and recycling might appear here.
    etc.

RENEWABLE NATURAL CAPITAL
Timber products: use, harvesting, recycling, etc.
Species exploitation: ditto.
Habitat destruction/remediation:
Leisure and visual environment, built environment, water, air, noise, etc.

---

ing practice, it *is* a simple concept and the accuracy of the actual sustainable cost is probably not important.

The notion of sustainable cost derives directly from accounting concepts of capital maintenance and the need, within all the definitions of sustainability, to maintain the natural capital for future generations. Translating the most basic concept of sustainability to the level of the organization we could say that *a sustainable organization is one which leaves the biosphere no worse off at the end of the accounting period than it was at the beginning.* It must be the case that the vast majority, if not all, organizations do not comply with this. The extent of this 'failure' can – potentially – be quantified. That is, it is theoretically possible to calculate the amount of money an organization *would* have to spend at the end of an accounting period to place the biosphere in the position it was at the start. We are, thus, dealing with a *notional* amount but one which is based on *costs* not *values*. The resultant number could be shown on the income statement as a notional reduction of profit or notional addition to operating expenditure. It is probable that the number would be very large and would wipe out any profit the organization had earned in the (or any previous) year; dividends will have been paid out of 'capital'. But broadly speaking, that is the 'right' answer. It is widely accepted that current organizational activity is *not* sustainable and the calculation of sustainable cost provides some broad 'ball-park' quantification of the degree to which this is the case.

This will not be a simple matter. First, any use of 'critical natural capital' will, by definition, have to be included at infinite cost because it is irreplaceable. Although that might be an uncomfortable conclusion it strikes us as being morally correct (and, perhaps, practically correct in terms of the survival of humanity). Second, there may be a very large number of ways of replacing a part of the biosphere; equally there may be no simple way. (What, for example, is the cost of replacing a net-full of cod?) Third, there is no simple agreement on the level at which resources can be sustainably harvested. Fourth, and perhaps most crucially, the very nature of ecology means that one rapidly finds oneself in an infinite regress. That is, each disturbance to the natural capital must have a potentially infinite number of other ripples in the pond.[26]

These are major practical problems and there is a real need to explore them in corporations, but until they are willing to work alongside researchers on matters of this sort, basically simple ideas like sustainable cost will remain academic pipe-dreams.

The third and final suggestion for approaching the problem of *reporting for sustainability* is the *resource flow/input–output approach.* This is derived from both a method well-established in economics and an approach used in many environmental audits. It is based upon a systems conception of the organization and attempting to report its resource flows. *It does not directly report sustainability* but provides a transparency to the organization which focuses upon resource use. This is done in a way that will enable participants to assess resource use – and, ultimately, therefore the sustainability of the organization's activities.

What one is seeking here is a catalogue of the resources flowing into an organization, those flowing out of it and the 'losses' or leakages (wastes and emissions, for example) from the process[27]. Such an 'account' would again be quantified – probably in both financial and non-financial numbers (including the profit and other distributions generated). The non-financial numbers would, in many ways be the most useful, being the most easily accessible and understandable, but the use of financial numbers may help in providing

---

[26] This is exactly the same problem as was encountered in life cycle assessment.

[27] This would not be that dissimilar from the approach taken by Danish Steel Works Ltd (see Chapter 12).

Figure 14.5

Resource flow statement for XYZ Lodge Ltd (extract)				
INPUTS	LEAKAGES			OUTPUTS
	loss/theft			
brought f/d	*breakages*	*emissions*	*wastes*	*carried f/d*
Building				Building
Fixtures	Deterioration			Fixtures
Furniture				Furniture
Fittings				Fittings
Furnishings	Deterioration			Furnishings
Sheets				Sheets
Crockery	Breakages			Crockery
etc.				etc.
additions to				
non-consumables				
Repairs				
New sheets			packaging	
New crockery			packaging	
etc.				
consumables				
Meat			scraps	
Groceries			packaging	2,700
Canned food			cans	bed-
Canned drink			alu cans	nights
Milk			bottles	
Bottled drink			bottles	
Cleaning materials		sewage	plastics	
Electricity		heat		
Oil		gases, heat		
Gas		gases, heat		
Car miles		gases		
Laundry		water		
etc.				Profit/loss
				Taxation paid
As far as possible all inputs, leakages and outputs would be described and/or quantified.				

summary data. Figure 14.5 is a tentative outline illustration of how a summary of this might look for a small hotel.[28]

Such a summary would probably need to be backed up by detail which analysed each of the categories and each category would need quantification – in simple numbers, in weights and measures or in financial numbers. Whilst perhaps *the* major problems with this suggestion are that it is cumbersome and would probably be wholly

[28] The hotel referred to is an actual organization and the example is used because it allowed access and a degree of experimentation with its resources and flows. The same organization is featured in Chapter 5 on environmental audits.

unacceptable to organizations on the grounds of confidentiality, the method could be used for internal reporting and *it could fulfil the requirements of transparency and of allowing society to make choices about resource use* (see below).

The resource flow/input–output approach has been independently pursued by Paul Ekins and New Consumer Ltd. Their approach is much more sophisticated and is more refined and developed than the approach described above. Under the Ekins/*New Consumer* proposal, the resources used by an organization/product and their flow are further separated into their source of origin, their function in the organization and their ultimate destination. The idea is to produce product/organization data sheets which can provide references for consumers and others wishing to assess the potential sustainability of an organization or product they intend dealing with. Yet again, the idea is experimental and the data shown in Figure 14.6 (taken from a 1990 New Consumer Ltd research proposal) have been collated from the public domain.[29]

In its concern with transparency, with informing the public and allowing society to decide, the *New Consumer* approach is clearly not a reporting *of* sustainability but a move towards reporting *for* sustainability.

At the time of writing, these three broad suggestions represent the full extent of the methods for reporting for sustainability of which we are aware.[30] We are therefore in a period when experimentation and research are critical. Until organizations take that need more seriously than they appear to be doing at present we must, of necessity, continue to work for, buy from and own organizations which are blatantly unsustainable. There is only one conclusion to such practice.

14.7   Accountability and Transparency

The essence of environmental accountability and transparency is that environmental matters are too complex and crucial to be left entirely in the already overburdened hands of corporations. Not only is it unreasonable to ask corporations to take even more

---

[29] The approach bears a passing resemblance to the methodology of the eco-labelling studies and the LCA methodology discussed in Chapter 9. Funding and access are being sought to enable the experiment to be further developed.

[30] There is at least one other attempt in progress but it is far too early to report on what it might look like. This is a UN CTC funded experiment in Canada being undertaken by Dan Rubenstein. Other methods to approximate sustainability can be considered though. For example, compliance with a public environmental charter such as the Valdez Principles (Chapter 4) could be taken as an approximation of sustainable activity. Actions could then be assessed against the charter in terms of whether they brought one closer to or moved one further away from the principles. Estimates of the costs of reaching this approximate sustainability could also be reported. (We acknowledge Paul Ekins's influence here as well.)

Figure 14.6 Example of Ekins/*New Consumer* sustainability report proposal

Emulsion paint Dulux, ICI		Raw materials/ Extraction	Processing/ Manufacture	Packaging	Use	Disposal
Resources	Renewable	Water Brine Sulphur dioxide Hydrogen sulphate	Chlorine gas Sulphuric acid			
	Non-renewable	Titanium dioxide, (ilmenite, rutile) Oil (Acrylates) Mercury	Oil (Acrylates) Gas Coal (coke)	Metal (tin) Oil (plastic)		Chalk (to neutralize metal salts)
Wastes	Emissions		Acrylic acid Sulphuric acid Chlorine gas Sulphur dioxide			
	Pollution		Acrylic acid Sulphuric acid Chlorine gas Sulphur dioxide			Sulphuric acid Heavy Metal Salts
Impacts	Global services Species/ Eco-systems	Mining (open cast & dredge)				
	Amenity	Mining (open cast & dredge)		Landfill sites		Marine life Marshland Landfill sites
Policy	I		Tioxide to spend £220 m over 5–10 yrs on environmental improvements. ICI spends 10% of the capital cost on safety and environmental protection			
	=		ICI's initatives include developing alternatives to CFCs, Aquabase car paint and Biopol, a biodegradable plastic.			

© *New Consumer* Ltd 1990

decisions which affect our futures but nobody has the information upon which to make such decisions in any unique and 'rational' way. As we have seen, the sustainability or otherwise of an organization cannot be reliably described.

Furthermore, it seems difficult to deny that those who are affected by the environmental actions of business have a right to information about those actions. This essential concept seems appropriate whether one is thinking in terms of democratic rights or concerned to help markets function – after all, neither democracy nor markets can function usefully without information.[31] The idea then is to 'open up' the organizations[32] in order to educate and inform stakeholders and thus enable them, rather than the management of organizations, to express their choices about critical environmental issues – to be given information on which to make personal judgements as to the sustainability or otherwise of the organization. In the absence of 'expert opinion'[33] this seems an inevitable and probably critically important road to travel.

The questions of how to fulfil this environmental accountability and the sorts of information which would be needed could also be resolved relatively simply (we have already considered four examples) were it not for the reluctance of organizations to collate and publish such data. Here again the problem of 'markets' rears its ugly head. Financial markets the world over have demonstrated – in general at least – an awesome indifference to the social and environmental activities of the companies they own. Indifferent, that is, except in so far as the social or environmental activities can be seen to have direct and fairly immediate *financial* implications.[34] Therefore we find little or no financial market pressure (or encouragement) to discharge environmental accountability. Furthermore, the singularly few organizations, anywhere in the world, which have voluntarily disclosed environmental (or social) information have rarely done so on a systematic and continuing basis. The current ACCA Environmental Reporting Awards Scheme has not been swamped by examples of environmental reporting that could be considered as accountability information – under the most generous of criteria.[35] So

[31] For more detail on these ideas see Gray, Owen and Maunders (1987, 1988, 1991); and Gray (1989, 1990d,e, 1991, 1992).

[32] Not as painful as it sounds. The well-documented case of Norsk Hydro, whose path-breaking environmental report in 1990 caused its management many sleepless nights but since publication has brought benefits far in excess of the costs, supports this.

[33] Or the less defensible concerns about secrecy in defence of the national or corporate interest – survival of ours and other species must surely transcend such petty concerns.

[34] For more detail see Mintzberg, 1983; Gray, Owen and Maunders, 1987, 1988, 1991; Owen, Gray and Maunders, 1987; Mathews, 1987.

[35] See Owen, Gray and Adams, 1992, and Chapter 12.

whilst we can expect to see initiatives like this encouraging more voluntary disclosure, there are no grounds for assuming that environmental reporting for accountability and transparency will become ubiquitous.[36] A faith in voluntary development of the mechanisms for environmental accountability is therefore misplaced. It, like all substantial developments in reporting and accountability, will require regulation. Whilst this might be heresy in the present climate, that does not, of itself, make it incorrect. Attachments to voluntary rather than regulatory solutions (at least in the accounting and reporting arena) can be held only if one chooses not to let mere evidence get in the way of a good prejudice.

14.8 Conclusions

The pursuit of sustainability represents an awesome challenge to humanity. Its definition raises enough problems, trying to understand it raises more. It is, however, the central concept by which humans may attempt to provide themselves (and the rest of the planet) with a future. Sadly, however, the term is being treated as a comfortable and easily circumscribed word. We hope that this chapter has shown that this is unlikely to be a defensible posture. We have also emphasized that with the current failures of global agreement on sustainability, more local agreement will be necessary; an essential element of this will be the actions of corporations. One way of operationalizing the concept of sustainability has been outlined – derived from the environmental economics literature.[37] We then used this basis to illustrate four approaches to accounting for the environment. Each of these approaches could be a useful management tool but their real value will lie in their publication. One might have hoped that a small matter like planetary survival might have transcended a concern with publicity effects of a company's information disclosure. Until the West in general, and Western corporations in particular, are able seriously to address sustainability in a climate of accountability and transparency we cannot see how substantive measures to mitigate environmental crisis can be developed. We deeply envy the optimistic protestations of Western business people and politicians that sustainability will be achieved without it hurting – in the sense of not costing us anything substantial in the short run in economic terms. This case has not been

---

[36] It should be noted that whilst a number of companies do, from time to time, respond to desires for new information – be it social, employee or value-added, for example – none of these voluntary efforts stays to become part of reporting orthodoxy and neither are they widespread. Value added statements, which are the 'success story' of voluntary disclosure, barely reached above 50 per cent of large companies and disappeared to nothing as companies became smaller.

[37] Other ways will emerge. For example, Clayton and Radcliffe (1992) employ positional analysis to try to get closer to what regional sustainability might look like.

made and until some careful analysis can show that the matters discussed in this chapter are irrelevant, mis-specified, misunderstood or in some other way grossly inappropriate we are forced to continue to assume that such optimism is devastatingly misplaced. The *Titanic* did go down, the *Exxon Valdez* did happen, the ozone is thinning . . . etc., etc. No amount of optimism, no growth in share price, no leaps in profitability can deny – or compensate – for that.

Further Reading

There is, as yet, not a great deal of material which addresses the issues of sustainability and its operationalization at organizational level directly. The following are recommended because they are heading well in that direction:

Daly, H. E. and Cobb, J. B. (1990) *For the Common Good*, Greenprint, London.

Jacobs, M. (1991) *The Green Economy: Environment, Sustainable Development and the Politics of the Future*, Pluto, London.

Turner, K. (ed.) (1988) *Sustainable Environmental Management*, Belhaven, London.

Furthermore, David Pearce has done more than most to develop the principles of sustainability in environmental economics – see the Bibliography. Watch out for *Sustainability* by A. Clayton and N. Radcliffe (still in preparation and due for publication). And for a deeper green view, see the publications from Ekins, Henderson, Robertson, Dauncey, Daly, Anderson, De La Court.

15. A Change of Paradigm?

15.1 Introduction

'The Earth Summit's real agenda is to bring it home to world leaders and politicians that we have no option but to change our ways.' Only last year (1991) he was heralding the Earth Summit as a 'last chance to save the world'. He is now more realistic. 'There will be failures. I see this just as a step on the way.' Privately, he admits he could make a philosophical case for saying there is no chance on earth of saving the earth; professionally, he cannot.[1]

At the start of this book we identified the initial major environmental problem as being one of belief. Attitude to and debate about the environment hung upon belief about the extent to which the planet was (or was not) in crisis; belief about whose responsibility it might be; belief about whether or not economic and business thought was responsible for causing the crisis; belief about whether or not the Western economic/business model could solve the crisis. But the behaviour by developed world political leaders and major business leaders in the run-up to and during the 1992 United Nations Conference of Environment and Development in Rio de Janiero (UNCED – the 'Earth Summit') suggested conflicting views about such beliefs. That is, the preliminary manoeuvring and eventual lukewarm response by most G7 leaders to the Rio agenda was entirely commensurate with a belief that the planet was in no real crisis – and if it was, it wasn't really G7's responsibility. The behaviour by very many businesses in lobbying to get elements of the Rio agenda diluted (e.g. on global warming) and businesses'

---

[1] Adapted from *Summitry*, in Vidal, 1992, which was written incorporating the views of and quoting from Maurice Strong, Organizer of the United Nations Conference on Environment and Development.

Figure 15.1

Some questions over which the deeper green and the greener business person tend to disagree

In essence, this difference of opinion centres upon:

(1) Are the causes of the problems business- and economic-related?
(2) If so, to what degree?
(3) Are the causes of the crisis distinct and separable or systemic?
(4) If the modern economic system and its baggage are part of the problem, can they also be part of the solution?
(5) Can the modern economic system be changed?
(6) Is there any will to try?

---

success in getting the whole issue of MNE (multinational enterprise) control removed entirely from the agenda suggested a similar belief. Throughout this book we have also seen the really very low level of response to the environmental crisis which has been undertaken by business at large across the world.

Such evidence leads us to conclude that:

(a) business as a whole does not believe in the seriousness of the environmental crisis; and/or

(b) it does not (or cannot) see business as part of the problem; and/or

(c) it is unable to take steps to do anything about it.

We tend to think that the present situation consists of a combination of all three. Whatever, a conclusion such as this has very serious consequences for our environmental future.

15.2   Can Business Really be Part of the Solution?

One of the few positive results of UNCED was the public recognition by Maurice Strong and Stephan Schmidheiny[2] (among others) that the problems facing the planet were critical for human, let alone non-human, existence. When two successful and 'hard-nosed' business people side with the environmentalists, then perhaps the twenty-plus years of pressure from environmentalists is starting to

---

[2] Maurice Strong is a self-made businessman of considerable wealth based on energy and mining corporations. He was secretary-general to the 1972 Stockholm UN conference on the human environment as well as organizer of UNCED in Rio de Janiero, 1992. He is a member of the World Economic Forum with Stephan Schmidheiny, who founded the Business Council for Sustainable Development and is himself a millionaire many times over. These are unlikely – and possibly implausible – champions of the environment and sustainability. (See, for example, John May, *The Independent on Sunday: The Sunday Review*, May 1992, pp. 6–7.)

pay off.[3] But such views are not especially widespread and, even when there is apparent agreement on the depth of the crisis, the deeper green environmentalists and the greener business people part company over the identification of causes of, solutions to, and timescales for the crisis[4] (see Figure 15.1).

We have carefully avoided anything which might smack of explicit theory throughout this book. Throughout much of the English-speaking world at least, the business person's contempt for theory is widely applauded[5] as part of a recognition of the pre-eminence of the practical, the pragmatic and the 'realistic'. Of course, no individual is free from theory[6] but as long as that theory stays implicit and unexamined then, for example, unexamined assertions such as that economic growth will lead to sustainability, or that the lesser developed countries must adopt Western standards of achievement, are taken as self-evident truths when, in fact, they are no such thing. They are simply the remaining tatters of a particular brand of economic thinking which is largely unsubstantiated.[7] This economic thinking might not matter if it had not pervaded business, provided justifications for actions, justified 'business ethics' which would be unacceptable in the individual, and provided the high moral tone that is adopted by governments and business people when talking of 'free markets' and 'level playing fields.'[8] Such economic thinking – and the business which has followed it – has also contributed mightily to the environmental crisis.

But debate upon such issues, upon such 'self-evident truths' as economic growth, would appear to be impossible because, at a minimum, even to discuss such matters requires an acceptance of

[3] The positive inference to draw is that when any individual chooses to review such evidence as exists about the state of the planetary environment, they will come to share the views of the deeper green environmentalists. Other inferences are always possible.

[4] Remember, that most commentators are speaking from the comfort of the 'developed' world where, apart from occasional minor droughts, algal bloom and the odd health scare the 'environment' has little, apparent, direct effect on life. In many lesser developed countries the effect of the 'environment' is brutally direct and apparent in that it is quite likely to kill one and/or one's children – and in many parts of the world is doing just that. Our somewhat precious Western concerns might look self-centred and callous in such a context.

[5] This is clearly evidenced by the vitriolic disdain in which universities are held by large proportions of business and business-centred politics throughout the English-speaking world.

[6] We might echo John Maynard Keynes's observation that every man who considers himself to be a free-thinker will usually be the slave to some defunct economist. This is exactly the case here.

[7] See e.g. Gray, 1990f; Gray and Morrison, 1991.

[8] See, for example, any of the Henderson, Ekins, Daly, Robertson, Schumacher references.

the *possibility* – *in principle* – that what is 'good for business' may perhaps not always be necessarily good for all life forms. For much of Western business and politics this is unthinkable, and so their world constructs the business and economics agenda under which we all live. That social construction continues into the environmental agenda.

Here the confusion begins. Businesses may be apparently leading the environmental agenda whilst simultaneously seeking profits and growth above all else; corporations may be striking important stands on the sustainability debate while lobbying British, EC or US governments to avoid any legislation on global warming, to support the motor car, or to tie environmental aid to the south into trade restrictions; or threatening to pull out of a country if an energy tax is introduced.[9] Whilst we can certainly speak positively about how far many organizations have advanced on the environmental agenda, it is difficult really to believe the assurances of 'business' when such duplicity is self-evident and, more importantly, to believe that the environmental agenda is safe in the hands of 'business'.

Of course, it would be foolish to fall into the trap of seeking simple tidy explanations. 'Business' – despite the propaganda – is not a homogeneous lump; individual organizations are frequently enormous and do not, unsurprisingly, speak with a single voice; and business exists within a system that is explicitly immoral, exploitive and combative and which frequently rewards behaviour wholly unacceptable in the individual (or punishes the absence of such behaviour). So whilst some who work in business and politics may believe that the planet faces a life-threatening crisis, a great many do not. And for those who do hold such beliefs, the cultural and institutional structure within which business operates makes substantial environmental, social and/or ethical initiative very difficult indeed. To expect the business world – as presently constituted – to solve the environmental crisis is naive in the extreme. Substantial, systemic change in the frameworks of business and the intellectual concepts within which business operates is an essential prerequisite for a more environmentally benign economic system. The quotation from Body Shop (see Chapter 14, Section 14.4, p. 289) captures the issue exactly – what it fails to recognize are the implications which arise from the observation.

15.3   Environmental Accounting?

What has been said for business applies with at least equal force to accounting and accountants. Whilst it is almost certainly true that

---

[9] Examples of these instances were all widely and publicly reported in 1991 and 1992. These contentions are also supported by the way in which business has lobbied for the terms of GATT (General Agreement on Tariffs and Trade) to override environmental considerations by reference to 'free market' motherhood statements, which are unexamined assertions at best and dishonest at worst.

business cannot change substantially until accounting does so, it is far from clear that accounting can change – or that accountants wish to change. Indeed, evidence and theory are against us. There are a number of strands of theory which suggest that not only can accounting not change in the ways we have suggested as necessary but that in attempting to address the environmental agenda accounting may do more harm than good.[10] It is impossible not to be sensitive to such points – in an ideal world. However, we do not live in such a world and, seeing the environmental crisis as requiring action of some sort, cannot see any likely force for benign systemic change in the immediate future. So one works with the tools to hand: business and accounting are those available. If the business and accounting environmental agenda are the only games in town, one can choose to play or not play. We choose to play – in the hope that it may be possible to change that agenda to reflect, more obviously, the real environmental exigencies and develop an accounting which *is* environmentally benign.

As the 1992 EC plan, *Towards Sustainability*, suggested, for any really significant environmental response from business, it will be necessary to redefine 'accounting concepts, rules, conventions and methodology' in order to permit accounting 'to internalize all external environmental costs'.[11] Radical, and welcome, though such a suggestion might be, genuinely environmentally sensitive business and environmentally sensitive accounting will require far more fundamental changes. The very framework of conventional accounting will have to be rebuilt from scratch. After all, the conventional accounting framework is hardly a roaring success for conventional business transactions and to expect it to incorporate environmental and social considerations sensitively – as a long-term prospect – is unwarrantedly optimistic.

In terms of this book, our view is that we hope to see three phases of development in accounting thought and accounting practice. First, we hope to see some development which clearly falls within conventional accounting – this is essentially the principal message of Chapters 1 to 9. The second develops from the first: that is, the evolutionary process – within which accounting begins to recognize environmental considerations – will produce changes in the accounting itself. There were hints of this in Chapters 1 to 9 and it becomes a little more explicit in Chapters 10 to 13. But it should be obvious that conventional accounting cannot really be fully responsive to the change in culture that comes with greater environmental sensitivity, and (the third phase) we introduced a

[10] Different strands of work from UK accounting academics Richard Laughlin, Michael Power and Christine Cooper all suggest this – from differing theoretical perspectives and with differing degrees of vitriol. But see also Gray (1992).

[11] COM (92) 23, Vol. II, *Towards Sustainability*, from DGXI, reported in *World Accounting Report*, May 1992, p. 1.

few developmental possibilities in Chapter 14. How will this happen? How might this look? – we have no crystal ball.[12] We are simply convinced that change is essential because any system – such as accounting – which reflects an economic theory which is so fundamentally socially and environmentally malign cannot itself lay legitimate claim to being environmentally benign.

15.4   Conclusions?

It is clear that the environmental crisis requires something far more profound than a green gloss to existing practices. It is increasingly apparent that what is needed – what is essential – is little short of a complete overhaul of our Western intellectual frameworks and a complete rethink of the institutional and ethical structure of our economic activity. Even if business believed in the necessity for this, there is no way in which business, by itself, could achieve it. It requires change throughout education, the professions, economics, politics, the ethics of modern society, and so on. And we do not come to such radical prescription lightly. This is not some anti-business knee-jerk or the rantings of the disadvantaged but the reluctant conclusion from a great deal of thought, reading, work and observation. Increasing numbers, from all walks of life, from countries around the world, are coming to the same reluctant conclusion. If fundamentally well-meaning individuals – be they politicians or business people – can operate a system which is intended to produce the greatest good for the greatest number but, instead, produces awesome inequality, profound poverty and destitution, staggering planetary damage, and a dehumanizing effect on people and communities – then we must eventually begin to suspect, however reluctantly, that there is something wrong with that system. Nothing short of basic and fundamental change can offer any hope to these problems.

But, in the meantime, whilst we start to wonder how such fundamental change might be set in motion, we are faced with the here-and-now. There is a need for immediate, practicable solutions to urgent issues. Preferably, such solutions might point towards the possibilities of future change – as opposed to simply a sticking plaster on the wounds of a fatally injured system. That is what this book has tried to be. We have laid out practicable possibilities, experiments and solutions, derived from considerable contact with organizations of all sorts whose help we are delighted to acknowledge. These we have derived in recognition of the immediacy of the problems. But each chapter has been written in the explicit recognition that none of these ideas is a final solution. Each is just a small step towards (hopefully) a more fundamental change.

We can see no alternative. We must develop and introduce such

---

[12] For more detail see Gray, 1992, and Gray and Laughlin, 1991.

incremental change as we can in order to mitigate the worst excesses of the system and sensitize us all to the issues at stake – this book suggests a large number of possibilities for this. But such incremental change will mean little without fundamental systemic change. Only a complete change of paradigm is likely to allow humanity to become part of 'environment' rather than its exploiter. Such a paradigm shift might save the human species from extinction – or at least, if we are to become dinosaurs, it would permit us to go extinct causing less widespread human and non-human suffering in the process and let us leave behind us a planet which has not been totally desecrated.

Appendix A

Further Reading and Information Sources

Throughout the text we have sought to provide extensive references, which are collected together in the bibliography, with directed further reading. This, together with the text, should provide a basis upon which further reading can be built and further information sought. Organizations have frequently suggested that their additional information needs fall into a number of specific categories.

Industry Support

There are many industry- and professionally based initiatives designed to help organizations adjust to the developing environmental agenda. Contact one's industry association or professional body directly or consider the addresses given in Appendix B.

Networks

There are many networks through which support and information can be obtained. These, for example Business-in-the-Environment, CEBIS, the Environment Council and CSEAR (see Appendix B for addresses), exist to keep organizations in touch and to help forge links between organizations. Similar initiatives exist across Europe and North America and in increasing numbers elsewhere (Appendix B gives little information for outside Europe).

Expert Advice

We are unable to offer specific suggestions on where one might go for this but a number of the organizations listed in Appendix B may be of assistance.

Keeping up-to-date

In addition to bulletins from organizations such as the Environment Council and UK CEED, for example, there is a plethora of relevant journals and newsletters, which include:

- *Business and the Environment* (Cutter Information, USA)
- *ENDS Report* (Environmental Data Services)
- *Environment Business* (Information for Industry)
- *Environment and Industry Digest* (Elsevier)
- *Environment Newsletter* (CBI)
- *Environment Briefing Notes* (KPMG Peat Marwick)
- *Environmental Finance* (Executive Enterprises, New York)
- *European Environment* (European Research Press)
- *Greenpeace Business* (Greenpeace)
- *Industry and Environment* (UNEP)
- *Integrated Environmental Management* (Blackwell Scientific)
- *International Environment Reporter* (Bureau of National Affairs, Washington, D.C.).
- *Social and Environmental Accounting*, CSEAR.

Appendix B

Selected Contact Addresses

Introduction

The following are just some of the organizations currently active in the environmental field and from whom further information, advice or encouragement can be obtained. In general the organizations have been chosen on the grounds that they constitute useful places to begin in the search for further information and contacts. It is intended that these names be used in conjunction with Appendix A.

The names and addresses were correct at the time of writing. They are in alphabetical order. *No endorsement of the quality of the organization or its information or advice is implied by its listing here. Furthermore no interpretation other than oversight should be made concerning the omission of any relevant and non-aligned body.*

Many further sources of addresses and information on organizations' activities exist. These include:

- M. Deziron and L. Bailey (1991) *A Directory of European Environmental Organizations*, Blackwell, Oxford.
- Environment Council (1992) *Who's who in the environment? (England)*, 2nd edn, Environment Council, London (edition for Scotland is planned).
- S. Forrester (1990) *Business and Environmental Groups – A Natural Partnership?*, Directory of Social Change, London.
- David Hover (1992) *Business and the Environment: A Survey of Management Educators in Western Europe*, International Academy of Environment, Geneva.
- J. Elkington and A. Dimmock (1991) *The Corporate Environmentalists – Selling Sustainable Development: But Can They Deliver?*, SustainAbility, London.

The British Library, Environmental Information Service, 25 Southampton Buildings, London WC2A 1AW
Business Council for Sustainable Development (BCSD), World Trade Centre Building, Case Postale 365, CH-1215, Geneva 15, Switzerland

Business and The Environment, Cutter Information Corp., 37 Broadway, Arlington, MA, 02174-5539

Business-in-the-Environment (BiE), 5 Cleveland Place, London SW1Y 6JJ

Business Information Marketplace, *Business Information Review*, Headland Press, 1 Henry Smith's Terrace, Headland, Cleveland TS24 0PD

Business Network, 18 Well Walk, Hampstead, London NW3 1LD

CMA – The Society of Management Accountants of Canada, P.O. Box 176, Hamilton, Ontario.

Centre for Economic and Environmental Development (CEED), 12 Upper Belgrave Street, London SW1X 8BA

Centre for Environment and Business in Scotland (CEBIS), 58/59 Timber Bush, Edinburgh EH6 6QH

Center for Human Ecology, Box 14, Mankato State University, Mankato, Minnesota 56001

Centre for Social and Environmental Accounting Research (CSEAR), Department of Accountancy & Business Finance, University of Dundee, Dundee DD1 4HN

Chartered Association of Certified Accountants (ACCA), 29 Lincoln's Inn Fields, London WC2A 3EE

Environment Management Unit, Confederation of British Industry (CBI), Centre Point, 103 New Oxford Street, London WC1A 1DU

Coopers & Lybrand, Chartered Accountants, Plumtree Court, London EC4

Council on Economic Priorities, 30 Irving Place, New York, NY 10033

Environmental Protection Technology Scheme, Department of the Environment, Room B 357 Romney House, 43 Marsham Street, London SW1P 3PY

The Business and the Environment Unit (BEU), Department of Trade and Industry, Ashdown House, Victoria Street, London SW1E 6RB

The Ecologist, Ecosystems Ltd, 1st Floor, Corner House, Station Road, Sturminster Newton, Dorset

Ecology Building Society, 18 Station Road, Cross Hill, Nr. Keighley, West Yorks BD20 7EH

Environment Council, 80 York Way, London N1 9AG

Environmental Data Services (ENDS) Ltd, Unit 24, The Finsbury Business Centre, 40 Bowling Green Lane, London EC1R 0NE

Environmental Finance, Executive Enterprises Publications Co., Executive Enterprises Building, 22 W. 21st St., New York, NY 10010-6904

Ethical Investment Research & Information Service (EIRIS), 4.01 Bondway, Business Centre, 71 Bondway, London SW8 1SQ

Euroenviron, Department of Trade and Industry, Business and the Environment Unit, Room 1010 Ashdown House, 123 Victoria Street, London SW1E 6RB

The European Environment Review, Graham & Trotman Ltd, Sterling House, 66 Wilton Road, London SW1V 1DE

Friends of the Earth, 26–28 Underwood Street, London NW1 7SQ

The Green Alliance, 60 Chandos Place, London WC2N 4HG

Green Party, 10 Station Parade, Balham High Road, London SW12 9AZ

Greenleap, Independent Association of Legal Engineering and Accounting Professionals for the Environment, 70 Richmond St. East, Suite 400, Toronto, Ontario, M5C 1NB, Canada.

Greenpeace, Canonbury Villas, London N1 2PN

Groundwork Foundation, Bennetts Court, 6 Bennetts Hill, Birmingham B2 5ST

Her Majesty's Inspectorate of Pollution, Romany House, Marsham Street, London SW1P 3PB

Institute of Chartered Accountants in England and Wales (ICAEW), PO Box 433, Chartered Accountants Hall, Moorgate Place, London EC2P 2BJ

Institute of Environmental Assessment, Holbeck Manor, Horncastle, Lincolnshire LN9 6PU

Institute for European Environmental Policy (IEEP), 3 Endsleigh Street, London WC1H 0DD

Integrated Environmental Management, Blackwell Scientific Publications, Osney Mead, Oxford OX2 0EL

International Chamber of Commerce (ICC) (UK), Centre Point, 103 New Oxford Street, London WC1A 1QB

International Chamber of Commerce, Cours Albert Ier 38, 75008, Paris, France

International Institute for Environment and Development (IIED), 3 Endsleigh Street, London WC1H 0DD

International Institute for Sustainable Development (IISD), 161 Portage Avenue East, Winnipeg, Manitoba, Canada R3B OY4

International Environment Reporter, Bureau of National Affairs Inc., 1231 25th St. N.W., Washington DC 20037

Jupiter Tarbutt Merlin, Knightsbridge House, 197 Knightsbridge, London SW7 1RB

KPMG Peat Marwick, Management Consultants, 8 Salisbury Square, London EC4Y 8BB

London Environmental Economics Centre (LEEC), 3 Endsleigh Street, London WC1H 0DD

Management Institute for Environment and Business (MEB), 1220 Sixteenth Street NW, Washington DC, USA 20036

National Centre for Alternative Technology, Machynlleth, Powys, Wales

New Consumer, 52 Elswick Road, Newcastle upon Tyne NE4 6JH

New Economics Foundation, 2nd Floor, Universal House, 88–94 Wentworth Street, London E1 7SA

Shared Interest Society 52 Elswick Road, Newcastle upon Tyne NE4 6JH

Social Investment Forum, 711 Atlantic Avenue, Boston MA 02111

Socially Responsible Investment Network, c/o Pensions Investment Resource Centre, 40 Bowling Green Lane, London EC1R 0NE

SustainAbility, The People's Hall, 91–97 Freston Road, London W11 4BD

Touche Ross, Management Consultants, Hill House, 1 Little New Street, London EC4A 3TR

Traidcraft, Kingsway, Gateshead, Tyne and Wear NE11 0NE

United Nations, Centre for Transnational Corporations, Room DC2-1244, United Nations, New York, NY 10017, USA

US Environmental Protection Agency, Public Affairs Office (A-107), Washington, DC 20460

Washington State Department of Ecology, Northwest Regional Office, 3190 160th Ave. SE, Bellvue, WA 98008-5452

Worldwatch Institute, 1776 Massachusetts Ave. NW, Washington DC 20036

Worldwide Fund for Nature, Panda House, Weyside Park, Godalming, Surrey GU7 1XR

Appendix C

Research Process and Method

Introduction

This text is the result of the third stage in the Chartered Association of Certified Accountants' (ACCA) 'Greening of Accountancy' project. Stage I was published in 1990 in *The Greening of Accountancy: The Profession after Pearce* (Research Report 17, London: ACCA). As a result of that publication, the ACCA determined to continue the project in a way which would specifically address a number of essentially practical and organization-based questions: What environmental accounting is being done? What is 'best practice'? Why is environmental accounting being adopted/not adopted? What environmental accounting *can* be done? What practical steps can accounting take to help organizations become more environmentally sensitive? *How* can accountants do more?

This was addressed in two stages. Professor David Pearce (who had advised on Stage I of the project) had recommended that future stages worked closely with industry and, in particular, that attempts at 'brainstorming' be undertaken. This 'brainstorming' – Stage II of the project – took a number of forms. First, a meeting of representatives of the researchers, ACCA, CBI, DTI and DoE, sketched out the sort of programme that was likely to address businesses' – and accountants' – needs. Secondly, the researchers took every opportunity to become involved with a number of other organizations, (notably Business-in-the-Environment but also the Environment Council, the Canada–UK Colloquium, the ACCA Environmental Reporting Awards and a range of other bodies – see Acknowledgements), through which wide-ranging discussion of the issues, needs and problems could be undertaken. This experience not only provided the basis for Stage III of the project but was a continuing activity throughout the project and remains so. The importance of this experience was considerable and we gratefully acknowledge the considerable benefit we have gained from all those involved in these bodies.

Stage III was the more formal, research-orientated part of the project and consisted of:

(1) extensive monitoring of published information – which is widely referenced in the text;
(2) attendance at conferences and meetings which permitted, *inter alia*, 'mini-interviews'
(3) visits to and interviews with various companies and other organizations;
(4) a postal questionnaire to the financial directors of large UK companies.

This appendix will provide some additional information on elements (2), (3) and (4) of Stage III. This text is the outcome of Stages II and III of the project.

Method of Data Collection

Our method of data collection was as 'creative' as possible in that we were seeking to gain – with regard to the impact of environmental issues on organizations in general and accounting in particular – as wide as possible an understanding of as many organizations as possible, across as many aspects of their operations as possible. We were seeking to understand how the vast and rapidly changing environmental agenda affected organizations and this ensured that we had to take as open-ended an approach as possible. Putting it slightly more formally, we have gathered data through reading published materials; attending workshops, colloquia and conferences; holding conversations with both corporate and other organizations (such as consultancies, trade associations, etc.); correspondence; action research; semi-structured interview; and postal questionnaire.

The initial approach was to seek access to a wide variety of organizations in order to undertake semi-structured interviews.[1] No attempt at formal sampling was made – a sample member was distinguished by a combination of personal contact, willingness to participate in the research and the probability of the organization having undertaken some environmentally related actions that might be relevant to a broad understanding of accounting. This led to eighteen semi-formal interviews with fourteen organizations (predominantly plcs in extractive, processing or manufacturing sectors)

---

[1] A checklist was sent to all organizations before the interview together with a covering letter explaining the research in more detail. Details are available from the authors to serious inquirers.

in two countries (the UK and New Zealand).[2] In each case, during the initial interview the organization was requested to allow follow-up interviews and, more especially, to allow the researchers to take part in the process of developing the organization's environmental accounting and information systems. Four organizations permitted this follow-up but only one allowed the researchers to work over a period of time with them. Where formal interview was not possible the opportunity was taken to discuss or correspond on issues. (This was the situation with a further twelve organizations in three countries: the UK, New Zealand and Canada.) Finally, opportunities presented themselves either to work, or spend time in discussion, with organizations which themselves dealt directly with corporate organizations. This had the effect of gaining from the experience of others, seeing other companies and public sector organizations discussing and working on the issues or gaining and providing suggestions on productive directions for further work. (This brought a further fourteen organizations into our ambit.)[3] This means that we have been able to benefit directly from the experience of forty organizations and, indirectly, from many others. To each of these we express our gratitude.

This eventually led to a postal questionnaire.[4] The other data collection methods had been broadly directed at senior management of the organizations and focused upon the organization's general response to the environmental issues, so allowing the interviewers to follow up on any issues of specific interest that arose. The questionnaires were much more focused and addressed specifically to financial directors in order to assess:

(1) Had our perceptions of very low involvement of accounting and accountants been correct?
(2) To what extent did the accountants know what was happening in their organizations and in what, if anything, were they involved?
(3) Was there any identifiable reason for the involvement/non-involvement and to what extent could this be related to background characteristics or those of the company, or the attitudes of the accountants?

[2] The average length of interview was one and a half hours, the shortest one hour, the longest three and a half hours. One organization was visited at two sites and three organizations permitted second, follow-up interviews. Of the eighteen interviews, seven were taped, and ten were conducted by a single researcher, eight by a pair of researchers.

[3] It had been anticipated that it would have been possible to work in more depth with one or two organizations in order to undertake in-depth case-studies. This has not proved possible and, as the apparent immediacy of the environmental agenda slipped in mid-1991 and the recession began to bite, four interviews were cancelled by the companies concerned.

[4] Copies are available from the authors.

The questionnaire was piloted among colleagues in the two departments in which we work, revised and then field-tested in five further interviews with companies. After minor amendment, the questionnaires were sent to the financial directors of all of *The Times* 1,000 companies. There was a follow-up mailing one month after the first mailing. Three hundred and fifty returns were received; 181 were usable replies for questionnaire analysis and 64 were blank but accompanied by usable comments in covering letters.[5] The questionnaires and the interviews are more formally analysed in a paper presented to the British Accounting Association Annual Conference in 1992 and in papers in preparation at the time of writing. Please contact the authors for more detail.

Conclusions

In formal terms, whilst we might be able to draw some cautious conclusions about the generalizability of the questionnaire to all companies in the UK top 1,000, we would not wish to place too great an emphasis on this alone.[6] And certainly, in a formal sense, we cannot claim any generalizability for the interviewing results or the applicability of our results to non-companies, to smaller companies or to non-UK organizations. Nevertheless, in the wide coverage that we managed we derive a degree of confidence in the relative accuracy of the overall picture we draw in the text. To a considerable extent, this picture is reinforced and confirmation provided by the questionnaires and discussion with others of wide, but differing, experience.

The overall conclusions are that whilst there is a reasonably high level of awareness of environmental matters as they affect business among accountants, this is rarely translated into innovative action. The amount of experience, therefore, on which one can draw in identifying 'best practice' in environmental accounting is relatively slight. In a crude sense, any practice is best practice. The text has therefore distilled this widely scattered experience and enhanced it with proposals which have been talked through extensively with practising managers and accountants. We conclude, reluctantly, that we are yet some way from an extensive experience in and practice of accounting for the environment.

[5] The non-response bias tests have not yet been performed.

[6] Not least because (a) it is widely recognized that questionnaires are not an especially reliable means of data collection, and (b) no means can realistically claim a fully reliable assessment of non-response bias.

Appendix D

References and Bibliography

3M/Environment Council *A guide to policy making and implementation* (London: 3M/Environment Council) 1991

Abt C. C. and Associates. *Annual Report and Social Audit* 1972 *et seq.*

Ackoff R. L. 'Systems, organisations and interdisciplinary research' *General Systems Theory Yearbook* Vol. 5 1960 (pp. 1–8)

Ackoff R. L. 'A Note on Systems Science' *Interfaces* August 1972 (pp. 40–41)

Accounting Standards Committee *The Corporate Report* (London: ICAEW) 1975

Adam J. A. 'Extracting power from the Amazon Basin' *IEEE Spectrum* 25(8) August 1988 (pp. 34–38)

Adams R. *Who Profits?* (Oxford: Lion) 1989

Adams R. 'The greening of consumerism' *Accountancy* June 1990 (pp. 80–83)

Adams R., J. Carruthers & S. Hamil, *Changing Corporate Values* (London: Kogan Page, 1991)

Adams R., J. Carruthers & C. Fisher, *Shopping for a better world* (London: Kogan Page) 1991

Ahmad Y. J., S. El-Serafy & E. Lutz (eds) *Environmental accounting for sustainable development* (Washington DC: UNEP/World Bank) 1989

Aitken P. 'Environmental pressures on business – the polluter pays' *Accountants Magazine* January 1991 (pp. 18–20)

Alexandre A., J. Barde & D. W. Pearce (1980) 'The practical determination of a charge for noise pollution' *Journal of Transport Economics and Policy* May 1980 (pp. 205–220)

Allen K. 'In pursuit of professional dominance: Australian accounting 1953–1985' *Accounting, Auditing and Accountability Journal* 3(1) 1991 (pp. 51–67)

American Accounting Association 'Report of the committee on environmental effects of organisational behaviour' *The Accounting Review* Supplement to Vol. XLVIII, 1973

American Institute of Certified Public Accountants *The measurement of corporate social performance* (New York: AICPA) 1977

Anderson E. R. 'Environmental loss control starts with Insurance' *National Underwriter* 87(31), 5 August 1983 (pp. 27, 30)

Anderson J. W. 'Can social responsibility be handled as a corporate investment?' *Business Horizons* March/April 1987 (pp. 24–25)

Anderson V. *Alternative Economic Indicators* (London: Routledge) 1991

Andrews B. H., F. A. Gul, J. E. Guthrie & H. Y. Teoh 'A note on corporate social disclosure practices in developing countries: The case of Malaysia and Singapore' *British Accounting Review* 21(4) December 1989 (pp. 371–376)

Angell D. J. R., J. D. Comer & M. L. N. Wilkinson (eds) *Sustaining Earth: Response to the environmental threats* (London: MacMillan) 1990

Anonymous (Mergers and Acquisitions) 'Roundtable: Managing the environmental risks in acquisitions' *Mergers and Acquisitions* July/August 1989 (pp. 28–41)

Antal A. B. (1985) 'Institutionalizing corporate social responsiveness: Lessons learned from the Migros experience' *Research in Corporate Social Performance and Policy* Vol. 7 1985 (pp. 229–249)

Antunes S. 'Your money or their life: ethical investment' *Guardian* 25 April 1987

Arthur Andersen *Environmental Liabilities: Is your company at risk?* (Houston: Arthur Andersen) 1990

Arvill R. *Man and environment: Crisis and the strategy of choice* (Harmondsworth: Penguin) 1976

Atkinson A. & A. Farooq 'Corporate social responsibility: a study in the West Midlands, UK' University of Aston Management Centre Working Paper No. 158. 1979

Aupperle K. E. 'An empirical measure of corporate social orientation' *Research in Corporate Social Performance and Policy* Vol. 6 1984 (pp. 27–54)

Austin D. 'Who pays for pollution?' *ReActions* December 1986 (pp. 40–43)

Bader A. H. 'Environmental-Risk Management' *Journal of Accountancy* 160(4) October 1985 (pp. 159–163)

Bailey P. E. 'Full Cost Accounting for Life-Cycle Costs: A guide for engineers and financial analysis' *Environmental Finance* Spring 1991 (pp. 13–29)

Bain S. 'How Green is Your Company?' *Scotland on Sunday* 3 February 1991 p. 13

Baker H. K. & J. A. Haslem 'Information needs of individual investors' *Journal of Accountancy* November 1973 (pp. 64–69)

Ball S. 'Implementation of the Environmental Assessment Directive in Britain' *Integrated Environmental Management* No. 5 August 1991 (pp. 9–11)

Ball S. 'BATNEEC: BAT v. NEEC?' *Integrated Environmental Management* No. 3 October 1991 (pp. 4–6)

Ball S. & S. Bell *Environmental Law* (London: Blackstone Press) 1991

Ball S. & J. Maltby 'The accounting implications of new and forthcoming environmental legislation' Paper presented to BAA National Conference, April 1992

Banks J. 'Mysteries of a nuclear audit' *Accountancy Age* 23 September 1977 (p. 11)

Barbier E. 'The concept of sustainable economic development' *Environmental Conservation* 14(2) 1987 (pp. 101–110)

Barnett A. H. & J. C. Caldwell 'Accounting for corporate social performance: A Survey' *Management Accounting* Vol. 55 November 1974 (pp. 23–26)

Baumhart R. C. 'How ethical are businessmen?' *Harvard Business Review* July/August 1961

Baumol W. J. 'Environmental protection at minimum cost: The Pollution Tax' in Seidler L. J. & L. L. Seidler (eds) *Social Accounting: Theory, Issues and Cases* (Los Angeles: Melville) 1975

Baumol W. J. & W. E. Oates *Economics, environmental policy and the quality of life* (New York: Prentice Hall) 1979

Baxter G. & C. Rarick 'The Manager as Kierkegaard's "Knight of Faith": Linking Ethical Thought and Action' *Journal of Business Ethics* 8(5) May 1989 (pp. 399–406)

Beams F. A. & P. E. Fertig 'Pollution control through social cost conversion' *Journal of Accountancy* Nov. 1971 (pp. 37–42)

Bebbington K. J. & R. H. Gray 'The Greening of Accountancy: The profession and the environment' *Accountants' Journal (NZ)* September 1990 (pp. 17–20)

Bebbington K. J. & R. H. Gray 'Where have all the accountants gone?' *Accountancy* March 1992 (pp. 28–9)

Beishon J. & G. Peters *Systems Behaviour* (London: Open University/Harper & Row) 1972

Belkaoui A. 'The impact of socio-economic accounting statements on the investment decision: an empirical study' *Accounting, Organizations and Society* 5(3) 1980 (pp. 263–83)

Belkaoui A. *Socio-Economic Accounting* (Connecticut: Quorum Books) 1984

Belkaoui A. & P. G. Karpik 'Determinants of the corporate decision to disclose social information' *Accounting, Auditing and Accountability Journal* 2(1) 1989 (pp. 36–51)

Bell R. 'Emissions to explain' *Independent on Sunday* 16 February 1992 (p. 55)

Benjamin J. J. & K. G. Stanga 'Difference in disclosure needs of major users of financial statements' *Accounting and Business Research* Summer 1977 (pp. 187–92)

Bennett A. 'Ethics Codes Spread Despite Scepticism' *Wall Street Journal* 15 July 1988 (p. 19)

Benson G. C. S. 'Codes of Ethics' *Journal of Business Ethics* 8(5) May 1989 (pp. 305–19)

Benston G. J. 'Accounting & Corporate Accountability' *Accounting, Organizations and Society* Vol. 7 No. 2 1982 (pp. 87–105)

Benston G. J. 'An analysis of the role of accounting standards for enhancing corporate governance and social responsibility' *Journal of Accounting and Public Policy* Vol. 1 No. 1 1982 (pp. 5–18)

von Bertalanffy L. 'General Systems Theory' *General Systems Yearbook* Vol. 1 1956 (pp. 1–10)

von Bertalanffy L. 'General Systems Theory – a critical review' in Beishon J. & G. Peters (eds) *Systems Behaviour* (London: Open University/Harper & Row) 1972

von Bertalanffy L. *General Systems Theory: Foundations, Development, Applications* (Harmondsworth: Penguin) 1971

Bierman H. & R. E. Dukes 'Accounting for research and development costs' *The Journal of Accountancy* April 1975 (pp. 48–55)

Bins-Hoefnagels I. M. J. & G. C. Molenkamp *Environmental Auditing* (The Hague: Touche Ross International) 1989

Bins-Hoefnagels I. M. J., G. C. Molenkamp & K. P. G. Wilschut 'De milieu-auditor en de accountant' (The environmental auditor and the accountant)' *Accountant* (Netherlands) 92(10) June 1986 (pp. 446–52)

Birnberg J. G. & N. M. Gandhi 'Toward defining the accountants' role in the evaluation of social programmes' *Accounting, Organizations and Society* 1(1) 1976 (pp. 5–10)

Bjork G. C. *Life, liberty and property: the economics and politics of land-use planning and environmental controls* (Heath: Lexington Books) 1980

Blake D. H., W. C. Frederick & M. S. Myers *Social Auditing: Evaluating the impact of corporate programs* (New York: Praegar) 1976

Bloom R. & H. Heymann 'The concept of social accountability in accounting literature' *Journal of Accounting Literature* Vol. 5 1986 (pp. 167–82)

Blowers A. *Something in the air: Corporate power and the environment* (London: Harper & Row) 1984

Blumenfeld K., R. Earle III, J. B. Shopley 'Identifying strategic environmental opportunities: A life-cycle approach' *Prism* Third Quarter 1991 (pp. 45–58)

Bossel H. 'Viability and sustainability: matching development goals to resource constraints' *Futures* 4/1987 (pp. 114–128)

Boulding K. E. 'General systems theory – The skeleton of science' *Management Science* 2 1956 (pp. 197–208)

Boulding K. E. 'The economics of the coming Spaceship Earth' in H. Jarratt (ed.) *Environmental quality in a growing economy* (Baltimore: John Hopkins Press) 1966 (pp. 3–14)

Boulding K. E. 'Review of *Ecodevelopment: economics, ecology and development – an alternative to growth-imperative models* ' *Journal of Economic Literature* Vol. XX(9) 1982 (pp. 1076–77)

Boustead I. & G. F. Hancock *Energy and Packaging* (London: Ellis Horwood) 1981

Bowen H. R. *Social responsibilities of the businessman* (New York: Harper & Row) 1953

Bowman E. H. & M. Haire 'A strategic posture towards corporate social responsibility' *California Management Review* Winter 1975 (pp. 49–58)

Bragdon J. H. & J. A. T. Marlin 'Is pollution profitable? The case of the pulp and paper industry' *Risk Management* April 1971

British Institute of Management *Social Responsibility: Management Checklist No. 51* (London: BIM) 1977

British Standards Institute *Draft British Standard: Environmental management systems (Parts 1–3)* (London: BSI) 1991

Brockoff K. 'A note on external social reporting by German companies: A survey of 1973 company reports' *Accounting, Organizations and Society* 4(1/2) 1979 (pp. 77–85)

Bromige D. J. & Partners, *Socially Responsible Investment in the United States of America* (London: Bromige and Partners) 1989

Brooks L. J. (Jnr) *Canadian Corporate Social Performance* (Hamilton: The Society of Management Accountants of Canada) 1986

Brown L. *Building a sustainable society* (New York: W. W. Norton) 1981

Brown L. 'Editorial: The other deficits' *World Watch* March/April 1991 (p. 2)

Bruce L. 'How green is your company?' *International Management* No. 1 1989 (pp. 24–9)

Bryce A. 'Business and law in a cleaner world' *Accountancy* June 1990 (pp. 75–8)

Bryer R. A. 'The status of the systems approach' *Omega* 7(3) 1979 (pp. 219–31)

Bunker N. 'War of words over the wasteland' *Financial Times* October 12 1987

Burchell S., C. Clubb & A. Hopwood, 'Accounting in its social context: towards a history of value added in the United Kingdom', *Accounting, Organizations and Society*, Vol. 10, No. 4, 1985 (pp. 381–413)

Burke T. & J. Hill *Ethics, Environment and Company* (London: Institute of Business Ethics) 1990

Burke T., N. Robins & A. Trisoglio (eds) *Environment Strategy Europe 1991* (London: Campden) 1991

Burkitt D. *The Costs to Industry of Adopting Environmentally Friendly Practices* (London: CIMA) 1990

Burman V. 'Budding friends of the earth' *Money marketing* 24 May 1990 (pp. 9–10)

Burton J. C. 'Commentary on "Let's get on with the social audit"' *Business and Society Review* Winter 1972 (pp. 42–43)

Business-in-the-Environment *Your Business and the Environment: A DIY Review for Companies* (London: BiE/Coopers & Lybrand Deloitte) 1991a

Business-in-the-Environment *Your Business and the Environment: An executive guide* (London: BiE) 1991b

Buzby S. L. 'Selected items of information and their disclosure in annual reports' *The Accounting Review* 49(1) January 1974 (pp. 423–35)

Buzby S. L. & H. Falk 'A survey of the interest in social responsibility information by mutual funds' *Accounting, Organizations and Society* 3(3/4) 1978 (pp. 191–201)

Buzby S. L. & H. Falk 'Demand for social responsibility information by university investors' *The Accounting Review* Vol. LIV(1) January 1979 (pp. 23–37)

Cairncross F. *Costing the Earth* (London: Business Books/The Economist) 1991

Campfield W. L. 'The accountants' opportunity for participating in the solution of socio-economic problems' in W. E. Stone (ed.) *The Accountant in a Changing Business Environment* (Florida: University of Florida Accounting Series) 1973 (pp. 2–11)

Capra F. & C. Spretnak *Green Politics: the global promise* (London: Hutchinson) 1984

Cardwell Z. 'Green Enlightenment' *AA(Accountancy Age)* January 1991 (pp. 30–3)

Carson R. *Silent Spring* (Boston: Houghton Mifflin) 1962

Carter R., J. Martin, B. Mayblin & M. Munday *Systems, management and change: a graphic guide* (London: Paul Chapman) 1984

Cartwright D. 'What price ethics?' *Managerial Auditing Journal* 5(2) Spring 1990 (pp. 28–31)

CEFIC *Guidelines for the communication of environmental information to the public* (Brussels: CEFIC) 1989

CEFIC *Guidelines on waste minimisation* (Paris: CEFIC) 1990

Charlton C. 'Lifecycle assessment: Making sense of environmental complexities' *CBI Environment Newsletter* No. 6 November 1991 (pp. 13–14)

Chartered Institute of Management Accountants *The Evaluation of Energy Use: Readings* (London: CIMA) 1982

Chastain C. E. 'Environmental Accounting: US and UK' *Accountancy* December 1973 (pp. 10–13)

Chastain C. E. 'Financial Accounting for Environmental Information' *Journal UEC* January 1, 1974 (pp. 46–51)

Chechile A. & S. Carlisle (ed.) *Environmental Decision Making: A multidisciplinary perspective* (London: Chapman Hall) 1991

Checkland P. B. 'The shape of the systems movement' *Journal of Applied Systems Analysis* Vol. 6 1979 (pp. 129–35)

Checkland P. B. *Systems thinking, systems practice* (Chichester: Wiley) 1981

Chester E. 'Acid Overload' *Green Magazine* 1(4) January 1990 (pp. 30–34)

Christophe B. 'L'environnement naturel: Source de rapprochement entre la comptabilité nationale et la comptabilité d'enterprise?' *Revue Francaise de Comptabilité* Novembre 1989 (pp. 67–73)

Christophe Bernard, 'Comptabilité et environnement: prise en compte des activités environnementales dans les documents financiers des entreprises' *Thesis* University of PARIS XII Val-de-marne 1989

Christophe B. & K. J. Bebbington 'The French Social Balance Sheet: An exploratory note on a possible approach to environmental accounting' *The British Accounting Review* 24(2) 1992 (pp. 149–56)

Churchill N. C. 'The accountants' role in social responsibility' in W. E. Stone (ed.) *The Accountant in a Changing Business Environment* (Florida: University of Florida Accounting Series) 1973 (pp. 14–27)

Churchill N. C. & A. B. Toan 'Reporting on Corporate Social Responsibility: A progress report' *Journal of Contemporary Business* Winter 1978 (pp. 5–17)

Churchman C. West 'On the facility, felicity and morality of measuring social change' *The Accounting Review* Vol. XLVI January 1971 (pp. 30–5)

Clarke M. & R. Tilman 'C. B. MacPherson's Contribution to Democratic Theory' *Journal of Economic Issues* Vol. XXII No. 1 March 1988 (pp. 181–96)

Clayton A. & N. Radcliffe *Sustainability: A Strategic Planning and Investment Guide* Working Paper Produced by IPAD for WWF, Spring 1992

Coker E. W. 'Adam Smith's concept of the social system' *Journal of Business Ethics* 9(2) February 1990 (pp. 139–42)

Commoner B. *The Closing Circle* (New York: Alfred Knopf Inc) 1971

Commoner B. 'The social use and misuse of technology' in Benthall J. (ed.) *Ecology: the shaping enquiry* (London: Longman) 1972 (pp. 335–62)

Cmnd 5391 *Company Law Reform* (London: HMSO) July 1973

Cmnd 6225 *Report of the inflation accounting committee* (Sandilands) (London: HMSO) 1975

Cmnd 6888 *The future of company reports – a consultative document* (London: HMSO) 1977

Cmnd 7654 *Company Accounting and Disclosure* (London: HMSO) 1979

Cmnd 310 *Best Practicable Environment Option* Royal Commision on Environmental Approval (London: HMSO) 1988

Cmnd 1200 *This Common Inheritance* (London: HMSO) 1990

Confederation of British Industry *The responsibilities of the British Public Company* (London: CBI) 1973

Confederation of British Industry *Clean Up – it's good business* (London: CBI) 1986

Confederation of British Industry *Narrowing the Gap: Environmental Auditing Guidelines for Business* (London: CBI) 1990

Confederation of British Industry *Local authority air pollution control* (London: CBI) 1991

Confederation of British Industry *Managing Waste: Guidelines for business* (London: CBI) 1992

Confederation of British Industry (1992b) *Environment means business: a CBI Action Plan* for the 1990s (London: CBI)

Confederation of British Industry (1992c) *Corporate Environmental Policy Statements* (London: CBI)

Confederation of British Industry/PA *Waking up to a better environment* (London: CBI/PA Consulting) 1990

Conseil national de la comptabilité, 'Bilan écologique', *Bulletin trimestriel* No. 45, 4th trimester 1980

Cook G. C. A. (with Woods Gordon Management Consultants) *Costs of*

Compliance Study: The Impact of Governmental Regulations on Business Economic Council of Canada Working Paper No. 13, January 1981

Cooper D. 'Developing an effective and practical waste management policy' *Integrated Environmental Management* No. 9 May 1992 (pp. 18–20)

Cooper D. J. 'A social analysis of corporate pollution disclosures: a comment' *Advances in Public Interest Accounting* M. Neimark (ed.) JAI Press Vol. 2 1988 (pp. 179–86)

Cooper D. J. & T. M. Hopper (eds) *Critical Accounts* (Basingstoke: Macmillan) 1990

Cooper D. J. & M. J. Sherer 'The value of corporate accounting reports: Arguments for a political economy of accounting' *Accounting, Organizations and Society* 9(3/4) 1984 (pp. 207–32)

Coppock R. 'Life amongst the environmentalists: an elaboration on Wildavsky's "Economic and environmental/rationality and ritual"' *Accounting, Organizations and Society* 2(2) 1977 (pp. 125–29)

Corson J. J. & G. A. Steiner *Measuring Business' Social Performance: The corporate social audit* (New York: Committee for Economic Development) 1974

Council for Economic Priorities *Economic Priorities Report* (New York: CEP) 1973

Counter Information Services *CIS Reports* (London: CIS) 1972 *et seq.*

Cowe R. 'The continental route to social information' *Accountancy Age* 26 September 1980 (p. 13)

Cowen S. S., L. B. Ferreri & L. D. Parker 'The impact of corporate characteristics on social responsibility disclosure: A typology and frequency-based analysis' *Accounting, Organizations and Society* 12(2) 1987 (pp. 111–22)

Daly H. E. (ed.) *Economy, Ecology, Ethics: Essays toward a steady state economy* (San Francisco: W. H. Freeman) 1980

Daly H. E. 'Ultimate confusion: The economics of Julian Simon' *Futures* 10/85 (pp. 446–50)

Daly H. E. 'Toward a measure of sustainable social Net National Product' in Ahmad *et al.* (1989) *op. cit.* (pp. 8–9)

Daly H. E. & J. B. Cobb Jr. *For the Common Good: Redirecting the economy towards the community, the environment and a sustainable future* (London: Greenprint) 1990

Dauncey G. *After the crash: The emergence of the Rainbow economy* (Basingstoke: Greenprint) 1988

Davis J. *Greening Business: Managing for sustainable development* (Oxford: Basil Blackwell) 1991

Davis K. & R. L. Blomstrom *Business and Society: Environment and Responsibility* (New York: McGraw Hill) 1975

Davis S. W., K. Menon & G. Morgan (1982) 'The Images that have shaped accounting theory' *Accounting, Organizations and Society* Vol. 7 No. 4 (pp. 307–18)

Deetz S. A. *Democracy in an age of corporate colonization* (New York: State University of New York) 1992

De La Court T. *Beyond Brundtland: Green development in the 1990s* (London: Zed Books) 1990

Department of the Environment *Sustaining Our Common Future* (London: DoE) 1989a

Department of the Environment *Environment in Trust* (London: DoE) 1989b

Department of the Environment *Clean Technology* (London: DoE) 1989c

Department of the Environment *Environmental Assessment: A Guide to Procedures* (London: HMSO) 1989d

Department of the Environment *Environmental Protection Bill* (London: HMSO) 1989e

Department of the Environment *The Government's proposals for the implementation in UK law of the EC Directive on freedom of access to information on the environment* Consultation Paper (London: DOE) 1991a

Department of the Environment *Digest of environmental protection statistics 1991* (London: DoE) 1991b

Department of the Environment *Waste management – The Duty of Care: A code of practice* (London: DoE) 1991c

Department of the Environment *Giving guidance to the green consumer: Progress on an eco-labelling scheme* (London: DoE) 1991d

Department of Trade and Industry *Your Business and the Environment* (London: DTI) 1989

Department of Trade and Industry *Cutting Your Losses* (London: DTI) 1990

Department of Trade and Industry *The Environment: A challenge for business* (London: DTI) 1991

Derwent R. 'A mandate for green reporting' *Accountancy* October 1989 (pp. 92–94)

Devarajan S. & A. C. Fisher 'Hotelling's "Economics of exhaustible resources", 50 years later' *Journal of Economic Literature* XIX(3) 1981 (pp. 65–73)

Devine P. & D. C. Mandelbaum 'Standby L/Cs for environmental self-indemnification' *Journal of Commercial Bank Lending* 72(4) 1989 (pp. 55–63)

Dewhurst J. 'The green resource audit' *The Accountant* December 1989 (pp. 8–9)

Deziron M. & L. Bailey *A Directory of European Environmental Organizations* (Oxford: Blackwell) 1991

Dibben M. 'Stainless Shares' *InterCity* March/April 1988 (p. 30)

Dick-Larkham R. & D. Stonestreet 'Save it! The accountants' vital role' *Accountants' Weekly* 15 April 1977 (pp. 22–3)

Dickson D. *Alternative technology and the politics of technical change* (Glasgow: Fontana) 1974

Dierkes M. 'Corporate Social Reporting in Germany: Conceptual developments and practical experience' *Accounting, Organizations and Society* Vol. 4 No. 1/2 1979 (pp. 87–107)

Dierkes M. & L. E. Preston 'Corporate Social Accounting and Reporting for the Physical Environment: A critical review and implementation proposal' *Accounting, Organizations and Society* 2(1) 1977 (pp. 3–22)

Dirks H. J. 'Accounting for the costs of environmental clean-up: Where things stand today' *Environmental Finance* Spring 1991 (pp. 89–92)

Dobbs M. 'Discounting, intergenerational equity and the almost anywhere dominance criterion' *Futures* 8/1987 (pp. 307–12)

Dobie C. 'Green becomes an issue for the fund managers' *The Independent* 14 May 1990

Dobson A. *Green Political Thought* (London: Unwin Hyman) 1990

Donaldson J. *Key Issues in Business Ethics* (London: Academic Press) 1988

Donlan T. G. 'Risk aversion: Insurers find few allies on Capitol Hill' *Barron's* 65(42) 21 October 1985 (pp. 14, 47–9)

Dowling J. & J. Pfeffer 'Organisational Legitimacy: Social values and organisational behaviour' *Pacific Sociological Review* January 1975 (pp. 122–36)

Drotning P. T. 'Why nobody takes corporate social responsibility seriously' *Business and Society Review* Autumn 1972

DRT International *Framework for corporate reporting on sustainable development* (Toronto: DRT/BCSD/IISD) 1991

Drucker P. 'Is business letting young people down?' *Harvard Business Review* Nov/Dec 1965 (p. 54)

Dunham R. 'Virtue rewarded' *Accountancy* June 1988 (pp. 103–5)

Dunham R. 'Ethical funds no bar to profit' *Accountancy* June 1990 (p. 111)

Dyckman T. R., D. H. Downes & R. P. Magee *Efficient capital markets and accounting* (Englewood Cliffs, NJ: Prentice Hall) 1975

Earth Works Group *50 simple things you can do to save the earth* (London: Hodder & Stoughton) 1989

Economist Intelligence Unit 'Environment Report' *European Trends* No. 4 1989 (pp. 31–7)

The Economist 'Business getting physical' *The Economist*, August 26, 1989 (p. 53)

Edelstein J. M. 'Managing environmental risks: Team approach' *National Underwriter* 5 August 1983 (pp. 10, 34–5)

Edgerton J. 'Investing: Tanker from hell' *Money* June 1989 (pp. 66–7)

Edwards D. 'An accountant's role in cost-effective energy conservation' *Accountants Weekly* 6 October 1978 (pp. 18–21)

Edwards P. & M. Mayer *Dangerous Substances in Water: A Practical Guide* (London: ENDS) 1992

EIRIS *The financial performance of ethical investments* (London: EIRIS) 1989

Ekins P. (ed.) *The Living Economy: A new economics in the making* (London: Routledge) 1986

Ekins P. *Wealth beyond measure: An atlas of new economics* (London: Gaia) 1992a

Ekins P. *A New World Order: Grassroots movements for global change* (London: Routledge) 1992b

Elkington J. 'Business through the looking glass' *New Scientist* 7 September 1978

Elkington J. 'The environmental pressure' *Management Today* January 1980 (pp. 62–5)

Elkington J. 'Converting industry to environmental impact assessment' *Environmental Conservation* 8(1) Spring 1981 (pp. 23–30)

Elkington J. 'Industrial applications of environmental impact assessment' *Journal of General Management* 7(3) Spring 1982 (pp. 23–33)

Elkington J. (with Tom Burke) *The Green Capitalists: industry's search for environmental excellence* (London: Victor Gollancz) 1987

Elkington J. *The environmental audit: a green filter for company policies, plants, processes and products* (London: SustainAbility/World-wide Fund for Nature) 1990

Elkington J. *Community Action: No Thanks, Noah* (London: British Gas) 1990

Elkington J. & Dimmock *The Corporate Environmentalists: Selling sustainable development: but can they deliver?* (London: SustainAbility) 1991

Elkington J. & J. Hailes *The Green Consumer Guide: High Street shopping for a better environment* (London: Victor Gollancz) 1988

Elkington J. & J. Hailes *The Green Consumer's Supermarket Shopping Guide* (London: Victor Gollancz) 1989

Elkington J. & V. Jennings 'The rise of the environmental audit' *Integrated Environmental Management* No. 1 August 1991 (pp. 8–10)

Elkington J., P. Knight & J. Hailes *The Green Business Guide* (London: Victor Gollancz) 1991

Emmanuel C. R. & D. T. Otley *Accounting for management control* (London: Van Nostrand Reinhold) 1985

Emery F. E. (ed.) *Systems Thinking* (Harmondsworth: Penguin) 1969

Environment Council *Who's who in the environment: England* 2nd Edition (London: The Environment Council) 1992

Enzenburger H. M. 'A critique of political ecology' in H. Rose & S. Rose (eds) *The political economy of science* (London: MacMillan) 1976 (pp. 161–95)

Epstein E. M. & D. Votaw (ed.) *Rationality, Legitimacy, Responsibility: Search for new directions in business and society* (California: Goodyear) 1978

Erlich P. R. & A. H. Erlich 'Humanity at the crossroads' *Stamford Magazine* Spring/Summer 1978 reprinted in Daly H. E. (ed.) *Economy, Ecology, Ethics: Essays toward a steady state economy* (San Francisco: W. H. Freeman) 1980 (pp. 38–43)

Ermann M. D. 'How managers unintentionally encourage corporate crime' *Business and Society Review* Vol. 59 Fall 1986 (pp. 30–4)

Ernst & Ernst *Social Responsibility Disclosure* (Cleveland, Ohio: Ernst & Ernst) 1976 *et seq.*

Estes R. W. *Corporate Social Accounting* (New York: Wiley) 1976

Fava J. A. 'Product lifecycle assessment: improving environmental quality' *Integrated Environmental Management* No. 3 October 1991 (pp. 19–21)

Ferguson A. 'Good to be green' *Management Today* February 1989 (pp. 46–52)

Filios V. P. 'Assessment of attitudes toward corporate social accountability in Britain' *Journal of Business Ethics* Vol. 4 1985 (pp. 155–73)

Finlayson R. A. 'Environmental consultants see business boom' *Business Insurance* 20(11) 17 March 1986 (pp. 18–20)

Finlayson R. A. 'Environmental studies useful, but risky' *Business Insurance* 20(11) 17 March 1986 (pp. 22, 24)

Finlayson R. A. 'Environmental audits reveal hidden liabilities before sale' *Business Insurance* 21(22) 1 June 1987 (pp. 42–3)

Firth M. 'A study of the consensus of the perceived importance of disclosure of individual items in corporate annual reports' *The International Journal of Accounting Education and Research* 14(1) Fall 1978 (pp. 57–70)

Firth M. 'The extent of voluntary disclosure in corporate annual reports and its association with security risk measures' *Applied Economics* 16 1984 (pp. 269–77)

Fisher A. C. *Resource and Environmental Economics* (Cambridge: CUP) 1981

Fisher A. C. & F. M. Peterson 'The environment in economics: a survey' *Journal of Economic Literature* 1976 (pp. 1–33)

Forrester S. *Business and Environmental Groups: a natural partnership?* (London: Directory of Social Change) 1990

Foster A. 'Decent, Clean and True' *Management Today* April 1989 (pp. 56–60)

Franc B. J. 'Wrestling with environmental compliance' *Pennsylvania CPA Journal* Spring 1989 (pp. 10–12)

Francis M. E. 'Accounting and the evaluation of social programs: A critical comment' *The Accounting Review* April 1973 (pp. 245–357)

Frankel M. *The Social Audit Pollution Handbook* (London: MacMillan) 1978

Frankel M. *A Word of Warning* (London: Social Audit) 1981

Frankel M. *Chemical Risk* (London: Pluto Press) 1982

Freedman M. & B. Jaggi 'An analysis of the association between pollution disclosure and economic performance' *Accounting, Auditing and Accountability Journal* 1(2) 1988 (pp. 43–58)

Friedman M. *Capitalism and Freedom* (Chicago: University of Chicago) 1962

Friedman M. 'The social responsibility of business is to increase its profits' *The New York Times Magazine* September 13 1970 (pp. 122–6)

Friends of the Earth *The Environmental Charter for Local Government* (London: FoE) 1989

Friends of the Earth *How green is Britain?: The Government's environmental record* (London: Hutchinson Radius) 1990

K. Fuller 'Reviewing UK's Experience in EIA' *Integrated Environmental Management* No. August 1991 (pp. 12–14)

Furkiss V. *The Future of Technological Civilization* (New York: Braziller) 1974

Galbraith J. K. *Economics and the public purpose* (Middlesex: England) 1973

Galbraith J. K. 'Revolt in our time: the triumph of simplistic ideology' in M. Kaldor (ed.) *Europe from below* 1991

Gambling T. *Societal accounting* (London: George Allen & Unwin) 1974

Gambling T. 'Magic, accounting and morale' *Accounting, Organizations and Society* 2(2) 1977 (pp. 141–51)

Gambling T. 'Accounting to society' in Carsberg B. V. & A. J. B. Hope (eds) *Current Issues in Accounting* (Oxford: Philip Allen) 1977 & 1984

Gambling T. 'The evolution of accounting man' *Accountants' Weekly* 10 November 1978 (pp. 30–1)

Gambling T. *Beyond the conventions of accounting* (London: Macmillan) 1978

Gambling T. 'The accountants' guide to the galaxy, including the profession at the end of the universe' *Accounting, Organizations and Society* 10(4) 1985 (pp. 415–25)

Geddes M. *Social Audits and Social Accounting: An annotated bibliography and commentary* School of Applied Economics and Social Studies, South Bank Polytechnic, London 1988

Geddes M. "The social audit movement' in D. L. Owen (ed.) *Green Reporting* (London: Chapman Hall) 1992 (pp. 215–41)

Georgescu-Roegen N. 'The entropy law and the economic problem' *Distinguished Lecture Series* No. 1 University of Alabama, 1971 reprinted in Daly H. E. (ed.) *Economy, Ecology, Ethics: Essays toward a steady state economy* (San Francisco: W. H. Freeman) 1980 (pp. 49–60)

Georgescu-Roegen N. 'Selections from "energy and economic myths"' *Southern Economic Journal* 41.3 January 1975 reprinted in Daly H. E. (ed.) *Economy, Ecology, Ethics: Essays toward a steady state economy* (San Francisco: W. H. Freeman) 1980 (pp. 61–81)

Gerboth D. L. (1973) 'Research, Intuition and Politics in Accounting Inquiry' *AR* (pp. 475–82)

Gerboth D. L. 'The Conceptual Framework: Not definitions but professional values' *Accounting Horizons* September 1987 1(3) (pp. 1–8)

Gerboth D. L. 'Commentary: On The Profession' *Accounting Horizons* 2(1) March 1988 (pp. 104–8)

Ghosh P. 'The green conundrum' *Management Today* August 1991 (p. 72)

Gibson W. D. 'Plant sites: Plentiful but risky' *Chemical Week* 139(17) 22 October 1986 (pp. 69–70)

Gilkinson B. 'Economic Instruments: Positive trend, positive signals' *Accountants Journal (NZ)* March 1992 (pp. 70–1)

Gilkinson B. 'What is a green economy?' *Accountants Journal (NZ)* February 1992b (pp. 25–6)

Goldsmith E. et al. *Blueprint for Survival* (Harmondsworth: Penguin) 1972

Goldsmith E. *The Great U-Turn: De-industrializing Society* (Devon: Green Books) 1988

Gorz A. *Critique of Economic Reason* (trans G. Handyside & C. Turner) (London: Verso) 1989

Gray R. H. 'Accountability, Financial Reporting and the Not-for-profit Sector' *British Accounting Review* 15(1) Spring 1983 (pp. 3–23)

Gray R. H. *Accounting for R&D: A review of experiences with SSAP13* (London: ICAEW) 1986

Gray R. H. 'Accounting and democracy' *Accounting, Auditing and Accountability Journal* 2(3) 1989 (pp. 52–56)

Gray R. H. 'Greenprint for Accountants' *Certified Accountant* March 1990 p. 18

Gray R. H. 'Corporate Social Reporting by UK Companies: a cross-sectional and longitudinal study – An Interim Report' Paper presented to British Accounting Association, University of Dundee, April 1990

Gray R. H. 'The accountant's task as a friend to the Earth' *Accountancy* June 1990 (pp. 65–9)

Gray R. H. 'Business ethics and organisational change: Building a Trojan horse or rearranging deckchairs on the Titanic?' *Managerial Auditing Journal* 5(2) Spring 1990 (pp. 12–21)

Gray R. H. *The Greening of Accountancy: The profession after Pearce* (London: ACCA) 1990

Gray R. H. 'Accounting and Economics: The Psychopathic Siblings – A Review Essay' *British Accounting Review* 22.4 1990 (pp. 373–88)

Gray R. H. 'Corporate social reporting in the UK: The British Petroleum Company plc' in Taylor & Turley (eds) *Cases in financial reporting* (Oxford: Phillip Allan) 1990 (pp. 98–122)

Gray R. H. 'Sustainability: Do you REALLY want to know what it means?' *CBI Environment Newsletter* No. 3 January 1991 (pp. 10–11)

Gray R. H. 'Accounting for the environment and sustainability in lesser developed countries' paper presented to the United Nations CTC ISAR March 1991

Gray R. H. *Trends in corporate social and environmental accounting* (London: BIM) 1991

Gray R. H. 'Corporate Reporting for Sustainable Development: Accounting for sustainability in 2000AD' (Winnipeg: International Institute for Sustainable Development) forthcoming. Discussion Paper 9106, University of Dundee.

Gray R. H. 'Accounting and environmentalism: an exploration of the challenge of gently accounting for accountability, transparency and sustainability' *Accounting, Organizations and Society* 17(5) July 1992 (pp. 399–426)

Gray R. H., K. J. Bebbington, D. Walters & I. Thomson 'The Greening of Enterprise: An exploration of the (non) role of environmental accounting and environmental accountants in organisational change' Paper presented to the British Accounting Association Conference, University of Warwick, 1992

Gray R. H. & D. J. Collison 'Disclosure: The movement towards environmental disclosure' *Environment Strategy Europe 1991* (London: Campden Publishing) 1991 (pp. 195–8)

Gray R. H. & D. J. Collison 'Environmental Audit: Green gauge or Whitewash?' *Managerial Auditing* 6(5) 1991 (pp. 17–25)

Gray R. H. & R. C. Laughlin 'The coming of the green and the challenge of environmentalism' *Accounting, Auditing and Accountability Journal* 4(3) 1991 (pp. 5–8)

Gray R. H. & R. C. Laughlin (eds) *Green Accounting: A special issue of Accounting, Auditing and Accountability* (Bradford: MCB Press) 1991

Gray R. H. & S. Morrison 'Accounting for the environment after the Pearce Report' *Radical Quarterly* No. 19 Spring 1991 (pp. 17–25)

Gray R. H. & S. Morrison 'The Physical Environment, Accounting and Local Development' *Local Economy* 1992 (pp. 336–50)

Gray R. H., D. L. Owen & K. T. Maunders 'Corporate social reporting: the way forward?' *Accountancy* December 1986 (pp. 6–8)

Gray R. H., D. L. Owen & K. T. Maunders *Corporate Social Reporting: Accounting and accountability* (Hemel Hempstead: Prentice Hall) 1987

Gray R. H., D. L. Owen & K. T. Maunders 'Corporate social reporting: emerging trends in accountability and the social contract' *Accounting, Auditing and Accountability Journal* 1(1) 1988 (pp. 6–20)

Gray R. H., D. L. Owen & K. T. Maunders 'Accountability, Corporate Social Reporting and the External Social Audits' *Advances in Public Interest Accounting* Vol. 4 1991 (pp. 1–21)

Gray R. H. & R. W. Perks 'How desirable is social accounting?' *Accountancy* April 1982 (pp. 101–102)

Gray R. H. & I. W. Symon 'An environmental audit by any other name. . . .' *Integrated Environmental Management* No. 6 February 1992a (pp. 9–11)

Gray R. H. & I. W. Symon 'Environmental Reporting: BSO/Origin' *Integrated Environmental Management* No. 7 March 1992 (pp. 8–10)

Gray Roger 'Social audit: responding to change?' *Management Accounting* December 1989 (pp. 8–9)

Gray S. J., L. H. Radebaugh & C. B. Roberts 'International perceptions of cost constraints on voluntary information disclosures: A comparative study of UK and USA multinationals' *Journal of International Business Studies* Fourth Quarter Winter 1990 (pp. 597–622)

Greenpeace *Whiter Than White?* (London: Greenpeace) 1985

Guthrie J. E. & M. R. Mathews 'Corporate social accounting in Australasia' *Research in Corporate Social Performance and Policy* Vol. 7 1985 (pp. 251–77)

Guthrie J. & L. D. Parker 'Corporate social disclosure practice: a comparative international analysis' *Advances in Public Interest Accounting* M. Neimark (ed.) JAI Press Vol. 3 1989 (pp. 67–93)

Guthrie J. & L. D. Parker 'Corporate Social Reporting: a rebuttal of legitimacy theory' *Accounting and Business Research* Vol. 9 No. 76 1989 (pp. 343–52)

Guthrie J. & L. D. Parker 'Corporate social reporting: a rebuttal of legitimacy theory', *Accounting and Business Research* Vol. 9, No. 76 1989 (pp. 343–52)

Guthrie J. & L. D. Parker 'Corporate social disclosure practice: a comparative international analysis' *Advances in Public Interest Accounting* Vol. 3, 1990 (pp. 159–76)

Haggerty A. G. 'Environmental RM: "Bad news game"' *National Underwriter* 90(27) 4 July 1986 (pp. 4, 14)

Hahn F. 'Reflections on the invisible hand' in Hahn F. *Equilibrium and Macroeconomics* (Oxford: Basil Blackwell) 1984 (pp. 109–33)

Hall C. A. *Social Responsibility Accounting: Doing Well vs Doing Good* Undergraduate Dissertation, Department of Accounting, Portsmouth Polytechnic, 1989

Haigh N. & D. Baldock *Environmental Policy and 1992* (London: Institute for European Environmental Policy) 1990

Hardin G. 'The Tragedy of the Commons' *Science* Vol. 162, 13 December 1968 (pp. 1243–1248) reprinted in Daly H. E. (ed.) *Economy, Ecology,*

Ethics: Essays toward a steady state economy (San Francisco: W. H. Freeman) 1980 (pp. 100–14)

Hardin G. 'Second Thoughts on "The Tragedy of the Commons"' Ch. 7 in Daly H. E. (ed.) *Economy, Ecology, Ethics: Essays toward a steady state economy* (San Francisco: W. H. Freeman) 1980 (pp. 115–20)

Hargreaves B. J. A. & J. Dauman *Business Survival and Social Change: A practical guide to responsibility and partnership* (London: Associated Business Programmes) 1975

Harte G. 'Ethical investment and corporate reporting' *The Accountants' Magazine* March 1988 (pp. 28–9)

Harte G. & D. L. Owen 'Fighting de-industrialisation: the role of local government social audits' *Accounting, Organizations and Society* 12(2) 1987 (pp. 123–142)

Harte G. & D. L. Owen 'Environmental disclosure in the annual reports of British Companies: A research note' *Accounting, Auditing and Accountability Journal* 4(3) 1991 (pp. 51–61)

Harte G. & D. L. Owen 'Current trends in the reporting of green issues in the Annual Reports of UK companies' in D. L. Owen (ed.) *op. cit.* 1992 (pp. 166–200)

Harte G., L. Lewis & D. L. Owen 'Ethical investment and the corporate reporting function' *Critical Perspectives on Accounting* 2(3) 1991 (pp. 227–54)

Haughton G. 'Impact analysis – the social audit approach' *Project Appraisal* 3(1) March 1988 (pp. 21–5)

Hawkshaw A. 'Status Quo Vadis' *CA Magazine* (Canada) March 1991 (23–7)

Heilbroner R. L. 'Economics and Political Economy: Marx, Keynes and Schumpeter' *Journal of Economic Issues* Vol. XVIII No. 3 September 1984 (pp. 681–95)

Held D. *Models of Democracy* (Oxford: Polity Press) 1987

Hemming C. R. 'Eco-labelling of washing machines: A UK pilot study' *Integrated Environmental Management* No. 2 September 1991 (pp. 17–19)

Henderson H. *Creating Alternative Futures* (New York: Berkley) 1978

Henderson H. *The Politics of the Solar Age: Alternatives to Economics* (Doubleday: New York) 1981

Henderson H. 'New Markets, New Commons, New Ethics' *Accounting, Auditing and Accountability Journal* 4(3) 1991 (pp. 72–80)

Her Majesty's Inspectorate of Pollution *HMIP's First Annual Report 1987–88* (London: HMSO) 1989

Herberger R. A. 'Making the ecology issue pay off' *SAM Advanced Management Journal* 39(2) April 1974 (pp. 41–4)

Hester E. J. 'Environmental issues for insurers and risk managers' *Integrated Environmental Management* 2. September 1991 (pp. 21–2)

Heuer M. A. 'Implementing the Control Data Corporation CSR Philosophy' *Research in Corporate Social Performance and Policy* Vol. 7 1985 (pp. 213–28)

Hewgill J. 'Can energy become the new currency?' *Accountants' Weekly* 9 September 1977 (p. 13)

Hewgill J. 'New frontiers: Into the unknown' *Accountants' Weekly* 7 February 1979 (p. 11)

Hillary R. 'Corporate environmental management attitudes' *Integrated Environmental Management* No. 7 March 1992 (pp. 10–12)

Hindle P. ' "More from less" in practice' *Moonbeams* Spring 1992 (pp. 14–18)

Hines R. 'The implications of stock market reaction (non-reaction) for financial accounting standard setting' *Accounting and Business Research* 15(57) Winter 1984 (pp. 3–14)

Hines R. D. 'Financial accounting: In communicating reality, we construct reality' *Accounting, Organizations and Society* 13(3) 1988 (pp. 251–61)

Hines R. D. 'The sociopolitical paradigm in financial accounting research' *Accounting, Auditing and Accountability Journal* 2(1) 1989 (pp. 52–76)

Hines R. D. 'The FASB's Conceptual Framework, Financial Accounting and the Maintenance of the Social World' *Accounting, Organizations & Society* 16.4 1991 (pp. 313–32)

Hines R. D. 'Accounting for Nature' *Accounting, Auditing and Accountability Journal* 4(3) 1991 (pp. 27–9)

Hines R. D. 'Accounting: Filling the Negative Space' *Proceedings of the Third Interdisciplinary Perspectives on Accounting Conference* Vol. 1 1991 (pp. 1.6.1–20)

Hjalte K., K. Lidgren & I. Stahl *Environmental Policy and Welfare Economics* (Cambridge: CUP) 1977

Hoggart C. 'Reducing the waste line' *Integrated Environmental Management* No. 8 April 1992 (pp. 18–19)

Holdgate M. 'Changes in perception' in Angell D. J. R., J. D. Comer & M. L. N. Wilkinson (eds) *Sustaining Earth: Response to the environmental threats* (London: MacMillan) 1990 (pp. 79–96)

Hopper T. & A. Powell 'Making sense of research into the organisational and social aspects of management accounting: A review of its underlying assumptions' *Journal of Management Studies* 22(5) September 1985 (pp. 429–65)

Hopwood A. G. 'Towards an organisational perspective for the study of accounting and information systems' *Accounting Organisations and Society* 3(1) 1978 (pp. 3–13)

Hopwood A. G. 'Economics and the regime of the calculative' in Bodington S., M. George & J. Michaelson (eds) *Developing the socially useful economy* (London: Macmillan) 1986 (pp. 69–71)

Hopwood A. G. 'Ambiguity, Knowledge and Territorial Claims: Some Observations on the Doctrine of Substance Over Form: A Review Essay' *British Accounting Review* 22(1) March 1990 (pp. 79–88)

Hopwood A. G. 'Accounting and organisational change' *Accounting, Auditing and Accountability Journal* 3(1) 1990 (pp. 7–17)

Houldin M. 'Can business change to green?' *AA (Accountancy Age)* November 1989 (pp. 34–9)

Houldin M. 'TQM and environmental management' *Integrated Environmental Management* No. 9 May 1992 (pp. 5–7)

Hueting R., P. Bosch & B. de Boer *Methodology for the calculation of sustainable national income* (Voorburg: Netherlands Central Bureau of Statistics) 1991

Huizing A. & H. C. Dekker 'Helping to pull our planet out of the red: an environmental report of BSO/Origin' *Accounting Organizations and Society* 17(5) July 1992 (pp. 449–58)

Humble J. *Social Responsibility Audit: A management tool for survival* (London: The Foundation for Business Responsibilities) 1973

Humphreys G. 'Superfund a l'europeenne? The draft directive on waste' *Integrated Environmental Management* No. 4 November 1991 (pp. 2–4)

Hundred Group of Finance Directors *Statement of Good Practice: Environmental Reporting in Annual Reports* (London: 100 Group) 1992

Hunt D. 'LCA of soft drink containers' *Integrated Environmental Management* No. 4 November 1991 (pp. 20–2)

Hunt D. 'Environmental management systems: BS7750 and beyond' *Integrated Environmental Management* No. 10 June 1992 (pp. 6–9)

Hunt S. M. 'Conducting a social inventory' *NAA Management Accounting* October 1974 (pp. 15–16, 26)

Hussey R. 'France has a social audit' *Accountancy* February 1978 (pp. 111–12)

Hutchinson C. *Business and the Environmental Challenge* (Reading: The Conservation Trust) 1991

Ingram R. W. & K. B. Frazier 'Environmental performance and corporate disclosure' *Journal of Accounting Research* Autumn 1980 (pp. 614–22)

INSEE (Institut national de la satellites de la statistique et des études économiques), 'Les comptes satellites de l'environnement' *Les collections de l'INSEE* Serie C, No. 130 March 1986

INSEE, 'Les comptes du patrimoine naturel', *Les collections de l'INSEE*, Serie C, No. 137–138 December 1986

Institute of Directors *Members' Opinion Survey: Environment* (London: IOD) 1992

International Chamber of Commerce *Environmental Auditing* (Paris: ICC) 1989

International Institute for Sustainable Development *Business strategy for sustainable development: Leadership and accountability for the 90s* (Winnepeg: IISD/BCSD/Deloitte Touche) 1992

Irvine G. 'Your brother's keeper? Duty of Care under the UK Environmental Protection Act' *Integrated Environmental Management* No. 2 September 1991 (pp. 2–4)

Jacobs M. *The Green Economy: Environment, sustainable development and the politics of the future* (London: Pluto Press) 1991

Jacobson R. 'Economic efficiency and the quality of life' *Journal of Business Ethics* 10. 1991 (pp. 201–9)

Jaggi B. 'An analysis of corporate social reporting in Germany' *International Journal of Accounting* 15(2) 1979 (p. 35)

Jenkins B. G. *Environmental audit: an auditor's perspective* (London: Coopers & Lybrand Deloitte) 1990

Johnson H. L. *Disclosure of corporate social performance: survey, evaluation and prospects* (New York: Praeger) 1979

Jones A. L. 'Planning for ecology and survival' *Managerial Planning* 23(2) 1974 (pp. 1–6)

Jones C. 'Corporate Social Accounting and the Capitalist Enterprise' in Cooper & Hopper (eds) 1990 *op. cit.* (pp. 272–93)

Kapp K. W. *The social costs of business enterprise* (Nottingham: Spokesman) 1978 (first published in 1950)

Karnes A., J. Sterner, R. Walker & F. Wu 'A Bicultural study of the independent auditor's perceptions of unethical business practices' *International Journal of Accounting* 24(1) 1989 (pp. 29–41)

Kast F. E. & J. E. Rosenweig *Organisation and Management: A systems approach* (McGraw Hill Kograkusha) 1974

Kemball-Cook D., M. Baker & C. Mattingly *The Green Budget: An emergency programme for the UK* (London: Greenprint) 1991

Kemp P. & D. Wall *A Green Manifesto for the 1990s* (London: Penguin) 1990

Kemp R. & S. Gerrard 'Risk and the management of UK landfill sites' *Integrated Environmental Management* No. 4 November 1991 (pp. 23–4)

Kestigan M. 'The greening of accountancy' *Australian Accountant* September 1991 (pp. 20–8)

Keynes J. M. 'National self-sufficiency' *Yale Law Review* Vol. 22 1933 (pp. 755–63)

Kiesche E. S. 'Facing the environmental chill on acquisitions' *Chemical Week* 143(12) September 1988 (pp. 26–9)

Kneese A. V. *Economics and the environment* (Harmondsworth: Penguin) 1977

Knight F. H. *The Ethics of Competition* (London: George Allen and Unwin) 1936

Kohls J. 'Corporate board structure, social reporting and social performance' *Research in Corporate Social Performance and Policy* Vol. 7 1985 (pp. 165–89)

Kopitsky J. J. & E. T. Betzenberger 'Bankers Debate: Should banks lend to companies with environmental problems?' *Journal of Commercial Bank Lending* 69(11) July 1987 (pp. 3–13)

Krietzman L. 'Packaging and design: Air Worthy' *Marketing* 28 July 1988 (p. 49)

Krohe J. Jnr 'Can we stop acid rain? And who should pay the bill?' *Across the Board* 21(2) February 1984 (pp. 14–25)

Landbank Consultancy *The Waste as a Raw Material (WARM) System* (London: Gateway Foodmarkets) 1992

Lander R. 'Funds of the Earth' *Management Today* February 1989 (p. 132)

Laughlin R. & L. K. Varangu 'Accounting for Waste or Garbage Accounting: Some thoughts from non-accountants' *Accounting, Auditing and Accountability Journal* 4(3) 1991 (pp. 43–50)

Laughlin R. C. 'Environmental Disturbances and Organisational Transitions and Transformations: Some Alternative Models' *Organisation Studies* 12(2) 1991 (pp. 209–32)

Laughlin R. C. & R. H. Gray *Financial Accounting: method and meaning* (London: Van Nostrand Reinhold) 1988

Lawrence J. 'Encouraging cleaner technologies' *Integrated Environmental Management* No. 4 November 1991 (pp. 15–16)

Lecomber R. *Economic Growth versus the environment* (London: MacMillan) 1975

Lehman C. Accounting ethics: surviving survival of the fittest, *Advances in Public Interest Accounting*, Vol. 13, 1990 (pp. 71–82)

Lessem R. 'Corporate Social Reporting in Action: An evaluation of British, European and American practice' *Accounting, Organizations and Society* Vol. 2 No. 4 1977 (pp. 279–94)

Lickiss M. 'President's Page: Measuring up to the environmental challenge' *Accountancy* January 1991 (p. 6)

Likierman A. *Rights and obligations in public information* (Cardiff: University College Cardiff Press) 1986

Likierman A. & P. Creasey 'Objectives and entitlements to rights in government financial information' *Financial Accountability and Management* 1(1) Summer 1985 (pp. 33–50)

Lindblom C. E. 'The accountability of private enterprise: Private – No. Enterprise – Yes.' in Tinker (ed.) 1984 *op. cit.*

Lindblom C. K. 'Organizational Legitimacy: Implications for Corporate Social Disclosure' University of Connecticut Working Paper May 1984

Linowes D. 'Let's get on with the social audit: A Specific Proposal' *Business and Society Review* Winter 1972 (pp. 39–42)

Litterick G. 'Charging for discharging to controlled waters' *Integrated Environmental Management* No. 5 December 1991 (pp. 2–5)

Ljung A. & O. Oftedal *Social Planning and Reporting* Stockholm School of Economics April 1977

Logsdon J. M. 'Organizational response to environmental issues: Oil companies and air pollution' *Research in Corporate Social Performance and Policy* Vol. 7 1985 (pp. 47–71)

Lovelock J. *Gaia: A New look at life on Earth* (Oxford: OUP) 1982

Lovelock J. *The ages of Gaia* (Oxford: OUP) 1988

Lowe A. E. 'The finance director's role in the formulation and implementation of strategy' *Journal of Business Finance* 4(4) 1972 (pp. 58–63)

Lowe A. E. & J. M. McInnes 'Control of socio-economic organisations' *Journal of Management Studies* 8(2) 1971 (pp. 213–27)

Lowe J. & D. Lewis 'Comprehensive versus piecemeal approaches to environmental control' *International Journal of Social Economics* 7(5) 1980 (pp. 274–85)

Luhmann N. *Ecological Communication* trans J. Bednarz (Cambridge: Polity Press) 1989

Luthans F. & R. M. Hodgetts *Social Issues in Business* (London: MacMillan) 1976

Lutz E., M. Munasinghe & R. Chander *A Developing Country Perspective on Environmental Accounting* (Washington DC: World Bank Environment Dept, Divisional Working Paper No. 1990-12) August 1990

Lynn M. 'Can environment survive the recession?' *Accountancy* September 1991 (pp. 76–7)

McBurney S. *Ecology into economics won't go (Or Life isn't a concept)* (London: Green Books) 1990

McComb D. 'Some guidelines on social accounting in the US' *Accountancy* April 1978 (pp. 50–2)

McCormick J. *British Politics and the Environment* (London: Earthscan) 1991

McKee A. 'The passage from theology to economics' *International Journal of Social Economics* 13(3) 1986 (pp. 5–19)

MacKenzie D. 'It makes money, being green' *New Scientist* 7 October 1989 (pp. 6–7)

MacKerron C. B. 'Conferees call for CO_2 and CFC cuts' *Chemical Week* 143(3) July 20. 1988 (pp. 26–7)

Macpherson C. B. *Democratic Theory: Essays in retrieval* (Oxford: OUP) 1973

Macpherson C. B. *The life and times of liberal democracy* (Oxford: OUP) 1977

Macpherson C. B. *Property* (Toronto: University of Toronto Press) 1978

Macrory R. 'Environmental policy in Britain: Reaffirmation or Reform' International Institute for Environment and Society, Berlin, W.P. No. 86–4 1986

Macrory R. *Universities and the Environment: Environmental regulation – opportunities and obligations* (London: CVCP) 1992

Magnet M. 'How acid rain might dampen the utilities' *Fortune* 108(3) August 8, 1983 (pp. 58–64)

Maheshwari G. C. 'Corporate characteristics and social responsibility reporting' *Asian Review of Accounting* 1(1) March 1992 (pp. 31–42)

Malachowski A. 'Business ethics 1980–2000: an interim forecast' *Managerial Auditing Journal* 5(2) 1990 (pp. 22–7)

Markandya A. & D. Pearce 'Natural environments and the social rate of discount' *Project Appraisal* 3(1) 1988

Marlin J. T. 'Accounting for pollution' *Journal of Accountancy* February 1973

Massachusetts Institute of Technology 'The MIT Report. Is Doomsday Really That Close?' *Business Week* March 11 1972 (pp. 97–8)

Mathews M. R. 'A suggested classification for social accounting research' *Journal of Accounting and Public Policy* Vol. 3 1984 (pp. 199–221)

Mathews M. R. 'Social accounting: A future need' *Accountancy* December 1985 (p. 139)

Mathews M. R. 'Social responsibility accounting disclosure and information content for shareholders' *British Accounting Review* 19(2) 1987 (pp. 161–68)

Maunders K. T. 'Social reporting and the employment report' in Tonkin D. J. & L. C. L. Skerratt (eds) *Financial Reporting 1981–1982* (London: ICAEW) 1981 (pp. 217–27)

Maunders K. T. 'Social reporting and the employment report' in Tonkin D. J. & L. C. L. Skerratt (eds) *Financial Reporting 1982–1983* (London: ICAEW) 1982 (pp. 178–87)

Maunders K. T. & R. Burritt 'Accounting and Ecological Crisis' *Accounting, Auditing and Accountability Journal* 4(3) 1991 (pp. 9–26)

Maunders K. T., R. H. Gray & D. L. Owen 'Managerial social accounting in developing countries: Towards the operationalisation of social reporting' *Research in Third World Accounting* Vol. 1 1991 (pp. 87–101)

Maxwell S. 'The rise of the environmental audit' *Accountancy* June 1990 (pp. 70–2)

Maxwell S. R. & A. K. Mason *Social Responsibility and Canada's Largest Corporations* ICRA Occasional Paper No. 9 (University of Lancaster: ICRA) 1976

Meadows D. H., D. L. Meadows, J. Randers & W. H. Behrens *The limits to growth* (London: Pan) 1972

Meall L. 'The ozone layer and its friends' *Accountancy* June 1990 (p. 124)

Medawar C. 'The social audit: a political view' *Accounting, Organizations and Society* 1(4) 1976 (pp. 389–94)

Medawar C. *The Social Audit Consumer Handbook* (London: MacMillan Press) 1978

Merlin Research Unit *The assessment process for green investment* (London: Jupiter Tarbutt Merlin) 1992

Miller A. 'Green Investment' Ch.11 in D. Owen (ed.) *Green Reporting: Accountancy and the challenge of the nineties* (London: Chapman Hall) 1992 (pp. 242–55).

Milne M. J. 'Accounting, Environmental Resource Values and Non-Market Valuation Techniques for environmental resources: A Review' *Accounting, Auditing and Accountability Journal* 4(3) 1991 (pp. 81–109)

Mintzberg H. 'The case for corporate social responsibility' *The Journal of Business Strategy* 4(2) 1983 (pp. 3–15)

Mishan E. J. *The costs of economic growth* (Harmondsworth: Penguin) 1969

Mitchell F., I. Sams & P. White 'Ethical investment: current trends and prospects' *The Accountants' Magazine* January 1990 (pp. 12–15)

Mobley S. C. 'Commentary on "Let's get on with the social audit"' *Business and Society Review* Winter 1972 (pp. 48–9)

Molinero L. (ed.) *Accounting and the Environment: Readings and Discussion* (Washington: Management Institute for Environment and Business) 1991

Moretz S. 'Industrial hygiene auditing: Allied Signal takes the "extra step"' *Occupational Hazards* Vol. 5 May 1989 (pp. 73–6).

Most K. S. 'Corporate Social Reporting: "Model report" by Deutsche Shell' *The Accountant* February 1977

Napier C. 'A reticence to lend and invest? A case study of financial institutions and environmental liability – Part two' *Integrated Environmental Management* No. 9 May 1992 (pp. 11–13)

Nash T. 'Green about the environment?' *Director* February 1990 (pp. 40–7)

National Rivers Authority *Guardians of the Water Environment* (London: NRA) 1989

Neale C. W. 'Post-auditing practices by UK firms: Aims, benefits and shortcomings' *British Accounting Review* 21(4) December 1989 (pp. 309–28)

Newell G. E., J. G. Kreuze & S. J. Newell 'Accounting for hazardous waste: Does your firm face potential environmental liabilities?' *Management Accounting (US)* May 1990 (pp. 58–61)

Nikolai L. A., J. D. Bazley & R. L. Brummett *The management of corporate environmental activity* (Washington: National Association of Accountants) 1976

Nixon B. and A. Lonie Accounting for R&D: the need for change, *Accountancy* February 1990 (pp. 90–1)

Nixon W. A. 'R&D disclosure: SSAP13 and after' *Accountancy* February 1991 (pp. 72–3)

Opschoor J. B. & H. B. Vos *Economic instruments for environmental protection* (Paris: OECD) 1989

Ordre des experts-comptables et des comptables agréés, '*L'evaluation des avantages et couts sociaux la responsabilité socio-économique de l'entreprise*' Conseil superieur de l'Ordre des experts-comptables Paris 1980

O'Riordan T. & R. K. Turner *An annotated reader in environmental planning and management* (Oxford: Pergamon Press) 1983

Owen D. F. *What is Ecology?* (Oxford: OUP) 1980

Owen D. L. 'Towards a theory of social investment: a review essay' *Accounting, Organizations and Society* 15(3) 1990 (pp. 249–66)

Owen D. L. *Green Reporting: The challenge of the nineties* (London: Chapman & Hall) 1992

Owen D. L., R. H. Gray & R. Adams 'A green and fair view' *Certified Accountant* April 1992 (pp. 12–15)

Owen D., R. Gray & K. Maunders 'Researching the information content of social responsibility disclosure: A comment' *British Accounting Review* 19(2) 1987 (pp. 169–76)

Owen R. & M. Dynes *The Times Guide to 1992* (London: Times Books) 1990

Owens S., V. Anderson & I. Brunskill *Green Taxes: a budget memorandum* Green Paper No. 2 (London: Institute for Public Policy Research) 1990

Packard V. *The Waste Makers* (Harmondsworth: Pelican) 1965

Papworth J. 'White into Green' *AA (Accountancy Age)* April 1990 (pp. 41–2)

Papworth J. 'Finding the green balance' *AA (Accountancy Age)* May 1990 (pp. 44&47)

Parker L. D. 'Polemical themes in social accounting: A scenario for standard setting' *Advances in Public Interest Accounting* Vol. 1 1986 (pp. 67–93)

Parker L. D. 'Accounting for social impact' Ch. 9 in Parker L. D., K. R. Ferris & D. T. Otley (eds) *op. cit.* 1989 (pp. 168–193)

Parker L. D., K. R. Ferris & D. T. Otley (eds) *Accounting for the human factor* (Sydney: Prentice Hall International) 1989 (pp. 168–193)

Parkin S. *Green Parties: An International Guide* (London: Heretic Books) 1989

Patten D. M. 'Intra-industry environmental disclosures in response to the Alaskan oil spill: A note on legitimacy theory' *Accounting, Organizations and Society* 17(5) 1992 (pp. 471–5)

Pearce D. 'Accounting for the future' *Futures* Vol. 9 1977 (pp. 365–74) reprinted in O'Riordan & Turner (*op. cit.*)

Pearce D. 'Resource scarcity and economic growth in poor developing countries' *Futures* 10/1985 (pp. 440–5)

Pearce D. (ed.) *Blueprint 2: Greening the World Economy* (London: Earthscan) 1991a

Pearce D. 'Towards a sustainable economy: Environment and economics' *The Royal Bank of Scotland Review* No. 172 December 1991b (pp. 3–15)

Pearce D., A. Markandya & E. B. Barbier *Blueprint for a Green Economy* (London: Earthscan) 1989

Pearce F. 'Waste is big business – but that's not all . . .' *Accountancy* December 1982 (p. 52)

Pearson M. & S. Smith 'Taxation: The environmental ally' *Accountancy* March 1990 (pp. 25–6)

Perks R. W. & L. Butler 'Accounting standards in practice: the experience of SSAP2' *Accounting and Business Research* No. 29 1977 (pp. 25–33)

Perks R. W. & R. H. Gray 'Corporate social reporting: an analysis of objectives' *British Accounting Review* 10(2) Autumn 1978 (pp. 43–60)

Perks R. W. & R. H. Gray 'Beware of social accounting' *Management Accounting* December 1979 (pp. 22–3)

Perks R. W. & R. H. Gray 'Social accounting: the role of the accountant' *The Accountants' Magazine* May 1980 (p. 201)

Perks R. W., D. Rawlinson & L. Ingram 'An exploration of ethical investment in the UK' *British Accounting Review* 24(1) 1992

Peskin H. M. 'Environmental and non-market accounting in developing countries' in Ahmad *et al.* (eds) *op. cit.* 1989 (pp. 59–64)

Peskin H. M. 'Alternative environmental and resource accounting approaches' in R. Costanza (ed.) *Ecological Economics: The science and management of sustainability* (New York: Columbia University Press) 1991 (pp. 176–93)

Peskin H. M. & E. Lutz *A survey of resource and environmental accounting in industrialised countries* (World Bank Environment Working Paper 37) August 1990

Peskin H. M., P. R. Portney & A. V. Kneese (eds) *Environmental regulation and the US economy* (Johns Hopkins University Press) 1981

Pezzey J. *Definitions of Sustainability* (No. 9) (UK CEED: 1989)

Pierro W. J. 'An environmental consultant's view of property transfer assessments' *Journal of Commercial Bank Lending* 72(4) 1989 (pp. 49–55)

Piesse J. 'Environmental spending and share price performance: The petroleum industry' *Business Strategy and the Environment* Spring 1992 (pp. 45–54)

Pike R. H. & T. S. Ooi 'The impact of corporate investment objectives and constraints on capital budgeting practices' *British Accounting Review* 20(2) August 1988 (pp. 159–74)

Pimm D. 'Environmental issues for auditors' *Audit Briefing* 2(1) October 1990 (pp. 1–3)

Plant C. & J. Plant *Green Business: Hope or Hoax?* (Devon: Green Books) 1991

Pollock J. 'Contaminated Land: Keep Out?' *CA Magazine* (Scotland) February 1992 (pp. 22–4)

Ponemon L. A. 'Ethical reasoning and selection-socialization in accounting' *Accounting, Organizations and Society* 17(3/4) 1992 (pp. 239–58)

Porritt J. 'Accounting for the planet's survival' *Accountancy* September 1989 (pp. 19–20)

Porritt J. 'How green is Britain?' *Telegraph Weekend Magazine* September 23 1989 (p. 19)

Porritt J. *How Green is Britain? The government's environmental record* (London: Hutchinson Radius/Friends of the Earth) 1990

Porritt J. (ed.) *Save the Earth* (London: Dorling Kindersley) 1991

Power M. 'Auditing and environmental expertise: between protest and professionalisation' *Accounting, Auditing and Accountability Journal* 4(3) 1991 (pp. 30–42)

Power M. 'Corporate responsibility and environmental visibility: the role of accounting and audit' paper to be presented at the conference 'Ecological responsibilities of enterprises' European University Institute, Florence 13–15 April, 1992

Power M. 'After calculation? Reflections on *Critique of Economic Reason* by Andre Gorz' *Accounting, Organizations and Society* 17(5) July 1992 (pp. 477–500)

Prakash P. & A. Rappaport 'Information inductance and its significance for accounting' *Accounting, Organizations and Society* 2(1) 1977 (pp. 29–38)

Preston L. E., F. Rey & M. Dierkes 'Comparing Corporate Social Performance: Germany, France, Canada and the US' *California Management Review* Summer 1978 (pp. 40–9)

Purkiss A. 'Gone with the wind' *Accountancy* January 1992 (pp. 70–2)

Puxty A. G. 'Social accounting as immanent legitimation: A critique of a technist ideology' *Advances in Public Interest Accounting* Vol. 1 1986 (pp. 95–112)

Puxty A. G. 'The Accountancy Profession in the Class Structure' in Cooper & Hopper (eds), 1990 (*op. cit.*) (pp. 332–65)

Puxty A. G. 'A critique of Parker and Gray, Owen & Maunders' *Advances in Public Interest Accounting* Vol. 4 1991 (forthcoming)

Quigley C. 'Our ecological crisis' *Current History* 59(347) July 1970 (pp. 9–12)

Quirke B. 'Accounting for the environment: Current Issues' *European Environment* 1(5) October 1991 (pp. 19–22)

Rabinowitz D. L. & M. Murphy 'Environmental disclosure: What the SEC requires' *Environmental Finance* Spring 1991 (pp. 31–43)

Raines J. P. & C. R. Jung 'Knight on Religion and Ethics as agents of social change' *American Journal of Economics and Sociology* 45.4 October 1986 (pp. 429–39)

Ramanathan K. V. 'Toward a theory of corporate social accounting' *The Accounting Review* 51(3) July 1976 (pp. 516–28)

Ramphal S. S. 'Endangered Earth' in Angell *et al.* (eds) *Sustaining Earth: Response to the Environmental Threats* (Basingstoke: MacMillan) 1990 (pp. 3–14)

Rawls J. *A theory of justice* (Oxford: Oxford University Press) 1972

Redmond S. 'Greens roll on after ozone win' *Marketing* 28 July 1988 (p. 15)

Rees J. *Natural Resources: Allocation, Economics and Policy* 2nd edition (London: Routledge) 1990

Reilly B. J. & M. J. Kyj 'Economics and Ethics' *Journal of Business Ethics* 9.9 September 1990 (pp. 691–98)

Repetto R. 'Wasting Assets: The need for national resource accounting' *Technology Review* January 1990 (pp. 38–44)

Rey Francoise, *Introduction à la comptabilité sociale (domaines techniques et applications)* Entreprise moderne d'editions Paris 1978

Rice F. 'Where will we put all that garbage?' *Fortune* April 11 1988 (pp. 72–6)

Richardson J. M. 'The resourceful earth: optimism and confrontation' *Futures* 10/85 (pp. 464–74)

Ridgers, B. The use of statistics in counter–information, in Irvine *et al.* (eds) *Demystifying Social Statistics*, London, Pluto Press, 1979

Roberts C. B. *International trends in social and employee reporting* (London: ACCA) Occasional Research Paper No. 6 1990

Roberts C. B. 'Environmental disclosures: a note on reporting practices in Europe' *Accounting, Auditing and Accountability Journal* 4(3) 1991 (pp. 62–71)

Roberts C. B. 'Environmental disclosures in corporate annual reports in Western Europe' in D. L. Owen (ed.) *op. cit.* 1992 (pp. 139–65)

Robertson J. 'Corporate Social Reporting by New Zealand Companies' *Journal of Contemporary Business* Winter 1978 (pp. 113–33)

Robertson J. *The Sane Alternative* (London: James Robertson) 1978b

Robertson J. 'Introduction to the British Edition' in Capra & Spretnak *op. cit.* 1984 (pp. xxiii-xxx)

Robertson J. *Future Work: Jobs, Self-employment and Leisure after the Industrial Age* (London: Gower/Temple Smith) 1985

Robertson J. *Future Wealth: A new economics for the 21st Century* (London: Cassell) 1990

Rock S. 'Splendour in the grass (Groundwork Foundation)' *Director* 43(4) November 1989 (pp. 123–30)

Rockness J. W. 'An assessment of the relationship between US corporate environmental performance and disclosure' *Journal of Business Finance and Accounting* 12(3) Autumn 1985 (pp. 339–54)

Rockness J. & P. F. Williams 'A descriptive study of social responsibility mutual funds' *Accounting, Organizations and Society* 13(4) 1988 (pp. 397–411)

Roney A. *The European Community Fact Book* (London: Kogan Page) 1990

Rose D. J., M. M. Miller & C. Agnew 'Reducing the problem of global warming' *Technology Review* 87(4) May/June 1984 (pp. 48–58)

Roslender R. *Sociological Pespectives on Modern Accountancy* (London: Routledge) 1992

Rowley D. A. & Witmer T. L. 'Assessing environmental risks before booking a loan' *Commercial Lending Review* 4(1) Winter 1988/89 (pp. 53–64)

Rubenstein D. 'Black Oil, Red Ink' *CA Magazine* (Canada) Nov. 1989 (pp. 28–35)

Rubenstein D. 'Lessons of Love' *CA Magazine* (Canada) March 1991 (pp. 35–41)

Rubenstein D. 'Bridging the gap between green accounting and black ink' *Accounting, Organizations and Society* 17(5) July 1992 (pp. 501–08)

Ruckelhaus W. D. 'Towards a sustainable world' *Scientific American* September 1989 (pp. 166–70)

Ryding Sven-Olof 'Environmental Priority Strategies in product design (EPS)' *Integrated Environmental Management* No. 4 November 1991 (pp. 18–19)

Sachs W. (ed.) *The development dictionary: A guide to knowledge as power* (London: Zed Books) 1992

Salamitou J. 'The environmental index: an environmental management tool for Rhône Poulenc' *Integrated Environmental Management* No. 4 November 1991 (pp. 7–9)

Sarokin D. & J. Schulkin 'Environmental concerns and the business of banking' *Journal of Commercial Bank Lending* February 1991 (pp. 6–19)

de Savornin Lohman A. F. 'Financial incentives: an idea whose time has come?' *Integrated Environmental Management* No. 4 November 1991 (pp. 4–5)

Scapens R. W. & J. T. Sale 'Performance measurement and formal capital expenditure controls in divisionalised companies' *Journal of Business Finance and Accounting* Autumn 1981 (pp. 389–419)

Schmidheiny S. *Changing Course* (New York: MIT Press) 1992

Schreuder H. 'Corporate social reporting in the Federal Republic of Germany: An overview' *Accounting, Organizations and Society* 4(1/2) 1979 (pp. 109–22)

Schumacher E. F. 'Buddhist Economics' *Resurgence* Vol. 1 No. 11 Jan-Feb 1968 reprinted in Daly H. E. (ed.) *Economy, Ecology, Ethics: Essays toward a steady state economy* (San Francisco: W. H. Freeman) 1980 (pp. 138–45)

Schumacher E. F. *Small is beautiful* (London: Abacus) 1973

Schumacher E. F. *The Age of Plenty: A Christian view* (Edinburgh: St. Andrews Press) 1974 reprinted in Daly H. E. (ed.) *Economy, Ecology, Ethics: Essays toward a steady state economy* (San Francisco: W. H. Freeman) 1980 (pp. 126–37)

Seabrook J. *The myth of the market: Promises and illusions* (Devon: Green Books) 1990

Sellen J. W. 'Positive savings from energy plans' *Accountant's Weekly* 18 January 1980 (pp. 22–3)

Shane P. & B. Spicer 'Market response to environmental information produced outside the firm' *The Accounting Review* July 1983 (pp. 521–38)

Sherman H. J. & E. K. Hunt 'Pollution in a radical perpsective' *Business and Society Review* Autumn 1972

Shiva V., P. Anderson, H. Schucking, A. Gray, L. Lohmann, D. Cooper *Biodiversity: social and ecological perspectives* (London: Zed Books) 1991

Sikka P., H. C. Willmott & E. A. Lowe 'Guardians of Knowledge and the Public Interest: Evidence and Issues of Accountability in the UK Accountancy Profession' *Accounting, Auditing and Accountability Journal* 2(2) 1989 (pp. 47–71)

Sikka P., H. C. Willmott & E. A. Lowe ' "Guardians of knowledge and the public interest": A Reply to our critics' *Accounting, Auditing and Accountability Journal* 4(4) 1991 (pp. 14–22)

Simpson S. *The Times Guide to the Environment* (London: Times Books) 1990

Singh D. R. & J. M. Ahuja 'Corporate social reporting in India' *International Journal of Accounting* 18(2) 1983 (pp. 151–70)

Singh J. 'Pollution risks may hamper acquisitions' *National Underwriter* 93(15) April 10 1989 (pp. 31, 33)

Skeel S. 'Rich on Rubbish' *Management Today* October 1991 (pp. 42–7)

Slaughter J. 'Spotlight on ethical funds' *Observer* 14 May 1989 (p. 63)

Smil V. 'A perspective on global environmental crises' *Futures* Vol. 6 1987 (pp. 240–53)

Smith D. 'The Kraken wakes: The political dynamics of the hazardous waste issue' *Industrial Crisis Quarterly* 5(3) 1991 (pp. 189–207)

Smith G. A. 'The teleological view of wealth: a historical perspective' Ch.14 in Daly H. E. (ed.) *Economy, Ecology, Ethics: Essays toward a steady state economy* (San Francisco: W. H. Freeman) 1980 (pp. 215–37)

Social Audit Ltd *Social Audit Quarterly* 9 Poland St, London. 1973–1976

Society of Environmental Toxicology and Chemistry (SETAC) *A Technical Framework for Life-Cycle Assessments* (Washington: SETAC) 1991

Society of Management Accountants of Canada (CMA) *Accounting for the Environment* (Hamilton: CMA) 1992

Specht L. 'What auditors don't know about environmental laws can hurt them!' *Proceedings of the Third Interdisciplinary Perspectives on Accounting Conference* Vol. 1 1991 (pp. 1.12.1–1.12.11)

Spellman J. D. 'Greenhouse effect: European Solutions' *Europe* 281 November 1988 (pp. 36, 37, 48)

Stephens M. 'Pressure turned on Green Movement' *Business Review Weekly* (Australia) August 17 1990 (pp. 87–91)

Stephenson L. 'Prying open corporations: tighter than clams' *Business and Society Review* Winter 1973 (pp. 66–73)

Stevenson M. A. & T. M. Dowell 'Energy for sustainable development' *Journal of Business Ethics* 9(10) October 1990 (pp. 829–36)

Stone C. D. *Where the law ends* (New York: Harper & Row) 1975

Stone C. D. *Earth and other ethics: The case for moral pluralism* (New York: Harper & Row) 1987

Stroup M. A. & R. L. Neubert 'The evolution of social responsibility' *Business Horizons* March/April 1987 (pp. 22–24)

Surma J. P. & A. A. Vondra 'Accounting for environmental costs: a hazardous subject' *Journal of Accountancy* March 1992 (pp. 51–5)

Teoh H. Y. & G. Thong 'Another look at corporate social responsibility and reporting: An empirical study in a developing country' *Accounting, Organizations and Society* 9(2) 1984 (pp. 189–206)

Thayer W. B. 'The role of the environmental audit in real estate transactions' *Secured Lender* 42(6) Nov/Dec 1986 (pp. 72–7)

Theobald J. 'Aggro for the Agrochemicals' *Management Today* March 1990 (pp. 62–7)

Thomas H. 'By appointment to the green consumer' *Accountancy* September 1989 (pp. 116–17)

Thomas V. 'Welfare cost of pollution control' *Journal of Environmental Economics and Management* Vol. 7 1980 (pp. 70–102)

Thompson C. *Environmental protection spending and the effect of tougher legislation in the chemical industry* CIA Conference Paper (London: CIA) 1991

Thompson H. J. 'The need for a secured lender exemption' *Integrated Environmental Management* 7. March 1992 p. 20

Tinker A. M. (ed.) *Social accounting for corporations* (Manchester: MUP) 1984

Tinker A. M. *Paper Prophets: a social critique of accounting* (Eastbourne: Holt Saunders) 1985

Tinker A. M., Lehman C. & Neimark M. 'Corporate Social Reporting: Falling down the hole in the middle of the road' *Accounting, Auditing and Accountability Journal* 4(1) 1991 (pp. 28–54)

Tonkin D. J. & L. C. L. Skerratt *Financial Reporting 1990–91: A survey of UK reporting practice* (London: ICAEW) 1991

Touche Ross *Head in the clouds or head in the sands? UK managers' attitudes to environmental issues – a survey* (London: Touche Ross) 1990

Touche Ross (I. M. J. Bins-Hoefnagels & G. C. Molenkamp) *Environmental Auditing* (The Hague: Touche Ross) 1988

Trades Union Congress *Greening the workplace* (London: TUC) 1991

Trotman, K. T. and G. W. Bradley, 'Associations between social responsibility disclosure and characteristics of companies', *Accounting, Organizations and Society*, 6(4) 1981 (pp. 355–62)

Turner R. K. 'Sustainable global futures: common interest, interdependence, complexity and global possibilities' *Futures* Vol. 10 1987 (pp. 574–82)

Turner R. K. (ed.) *Sustainable Environmental Management: Principles and Practice* (London: Belhaven Press) 1988

Turner R. K. 'Interdisciplinarity and holism in the environmental training of economists and planners' Symposium on education for economists and planners, International Environment Institute, University of Malta, December 1989

Turner R. K. *Towards an integrated waste management strategy* (London: Business Gas) 1990

Turner R. K. & D. W. Pearce 'Ethical foundations of sustainable economic development' International Institute for Environment and Development/ London Environmental Economics Centre Paper 90-01 March 1990

Ullmann A. E. 'The corporate environmental accounting system: a management tool for fighting environmental degradation' *Accounting, Organizations and Society* 1(1) 1976 (pp. 71–9)

Ullmann A. E. 'Corporate social reporting: political interests and conflicts in Germany' *Accounting, Organizations and Society* 4(1/2) 1979 (pp. 123–33)

Ullmann A. E. 'Data in Search of a Theory: A Critical Examination of the Relationships Among Social Performance, Social Disclosure and Economic Performance of US Firms' *Academy of Management Review* 10(3) 1985 (pp. 540–57)

United Nations World Commission on Environment and Development *Our Common Future* (The Brundtland Report) (Oxford: OUP) 1987

Van Den Bergh R. *The Corporate Report – The Deutsche Shell Experience* December 1976

Victor P. A. *Economics of pollution* (London: MacMillan) 1972

Victor P. A. 'Economics and the challenge of environmental issues' W. Leiss (ed.) *Ecology versus Politics in Canada* (Toronto: University of Toronto Press) 1979, reprinted in Daly H. E. (ed.) *Economy, Ecology, Ethics: Essays toward a steady state economy* (San Francisco: W. H. Freeman) 1980 (pp. 194–214)

Vidal J. (ed.) *Earth* (London: The Guardian/Oxfam) 1992

Wainman D. 'Balancing Nature's Books' *CA Magazine* (Canada) March 1991 (pp. 17–21)

Walesby N. J. *Business and the Environment: a pilot study of attitudes and strategic preparation amongst East of Scotland businesses with consented discharges of trade effluent* MBA Dissertation, University of Dundee, 1991

Walton C. W. 'Corporate social responsibility: The debate revisited' *Journal of Economics and Business* 3(4) 1983 (pp. 173–87)

Ward B. *Spaceship Earth* (Harmondsworth: Penguin) 1966

Ward B. *Progress for a small planet* (Harmondsworth: Penguin) 1979

Ward B. & R. Dubos *Only one Earth: The care and maintenance of a small planet* (Harmondsworth: Penguin) 1972

Ward S. *Socially Responsible Investment* (London: Directory for Social Change) 2nd edition 1991

Wartick S. L. & P. L. Cochran 'The evolution of the corporate social performance model' *Academy of Management Review* 10(4) 1985 (pp. 758–69)

Weston D. 'The rules of lucre' *Geographical Magazine* April 1991 (pp. 38–40)

Weston J. (ed.) *Red and Green: the new politics of the environment* (London: Pluto Press) 1986

Wheatley D. 'Greener than green?' *New Law Journal* February 15 1991 (pp. 208–09)

Which? 'A fair profit?' *Which?* February 1989 (pp. 88–9)

Winter G. *Business and the Environment* (Hamburg: McGraw-Hill) 1988

Wiseman J. 'An evaluation of environmental disclosure made in corporate annual reports' *Accounting, Organizations and Society* 7(1) 1982 (pp. 53–63)

Wolfson K. 'Ethics – The investment criterion of the 1990s' *Financial Weekly* November 3–9 1989 (pp. 18–21)

Worcester R. 'Monitoring and forecasting public opinion about business' *Journal of General Management* No. 1 Autumn 1973 (pp. 61–5)

World Wide Fund for Nature (WWF) *South-North Terms of Trade, Environmental Protection and Sustainable Development* (Gland: WWF) 1992

Wright C. & E. Kaposi 'Reports: Could do better' *AA (Accountancy Age)* March 1992 (pp. 35–6)

Wright J. C. *Natural resource accounting – a technique for improving planning in New Zealand* (Christchurch: Centre for Resource Management) 1989

Wynne-Davies C. 'BT – Working for the environment' *Integrated Environmental Management* No. 7 March 1992 (pp. 16–17)

Yankelovich D. *Corporate Priorities: A continuing study of the new demands on business* (Stamford, Conn: Daniel Yankelovich Inc) 1972

Zaikov G. 'Political and economic problems of accounting for ecological factors in social production' *Problems of Economics* 28(9) 1986

Zeigler C. E. 'Essay: the second bottom line' *Scientific American* August 1991

Zyber G. R. & C. G. Berry 'Assessing environmental risk' *Journal of Accountancy* March 1992 (pp. 43–8)

Index